To Make Your Composition More Reasonable

- Maintain a questioning attitude about all ideas.
- Separate fact from opinion and taste from judgment.
- Be sensitive to the connections between ideas.
- Raise important questions:

    Which of my ideas are judgments?

    To what extent have I been influenced by preconceived notions?

    To what extent is my reasoning self-serving?

    Have I judged anything too hastily?

    Have I assumed too much?

    Have I overlooked any important distinctions?

    Are my judgments reasonable?

- Avoid logical fallacies: either–or thinking, stereotyping, attacking the person, contradiction, faulty analogy, faulty causation, irrational appeal, hasty conclusion, overgeneralization, and oversimplification.

Vincent Ryan Ruggiero *State University of New York at Delhi*

Composition: The Creative Response

Wadsworth Publishing Company
Belmont, California
A Division of Wadsworth, Inc.

English Editor: Cedric W. Crocker
Production Editor: Gary Mcdonald
Managing Designer: Cynthia Bassett
Print Buyer: Karen Hunt
Designer: Janet Bollow
Copy Editor: Elaine Silverstein
Technical Illustrator: Joan Carol
Cover: Janet Bollow
Cover Photograph: © Robert Llewellyn
Composition: Thompson Type, San Diego
Chapter opening photos are from the following sources: 1 John Blaustein/ Woodfin Camp & Associates   2 © Peter Menzel   3 Evelyn Hofer/Archive Pictures Inc.   4 John Spragens Jr./Picture Group   5 Carrie Boretz/Archive Pictures Inc.   6 David A. Krathwohl/Stock, Boston   7 © Peter Menzel   8 Laurie Cameron/Jeroboam, Inc.   9 Peter Menzel/Stock, Boston   10 Cary Wolinsky/Stock, Boston   11 © Peter Menzel

© 1985 by Wadsworth, Inc. All rights reserved. No part of this book may be reproduced, stored in a retrieval system, or transcribed, in any form or by any means, electronic, mechanical, photocopying, recording, or otherwise, without the prior written permission of the publisher, Wadsworth Publishing Company, Belmont, California 94002, a division of Wadsworth, Inc.

Printed in the United States of America
1 2 3 4 5 6 7 8 9 10—89 88 87 86 85

ISBN 0-534-04398-4

Library of Congress Cataloging in Publication Data

Ruggiero, Vincent Ryan.
   Composition : the creative response.

   Bibliography: p.
   Includes index.
   1. English language—Rhetoric.   I. Title.
PE1408.R835   1985   808'.042   84-25704
ISBN 0-534-04398-4

TO EDITH THEISSELMANN
Who gave me a home when I needed one and through her quiet example taught me some of the most valuable lessons in life—that time is precious and should not be squandered, that honesty with others depends upon honesty with self, and that success is measured by how well one performs a task and not by how much recognition one receives for performing it.

Contents

Preface — xiii

Part I
Overview — 1

Chapter 1
The Composition Process — 3

What Is a Composition? — 5
The Role of Creativity — 5
Stages in Composition — 11
Your Contract with Your Readers — 14
Learning by Doing — 15
What Your Instructor Expects — 16
Some Preliminary Guidelines — 16
   1. Select the Best Time, Place,
      and Circumstances in Which to Write — 17
   2. Plan Your Paper Before You Begin to Write — 17
   3. Write the Rough Draft — 18
   4. Revise the Rough Draft — 18
   5. Rewrite the Paper — 19
Composition Assignment — 19

Part II
Planning the Composition — 21

Chapter 2
Finding a Topic and Generating Ideas — 23

Finding a Topic — 23
Topic Possibilities — 24

v

Exercise	28
Generating Ideas	28
Freewriting	29
Forcing Associations	31
Imaginary Dialogue	32
Narrowing Your Topic	37
Exercises	39
Composition Assignment	39

Chapter 3
Selecting the Composition Form and Controlling Idea — 41

Basic Composition Forms	41
The Narrative Composition	42
The Informative Composition	44
The Persuasive Composition	46
The Forms in Combination	48
Selecting the Composition Form	49
Exercises	51
The Controlling Idea	53
Selecting a Controlling Idea	54
What Do You Really Want to Say?	54
How Much Time and Space Do You Have?	54
What Idea Will Others Find Most Interesting?	55
Expressing the Controlling Idea	56
Make the Subject Appropriately Specific	57
Make the Predicate Precise	57
Include All Necessary Qualifications	58
Make the Statement as Complete as You Can	59
Exercises	61
Composition Assignment	61

Chapter 4
Evaluating Your Ideas — 63

Characteristics of Critical Thinking	64
A Questioning Attitude	65
Separation of Fact from Opinion and Taste from Judgment	66
Sensitivity to the Connections Between Ideas	68
Exercises	70
Raising Important Questions	72
Which of My Ideas Are Judgments?	72
To What Extent Are My Judgments Influenced by Preconceived Notions?	73
To What Extent Is My Reasoning Self-Serving?	75

Contents

Have I Judged Too Hastily? ... 75
Have I Assumed Too Much? ... 76
Have I Overlooked Important Distinctions? ... 76
Are My Judgments Reasonable? ... 77
Exercises ... 79
Composition Assignment ... 80

Chapter 5
Considering Your Readers ... 83

Writing *to* Versus Writing *for* Readers ... 83
   Familiar Audiences ... 85
   Unfamiliar Audiences ... 86
   Exercises ... 87
How to Be Persuasive ... 88
Principle 1: Understand the Opposing Side of the Issue ... 88
   There's More than One Side to an Issue ... 88
   Show that You Understand the Other Side ... 89
Principle 2: Respect Your Readers ... 89
   Separate the Person from the Idea ... 90
   Write When You Are Calm ... 91
Principle 3: Build a Balanced Case ... 91
   Limit the Number of Arguments ... 92
   Use Understatement ... 92
   Concede a Point or Two ... 92
   Begin on a Point of Agreement ... 93
Principle 4: Support Your Judgments with Appropriate Evidence,
Carefully Interpreted ... 93
   Kinds of Evidence ... 94
   When Is Your Evidence Adequate? ... 96
   Interpreting Evidence ... 96
Principle 5: Anticipate Your Readers' Reactions ... 98
Two Sample Papers ... 99
What to Expect from Your Readers ... 102
   Exercises ... 102
   Composition Assignment ... 104

Part III
Writing the Composition ... 107

Chapter 6
Writing a Narrative Composition ... 111

Characteristics of a Narrative Composition ... 111

Basic Narrative Techniques	113
Narrating	113
Describing	116
Defining Figuratively	118
Dialogue	119
Exercises	120
Combining Narrative Techniques	121
Exercises	124
Four Helpful Strategies	125
A Sample Composition	126
Suggested Topics for a Narrative Composition	128
A Checklist for Your Narrative Composition	129

Chapter 7
Writing an Informative Composition   131

Characteristics of an Informative Composition	131
Basic Informative Techniques	133
Presenting Factual Data	134
Citing Examples	135
Making Analogies	137
Defining Literally	138
Presenting a Process	139
Tracing	140
Summarizing	141
Quoting and Paraphrasing	142
Exercises	145
Combining Informative Techniques	148
Defining Literally and Tracing	149
Presenting Factual Data and Describing	149
A Combination of Several Techniques	149
A Combination of Several Techniques	150
Exercises	151
Four Helpful Writing Strategies	153
A Sample Composition	158
Suggested Topics for an Informative Composition	160
A Checklist for Your Informative Composition	161

Chapter 8
Writing a Persuasive Composition   165

Characteristics of a Persuasive Composition	165
Basic Persuasive Techniques	168
Presenting Reasons	168
Explaining	168

Contents

Classifying	170
Comparing	171
Interpreting and Evaluating	173
Speculating	174
Exercises	175
Combining Persuasive Techniques	177
Exercises	183
Four Helpful Strategies	185
A Sample Composition	187
Suggested Topics for a Persuasive Composition	189
A Checklist for Your Persuasive Composition	191

Part IV
Revising the Composition 195

Chapter 9
Revising for Logic 199

Ten Common Fallacies	199
Either–Or Thinking	200
Stereotyping	200
Attacking the Person	201
Contradiction	202
Faulty Analogy	203
Faulty Causation	204
Irrational Appeal	206
Hasty Conclusion	207
Overgeneralization	208
Oversimplification	210
A Brief Revision Guide	211
Exercises	212
Composition Assignment	215

Chapter 10
Revising for Sentence Style 219

The Simple Sentence	219
Coordination and Subordination	221
Exercises	223
Expanding Your Sentences	224
A Strategy for Expanding Sentences	226
Exercises	227
Maintaining Clarity	228

Exercises	230
Varying Word Order	230
Invert Subject–Verb Order	231
Open with a Prepositional Phrase	231
Open with an Adjective	231
Open with an Adverb	232
Open with a Participle	232
Open with an Infinitive Phrase	233
Change the Order of Clauses in a Complex Sentence	233
Exercises	233
Revising Sentences for Exactness	236
Two Kinds of Meaning	237
How Inexactness Occurs	238
Three Important Choices	239
Exercises	243
Revising Sentences for Economy	245
The Basic Principles	247
Three Kinds of Inflatedness	247
Dealing with Profound Ideas	250
Exercises	251
Revising Sentences for Liveliness	254
Eliminate the Predictable	254
Put Yourself in the Background	256
Substitute Active for Passive Voice	256
Substitute Vivid Words for Bland Words	257
Substitute Figurative for Literal Language	258
Vary Your Sentence Style or Structure	260
Summary of Sentence Strategies	261
Exercises	262
Composition Assignment	265

Chapter 11
Revising for Paragraph Effectiveness — 269

Basic Paragraph Patterns	270
Exercises	273
Revising for Paragraph Length	273
Make Your Paragraphs Average About Ten Lines in Length	273
Vary the Length of Your Paragraphs to Avoid Monotony	274
Break Your Paragraphs at the Natural Junctures of Your Ideas	274
Exercises	278
Revising for Paragraph Coherence	283
Use Pronouns Effectively	284
Repeat Words Skillfully	284
Use Echo Words	285
Use Relationship Words	285

Contents   xi

   A Sample Passage   289
      Exercises   290
      Composition Assignment   292

Part V
The Research Paper   295

Using Your Library's Resources   296
   General/Circulating Collection   296
   Reference   297
   Periodicals   297
   Nonprint Materials   297
   Government Publications   297
The Library Classification System   297
The Library Catalog   299
A Strategy for Research   301
Taking Notes   306
Manuscript Mechanics   308
   Materials   308
   Margins and Indentation   309
   Spacing   309
   Syllabication   309
   Page Numbers   310
   Tables and Illustrations   310
   Titles and Other Headings   310
   Abbreviations   311
   Corrections   311
Deciding on Form   311
   The Informative Research Paper   312
   The Persuasive Research Paper   312
Deciding on Format   313
   The Separated Format   313
   The Integrated Format   314
Documentation Defined   314
Kinds of Documentation   316
   Guidelines for Brief Documentation   316
   Guidelines for the Works Cited List   318
   Citing Books   318
   Citing Periodical Articles   320
   Citing Nonprint Materials   322
Sample Research Papers   323
An Informative Research Paper   324
A Persuasive Research Paper   334
   Suggested Topics for a Research Paper   343
   Checklist for Your Research Paper   344

Part VI
The Handbook   347

Editing the Composition   347
Solving Verb Problems (VB)   348
   1. Know the Principal Parts of the Verbs You Use   348
   2. Use the Principal Parts to Form Tenses   351
   3. Use -s and -ed Endings Correctly   354
   4. Make Your Subjects and Verbs Agree   356
   5. Use the Correct Sequence of Tenses   360
   6. Use the Correct Mood of the Verb   362
Solving Pronoun Problems (PRON)   364
   Incorrect Pronoun Case   364
   Faulty Pronoun Reference   367
Solving Adjective and Adverb Problems (ADJ/ADV)   370
   Learn to Distinguish Adjectives from Adverbs   370
   Use Adjectives and Adverbs Correctly   371
   Use Comparative and Superlative Forms Correctly   372
Solving Sentence Problems   374
   Sentence Fragments (FRAG)   374
   Run-On Sentences and Comma Splices (RUN-ON, CS)   378
   Faulty Predication (PRED)   380
   Faulty Modification (MOD)   382
   Mixed or Incomplete Construction (CON)   385
   Unnecessary Shifts in Person or Tense (SHIFT)   388
Solving Spelling Problems (SP)   390
   Words That Are Often Mispronounced   391
   Words That Are Similar in Sound   392
   Related Words That Are Spelled Differently   393
   Words with Prefixes, Suffixes, or Troublesome Internal Letter Combinations   393
   Words with Unusual Plural Forms   394
   A Basic Spelling List   395
Solving Punctuation Problems (PUNCT)   403
   End Punctuation   404
   Internal Punctuation   405
   Punctuation of Quoted Material   413
   Punctuation of Words   417
   Punctuating Paragraphs   423
A Glossary of Usage   430

Notes   451
Index   457

Preface

Why is it so difficult to teach Freshman English? First, because composition is an art whose mastery depends on disciplined practice—and our society has little regard for practice and less for discipline. Then, because learning to write well is a slow process involving the building of good habits over a period of years—and we are expected to reverse eighteen years of bad habits in fifteen weeks. And finally, because teaching composition effectively requires small classes of students with like proficiencies and readiness to learn—and our classrooms are overcrowded with students ranging from the barely literate to the verbally accomplished, from those who hate composition with the considerable passion of a captive audience to those who delight in writing, from those whose confusion seems invincible to those for whom the briefest direction or explanation is more than adequate.

Because teaching Freshman English is unusually difficult, the composition textbook must meet more exacting standards than other texts if it is to be useful. Moreover, authors of composition texts have a special obligation to make clear the premises that underlie their choices of content and organization and to specify the features that justify the addition of another volume to the lengthy list of textbooks already in print.

Premises Underlying This Book

Composition: The Creative Response is constructed on the following premises:

The composition course should include instruction in creative thinking. The concept of creative thinking has come to us from another discipline, cognitive psychology, but it is not foreign to English. We have always honored it in our literature classes, and it is closely related to an important concept in classical rhetoric, the concept of *invention*. By teaching students the basic principles and strategies of creative thinking, we help them identify their topics and generate ideas more effectively, combine writing techniques more imaginatively, and develop a pleasing writing style. By reminding them that composition writing is (or at least can be) a creative response, we assist them to overcome the crippling attitude that writing is a chore and Freshman English a burden to be suffered rather than an opportunity to be seized enthusiastically.

The composition course should include instruction in critical thinking. The critical-thinking movement began some years ago when the business and professional communities and several educational commissions called attention to the lack of reasoning skills in employees and students. The movement has already resulted in critical-thinking requirements in one state (California) and plans for such requirements in many others. Although other disciplines, notably philosophy and psychology, have made substantial contributions to our understanding of critical thinking, the close relationship between thought and language makes the composition course the most natural place for critical thinking instruction. (In fact, prior to the sixteenth century it *was* an important part of rhetorical instruction.)

The composition course should address, directly and thoroughly, the tasks of planning and revising the composition. When students produce boringly predictable, repetitive compositions, the cause is not so much lack of imagination as ignorance of when and how to apply it. The solution to this problem is to teach them to postpone writing in any formal sense until they have done some planning—that is, until they have thought about what they want to say (on paper, of course), letting their minds range over the subject, forcing associations, freewriting, and then deciding on a purpose, a controlling idea, and an audience. Similarly, when students' compositions are poorly paragraphed (or unparagraphed) and filled with vague or bloated language expressed in primer-style sentences, the problem is not so much a lack of writing talent as the lack of a strategy for revising their first drafts. The solution to this problem is to present them with a practical, easy-to-use strategy and to guide them in applying it to their writing.

The composition course should provide instruction in the fundamentals of grammar and usage. Ideally, students would come to us from grade and high school with a firm grounding in grammar and usage, and we would not have to devote a moment of Freshman

English to instruction in those matters. Unfortunately, the ideal is far from being realized. For the short term at least, there seems no way to avoid the responsibility of offering instruction in grammar and usage. The challenge is to find ways of doing so without neglecting the larger rhetorical aim of Freshman English.

Distinguishing Features of This Book

This book differs from most other composition texts in a number of ways, the most important of which are the following:

It begins with an overview chapter that presents a capsule view of the entire book and thus enables students to begin writing whole compositions from the outset of the course.

It devotes an entire chapter to the task of finding a topic and generating ideas, emphasizing how to discover unusual topics and how to get beyond predictable ideas.

It devotes a separate chapter to selecting the most appropriate composition form and framing an effective controlling idea statement.

It discusses the concept of audience in a separate chapter and presents a strategy for designing the composition to be effective with its audience.

It offers detailed instruction in the writing of three composition forms—narrative, informative, and persuasive—with clear explanations of the characteristics and strategies of each, together with an annotated sample paper.

It provides annotated examples of eighteen important writing techniques, including citing examples, presenting factual information, presenting reasons, interpreting, and evaluating—and explains which form each is associated with and how and where to use it.

It demonstrates how to combine composition techniques creatively to enrich the texture of student writing and make it more effective.

It presents two chapters on reasoning (Chapters 4 and 9), reflecting the fact that judgments must be analyzed twice and in different ways—before the rough draft is written, to ensure that the writing effort will not be wasted on an unreasonable idea, and after the rough draft is written, to ensure that the act of writing has not produced a fallacy.

It presents two complete research papers to illustrate the differences between the informative and the persuasive approaches and includes the 1984 *MLA Handbook* guidelines.

It offers a detailed treatment of the sentence (Chapter 10), including explanations of sentence combining and sentence expanding, but presents this treatment in the context of *revision* to reflect the writing practice of professionals, who polish their sentences in later stages of the writing process.

It offers a thorough explanation of paragraphing (also in the context of revision), blending the traditional view of the paragraph as minicomposition with the paragraphing guidelines used by professionals.

It includes a complete handbook with a problem-solving approach to errors in grammar and usage and a generous number of exercises.

It is arranged to reflect the way the writing process unfolds—that is, planning followed in turn by writing, revising, and editing, making it easy for students to follow.

I wish to express my gratitude to all who had a part in the making of this book. Special thanks go to Herbert Sorgen, Anna Zilles, and their associates at the SUNY Delhi library for their research assistance; to Mary Jane Platou of the University of Scranton Media Resources Center for her contribution to the research paper section; to Kevin Howat and Gary Mcdonald of Wadsworth Publishing Company for their guidance in moving the book smoothly through all the stages of production from signing to publication; and to the following English professors for their helpful suggestions for improving the book's substance and organization: Hilda Attride, Riverside City College; Dean S. Barnard, Jr., York College of Pennsylvania; William Condon, Arkansas Tech University; Marya M. DuBose, Augusta College; Elizabeth Hanson-Smith, California State University, Sacramento; A. Leslie Harris, Georgia State University; Nancy W. Johnson, Northern Virginia Community College; Larry P. Kent, Harper College; Susan Petit, College of San Mateo; David Rankin, California State University, Dominguez Hills; and Victor J. Vitanza, University of Texas, Arlington.

Vincent Ryan Ruggiero
Delhi, New York   January, 1985

❦ *Composition, at its best, is a creative response to the need or desire to communicate. Even though millions of compositions are produced each year by amateurs and professionals, every successful composition is in some way unique. The opportunities for creativity in writing are inexhaustible. That they are often unrealized is largely attributable to the popular misconception that originality lies in ignoring convention. The fact is that originality in writing is more readily achieved by honoring discipline and tradition than by opposing them. The greater a writer's mastery of both self and the rhetorical principles and strategies proven effective over the centuries, the freer that writer is to make the choices that will express his or her creativity.*

Part I

Overview

In a composition course, as in any college course, a good start can make a significant difference in your level of achievement. The more quickly you become acclimated and understand the nature of the subject and the objectives you will be expected to meet, the sooner you can begin mastering the specific skills of the discipline and experiencing the confidence that mastery brings. This overview will help you make that good start.

Chapter 1

The Composition Process

This chapter begins by examining a common myth about writing. Next it defines the term composition, *explains the role of creativity in the writing process, and discusses the stages of composition and the writer's obligation to his or her readers. Finally, it outlines your instructor's expectations for your compositions and provides preliminary guidelines to get you started writing.*

There is a myth that professional writers produce their work with ease. According to this notion, all they have to do is sit down at the typewriter and let their fingers record the torrent of words that gushes forth in just the right arrangement to delight their readers. Presumably they never have to grope for an expression or ponder an idea the way amateurs do. Their art just happens, bursting forth effortlessly from their gifted minds.

This myth has managed to survive innumerable attempts to dispose of it. It persists today, and more than likely you have been affected by it. From the time you started school until now, you have undoubtedly seen only *published* books, *finished* products. Your earliest grade school readers gave no hint of the author's fumbling for the right word or the most graceful phrasing. And all the books that followed were models of completeness and polish. Having never been permitted to see professional work in progress, you received the subliminal message that professionals write with ease.

Had you been allowed to see writers at work and examine their early drafts, you would have found not only that the popular notion is a myth but also that the truth of the matter is almost exactly the opposite! All the difficulties you experience with your writing—the struggle to unscramble disordered fragments of thought; to overcome confusion, vagueness, and ambiguity and discover what you want to say; to conquer awkwardness and dullness and repetition—all these difficulties exist for professional writers as well. The only difference is that professionals' wastebaskets are not half-filled but *overflowing* with false starts; their desks are not sprinkled with scraps of paper containing scratched-out notes, shorthand reminders, and personal hieroglyphics, but *littered* with them.

Humorist James Thurber once explained to an interviewer that the act of writing was for him essentially rewriting. "It's part of a constant attempt on my part," he said, "to make the finished version smooth, to make it seem effortless." That is the truth that has largely been obscured. *The writing of the masters is not effortless: it is made to seem effortless by their extraordinary effort.*

When asked how often his work came out right the first time, Thurber recounted his wife's negative reaction to the first draft of something he'd written (she had called it "high school stuff") and went on to explain:

> I have to tell her to wait until the seventh draft, it'll work out all right. I don't know why that should be so, that the first or second draft of everything I write reads as if it was turned out by a charwoman. I've only written one piece quickly. I wrote a thing called "File and Forget" in one afternoon—but only because it was a series of letters just as one would ordinarily dictate. And I'd have to admit that the last letter of the series, after doing all the others that one afternoon, took me a week. It was the end of the piece and I had to fuss over it.[1]

Seven drafts! And that from a man who was nearly blind and had to write every draft in a large scrawl. Nor was Thurber's dedication to perfecting his work much different from that of other successful writers. When asked whether he rewrote his work, short-story writer Frank O'Connor answered, "Endlessly, endlessly, endlessly. And keep on rewriting, and after it's published, and then after it's published in book form, I usually rewrite it again."[2]

As these examples suggest, what it takes to become an effective writer is not so much natural talent (though admittedly that helps) as a willingness to work. If you have that, you have no reason to fear your writing course or the lessons in this book.

What Is a Composition?

The term *composition* can mean a short story or a poem, as well as an essay. In this book, however, we will use a more restrictive meaning. A composition, as we will refer to it, is a brief essay that expresses your thoughts and feelings in direct prose statements—that is, statements in which you make your ideas explicit rather than leaving your readers to discern them through interpretation (as is often done in the writing of fiction and poetry).* If you have come to think of a composition as a specified number of words about some topic, with a title, introduction, body, and conclusion, it will be helpful for you at the outset of this course to reflect on the root meaning of the word. To *compose* means to select, shape, and arrange. It means to take the raw material and work it as sculptors do their stone, potters their clay, turning random thoughts into focused thoughts, rough sentences into polished sentences, disorganized paragraphs into organized paragraphs.

The key to good composing is making intelligent choices. From the moment you think of a topic to the final draft of your composition, a host of choices will confront you: How will you narrow the topic? What ideas will you include in the composition? Which will be the controlling idea? What form do you want the composition to take? For whom are you writing? How will you develop your important points? What organizational pattern will you use? The more carefully you consider and make these choices, the better your composition will be.

The Role of Creativity

A composition is properly called creative if it bears the stamp of uniqueness; in other words, if something about it sets it apart from other compositions. Sometimes that something is the topic itself

---

*As we shall see in subsequent chapters, this definition of composition does not rule out the use of some of the *techniques* of fiction or poetry. It does mean, however, that where such techniques are used, they are made to serve direct prose statement.

(though it is possible to write an uncreative paper about a creative topic). But more often the creativity lies in what is said about the topic, in how the ideas are developed, or in the writer's choice of words. In any case, creative compositions do not occur automatically. One of the biggest mistakes you can make in this course is to pretend that your writing will be different from everyone else's merely because you want it to be.

To clarify this point, let's compare some less creative passages with more creative passages and note the differences.

Less Creative

I shot the elephant and heard the crowd roar. He remained standing for a while, looking very old and almost paralyzed. Then he fell to his knees. He struggled slowly to his feet. I fired a third time and he fell for good.

More Creative

When I pulled the trigger I did not hear the bang or feel the kick—one never does when a shot goes home—but I heard the devilish roar of glee that went up from the crowd. In that instant, in too short a time, one would have thought, even for the bullet to get there, a mysterious, terrible change had come over the elephant. He neither stirred nor fell, but every line of his body had altered. He looked suddenly stricken, shrunken, immensely old, as though the frightful impact of the bullet had paralysed him without knocking him down. At last, after what seemed a long time—it might have been five seconds, I dare say—he sagged flabbily to his knees. His mouth slobbered. An enormous senility seemed to have settled upon him. One could have imagined him thousands of years old. I fired again into the same spot. At the second shot he did not collapse but climbed with des-

More Creative

perate slowness to his feet and stood weakly upright, with legs sagging and head drooping. I fired a third time. That was the shot that did for him. You could see the agony of it jolt his whole body and knock the last remnant of strength from his legs. But in falling he seemed for a moment to rise, for as his hind legs collapsed beneath him he seemed to tower upward like a huge rock toppling, his trunk reaching skywards like a tree. He trumpeted, for the first and only time. And then down he came, his belly towards me, with a crash that seemed to shake the ground even where I lay.[3]

Comment   The writer of the more creative passage was George Orwell, perhaps best known for his novels *1984* and *Animal Farm*. This passage, however, is not from a novel. It is from an essay, a literary form at which Orwell excelled. The reason Orwell's treatment is more creative than the other is not that it is longer (that is incidental) but that it reconstructs the actual experience, allowing the reader to share it, to see and hear what Orwell did, to feel the shiver of excitement Orwell felt. Where others might have been content with telling, Orwell *showed* his readers, and so created a memorable passage.

Less Creative

When a migraine headache comes now, I don't fight it. I lie down and wait for it to go away, however long that takes. And when it's over I feel much better.

More Creative

And once it comes, now that I am wise in its ways, I no longer fight it. I lie down and let it happen. At first every small apprehension is magnified, every anxiety a pounding terror. Then the pain

More Creative

comes, and I concentrate only on that. Right there is the usefulness of migraine, there in the imposed yoga, the concentration on the pain. For when the pain recedes, ten or twelve hours later, everything goes with it, all the hidden resentments, all the vain anxieties. The migraine has acted as a circuit breaker, and the fuses have emerged intact. There is a pleasant convalescent euphoria. I open the windows and feel the air, eat gratefully, sleep well. I notice the particular nature of a flower in a glass on the stair landing. I count my blessings.[4]

Comment   The passage on the right, written by Joan Didion, is more creative for two reasons: first, its greater range of meaningful associations; and secondly, the richness of its phrasing (none of it merely decorative, but contributing to the message).

Less Creative

There seems to be a general assumption that brilliant people need excitement in order to work well. But there's no evidence that great achievers in the past led such lives. Most, in fact, led uneventful lives. They just took the common, everyday events and transformed them.

More Creative

There seems to be a general assumption that brilliant people cannot stand routine; that they need a varied, exciting life in order to do their best. It is also assumed that dull people are particularly suited for dull work. We are told that the reason the present-day young protest so loudly against the dullness of factory jobs is that they are better educated and brighter than the young of the past.

  Actually, there is no evi-

More Creative

dence that people who achieve much crave for, let alone live, eventful lives. The opposite is nearer the truth. One thinks of Amos the sheepherder, Socrates the stonemason, Omar the tentmaker. Jesus probably had his first revelations while doing humdrum carpentry work. Einstein worked out his theory of relativity while serving as a clerk in a Swiss patent office. Machiavelli wrote *The Prince* and the *Discourses* while immersed in the dull life of a small country town where the only excitement he knew was playing cards with muleteers at the inn. Immanuel Kant's daily life was an unalterable routine. The housewives of Königsberg set their clocks when they saw him pass on his way to the university. He took the same walk each morning, rain or shine. The greatest distance Kant ever traveled was sixty miles from Königsberg.

The outstanding characteristic of man's creativeness is the ability to transmute trivial impulses into momentous consequences. The greatness of man is in what he can do with petty grievances and joys, and with common physiological pressures and hungers. "When I have a little vexation," wrote Keats, "it grows in five minutes into a theme for Sophocles."[5]

Comment Unlike the Didion passage, the more creative passage here, by Eric Hoffer, has no unusual associations, nor is its phrasing especially rich. What makes it creative is the specific details the author has taken from the lives of great achievers to support his assertions. Though a hundred other writers might write essays expressing the same general view as Hoffer's, the particulars that fill his essay make it unique.

Less Creative

This is the story of an American invention, blue jeans. Everyone wears them and not just in the United States, but around the world as well, even in Russia. They've been with us for a long time and will undoubtedly stay.

More Creative

This is the story of a sturdy American symbol which has now spread throughout most of the world. The symbol is not the dollar. It is not even Coca-Cola. It is a simple pair of pants called blue jeans, and what the pants symbolize is what Alexis de Tocqueville called "a manly and legitimate passion for equality. . . ." Blue jeans are favored equally by bureaucrats and cowboys; bankers and deadbeats; fashion designers and beer drinkers. They draw no distinctions and recognize no classes; they are merely American. Yet they are sought after almost everywhere in the world—including Russia, where authorities recently broke up a teen-aged gang that was selling them on the black market for two hundred dollars a pair. They have been around for a long time, and it seems likely that they will outlive even the necktie.[6]

Comment The creativity in the passage on the right lies in its wealth of factual detail and its concrete reference. (Even the title of the essay from which this passage is taken, "The Jeaning of America—and the World," is creative.)

Note that with the exception of the Orwell passage, these passages are written about common topics. What could be more prosaic than headaches, uneventful living, and jeans? And yet each topic yielded a creative response. You may of course believe, as many people do, that certain writers produce creative responses because of what they, the writers, are. That view is essentially wrong. Though talent does vary among people, creative work of any kind is more a reflection of what people do than of what they are.

Research has established conclusively that creativity can be learned.[7] Accordingly, all that is necessary is to learn the techniques and strategies that produce creative responses, the same techniques and strategies that guided the writers quoted above and guide all other effective writers. Those techniques and strategies will be detailed in the chapters that follow. But you can anticipate them by applying the following guidelines in your early composition efforts:

Press yourself to go deeper than the first layer of thought about your topics. Early ideas tend to be common ideas, those you have heard so often that they are little more than a conditioned response. They are the ideas that everyone else writing about your topic will tend to think of. By making yourself produce not your usual ten ideas but fifty or a hundred, you increase your chances of producing some original ones.

Focus on specifics. General statements are seldom very creative, so concentrate on particulars in your composition. If you are recounting a personal experience, include lots of concrete details. If you are informing your readers about an interesting or famous person, place, or thing, pack your composition with factual data. And if you are arguing for a particular point of view on a controversial issue, give much more space to the evidence and the reasoning that support your judgment than to the judgment itself.

Stages in Composition

Broadly speaking, there are three stages in composition—planning, writing, and revising. Each has a special importance. Careful planning helps you anticipate problems and address them. It ensures a clear and unified piece of writing with a single, well-focused topic, sensible ideas, and sensitivity to your readers' needs and expectations. Careful writing adds form and substance to your ideas. Careful revising adds refinement and polish, giving you an opportunity to eliminate weaknesses and create a sense of effortlessness and spontaneity in the writing.

It is true that a composition can be written without devoting any time to the planning and revising stages, but the result is seldom a creative response. In fact, it often lacks basic coherence. Here is an example of such a composition.

> Marriage is still useful, not just to meet the demands of traditional morality, but to provide a sense of belonging and of self-discipline. Being married helps people to think twice before they do something, whether that something is cheating on their mates or breaking off the relationship. This is especially true where children are involved.
>
> People living together before they marry should have some understandings. They shouldn't just get up and walk away when there is a problem. It's probably more easily said than done, but they should talk their problems out instead of keeping them inside and letting them grow. Such communication can even help bring them closer together.
>
> Living together offers one great advantage over being married. If the couple prove to be incompatible, they can end their relationship neatly and without legal complications.
>
> If a couple is thinking of getting married, I think they should live together first. Then they can see each other as they really are, discovering the quirks and faults that are usually hidden during the dating period. That way they can discover whether their relationship is a good one and gain some assurance that if they ever should decide to marry, their marriage will last.

It would take a very casual reading to miss the fact that these four paragraphs are not sufficiently connected. The first paragraph speaks of the usefulness of marriage; the second, of the importance of communication in living together before marriage; the third, of the advantage of living together instead of marrying; and the fourth, of the value of living together before marriage. There is no single idea that draws all these thoughts together. It seems clear that the writer was content to meander along, jotting down whatever thoughts happened to occur to him and in whatever order. He appears not to have planned or edited his paper at all.

Such writing is hard to take seriously, particularly when the topic is a complex one requiring careful thought and judgment. Yet this is precisely the way the vast majority of unplanned and un-

The Composition Process

edited writing appears. The point cannot be made too strongly—whenever you ignore or skimp on any one of the three stages of composition, you run the grave risk of producing a rambling or shallow or confusing or boring or insulting composition.

Had the writer of the composition on marriage appreciated this point, he would have given more attention to planning and editing and produced a more effective paper, like one of the following.

> a. Many people believe that marriage has outlived its usefulness. They point to the rising divorce statistics and the terrible emotional and financial toll divorce takes on everyone concerned, and they argue that people would be better off not marrying at all.
>
> I disagree with this view. I concede that divorce statistics suggest something is wrong with many marriages and that the break-up of a marriage is a painful experience. Yet those dark realities do not change the fact that *some marriages do work*. And when they do, they affect lives in powerful, positive ways.
>
> My parents have such a marriage. Several months ago they celebrated their thirty-fifth anniversary. Everyone who knows them says they are as devoted as newlyweds. Naturally, they have their bad moments—disagreements over some family matter, the inevitable minor frictions between personalities. But they survive them, and in so doing, they seem to grow and develop. My brother and sister and I have often commented that our greatest blessing in life has been the opportunity to observe in our parents how love and commitment can bring understanding and peace of mind.
>
> What of the marriages that don't work? They are tragedies, to be sure. But they do not prove that people are better off not marrying. To be human means to run the risk of failing, of making a mistake, of being wounded. To go through life in fear, unwilling to make a commitment, is a denial of our humanity. People who never marry because they fear divorce will never become divorce statistics, it is true, but they may lose a great deal more than they gain.
>
> b. Mary and Paul were high school sweethearts. In May of their senior year, they announced their engagement. That summer they were married in a big church ceremony. Five years, two children, and countless shouting matches later, they were divorced.
>
> Mary and Paul's case is not typical of all divorce cases. But it is typical of many. And it illustrates clearly one of the major causes of divorce. That cause is early marriage, marriage before the couple know who they are and what they want from life, and before they are

ready to accept the responsibilities of marriage. In such marriages, when greater maturity brings clearer self-images and better understanding of goals and expectations, the couple often feel cheated and trapped. In such a setting, love can quickly turn to resentment and hate.

The solution to the problem of early marriage is as obvious as it is difficult to persuade young people of—postpone marriage. Later marriage carries no guarantee of success, of course, but it offers better odds. A twenty-eight-year-old couple are in a better position to decide whether they are compatible and whether their ideas and attitudes and values harmonize than an eighteen- or twenty-one-year-old couple are. So the danger of deciding carelessly or impetuously is lessened.

The greatest obstacle to postponing marriage is a young couple's desire to share their lives with each other right away. That obstacle is easily overcome by their deciding to live together for a while to gain time to mature and to test their compatibility. But society has traditionally frowned on that arrangement, and many parents continue to oppose it even in this age of sexual liberation.

So each year across the land, as thousands of Marys and Pauls march down the aisle, society rests secure in its tradition, parents beam in pride . . . and the future of divorce is assured.

These compositions are rather different from each other in point of view and development. Yet they are similar in two important respects: each is centered around a single idea and hence is a unified piece of writing; and each has the connections between sentences and paragraphs clearly signaled. In short, each has been carefully planned and revised.

Your Contract with Your Readers

Seldom do you write only for yourself.* Most of your writing is intended to be read by others. Thus whether your writing succeeds or fails depends in part on the reaction of your readers. For this reason, it is important to be sensitive to the attitude your writing conveys. If your attitude is, "Here's a rough statement of my ideas—if the readers want to understand it, let them figure it out," you should not be surprised if your readers feel insulted and decide they can't spare time to struggle with your message.

---

*Even that most private form of writing, the diary, is sometimes published.

The safest and most realistic approach to writing is the attitude that *you* owe *the readers* something, not the reverse. However enamored you are of your own ideas (and it's human nature to have a special regard for one's own views), it is foolish to assume that others are waiting with great anticipation to hear them. When you write for readers, you are making a claim on their time; therefore, you owe them a careful effort to make your thoughts clear and meaningful.

Think of your relationship with your readers as a *contractual* one: you offer, in return for their attention, a worthwhile and pleasurable experience. With this perspective, you will not be likely to take your readers for granted.

Learning by Doing

At this point you have only a general outline of what you will be studying in your writing course. Subsequent chapters will fill in that outline and deepen your understanding of the writing process. Yet you will begin writing at once. That may make you a bit uncomfortable; you may feel you are being asked to do something before you have learned how to do it. However, a look at the reason for this approach should put you more at ease.

Writing is a skill, and skills are learned by doing. When you were younger, you undoubtedly played basketball before you mastered all the skills of the game. Even if you spent some time every day working on the individual skills of dribbling, passing, shooting, and playing defense, you probably spent some time trying to put all the skills together in a game. Imagine how different it would have been if your instructor had said, "You may play a game of basketball only *after* you've learned all the skills individually—we'll spend a week on dribbling, a week on passing, two weeks on shooting, and a month on playing defense." By the time you'd gotten around to playing a game, you'd have been bored with basketball, perhaps even hated it. Moreover, you would not have become skilled at the game, because playing basketball is not a matter of having a group of skills: it is *blending those skills as the game demands*. If you had never played a game, you wouldn't know how to fit the skills together.

Just as there is much to learn from playing a game before you have polished all the skills, so there is much to learn from writing compositions before you have learned all the skills of writing. That is why you will be writing throughout the term as you learn about the various principles and techniques of composition.

What Your Instructor Expects

How will your instructor grade your efforts? Is it fair for him or her to expect as much of you at the beginning of the term as at the end? What expectations would be reasonable? To begin with, your instructor will expect you to have done some composition writing in high school and to have read enough books, essays, magazine articles, editorials, and letters to editors to have developed some feeling for what is clear and intelligible writing. Moreover, he or she will expect you to be generally aware of the standards of acceptable grammar and usage and conscientious enough to refer to the handbook in this text or to a dictionary when in doubt. In addition, while your instructor may not demand adherence to principles you have not yet learned, he or she will expect you to apply those you have learned. For example, after you have completed this overview, you will be expected to apply the writing guidelines it presents.

Most important, your instructor will expect you to take the initiative in answering your own questions about writing and in expanding your skills. In other words, instead of waiting for your instructor to cover a topic that confuses you, you should make an attempt to overcome your confusion by consulting the table of contents or the index, finding where in this book the topic is discussed, and looking there. This approach will expedite your development as a writer.

Consider the problem of grading from your instructor's standpoint. No matter how understanding and sympathetic he or she might be about the weaknesses and blank spots in your writing background, it will be necessary to use *some* standard in evaluating your writing. The higher that standard (within reason, of course), the more motivated you will be to extend yourself. If you set yourself a demanding standard at the outset of this course, you will have no reason to fear your instructor's evaluations of your work.

Some Preliminary Guidelines

The following guidelines will help you get started writing compositions. They are a capsule version of the principles and techniques developed later in the text.

1. Select the Best Time, Place, and Circumstances in Which to Write

No two people respond identically to the same conditions, so there is no one set of conditions that suits everyone. Your writing will proceed much better if you choose the right conditions for you. Are you a morning person, one who functions better at 6 A.M. than at 6 P.M.? Then try to set aside time early in the morning to do your writing. Do you work better at a desk or table or in an easy chair? Using a pen, pencil, or typewriter? What conditions best stimulate your thought process? Quiet or noise? Soft music, rock music, or no music? (A word of caution: Just because you *like* Michael Jackson's music does not mean it helps you write better.) Do you work better alone or around others? If you are not sure what you find stimulating and what you find distracting, experiment and find out. By choosing your working conditions with care, not only will you save time and effort, but you will also be more satisfied with what you write.

2. Plan Your Paper Before You Begin to Write

You may think that you'll save time by plunging right into the writing stage with no more than a general idea of what you want to say. But in the long run you'll lose time. That approach is like starting out in a car without knowing in which direction you really want to go, hoping that you'll decide on a destination while you're driving. The problem is that by the time you decide, you may have already gone miles and miles in the wrong direction. In writing, as in travel, the trip is likely to be faster and smoother if you know your destination in advance.

Here's how to plan. Choose a topic that interests you and that you know something about. Or, if your instructor assigns the topic, choose *an aspect* of it that interests you and that you know something about. (If you know nothing about a topic, then no matter how exciting it may seem, you'll have nothing to say about it.) Then list everything you can think of to say about the topic—bits of information, questions, views you've heard others express, experiences you or others have had, your feelings, anything even remotely related to the topic. Don't skimp on this list; press yourself to produce as many ideas as possible. The more ideas you get down now, the more you'll have to choose from later.

Next, look over your list of ideas and decide whether your

paper will be mainly *narrative* (recounting an experience dramatically), or *informative* (presenting factual details), or *persuasive* (arguing for a particular position). Decide, too, what the main idea of your paper will be (it may be a combination of several ideas on your list) and how every other idea relates to the main idea. Be sure to discard all ideas that are unrelated or only remotely related to the main idea.

Now examine your list critically. Does everything you want to say make sense? Will your readers find anything unclear? Will they disagree with anything? If so, is there a better way of expressing the idea to make it more meaningful or reasonable? Also, consider what arrangement of your ideas will be most effective in conveying your message, and decide which ideas or parts of your composition are important or complex enough to deserve expanded treatment.

3. Write the Rough Draft

Write the paper as well as you can, following the arrangement you decided upon in step 2. However, don't be overly concerned about polishing your expression. There'll be time for that later. Give most of your attention and space to major points by expanding on them—for example, by adding more description or explanation. Indicate the connections between your ideas so your readers will not be confused. Write in a style you think readers of average intelligence will find appealing; more specifically, keep your choice of words precise, simple, yet lively. Don't use a lot of words unnecessarily or insert big words for their own sake, and don't always use the same type of sentence. Finally, be sure to break the paper into paragraphs of reasonable length and to use standard punctuation. When you've finished writing—*not before*—choose an appropriate title. Choosing a title too early in the composition process can block the flow of ideas.

4. Revise the Rough Draft

The best way to revise the composition is to put yourself in your readers' place. The idea is to get beyond the "Of course it's excellent because I wrote it" attitude. Be honest with yourself in appraising your paper's strengths and weaknesses. The more *you* find to correct, the less your readers (or your instructor) will find. Read your paper at least three times—once for logic, once for sentence style, and once for paragraph effectiveness. Then check for correctness, consulting the handbook as necessary. Make notes for revision in the margins and between the lines.

5. Rewrite the Paper

Completely rewrite the paper or, if your instructor prefers, type it, incorporating all the revisions you made in step 4. If you type the paper, proofread it carefully for typing errors.

These guidelines may seem cumbersome at first. Any new approach or activity does. When you first attempted to form your letters or to whistle or to tie your shoelaces, you probably thought you'd never succeed. Yet the more you practiced, the less strange the process felt and the more skilled and confident you became. In the same way, when the newness of these guidelines wears off, you'll find them as natural as they are effective.

Composition Assignment

Review the guidelines presented in the chapter. Then write a brief composition on one of the following topics. (Unless your instructor specifies a different length, aim for about 300 words.) Be sure to give sufficient attention to each part of the composition process: planning, writing, and revising.

- Why I support (oppose) the Equal Rights Amendment (ERA)
- The worst mistake parents make with teenagers
- The childhood experience I remember most vividly
- How TV commercials affect us
- My first (worst) date
- The most interesting job I ever had
- The oddest person I ever met
- Some rules make no sense
- The biggest show-off I ever met
- What most surprised me about college
- The best (worst) advice I ever received
- Good lessons I learned in bars
- The best (worst) teacher I ever had
- Small-time politics
- A clear case of hypocrisy

Part II

Planning the Composition

Planning is the first stage of the composition process, the stage in which you create a blueprint to guide you in writing the composition. In essence, this stage consists of raising and answering a number of questions: What topic will you write about? What will you say about the topic? What form will your composition take? What will be your controlling idea? How reasonable are your judgments on the subject? Whom will you be writing for?

The quality of your final paper will depend on how well and thoroughly you address these questions and make the choices involved. If you wish to produce a creative response, this is the time to use your imagination and force yourself beyond predictable topics and safe, familiar ideas. The four chapters in part II offer you a number of effective approaches to use in planning your composition. The more conscientiously you employ them, the surer, smoother, and more satisfying the writing stage will be for you.

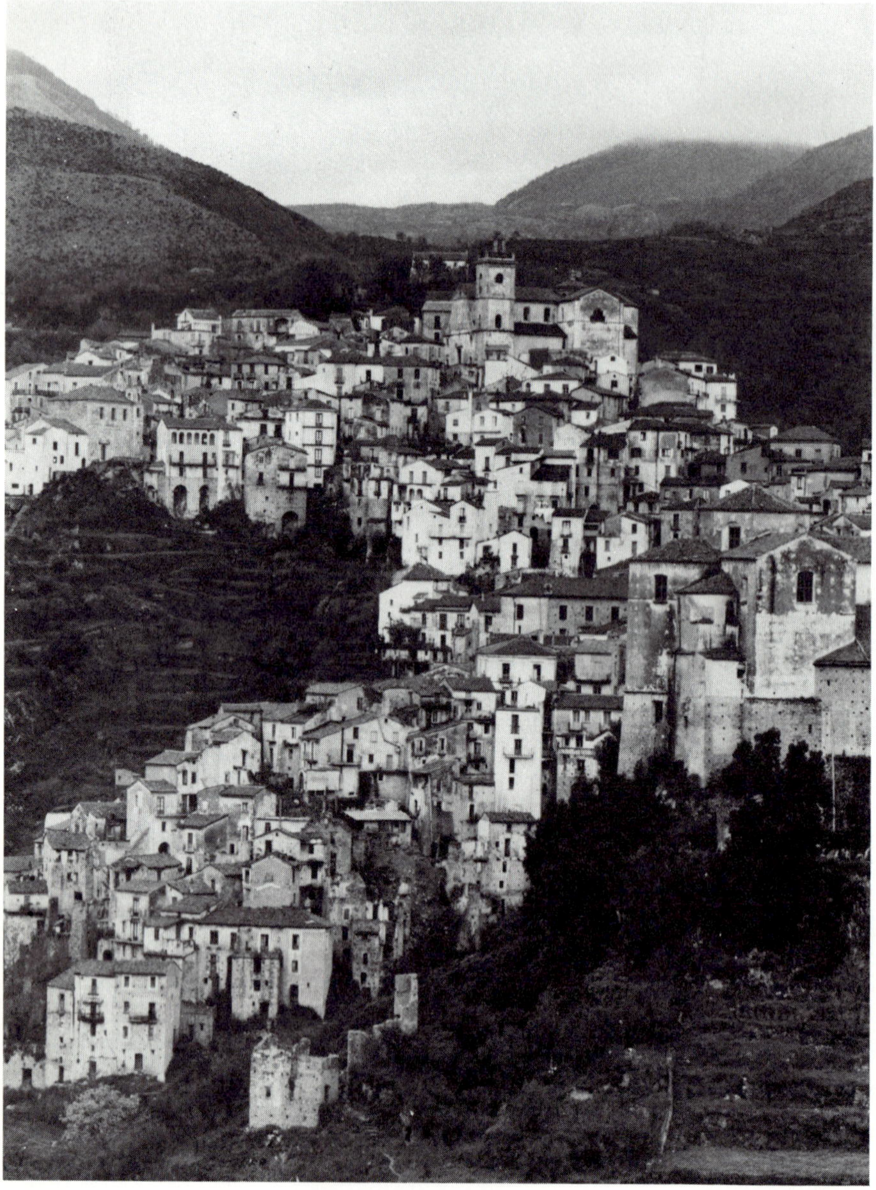

Chapter 2

Finding a Topic and Generating Ideas

🍎 *This chapter explains how to select topics you can write about most enjoyably and effectively. It also details three helpful approaches you can use to produce more ideas and more creative ideas.*

If you're like most people, you've suffered on more than one occasion from the "I'm afraid I've got nothing to say" syndrome. That is, you've sharpened a dozen pencils, opened a notebook full of paper (or uncovered your typewriter and unwrapped a ream of paper), shaken your wrists to loosen the muscles, and proceeded to sit there. And sit there. After a while you drummed the desk, stared alternately at floor and ceiling, fiddled with the paper, wiped a speck of dust from the desk, chewed your eraser, and waited for the flood of ideas that never came.

The problem is not limited to student writers. Professionals, too, encounter it. It even has a name—*writer's block*. Fortunately, it is not incurable. There are quick and effective techniques you can use to find a topic and generate ideas to write about, thereby sparing yourself the anxiety of waiting in vain.

Finding a Topic

Your best guides to selecting a topic are your *interests* and your *knowledge*. It's hard enough to keep a reader's attention on a topic that excites you. Choosing a topic that you yourself are bored with dooms your efforts from the start. Similarly, you are not apt to produce a worthwhile paper on a topic you know little about (unless, of course, you have the time and inclination to do research). Your ignorance will make your treatment trite, shallow, or opinionated.

Having knowledge about a subject does not mean being an "authority" on the subject. If only those with M.A.'s or Ph.D.'s expressed their views, very little would ever be written, and many valuable contributions would be lost. Nevertheless, the more thoroughly you are acquainted with a subject, the more you will have to say and the more valuable your ideas are likely to be.

There is no foolproof test for when you know enough about a subject to write about it effectively. You might write perceptively about the subject of divorce without knowing a single divorced person. A little reading or television viewing, followed by some reflection on the subject, particularly on the various effects of divorce on all the people involved (including children), can be enough to produce insights. On the other hand, you may have witnessed divorce numerous times in your own family, have been strongly affected by it yourself, and yet be unable to write effectively about it because you have never really stopped to think about it.

Knowledge, then, is not just a matter of having had real or vicarious experience. It is a matter of experience plus analysis. All things being equal, the best subjects for you to write about are the ones that you have had significant experience with and that you have examined and interpreted.

Topic Possibilities

You may think there is no topic you know well enough to write about. That would be a mistake. You've had countless contacts with people and places and things, you've enjoyed (in some cases not enjoyed) hundreds of thousands of experiences, and you've drawn and revised innumerable conclusions about those experiences. If you were able to remember all these things clearly and were to begin writing them down in detail, you would be an old man or woman before you finished writing. And you would not even have tapped your potential for *new* thoughts, *new* conclusions. Nothing to write about? Nonsense. The problem is usually not so much a lack of knowledge as a failure to remember, to retrieve relevant material from the storehouse of information in your mind.

What you need most, therefore, is a quick way to review the range of topic possibilities—to jog your memory, trigger associations, and reveal areas of interest and knowledge to choose from. Here are six such procedures.

1. *Review your special areas of experience and competency: your hobbies, jobs you've had, your relationships with your parents and brothers or sisters, singing or playing an instrument, driving or fixing cars, leisure activities.* Be sure not to overlook the obvious. A student who once lamented he had nothing to write about realized, after a little prodding, that his job the previous summer was a goldmine of composition possibilities. He had been a seaman on a freighter that sailed the Atlantic and Mediterranean.
2. *Consider interesting places you've visited, extraordinary people you've met, unusual situations you've been in, and memorable experiences you've had.*
3. *Consider emotions you've felt and the occasions they call to mind.* Consider the following emotions:

hatred	aggravation	depression
pity	satisfaction	worry
fear	jealousy	greed
grief	resentment	anger
love	remorse	shame
passion	sorrow	pride
disgust		

4. *Review good and bad qualities that people display, and let these qualities suggest particular experiences, feelings, and ideas.* Consider these qualities and their opposites:

humility	kindness	helpfulness
friendship	courtesy	prudence
concern	courage	fairness
thrift	selflessness	gratitude
tact	respect	wisdom
mercy	honesty	responsibility
charity	patience	sincerity
sympathy	generosity	enthusiasm

5. *Consider interesting quotations and the thoughts they bring to mind.* For example:
   a. "A fool sees not the same tree that a wise man sees." (William Blake)
   b. "Calling attention isn't the same thing as explaining." (John Ashbery)

c. "Everyone is his own enemy." (St. Bernard)
d. "Perhaps the greatest of all generosities is that which gives the benefit of the doubt—which refuses to retail malicious gossip, which believes the best rather than the worst." (I.A.R. Wylie)
e. "Whoever lies for you will lie against you." (Bosnian proverb)
f. "Nothing is so stupid as an educated man if you get him off the subject he is educated in." (Will Rogers)
g. "That man is richest whose pleasures are the cheapest." (Henry David Thoreau)
h. "The Christian ideal has not been tried and found wanting. It has been found difficult and left untried." (G. K. Chesterton)
i. "If we all pulled in one direction, the world would keel over." (Yiddish proverb)
j. "Travel makes a wise man better but a fool worse." (Thomas Fuller)
k. "The wise man does at once what the fool does finally." (Gracian)
l. "The unexamined life is not worth living." (Socrates)
m. "The cruelest lies are often told in silence." (Stevenson)
n. "How glorious it is—and how painful—to be an exception." (Musset)
o. "Conscience is, in most men, an anticipation of the opinion of others." (Sir Henry Taylor)
p. "Men are not punished for their sins, but by them." (E. Hubbard)
q. "Anger is seldom without an argument, but seldom with a good one." (Lord Halifax)
r. "No pleasure lasts more than a moment." (Anonymous)
s. "If there has been a decline of decency in the modern world and a revolt against law and fair dealing, it is precisely because of the decline in the belief in each man as something precious." (James Reston)
t. "We believe whatever we want to believe." (Demosthenes)
u. "Laws are good or bad, less by themselves than by the manner in which they are applied." (Anatole France)
v. "One is always changed into the image of what one admires." (Paul Sabatier)
w. "I am afraid most parents don't know what they want and don't mean what they say because they have no convictions." (Erich Fromm)

Finding a Topic and Generating Ideas

    x. "Friendship is always a . . . responsibility, never an opportunity." (Kahlil Gibran)
    y. "No one fails who does his best." (Anonymous)
    z. "How awful to reflect that what people say of us is true." (L. P. Smith)
   aa. "In quarreling the truth is always lost." (Publilius Syrus)
   bb. "The greatest mistake you can make in life is to be continually fearing you will make one." (E. Hubbard)
   cc. "The girl who can't dance says the band can't play." (Yiddish proverb)
   dd. "People hate those who make them feel their own inferiority." (Chesterfield)
   ee. "The moment we understand and feel sorry for the next man and forgive him, we wash ourselves, and it is a cleaner world." (Albert Schweitzer)
   ff. "Those who cannot remember the past are condemned to repeat it." (Santayana)
   gg. "A man's worst difficulties begin when he is able to do as he likes." (T. H. Huxley)
   hh. "There is nothing noble in being superior to some other man. The true nobility is in being superior to your former self." (Hindu proverb)

6. *Consult a list of general topics to stimulate your thinking.* Here is a brief list:

America	marriage	religion
self-interest	dieting	astrology
pranks	careers	insanity
habits	violence	cigarettes
bigotry	inventions	television
pretending	suicide	pornography
food	alcohol	censorship
ESP	jogging	prejudice
sports	pollution	self-defense
death	intuition	dormitories
cars	childhood	borrowing
war	roommates	swearing
movies	cheating	evil
sex	manners	trash
fashion	hypocrisy	illiteracy
recreation	high school	punctuality
money	rudeness	the seasons
dreams	virginity	morality

art	gambling	nature
nudity	marijuana	snobbery
beauty	toys	English class
dating	privacy	poetry
poverty	sleep	imagination
health	humor	confusion
phobias	sanitation	saving face
travel	mercy killing	paranoia
dancing	homosexuality	pets
crime	advertising	filth
security	prostitution	aggression
competition	music	anxiety
depression	flying saucers	communism
professors	cannibalism	the human body

Exercise   Take a sheet of paper and go through the six ways of finding a topic detailed above. List all the topics about which you have some knowledge and in which you are interested. Don't skimp on this list—aim for at least twenty-five topics.

Generating Ideas

Once you have selected your topic, your next task is to decide what you will say about it. This stage should not be confused with the writing stage. Here you will merely be producing ideas, not arranging and developing them in a composition.

We will be examining three helpful techniques for generating ideas. First, however, let's note the important principles that underlie all three techniques.

Thinking on paper is more effective than thinking within your mind. Many studies have documented what serious writers have long realized—that the act of writing down one idea often triggers a whole series of ideas.

Once ideas begin to flow, your only concern should be to record them as quickly as possible. Sometimes ideas come slowly, allowing time for careful, legible expression, and even for a sentence or two of elaboration. However, at other times they come so rapidly that you will be hard pressed to scribble them down in fragments. Never be so concerned with legibility or elaboration that you stop the flow of ideas or postpone recording them; otherwise you may lose valuable ideas.

The more ideas you produce, the more likely you are to have good ideas. There is a definite connection between the quantity and the quality of ideas. Studies have demonstrated that the original idea, the penetrating insight, the creative breakthrough are more apt to come when you make an extended effort to produce a number of ideas than when you settle for the first few that come to mind.[1] Such studies reveal that the early ideas are often not particularly good. They tend to be more predictable, more common, less original. But if you let them, they can stimulate the production of the later, better ideas. It is almost as if the mind requires a warming-up exercise before performing at its best.

Now let's turn to the techniques for generating ideas. They are *freewriting, forcing associations,* and *imaginary dialogue.*

Freewriting

Freewriting is useful in two very different situations. One is when you want to write about your topic but the blank page creates a mental block for you. The other is when you know you have a great deal to say but the sheer number of your ideas leaves you undecided where to begin recording.

Your aim in freewriting is simply to fill a page (or two or three pages) with writing. In freewriting, you are completely unconcerned about the usefulness of your words, or their organization, or even their coherence. Since no one but you will see the writing, there is no need to make it meet any standard—and that includes the standards of spelling, grammar, and usage.

Freewriting has only one guideline: *don't stop writing.* Pausing to ponder a thought or to decide what to say next are acceptable in other idea-producing strategies and in later stages of the composition process, but they are unacceptable in freewriting because they aggravate the problem you are trying to solve. So don't let your pencil or typewriter be idle for a moment. If a dry period occurs, write through it. Make yourself continue, even if you are writing no more than the same word over and over. Merely writing "courage" over and over, and keeping your mind open to associations, may eventually stimulate you to write, "Aunt Sarah's final illness," and from there it's a short step to wondering (and writing), "Was she

Sample of Freewriting

The underlined words show how to deal with pauses when they threaten to interrupt the flow of words.

<u>The human body.</u> Where should I begin? Some bodies are big, some small. My back aches. Probably a result of sitting in this chair and trying to write about the body. <u>Can't pause here, have to keep moving. The human body.</u> It's a marvelous thing. All the parts. My fingers on the pen, guiding its movement, providing just the right pressure. <u>The human body.</u> The head, the brain, with its thinking ability, its ability to reason. Few people reason well. Their egos get wrapped up in the process. Still, the ability to be correct once in a while is marvelous. The eye, the amazing way it is able to see, to put the body in touch with things outside itself. Not a perfect thing, the eye, because some people need eyeglasses. Creative invention, eyeglasses. A tribute to the human mind. I wonder what the connection is between mind and brain. Are they the same? Is the mind a spiritual thing? <u>The human body. The human body. I've got to write something besides "the human body." </u> Seems silly, but <u>I'm going to keep writing something down here, just keep going until I get an idea that's about the topic, the topic, the human body.</u> I almost died from a ruptured appendix when I was ten. How I suffered from that pain. A little thing like an appendix. Not even necessary to the body. Yet it almost killed me. That shows just how fragile the body is. My friend Ed should have reflected on that. He wouldn't have tried to push his car so fast. He might be alive today. The human body....

really courageous or was she just foolish?"; "What distinguishes the hero from the foolhardy person?"; "Can you be afraid and still be courageous?"; "Maybe the hero is more afraid, not less, but just handles her fear differently."

If you are meticulous about your work and feel guilty about producing a messy page, remember that you are working to *discover* ideas at this stage—not to *communicate* them. Although neatness is a virtue in final drafts intended for other people's eyes, it is a vice here if it slows you down or distracts you. When the ideas begin to flow, you may not be able to write fast enough to get them down. So sacrifice neatness and forget about grammar and usage, paragraphing and organization. Write in fragments and your own personal shorthand. As long as you can decipher your notes later, they're neat enough.

Let's say that you chose the topic "The Human Body" to write about. Page 30 illustrates how your freewriting might look.

Later, when you've filled one or more pages with freewriting, you can sort out what you've written and decide what you wish to include in your composition. Your work may be even less presentable than this, but that is nothing to worry about. Your freewriting will have helped you begin producing ideas, and that is all you want it to do.

Forcing Associations

The aim of this technique is twofold: to discover the various aspects and dimensions of your topic that you might wish to include in your composition, and to identify all the associations that the broad topic and its specific subheadings have for you. To use this approach you need only ask the following questions about your topic and answer each as thoroughly as you can:*

What are the *divisions or classifications* of the topic? (What subtopics does it cover?)

What special *occasions* in the history of the topic are of major importance or unusual interest?

What important *places* are associated with the topic?

What special *principles and practices* are associated with the topic?

---

*Occasionally one or more of these questions will be inapplicable to your topic. However, most of them will apply to any topic you choose.

What *implements* are associated with the topic?

What *individuals, organizations, or agencies* have contributed to the development of the topic?

What significant *personal experiences* have you or people you know had with the topic?

Do you have a *strong opinion* about some part of your answer to one of the questions above? If so, what is that opinion?

See pages 33–37 for illustrations of this technique.

Imaginary Dialogue

The imaginary-dialogue approach enables you to see a subject through someone else's eyes. Naturally, it is impossible to enter other people's perspectives totally. But you can approximate their views. Even the least perceptive person is aware of how others may react in some situations. How many times have you said, "I know what my mother is going to do when she finds out about this"? Obviously you were familiar enough with her past reactions to predict with some accuracy how she would react in a similar situation. It's the same with other people and other situations.

With a little effort and imagination, you could probably predict how a teacher from high school or a friend from your hometown would react to something you've seen or experienced in college. And by making an even greater effort, you could predict (granted, a little more tentatively) how a storeowner who had been robbed half a dozen times would feel about lenient judges and parole boards. Or how a woman whose husband was killed in Vietnam would feel about draft evaders.

In addition to generating ideas, this technique can raise aspects of a topic you might not otherwise have considered. It can also challenge you to respond more precisely and more completely than you would otherwise have done. Here's how to use this approach.

> Think of someone you know who has a firm viewpoint on the topic, preferably someone you've discussed it with before. Imagine yourself discussing the topic with that person now. Take the notes you produced through freewriting and forcing associations and look at each of your points as that person would view it. Jot down next to each point the response that person would make to it. Then write down your reaction to the response.

Finding a Topic and Generating Ideas

TOPIC: SPORTS

aquaplaning   archery   bullfighting   canoeing   croquet
curling   yachting   football   trapshooting   water polo   fencing   hiking
hang gliding   baseball   horseshoe pitching   basketball   lacrosse   golf
platform tennis   surfing
skydiving   snowmobiling   scuba diving   iceboating
horseracing   windsurfing   weightlifting
       mountain climbing   skiing

DIVISIONS OR CLASSIFICATIONS

First superbowl   First college football   First ascent of
                  game in U.S.   Mt. Everest
Origin of lacrosse   Induction ceremony –
                          Hall of Fame

OCCASIONS

Lou Gehrig's retirement speech   1983 America's Cup race
        Invention of snowmobile   Highlights of Babe Ruth's career

Basketball   The coach's office
Hall of Fame   in your high school
     The college weight room   Wrigley Field
                Dodger Stadium   Your favorite ski resort

PLACES

                                              The highest mountain
Your favorite surfing beach   you've climbed

The "T" formation   The "back door" play   Techniques
in football   in basketball   of climbing
       Folding a parachute   The zone defense   a mountain
The infield fly
rule in baseball   Slalom racing
Training a   on skis
racehorse   Varieties of the
               serve in tennis
Formations in skydiving   Cheerleading then + now   The goalie's job

PRINCIPLES AND PRACTICES

The making   A mountain climber's equipment
of a baseball   The evolution of
          Changes in   Racing yacht design   the archer's bow
          parachute
          design   Variations in
The evolution of   tennis racquets
football helmets
          Cross country ski equipment

IMPLEMENTS

INDIVIDUALS, ORGANIZATIONS, AGENCIES

- The origin of Little League
- Jim Thorpe
- Bear Bryant
- Dr. James Naismith
- Your high school coach
- Billy Martin and George Steinbrenner
- Abner Doubleday
- Willie Mays
- Vince Lombardi
- Pelé

PERSONAL EXPERIENCES

- Your first time at a professional game
- Learning to throw a curve ball
- The day you won (lost) the championship
- Being cut from the team
- Locker room pranks
- Your most memorable sports experience
- Playing catch with your mother or father
- Playing golf at a famous course
- Sitting on the bench

YOUR STRONG OPINIONS

- TV commercials are ruining sports
- The designated hitter is hurting baseball
- High school coaches shouldn't imitate college and professional coaches
- Parents shouldn't demand that children fulfill their athletic fantasies
- High schools and colleges spend too much money on sports
- I'm sick and tired of sports-talk
- Howard Cosell should be neither seen nor heard
- Let's open the Olympics to all athletes and end the hypocrisy of the amateur rule
- Most fans are fanatical
- Sitting on the bench doesn't build character — it breeds resentment
- Sports should be for everyone, so let's have more emphasis on <u>intramurals</u>

Finding a Topic and Generating Ideas

TOPIC: THE HUMAN BODY

Heart, Lungs, The mind, Tendons, Pancreas, Hair, Knees, Elbows, Muscles, Ligaments, Skin, Ankles, Nose, Liver, Stomach, Kidneys, Teeth, Sinuses, Brain, Arms, Eyes, Ears, Appendix, Spine, Legs, Tongue, Genes, Hormones

DIVISIONS OR CLASSIFICATIONS

Heart disease, Acne, Occasions of illness, Emphysema, Tonsillitis, Psoriasis, Diabetes, Allergies, Occasions of health, Cancer, Asthma, Epilepsy

OCCASIONS

The library, Sanitation, Hospital, Health spa, Barber shop, Dentist's office, Doctor's office, Hospital laboratory, Physical therapy, Classroom, Cemetery, Optometrist's office, Drug store, School, Beauty parlor, Chiropractor's office

PLACES

Dieting, False teeth, Pacemaker, Nutrition, Birthing: old practices and new, The autopsy, Body building, Heart transplant, Teeth flossing, Periodontal surgery, Facelift operation, Bloodletting, Discovery of X-ray, Evolution of medical profession, History of bathing, Acupuncture, Knee surgery

PRINCIPLES AND PRACTICES

The polio vaccine, The invention of eyeglasses, The invention and development of false teeth, Medicine, Schoolbooks

IMPLEMENTS

INDIVIDUALS, ORGANIZATIONS, AGENCIES

Alexander Graham

Louis Pasteur

Elderhostel: a unique senior citizens' organization

World Health Organization

Jonas Salk

Galen

UNESCO

The best teacher I ever had

The Environmental Protection Agency

PERSONAL EXPERIENCES

My ruptured appendix

My automobile accident

A trip to the beauty parlor

My first visit to the doctor's office

My first pair of glasses

My first encounter with death

Getting a tooth pulled

Having my tonsils out

YOUR STRONG OPINIONS

It's stupid to abuse drugs, including booze

Schools should prepare students for parenthood

Rich countries have a moral obligation to give economic and technological aid to poor countries

Doctors earn too much money

It's better to leave one's wealth to charities than to relatives

We should get tough with child molesters

The TV industry should be forced to use its potential for educating people instead of squandering that potential

Life is short, so time is precious — it's a sin to waste it

When I die, I want to be cremated

Boxing should be outlawed

Health care should be considered the right of every citizen regardless of economic level

Finding a Topic and Generating Ideas

Let's say the topic you're exploring is peer pressure to smoke cigarettes. You might imagine yourself discussing the matter with one of your childhood friends who exerted the most pressure on you and others. Here's the way part of your idea sheet would look:

Original Note	Imaginary Response from Friend	Your Reaction to Her Response
The first time I smoked a cigarette I really didn't want to.	Why didn't you refuse?	I was afraid the group would ostracize me. I needed their acceptance because I was insecure.
There was a lot of pressure to conform.	That's crazy. Nobody pressured anyone else.	It wasn't obvious pressure but subtle. For example....
If Jane hadn't smoked, I don't think I would have.	Jane was only one member of the group. Why did she have such an influence on you?	She was my best friend. I looked up to her. Though I'm ashamed to admit it even now, I followed her in many ways.

As you use the three techniques for generating ideas, remember that ideas will not come to you only when you are making a formal effort to produce them. Many good ideas occur at odd moments and in strange places. The principle of specific gravity occurred to Archimedes as he slid into a bath and noticed how his body displaced the water in the tub. Insights can come while you are in church, driving a car, even sleeping. Many an artist or inventor has awakened with the solution to a problem that seemed unsolvable the night before. But such ideas fly away as quickly as they come to you. They must therefore be captured and recorded the moment they appear. So keep a notebook handy.

Narrowing Your Topic

Even a casual look at the ideas shown above for the topics *sports* and *the human body* will suggest the foolishness of expecting to write a meaningful composition on a broad topic. Thus, after you generate ideas you must narrow your topic. To do this, examine all the aspects and dimensions you have identified and decide which you will write about.

You will have no difficulty narrowing your topic if you keep two simple principles in mind. The first is that *the unusual is generally more interesting than the usual.* This does not mean, of course, that you cannot make a common topic interesting. (As we noted in Chapter 1, a creative treatment is possible with any topic.) It merely means that choosing an unusual, less-discussed aspect of a broad topic increases the chances that your composition will be interesting.

The second principle is that *less is more.* This means that the narrower your topic, the more fully and effectively you can move from surface matters to subtleties and complexities and from the general to the specific. Although a 300–500-word composition may seem quite long if you have had little writing experience, such a composition affords you very little room for development. To produce a successful effort, therefore, you must resist the temptation to make your topic broader than you can do justice to.

Here are some examples of effectively narrowed topics. Each is somewhat unusual and is suitably limited for a brief composition.

Broad Topic	Effectively Narrowed Topic
Crime	The Reliability of Lie Detectors
	Lombroso's Strange Theory of Criminality
	Does the Insanity Defense Make Sense?
	Colonial Methods of Punishment for Criminals

Finding a Topic and Generating Ideas

The Human Body
- Common Knee Injuries
- The Pancreas
- Vocal Chords
- Why Funerals Are a Ripoff

Sports
- Sportscasters, Famous and Infamous
- The Legendary Jim Thorpe
- The Effects of Being Punched in the Boxing Ring
- Sports in Primitive Cultures

Exercises

1. Examine the associations for sports (pages 33–34) and for the human body (pages 35–36). Then develop four narrowed topics for each. Be sure they follow the principles of narrowing discussed in the chapter, as do the examples shown on pages 38–39.
2. Select one of the topics you listed in your response to the mid-chapter exercise on page 28. Apply the three techniques for generating ideas. Then develop at least four narrowed topics suitable for a 300–500-word composition. Be prepared to submit your worksheets.

Composition Assignment

Write a 300–500-word composition on one of the narrowed topics you produced in exercise 2 above. Be sure to give sufficient attention to each part of the composition process: planning, writing, and revising.

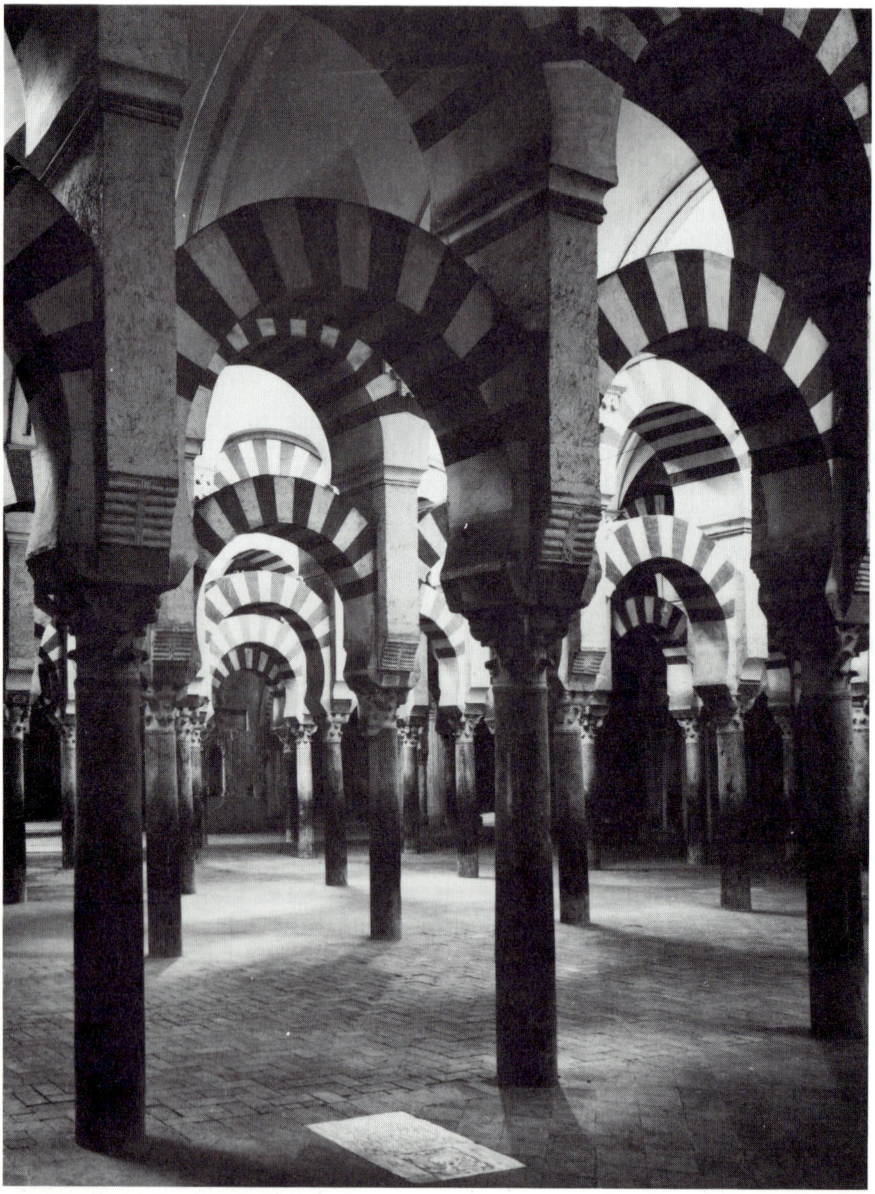

Chapter 3

Selecting the Composition Form and Controlling Idea

This chapter illustrates the basic composition forms and explains how to decide which is best for your paper. It also explains how to select and express your controlling idea.

After finding your topic and generating ideas for it, the next step in planning is to decide what form your composition will take and exactly what you will say in it. The importance of this step is best appreciated by reflecting on how you produced your ideas. It was not an organized, carefully controlled, highly focused process. Rather, it was—it *had* to be—free and random. It would be naive, however, to think that others would find that random collection of ideas meaningful. To be meaningful to others, those ideas must be given a specific shape and direction.

Basic Composition Forms

Let's first consider composition form. Broadly speaking, there are three forms to choose from: *narrative, informative,* and *persuasive.** Each has its own special characteristics that distinguish it from the others.

---

*There are, of course, many subdivisions within each form.

The Narrative Composition

Narrative writing recounts actual experiences.* It aims not merely to tell the readers what happened but to *show* them, so that they participate in the experience vicariously. This showing may be accomplished through various techniques. For example, a composition on the terrifying experience of almost drowning in a raging river during a canoe trip might go beyond a simple presentation of events to a dramatic account of the incident, complete with vivid depiction of the actions and emotions that accompanied it. On the other hand, a "travel" article about a New Jersey family's trip to the western United States might be more matter-of-factly presented.

Besides providing a logical sequence of events, effective narrative writing also provides appropriate sensory impressions—descriptions of persons, places, things, thoughts, and feelings as they occurred during and after the experience. Here is a good example of narrative writing.

Note that this composition is intensely personal and dramatic in its expression. The writer is not merely explaining the sequence of events; she is sharing the sensations, impressions, and emotions she experienced during the events. Her objective is not merely to have the readers understand, but to have them feel what happened.

It happened September 2, 1971, five days before the beginning of my senior year in high school. I was working part-time evenings at a self-service gas station in Northville. At nine o'clock, just as I was locking up, some of my friends drove in and asked if I'd like to ride around with them. It sounded like fun so I climbed into the crowded station wagon. In the front were Doug, Dennis, and Dave, the driver, whose father owned the car. I sat behind Dave with Gail; Marilyn and Kathy were in the rear seat.

After riding around town for a while we began to get bored. Someone urged, "Let's drive to Amity." Dave explained that his father had told him to stay in town, but after some good-natured needling, he agreed to go. We headed out of town on Route 40.

After we'd gone a few miles, Gail asked if she could drive. Dave stopped the car and moved over, Dennis got in back, and Gail took over. About half a mile down the road, she began to swerve back and forth, at about fifty miles per hour, first touching the far left edge of the highway and then the far right, the whole wagon leaning precariously at each turn. She was laughing wildly, obviously very pleased with her daring maneuvers. I suddenly became very nervous

---

*In fiction, which does not concern us here, the experiences are at least in part imaginary.

and shouted, "Gail, what are you doing that for? It's dangerous. Please stop it."

Before she had a chance to answer, the car slipped off onto the low shoulder. She pulled it out too quickly and was on the wrong side of the road when someone in front grabbed the wheel in an attempt to help. But this over-corrected the car, causing us to head for the guardrails on the right.

I never felt the impact; I must have closed my eyes. All I remember was floating in space, weightless in a black sea, for what seemed like hours. I woke to the sound of a blaring horn. My mind flashed to three months before when my cousin was dragged from his car only seconds before it exploded into flames. I realized I had to get out.

There were only two of us left in the car—Gail and I. Then Gail slid out through the windshield and was gone. I unhooked my seatbelt and tried to open the door but couldn't. (I later learned that the car had turned to face the direction from which we had come and landed on the driver's side, with only a few small trees preventing it from rolling down a steep hill.) So I crawled into the front seat, and slid out through the windshield and down the hill. There I found Gail. When I asked her if she was all right, all she said was, "I can't move." Panicked, I scrambled up the hill where I figured I could get help.

It was very dark, and I didn't know exactly where I was, when I looked up and saw before me the twelve-foot wall we had come over. It had not been visible from the road. Hysterically, I screamed for help, not knowing that only a few yards away was a path that led to the road. I heard something and turned to find a woman next to me. She lived nearby and had come to investigate when she heard the horn. Her son had gone to call the ambulance.

As I was led to the road, I could hear Marilyn below, yelling for help. On the road I found Dave and Kathy. Kathy had been thrown out the rear window. Her head was bleeding. She was in a daze and unaware of what had happened. (Only five weeks before she had rolled over in a Volkswagen and had badly scraped up her back.)

The ambulance arrived. The attendant bandaged Kathy's head and asked her to lie down in back. Dave and I rode in front to the hospital, where we found Doug and Dennis, who had ridden in with friends. By that time the waiting room was full of nervous parents and concerned friends. "Where were Gail and Marilyn?" The question was on everyone's mind. The minutes passed slowly. People paced, stared at the walls. The silence was strangely awkward . . . in a funny way, almost too *loud*.

About an hour and a half later the ambulance pulled in and Gail and Marilyn were wheeled into the emergency room. Marilyn, we learned, had been thrown out through the rear window with Kathy, then had slid down the gravel bank on her back. Because of the wall and the steep hill, she and Gail had had to be rescued by way of some old railroad tracks below.

Kathy, Marilyn, and Gail were admitted to the hospital. Kathy required twelve stitches for a deep gash on her forehead. Marilyn's back was torn raw from contact with the rough gravel. But Gail was much worse. She had numerous cuts and bruises, a punctured lung, three broken ribs, and two broken teeth. Her three-week stay in the hospital included four days in intensive care. Yet despite her condition, Gail was very lucky, as we all were. For after seeing the car and the place it had landed, many people wondered how any of us had survived.

It's been years since that accident happened. And I've driven that road hundreds of times. But every time I pass that section of road I unconsciously ease up on the accelerator. And frequently, as the memory of the experience recurs, I find myself shuddering.

The Informative Composition

Informative writing presents factual data in an impersonal way. It aims to improve the readers' understanding of the topic rather than to affect their emotions or persuade them of something. The focus in informative writing is on details: Who? What? When? Where? Why? In what manner? With what results? The emphasis is more on objective reporting than on the author's personal point of view. Examples of informative writing are business reports, news articles, encyclopedia articles, and textbooks. Here is an example of informative writing.

If you examine this passage carefully, you will note that it contains a wealth of details about caravans: what they are, how they developed, where they were used, and so on. Not a single sentence expresses the author's personal opinion about caravans. The

CARAVAN, kar′-ə-van. Since ancient times, men traveling through inhospitable territory in various parts of Africa and Asia have sought safety by organizing caravans. The word comes from the Persian *karwan*, meaning "a company of travelers." Caravans differed greatly in size, ranging from half a dozen members to processions of thousands extending from horizon to horizon. The use of pack animals to carry passengers and baggage was a distinct feature of such groups. In desert areas, camels—either the single-humped (dromedary) type of Southwest Asia and North Africa or the double-humped (Bactrian) Central Asian breed were customarily used. In mountainous, forested, or prairie country, horses and donkeys were preferred, and in some places human porterage was used.

Although caravans were organized for many reasons, the conduct of trade was a primary purpose. Until the growth of large-scale maritime commerce, overland transport by caravan was the main means for the exchange of goods between widely separated peoples. The rise of Islam furnished an additional stimulus to caravan travel, for pilgrims journeying to the sacred city of Mecca often had no other way of travel available to them.

Caravan trips, which often required months or years to complete, were costly enterprises. Men and animals had to be maintained, and hazards from brigands, climate, and terrain were formidable. Caravaners therefore trafficked chiefly in goods of small bulk and high value. Fine cloth, ceramics, glassware, hides, salt, ivory, gems, and rare metals were typically found in caravan shipments.

Caravans apparently first flourished in the ancient Near East and linked the principal urban centers of the region extending from Persia to Egypt. In time these caravan routes reached further, to India, Central Asia, and China. The Great Silk Road through Central Asia is renowned as the path by which the wonders of Chinese civilization became known to the West.

The introduction of the camel from Southwest Asia into North Africa about the first century A.D. spurred the growth of communications between the lands along Africa's Mediterranean coast and the Sudan and forest regions south of the Sahara. Timbuktu, Gao, Takedda, Walata, and many other African cities flourished as "ports" situated along the trans-Saharan caravan trade route.

In the New World, the wagon train, in which people migrated westward, was the counterpart of the Old World caravan. Settlement more than trade, however, was the driving force behind the organization of the American and Canadian version of the caravan.[1]

focus is exclusively on what authorities agree is true about the subject.

There is no restriction on the kind of subject that can be treated in a purely informative way. Even controversial subjects can be treated in this manner. You might, for example, write an informative composition on mercy killing or capital punishment or the danger of nuclear war. It would not, of course, present arguments for a particular position. It would rather present what is known about the subject—its origin, history, and development. Where controversy existed, it would describe the situation as objectively as possible, stating what positions the various factions took but not favoring one side over another.

The Persuasive Composition

Persuasive writing (also known as argumentative writing*) evaluates issues by presenting the writer's judgments and the evidence that supports them. In such writing the issues are always to some extent controversial—that is, they are open to more than one interpretation, so informed and intelligent people may differ in their views of them. Persuasive writing, therefore, aims to persuade the readers of the reasonableness of the writer's views. In many cases, it also aims to move the readers to some kind of action. A newspaper editorial, for example, may argue in favor of the high school budget with the aim of having the readers vote for it. A letter to a dormitory director may argue that her expulsion of a student was unfair, in the hope that she will allow the student to return. Here is an example of persuasive writing.

Note that the issue here—how to bring up children—is a controversial one, admitting of many different views. The author's purpose is to persuade his readers that his view is the most reasonable one. His approach, therefore, is to state his position and the reasoning that supports it. (Notice how he is careful to explain any point the reader might misunderstand, such as his definition of objective *in paragraph 2 and his distinction between* letting children learn *and* teaching them *in paragraph 4.)*

There's an old saying that advises anyone who wants a tree to grow in a certain direction to bend it that way when it's young, because trees don't bend easily when full-grown. The statement, of course, refers not only to trees but to people as well. I believe it makes a great deal of sense. Human beings are creatures of habit, and the habits that are formed early in life are very difficult to break later. Those who develop good habits in childhood have an easier time adjusting to adulthood. Nevertheless, I also believe that some parents apply the old saying too literally in raising their children. They forget that children and trees are not exactly the same.

When children are young, parents should teach them values. Specifically, they should teach them the basic rules of etiquette and some objective moral standard to guide their behavior. By "objective" I mean something that takes them beyond their own feelings and makes them mindful of the rights of others. The Golden Rule is a good example of such a standard. Such parental teaching is not only normal—the majority of people in all places and times have apparently passed on their values to their young—but it is reason-

---

*Argumentative writing is the more traditional term. However, popular usage has blurred the distinction between the words argumentative *and* quarrelsome. *As a result,* argumentative *has unfortunately come to suggest heated, emotional, and therefore somewhat illogical discourse, rather than reasoned discourse. The term* persuasive *is used here and elsewhere in this text because it is less open to misinterpretation.*

able as well. For when children are left to act as they please, they do harm to others and so are often resented and rejected.

Parents should also teach their children their religious and political views. They should take them to their church or temple, if they attend one, teach them their prayers and rituals, and share with them their beliefs about man's relation to man and God. To do less would cheat their children. It would be a refusal to share with them the best they have to offer—the beliefs that give meaning and direction to their lives.

What parents should not do is brainwash their children, keep them ignorant of the fact that honest and well-meaning people do differ in their views of life, or pretend that they have the Truth, capital T, and that it's therefore wrong to ask questions about or to doubt their views. They should let their children learn about other religions, other political philosophies, and other conceptions of right and wrong. I don't think they have to go out of their way to *teach* such things, but they shouldn't stand in the way of their children's learning them when the children become old enough to understand them. Above all, they should encourage their children to use their minds— to ask any question without feeling guilty. After all, asking questions and working out answers is the way to intellectual maturity.

Similarly, when children enter the teen years, their parents should increase their freedom and self-determination even more. Just as young people need to learn to accept greater responsibility as they get older, so they need to learn how to make wise choices and decisions. Of course, parents can and should continue to offer their advice and provide guidance whenever the teenagers want or need it. But they should avoid making decisions for them unless the teenagers' health or safety is threatened. It may be necessary to answer with a flat "No" when a fifteen-year-old wants her boyfriend to sleep with her in her room or wants to invite friends over to a drinking party. But it is not necessary to choose her courses in school or to deny her a choice in whether to continue with piano lessons. It's just as irresponsible for parents to deny their children the chance to make mistakes as it is to deny them assistance when they need it. After all, mistakes can sometimes be our best teachers.

In short, I think children should be taught when they are young, but be allowed to teach themselves more and more as they get older. This prepares them for adulthood gradually, sparing them the trauma of adjusting to it all at once. But even more important, I believe that at every stage they ought to be treated with care. To bend a child's mind makes good sense, as it does to bend a young tree, but not if the mind is *broken* in the process.

The Forms in Combination

Although the three composition forms are often used alone, the writing techniques associated with one form may be combined with those of another form. A film review, for example, may inform the readers about the subject and treatment of the film and then evaluate it. A magazine article may narrate the author's experience of watching a friend die from an overdose of drugs, present information on the number of such incidents around the country, and develop the author's idea about the best way to head off such tragedies before they occur. An article in a professional journal for English teachers may inform the readers about a new technique for teaching literature, narrate the writer's experiences using that technique in her classroom, and present her judgment that it is preferable to traditional teaching techniques. Here is an example of such a combination. (Further examples will be presented in Chapters 6 through 8, which examine in more detail the individual writing forms and their respective techniques and strategies.)

This combination of forms is informative and persuasive. It begins with several paragraphs of informative writing to provide background.

    In the time of the early Greeks, we are told, there was originally no concept of the body as separate from the mind and spirit. The tingling aliveness of every limb after a run might trigger an intellectual discussion, no less alive and tingling. The flight of the javelin was akin to the flight of the spirit. Life was whole and unified, and we still admire that classic unity in the masterpieces of Greek sculpture.

    But then the great games at Olympia and Delphi, Nemea and the Corinthian Isthmus, fell under the spell of professionalism. The pressure for winners became intense. Bribes became commonplace. Olympic victors were given the most extravagant prizes and privileges. The ancient idea—the unity of body, mind, and spirit—was degraded beyond repair.

    By the time of Alexander the Great, Olympic athletes were generally held in disrepute. Finally, under the Romans, the Olympics themselves were disgraced. The Emperor Nero was allowed to enter the games (which had been put off for two years at his request) as a chariot racer. He fell out of the chariot twice and finally had to give up, after which the judges awarded him the olive crown of victory.

This paragraph is mainly persuasive, setting forth the author's judgment of the effects of the present approach to physical education.

    Our present big-time sports have not descended that far, but we of the West have never regained the ancient ideal of body/mind/spirit, pure and whole, and that loss is not merely a theoretical one. As a matter of fact, our present fragmented approach to physical education and the body imposes serious handicaps on every administrator, teacher, and student in our school systems today.

Too often, we tend to think of our elementary school children as little bundles of thought and emotion who also happen to have bodies. These bodies are . . .

Surely we are due for a reform in the education of body/mind/spirit. In doing the research for my new book, *The Ultimate Athlete*, I discovered that such a reform is not only possible, but, in my view, inevitable. Away from the Super Bowl hullabaloo, away from the frantic cries of Number One, other games are being played and played very well. Another movement is now well under way, one that can transform our attitude toward sports, physical education, and the body.

This movement is exemplified by the growing army of joggers, hikers, swimmers, and cyclists, who are becoming increasingly knowledgeable about the benefits—and the long-term joys—of cardiovascular conditioning.

It is exemplified by . . .

The New Physical Education has not yet swept the field. The most optimistic estimate has less than a fourth of the nation's schools involved. But it enjoys the full support of AAHPER's [American Alliance for Health, Physical Education, and Recreation] leadership and holds tremendous appeal for teachers and parents, once they become acquainted with it. Here, indeed, is an idea whose time has come.

The splitting off of the body from the mind and spirit constituted a major error in Western thought, one that must never be repeated. In returning the body to the educational enterprise, everyone involved stands to gain. Moreover, as I point out in *The Ultimate Athlete*, "We may well discover that sports and physical education, reformed and refurbished, may provide us the best possible path to personal enlightenment and social transformation in this age."[2]

The ellipses (spaced periods) indicate the omission of the end of the sentence and a number of paragraphs that followed in the original.

This passage is a blend of information and judgment. (The idea that the reform is "inevitable" is a judgment, since it is open to dispute.) The author's evidence for this judgment is presented in a number of paragraphs; only the first ("This movement is exemplified by the growing army . . .") is presented here.

These two paragraphs also combine information and judgment. The first three sentences of the first paragraph are informative. The final sentence of the first paragraph and the entire second paragraph present judgments.

Selecting the Composition Form

To select the form for your composition, you should *examine closely the list of ideas you have produced and decide what form would be most suitable for them*. If those notes include a reference to a very significant experience you have had, you should consider limiting your paper to a narrative account of that experience. If most of your notes are factual data, you should consider doing an informative composition. If you have mainly opinions and supporting evidence, a persuasive paper might be your best choice.

Choosing one composition form, however, necessitates discarding all the notes that do not fit that form. Unfortunately, sometimes many of your best notes will not fit. Whenever that is the case, you should consider using a combination of two or three composition forms so that you can include more of your notes. Anytime you use a combination of forms, you must decide which one, if any, will dominate. If your notes are equally informative, narrative, and persuasive, you may want to assign equal space and emphasis to the three forms in your composition. If, on the other hand, one is more important, it should be given more space and emphasis.

An example may make this process a little clearer. Let's assume you are writing on the topic of violence in the high school you graduated from. You have generated a number of ideas and are now ready to select your composition form. Here, together with your comments on possible choices, is a selection from your notes.

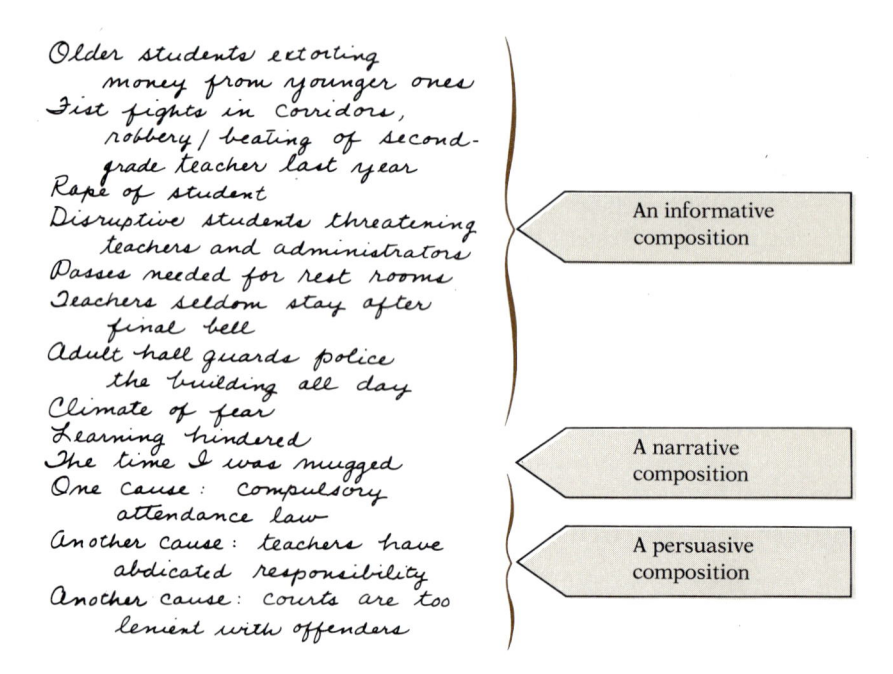

> Older students extorting money from younger ones
> Fist fights in corridors, robbery/beating of second-grade teacher last year
> Rape of student
> Disruptive students threatening teachers and administrators
> Passes needed for rest rooms
> Teachers seldom stay after final bell
> Adult hall guards police the building all day
> Climate of fear
> Learning hindered ⟵ An informative composition
> The time I was mugged ⟵ A narrative composition
> One cause: compulsory attendance law
> Another cause: teachers have abdicated responsibility
> Another cause: courts are too lenient with offenders ⟵ A persuasive composition

The other alternative, of course, is to combine the forms. In this case the combination with the greatest potential for effective development is informative and persuasive. Such a combination would enable you to use all your notes with the exception of the one about your being mugged. (Even that one could be used if you

Selecting the Composition Form and Controlling Idea

treated it objectively as just another example of violence.) If you decided that the dominant form would be persuasive, you would give more attention to your view of the causes of violence and to your reasons for supporting that view, using the secondary informative material to establish the seriousness of the matter.

Exercises

1. Assume that you have selected the topic "Part-time and Summer Jobs during High School" and have produced the list of ideas shown below. Examine the list carefully and decide what composition forms could be used for it. Then select the form (or combination of forms) you would prefer to use. You may wish to rearrange the ideas to clarify relationships.

   My friend waxed cars.
   My sister worked at Burger King.
   I worked as an aide at a hospital.
   A job teaches you how to deal with people.
   It can help clarify career plans (one way is by deflating unrealistic notions).
   It helps parents financially by letting a teenager pay for his or her own clothing, books, movies, and so on.
   It builds a sense of confidence and self-worth.
   It teaches a teen to budget time.
   My job in the hospital made me more aware of how fragile (and precious) life is.
   I became a more careful driver by seeing what takes place in emergency rooms after auto accidents.
   It's difficult today for kids to get jobs.
   A job teaches a teen to deal with a routine without losing creativity or enthusiasm.
   It makes a teenager grow up faster.
   Several of my friends applied at lots of places but didn't find work.
   Sometimes kids "turn off" employers by their appearance or attitude.
   Parents should encourage their kids to get part-time and summer jobs as soon as the kids are old enough.

2. Assume you have selected the topic "Criminals' Rights versus Victims' Rights" and have produced the list of ideas shown

below. Examine the list carefully and decide what composition forms could be used for it. Then select the form or combination of forms you would prefer to use. You may wish to rearrange the ideas to clarify relationships.

A criminal's chances of getting off easily (sometimes completely free) are usually very good.

Our legal system today is more concerned for criminals' rights than victims' rights.

Some say the solution is to let policemen use any means at their disposal to deal with suspects.

I believe the solution to the problem lies with legislators, lawyers, and judges meeting their responsibilities to society more fully.

Policemen are the closest ones to the problem of crime, I realize.

Policemen should not be allowed to act as judge and jury.

A suspect is just that—one *suspected* of a crime—not one convicted of a crime.

When police have too much freedom, our liberty is in danger.

Sometimes the police are too close to crime to be objective.

If a policeman has to use strong measures to protect his own life or the lives of innocent bystanders, then he should be free to use those measures.

The temptation to kick, punch, and even shoot suspects is at times very strong, particularly suspects in certain crimes, such as physical assaults on the elderly and child molestation.

Racial and ethnic prejudice can too easily influence one's judgment of who is a suspect.

Personal animosities can hide as justice.

Even criminals must be granted some rights—such as the right to personal safety during and after arrest, the right to legal counsel, and the right to a fair trial.

Defense lawyers should be less concerned with finding loopholes for their clients and more concerned with seeing justice done and keeping society safe from criminals.

A good example of the law being too concerned with criminals' rights is the case where a conviction for a violent crime is overturned by a court because a freely offered confession did not meet some minute legal standard.

Before handing down decisions, judges should weigh the effects of those decisions on the community.

Penalties should be stiffened by the legislature, particularly penalties for second offenders.

The Controlling Idea

After selecting the composition form, the next step in planning is to select the controlling idea. A controlling idea is an idea around which a piece of writing revolves.* It is the idea central to the meaning you want to convey, the essential message. It is this idea that governs most other considerations in writing: which ideas are judged relevant and which irrelevant; the organizational pattern used; the stylistic choices made; and so on. *Unless you want to do extensive revision later, be clear about your controlling idea before you begin writing.*

Almost every piece of writing you do for others should have a controlling idea. (An exception is the personal letter, which is often composed of a series of ideas, none of which is central.) In narrative writing, in which your aim is to re-create an experience for your readers, that idea may be largely unexpressed. The step-by-step account of the experience with appropriate descriptive detail will convey the meaning indirectly. Thus if you were relating an embarrassing situation, you might choose to let the story itself create the message without actually saying, "This was the most embarrassing experience of my life." However, even where you elect not to *express* the controlling idea, such an idea must still exist, and you can usually re-create the experience more effectively if you decide exactly what that idea is before you begin writing.†

In informative and persuasive writing, the controlling idea is not only expressed, but given prominence. Therefore, taking the trouble to construct it with care and precision will both make your writing effort easier and more enjoyable and protect against misunderstanding by your readers.

---

*Some instructors use other terms to signify the main idea in a piece of writing. *Thesis, thesis idea,* and *central idea* are the most common ones.

†Fiction writer Frank O'Connor approached his short stories in this way. "If somebody tells me a good story," he once explained, "I'll write it down in my four lines; that is the secret of the theme.... I always confine myself to my four lines. If it won't go into four, that means you haven't reduced it to its ultimate simplicity, reduced it to the fable." [In *Writers at Work,* edited by Malcolm Cowley (New York: Viking, 1959), p. 168.]

Selecting a Controlling Idea

There are certain considerations you should keep in mind when deciding on a controlling idea.

What Do You Really Want to Say?

This question may seem too obvious. After all, what could you say other than what you want to say? Unfortunately, it is easy to fall into the trap of saying what you think others want you to say, what you feel you are *expected* to say. To gain the satisfaction that comes from expressing your thoughts well, you must first be sure they *are* your thoughts. Not every writing situation, of course, allows total freedom. (In a business letter or memo, for example, you might be expressing your supervisor's judgment or a committee's decision.) But you should exercise whatever freedom the situation affords.

Consider the following situation. You have chosen the topic "The Value of the Honor Society in My High School." You may want to say that in your high school the honor society was a joke, that really deserving students were often passed over while less worthy students who "played the game" or came from important families were selected. You may believe, further, that one of the causes of this unfortunate situation was that selections were made by a secret committee. Yet you may shy away from saying what you really believe. Instead, you may decide that the teacher expects you to write that the National Honor Society had a positive influence on students, encouraging them to pursue excellence not only in school but in later life as well. And so you may suppress your own ideas. That decision is a disservice to your own thoughts and a compromise to your integrity, and it will almost certainly produce a less forceful paper. It's much better to say what you truly believe than what you think others want you to say.

How Much Time and Space Do You Have?

As we saw in Chapter 2, it is important to narrow the topic so that it can be *adequately* treated in the time and space available. This same concept applies when you are deciding on a controlling idea. It may be stated this way: in writing, *less can be more*. That is, the less you choose to write about, the more you can say about it in a limited space. In a given number of words, you can achieve greater depth discussing your favorite rock musician than discussing the history of rock music. Similarly, you can more easily cover discrimination against women in sports than you can discrimination in general.

What Idea Will Others Find Most Interesting?

This is seldom an easy question to answer, because what people find interesting depends largely upon their tastes, inclinations, and interests. Often the question is best approached in reverse, by considering what others will *not* find interesting. That is not so difficult to determine. To begin with, they are sure to be bored with a recitation of the obvious. Most people already believe that there is too much violence on television, that professional athletes are overpaid, and that institutional religion has declined in popularity. So you will do your readers and yourself a favor by not making any of these ideas the controlling idea of a composition. That does not mean you can't use these ideas in the course of developing another controlling idea on a related subject. It just means that any such statement should be made without belaboring the point, or you will risk boring your readers.

Try not to make your controlling idea anything you have often heard said by others. If you have heard the idea many times before, chances are your readers have too. Try to be original, to develop the habit of saying what other people have not said. To be sure, this effort can lead you to say some bizarre things, to make you more concerned with shocking the reader than with saying something sensible. But so long as you are also testing your ideas for reasonableness, you will be able to maintain a proper balance.

The trick is to develop a sense for what needs to be said about an issue, for what perspective has been neglected. In dealing with any kind of problem, you'll often find that the neglected side holds the solution. In other words, you'll find writer after writer identifying a problem, deploring it, and attacking the conditions and people responsible for it—but far fewer writers offering ways to overcome the problem. Take, for example, the issue of abortion. A great deal has been written about it. Yet much of what is written misses the real problems, pretends they don't exist, or deals with them too simplistically. To be specific, most discussions of abortion argue either that the mother has a right to do anything she wants with her body or that the fetus is a human being and therefore has the right to live. But the real problem is not either of the rights mentioned. It is the *conflict between them.* Both arguments make valid claims. Each should be honored. The dilemma is, which should take precedence? Perhaps one should all the time, or perhaps the other should, or perhaps one should in some circumstances but not in others. By writing about this neglected aspect of the topic, which your readers are not so likely to have encountered before, you increase your chances of interesting them.

But it is even possible to take a *common* idea and give it an uncommon treatment. Here's how it can be done. Instead of writing about how much violence there has been on television in recent years, you could present the idea that it is possible to produce exciting, action-filled shows without a lot of on-screen violence, supporting the idea, perhaps, with details about one or more shows that have done just that. The basic topic—TV violence—would remain the same. But the controlling idea would be a little different from the obvious or the expected.

If you can construct a good argument for the idea that professional athletes are *under*paid, or for the idea that institutional religion is *more* popular than ever, the unusualness of your position will create reader interest. Such ideas are not quite as absurd as they appear. Not all athletes make the salaries of the superstars. Many, particularly in less popular sports, are paid relatively modest sums. Similarly, there are places in this country and other countries where institutional religion is thriving. If you know of some such little-emphasized reality, you have the basis of a lively, out-of-the-ordinary paper.

Even if you lack such knowledge, you can still write an interesting paper by considering an unusual *perspective* on a problem. Perhaps you will decide to argue that players who are thought to be overpaid (such as a Moses Malone or a Reggie Jackson) are in fact paid only a small portion of the money their popularity generates, so they are really paid no more than they are worth. Or you may present the idea that people are making a mistake by ignoring institutional religion, that despite its shortcomings, no other means of meeting people's spiritual needs has proved as effective.

Expressing the Controlling Idea

In informative and persuasive writing, where the controlling idea is stated directly, it is important not only to select it with care but also to express it with care. Surely you have experienced the frustration of coming up with a good idea only to find yourself unable to express it clearly, perhaps saying even the opposite of what you really meant. The following guidelines can help you

Selecting the Composition Form and Controlling Idea

avoid such frustrating experiences and ensure that the controlling idea that comes out on paper is the one you had in your mind.

Make the Subject Appropriately Specific

If the subject of your controlling idea statement is too general, you will not be sure how to develop the paper in the later planning stages, how to decide what to include and what to exclude. Thus you increase the chances of writing a paper that wanders from point to point, never achieving the focus it needs. As we saw in Chapter 2, the subject "Crime," "The Human Body," or "Sports" is too broad for a composition (even one of 750 or 1,000 words).

Make the Predicate Precise

The predicate is what you say about the subject of your sentence, and it consists of the verb and its modifiers. For example, in the sentence "Few nations have learned to find peaceful ways to settle their differences," the subject is "few nations" and the predicate is everything else. Any imprecision in the predicate will result in failure to say what you want to say.

Many beginning writers are careless about their choice of predicates and end up saying something quite different from what they intended. Such mistakes often appear to be failures of thought. But they may not be that at all. They may be merely failures to translate thoughts into words.

Even the simple matter of verb tense can make a significant difference in meaning. Saying your town *has* numerous recreational activities for teenagers is not the same as saying your town *had* numerous recreational activities for teenagers. (The latter implies it no longer has such activities.) Moreover, the sentence "The mayor of Plainview lied about his opponent during the campaign" may look very much like the sentence "The mayor of Plainview made some incorrect statements about his opponent during the campaign," but their meanings are very different. The first sentence says the mayor knowingly misrepresented the facts. The second sentence merely says that what the mayor said, perhaps innocently, was false.

In most cases the choice of the predicate is not made from only two possibilities, but from many. Thus it is necessary to consider all the possibilities. Let's see how this works in an actual situation. Suppose you wanted to say something about people not believing in an afterlife. Here are some of the different predicates you should consider:

Many people no longer *believe* in an afterlife.
Many people no longer *want to believe* in an afterlife.
Many people no longer *are able to believe* in an afterlife.
Many people no longer *are certain* there is an afterlife.
Many people no longer *act as if there were* an afterlife.
Many people no longer *care if there is* an afterlife.
Many people no longer *accept some particular conception* of an afterlife.
Many people no longer *publicly profess belief* in an afterlife.

It would be a mistake to think that you must always choose one simple predicate. In many cases, particularly in such a complex matter as the question of people's belief in an afterlife, what you really want to say is a combination of possibilities. The best expression of all the strands of thought you have in mind, for example, may be something like this:

It has been reported that many people no longer believe in an afterlife. Yet it is possible that a large number of these people haven't renounced *all* such belief. Instead, they may have merely lost their certainty about some particular conception of an afterlife, and have therefore stopped professing their belief publicly.

Include All Necessary Qualifications

Saying something "happens" is different from saying it "usually happens" or that it "happens every other Thursday." Saying something "is" is different from saying it "may be" or "probably is." It is important to include in the controlling idea statement all necessary qualifications. These include qualifications of time, place, degree of certainty, and condition.

Qualifications of Time   Does it really happen *all the time* (or *never*)? Or rather, *usually, often, sometimes, occasionally, infrequently, or only on the third Tuesday of each month?*

Qualifications of Place   Is it really *everywhere* (or *nowhere*)? Or rather, in *most* places, *many* places, *some* places, *a few* places, or *only in Dubuque?*

Qualifications of Certainty   Is what you are saying *absolutely certain?* Or is it, instead, *probable* or only *possible?*

Qualifications of Condition   Does it happen in *all circumstances* (or *no circumstances*)? Or rather, in *most* cases, *many* cases, *some* cases, a *few* cases, or *only when it has rained for seven days immediately after a full moon in early summer?*

Make the Statement as Complete as You Can

The most helpful controlling ideas are those that not only state the essential idea but also suggest the context in which that idea will be presented. That is, they specify the particular aspects of the idea that will be presented and the relationships among those aspects. To understand this better, think of a controlling idea statement as a brief summary of the entire composition that captures all its proportions and emphases. One of the best models for such a statement is the explanatory note usually provided just after the title of a *Reader's Digest* article. Here are some examples.

> From an informative article entitled "Nature's Elegant Oddity: the Giraffe":[3]
>
> A mixture of the graceful and preposterous, the high lord of the animal kingdom is among the most beguiling of creations.
>
> From an informative/persuasive article entitled *"Donahue! Darling of the Daytime Dial"*:[4]
>
> Every weekday, 6½ million adoring women cling to his every word. And why not? For Phil Donahue brings to television a rare blend of intelligence and charm, controversy and conscience.
>
> From a narrative article entitled "The American in Cell No. 5":[5]
>
> The world of young Ken Kraus, U.S. Marine, had turned into a nightmare. On duty at our embassy in Iran, he had been shot by revolutionaries, then kidnapped from the hospital, charged with murder, and thrown into a foul dungeon. And there he waited, while the fusillades of a rooftop firing squad drifted down from above.
>
> From a persuasive article entitled "Football's Unfolding Tragedy":[6]
>
> At every level of the game, skill, teamwork, and sportsmanship have given way to intimidation and brutality. Unless changes are made, a great American sport may soon play out its final bloody quarter.

As all the above guidelines suggest, the best controlling idea statements grow out of a preliminary statement; a careful examination of the preliminary statement to determine whether the subject is appropriately specific, the predicate is precise, all necessary qualifications have been included, and the statement is complete; and a revision of the preliminary statement, if necessary, to improve it. The following revisions illustrate the process:

Preliminary Controlling Idea Statement	Revised Controlling Idea Statement
My roommate gets drunk all the time.	Whether my roommate is going to a movie with his friends or to a dance with his girlfriend, he begins the evening by getting drunk and embarrassing everyone around him.
Our college basketball team will probably get an NCAA bid.	Our college basketball team is virtually assured of an NCAA bid if several key players remain eligible and uninjured and if we defeat our arch-rival, Southwestern Tech.
The poor are going to revolt against the rich.	In countries where the rich minority openly exploit the poor majority, there is great potential for revolution; and though American military aid may postpone the overthrow of governments, it will not prevent it.
Ethnic jokes may seem harmless, but they are actually harmful.	Though many people consider ethnic jokes to be harmless, they are actually quite harmful. They not only cause people embarrassment but also perpetuate stereotyping and scapegoating, thereby denying many people a basic right—the right to be regarded as individuals.

Selecting the Composition Form and Controlling Idea

Exercises

1. Each of the following preliminary controlling idea statements is less than effective. Following the guidelines given in the chapter, revise each statement to make it effective. (You may add ideas or change the focus of the statements if you wish.)
   a. Many male supervisors use their positions to harass female subordinates sexually.
   b. I think Cabbage Patch dolls are ugly.
   c. People who marry to escape boredom are running a great risk.
   d. It's not up to the professor alone to make the class interesting. Students share the responsibility.
   e. Getting along with one's in-laws is an art.
   f. Most TV commercials are boring.
   g. I am (am not) impressed by the food at the college dining hall.
   h. The teachers in the high school I attended weren't demanding enough.
   i. I never anticipated the confusion of my first registration day at college.
   j. Growing up in a large family is better than growing up in a small family.
   k. Every student should be made to take a foreign language in high school.
2. Turn back to the exercise on the topic "Part-time and Summer Jobs during High School," presented on page 51. Review the ideas given for that topic and your decision about composition forms. Then construct an effective controlling idea for a composition. Be sure to apply the principles explained in the preceding pages.
3. Turn back to page 52. Review the notes presented there for the topic of "Criminals' Rights versus Victims' Rights," and your decision about composition forms. Then select an appropriate controlling idea for a composition. Be sure to apply the principles explained in the preceding pages.

Composition Assignment

Select one of the topics you identified as interesting in Chapter 2. Then generate ideas for your composition by freewriting, forcing associations, and imaginary dialogue, and narrow your topic. Finally, select an appropriate composition form and a controlling idea and write a 300–500-word composition. Be sure to give sufficient attention to each part of the composition process: planning, writing, and revising.

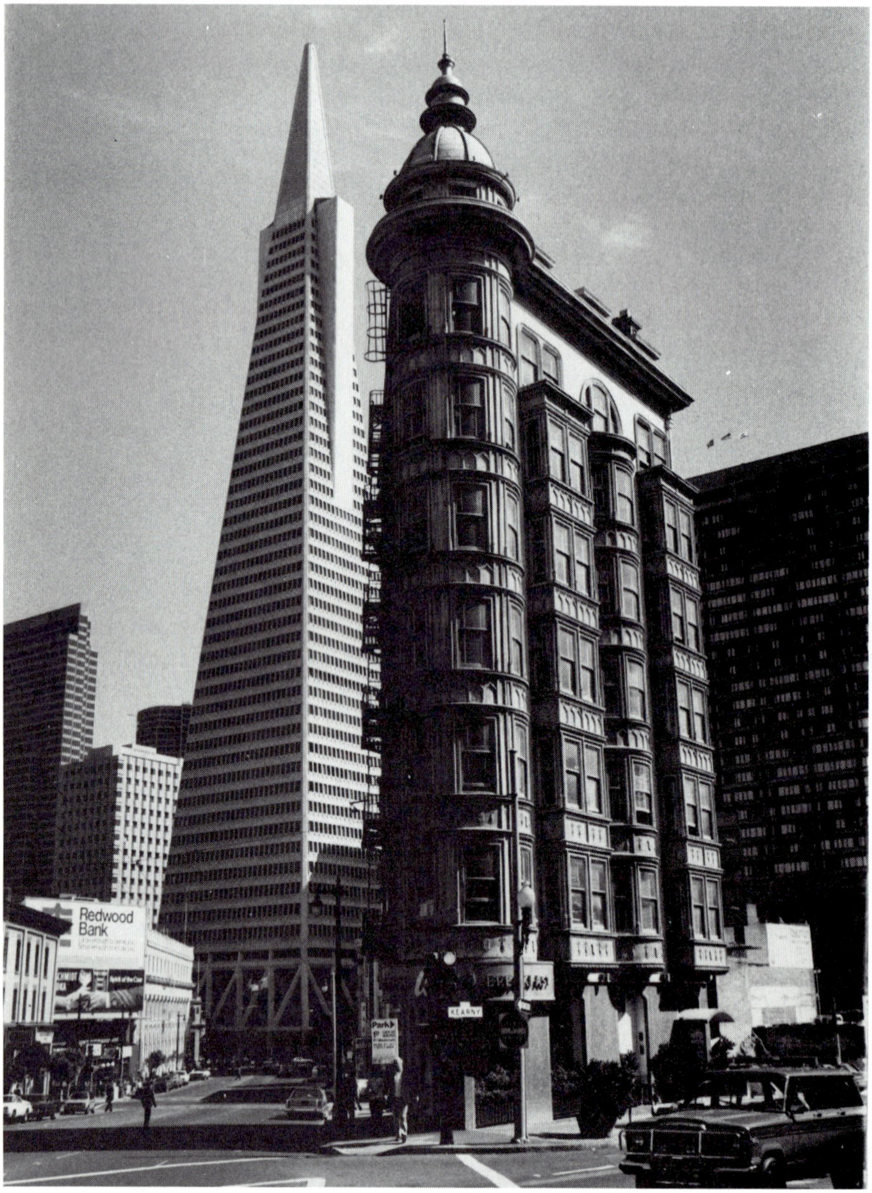
Redwood
Bank
KEARNY
Park

Chapter 4

Evaluating Your Ideas

🍎 *This chapter explains the characteristics of critical thinking—a questioning attitude, the separation of fact from opinion and taste from judgment, and sensitivity to the connections between ideas. It also describes how to test the quality of your reasoning and provides standards to apply in making your judgments.*

As we observed in Chapter 1, a special kind of thinking is needed to produce good ideas. That kind of thinking—called creative thinking—is unconcerned with correctness or reasonableness, which can stifle the flow of ideas; and it refuses to discriminate against any idea, however unfamiliar, unpopular, or seemingly farfetched. It is open, uninhibited, and daring. And that is the secret to its effectiveness.

But although creative thinking can lead to unusual insights and ingenious solutions, you should not regard it as infallible. Much of what it produces is at least flawed and at most worthless. This should neither surprise nor discourage you. The writer who expects his every idea to be valuable is as foolish as the pearl diver who expects every oyster to contain a pearl. Not everything a person thinks makes sense, as Harold A. Larrabee illustrates in this little story:

There is an old story about an American frontiersman who never had any medical instruction, but who decided to try his hand at practicing medicine. When his first patient, a blacksmith who seemed to be very ill indeed with what looked like typhoid fever, demanded some pork and beans, the amateur doctor said "All right" on the theory that he might as well die happy. The blacksmith, however, promptly began to improve, and ultimately recovered; whereupon the doctor made the notation: "For typhoid fever—prescribe pork and beans."

Somewhat later came another patient, a shoemaker, who seemed to have the same trouble as the blacksmith, but who, on being fed pork and beans, inconsiderately proceeded to die. The undaunted "doctor" then wrote in his notebook: "Pork and beans good for blacksmiths with typhoid fever, but not for shoemakers."[1]

We are a little bit like the amateur doctor. Despite our best intentions and most painstaking efforts, we make mistakes. Our errors may not be as laughable as his, but they are as real. And they affect all of us, from students to professors to experts in every field. *Error is a natural consequence of the imperfect human condition.*

Characteristics of Critical Thinking

If you want your writing to be reasonable, to make sense—and this is an important goal, particularly in persuasive writing—you cannot merely *assume* that your ideas are sound. You must *prove* to yourself that they are. That means examining and evaluating all the ideas you have produced, especially the controlling idea, being alert to every shallow, narrow-minded, or illogical interpretation or conclusion. To do this you must employ another kind of thinking: critical thinking.

Critical thinking is an active mental process in which you scrutinize your ideas (or other people's ideas), probe their stated and implied meaning, and decide whether that meaning is defensible. Such thinking depends on three characteristics: a questioning attitude toward all interpretations and conclusions, skill in separating fact from opinion and taste from judgment, and sensitivity to the connections between ideas. Let's look at each of these characteristics more closely.

A Questioning Attitude

Most of us think there is only one *right* way to do things—and that is *our* way. For example, take our attitude toward bathing. In Western culture, bathing is a private act for which the sole purpose is cleanliness. When we hear of the Oriental practice of family bathing, we are apt to get nervous or consider it evidence of a lower or debased culture. Western societies would never permit such a custom, we believe. And yet there was a time when public bathing was very much a part of Western culture.

In Roman times, the purpose of bathing was not only cleanliness but also regeneration; that is, renewing the body. More significantly, this view of bathing continued into the Middle Ages. Our picture of medieval people as unwashed and foul smelling is a great distortion. As a matter of fact, there were better bathing facilities in Europe in the Middle Ages than there were at the turn of the twentieth century in New York City's tenements. And the baths were public. They were places for socializing, relaxation, and renewal. Men, women, and children bathed and steamed themselves together without embarrassment or shame. It was only with the Protestant Reformation and the Catholic Counter-Reformation that nakedness became sinful and bathing began to be viewed as a private matter.[2]

The assumption that the present way of viewing things is the only way undermines a questioning attitude. Similarly, the assumptions that what the majority of people *say is so* must really *be so* and that the way things *are* is the way they *should be* paralyze the critical sense. All three assumptions imply that human beings are perfect creatures who cannot err. But a questioning attitude depends on the expectation of error. It begins with the realization that humans are imperfect and that anything of human invention or design (including statements of belief) can be flawed.

To be a good critical thinker, you must learn to ask questions about every significant idea you encounter or produce. You should be especially inquisitive about ideas you feel strongly about and ideas that are familiar to you because people around you accept them. In other words, develop the habit of suspending your allegiances long enough to examine them closely.*

---

*This approach does not deny the value of faith. There is an important difference between a questioning attitude and a doubting attitude. The former is insurance against misplaced faith; the latter makes faith impossible.

For example, if an editorial in your local newspaper proclaims, "The high school's athletic budget should be eliminated because taxes are too high," then you should ask: "How high are the taxes in comparison with those of other districts? Are they out of line? Why single out the athletic budget? Is it the biggest item in the overall budget? Has it risen dramatically in recent years? Why not cut other items such as administrative expenses? Why not trim several items instead of eliminating one? How many students would be affected by this? Would the negative results outweigh the positive?"

Or if you see in your notes for a composition the sentence "Technology dehumanizes mankind," then ask yourself: "What do I mean by 'technology'? Do I mean all inventions, all industrial processes, all labor-saving devices? Do such things necessarily dehumanize? Isn't it possible that in some cases, perhaps most, they *humanize* mankind—that is, make it possible for people to realize more of their human potential?"

Separation of Fact from Opinion and Taste from Judgment

Facts are ideas that have been shown beyond a reasonable doubt to be so. They are commonly found in encyclopedias, dictionaries, biographical reference books, and almanacs. *Opinions* are ideas that lack the certainty of facts; they are ideas that knowledgeable people still disagree about.*

The word *opinion* often causes a great deal of confusion because it has such a wide range of meaning, covering everything from expressions of taste to expressions of judgment. *Tastes* are personal preferences, whereas *judgments* are conclusions and are therefore open to debate.

Thus when someone says, "It's my opinion that . . . ," he can mean "I prefer to believe . . ." (taste) or "I haven't really thought about the matter, but I have a feeling that . . ." (mixture of taste and judgment) or "I have researched the matter and after careful

---

*Research, experimentation, or deliberation may either discredit opinions or lead to their general acceptance. In the latter case, they are no longer considered opinions, but facts. Some of our most solid facts began as private opinions vigorously rejected by the majority of people. The fact that the sun is the center of our solar system, for example, began as an opinion held by Copernicus and Galileo. And Einstein's theory of relativity, an opinion about the nature of the universe, appears to be reaching the point where it is regarded as fact.

Evaluating Your Ideas

deliberation have concluded that . . ." (judgment). The problem is that these meanings are not interchangeable.

Everyone is, of course, entitled to his or her preferences. What's more, the idea that taste can't be dictated is not a new one. The Romans affirmed it in their saying, *"De gustibus non disputandum est"* ("It's foolish to argue about matters of taste"). Some people's idea of art is a Marlboro advertisement. Some think the epitome of automobile style is the Volkswagen Rabbit. And some believe that obesity is beautiful. But there will always be others who will disagree. And though each person may feel the other's taste is bad taste, there is seldom much to be gained by arguing, because taste is an intensely personal matter.

Problems arise when people assume that every opinion is a matter of taste and that there is no standard by which to test opinion other than personal preference. "I'm entitled to my opinion," they say, as if the right to have an opinion guarantees the rightness of that opinion. If this were true, then the modern medical idea that severe chest pains can be a symptom of a heart attack is no better than the centuries-old standard diagnosis of acute indigestion; then, too, the ancient idea that the *earth* is the center of our solar system was as right as the modern idea that the sun is; and Hitler was right to invade other countries, draw the world into war, and exterminate over nine million human beings. (After all, he was following his opinion.)

Personal preference can't be the measure of the above cases because they are not matters of taste. They are matters of judgment. And *no matter of judgment is purely subjective.* However strong opinions in such matters may be, they can be mistaken. For example, in dealing with the question of whether cigarette smoking causes lung cancer, it makes no sense to say that one opinion is as good as another. Either smoking is a causative factor or it isn't. If it is, then those who believe it isn't are wrong.

Here is another example. Let's say your roommate's books are missing from the cafeteria bookshelf. Your theory is that another student stole them. Your roommate believes that an off-campus visitor did. Perhaps you are both wrong. (It may have been a cafeteria employee or a kleptomaniacal professor. Or perhaps the books were not stolen at all, but merely misplaced.) But one thing is certain—you cannot *both* be right!

Or say you are having a class discussion on the question of whether premarital sex is helpful in developing a mature, responsible attitude toward others. Some argue that it is; others argue that it isn't. Who's right? The question is complex. Perhaps it is helpful for some people but not for others. There may be a dozen qualifications necessary to reach a reasonable answer. Thus, not all answers will be good answers. Some may be wise, others foolish. How can you tell which are which? By how logical and how well supported with facts they are.

To be a good critical thinker, you must avoid confusing matters of taste and matters of judgment. If you are writing about your likes and dislikes in music or films or people or food, you may limit your treatment to description and explanation. No one has a right to demand that you defend your choices in such matters. But whenever you are writing about matters of judgment, remember that uninformed and unsupported opinions carry no weight.

Sensitivity to the Connections Between Ideas

Careful writers realize that the validity of conclusions depends on how logical the relationships are between ideas and how accurate the individual ideas are. Consider this example:

Cheating is dishonest.
Plagiarism is cheating.
Therefore, plagiarism is dishonest.

The conclusion here is valid because (a) it is true that, according to the ethical values of our culture, cheating is dishonest; (b) it is true that plagiarism is, by definition, a form of cheating; and (c) the conclusion follows logically from those two ideas (which logicians call *premises*). But consider the two examples that follow:

The conclusion is flawed because it is based on a misreading of the first premise. That premise doesn't say that only fish live in water. It allows for the possibility that life forms other than fish may also live there.

Fish live in water.
Whales live in water.
Therefore, whales are fish.

The first premise is incorrect. Low grades may *be a sign that a teacher doesn't like a student. But they are not* necessarily *such a sign. So the conclusion is flawed.*

Low grades are a sign a teacher doesn't like a student.
Mr. Snipswitch gave me a low grade on my composition.
Therefore, Mr. Snipswitch doesn't like me.

In many cases the judgments you deal with or reach yourself will not be expressed in logical format. Instead of appearing as two premises and a conclusion, they will be expressed as a single, seemingly self-evident idea. For example, you may say, "Mr. Snipswitch gave me a low grade on my composition because he doesn't

Evaluating Your Ideas

like me." The error of that idea, however, is precisely the same as the one noted above. It is merely more hidden and therefore more difficult to see.

Let's take another example of a hidden error. You might write, "Use of the masculine pronoun 'his' after the word 'everyone' (as in '*Everyone* took off *his* coat') is a sign of male chauvinism." It might seem a perfectly reasonable conclusion to you. But viewed more closely, its error becomes evident.

> Preference for male over female is a sign of male chauvinism.
> Use of the pronoun "his" after "everyone" is a sign of preference for male over female.
> Therefore, use of the pronoun "his" after "everyone" is a sign of male chauvinism.

The second premise is flawed. Use of the pronoun "his" in that way is not necessarily a sign of such preference. It may be a sign of grammatical consistency. So the conclusion is flawed.

Naturally you don't have time to break down every complex idea into its components and scrutinize them (though you would do well to do so with your controlling idea). But you can try to be sensitive to the stated and implied connections between your ideas. Such sensitivity can help you in three ways. First, it can help you see any inconsistencies in your thinking. Psychiatrist Thomas Szasz, for example, criticizes many of his colleagues for classifying transsexualism as an illness. He points out that the only way the transsexual differs from others of his sex is by his desire to *be* the other sex. "If such a desire qualifies as a disease," Szasz argues, "then the old person who wants to be young is a 'transchronological,' the poor person who wants to be rich is a 'transeconomical,' and so."[3] (If the psychiatrists Szasz is criticizing had considered the connection Szasz points out, they might have changed their minds about their classification.)

Moreover, sensitivity to the connections between ideas can help you recognize unwanted effects. In 1979 the New Jersey legislature proposed that the age of sexual consent be lowered from sixteen to thirteen. Their intent was to put an end to the criminal prosecution of teenaged boys who had sexual contact with girls a few years younger. The many critics of the legislation pointed out that it had a serious negative effect as well—it left older men free to take advantage of young girls. Had the legislators been more sensitive to the connections between the ideas in this case, they might have decided not to propose a change in the age of consent.

Finally, such sensitivity can help you identify irrelevant ideas—that is, ideas falsely seen as logically connected to other ideas. The following letter to the editor provides an example of such irrelevancies.

Your editorial said Mayor Slither's handling of the street-paving contract bids should be investigated. That suggestion is outrageous. The mayor is one of the most hard-working officials who has ever held office in this city. He has never taken a vacation and in spite of his busy schedule has always found time to assist in fund-raising drives and to mediate community disputes.

The problem is that there is no necessary connection between hard work and honesty. The mayor could be generous with his time and yet still be a crook. For that reason, the writer's suggestion that the mayor must have been honest in the street-paving contract matter simply does not follow logically.

Exercises

Each of the following brief dialogues contains at least one shallow, narrow-minded, or illogical idea. Read each dialogue carefully and determine what is wrong with it. Be sure to approach your evaluation with a questioning attitude; with alertness to the distinctions between fact and opinion, taste and judgment; and with sensitivity to the connections between ideas.

1. *Alice:* My girlfriend back home just got married. She's eighteen and he's twenty.

   Mae: That's a shame. With so many marriages ending in divorce, nobody should get married until he or she is at least twenty-five.

   Alice: I don't agree. I mean, it's up to the individual couple to decide what's right for them. They know what's best for them. Besides, there's no right or wrong time to get married.

2. *Merv:* Did you read the latest news about mercy killing? Some group is up in arms about it. They say they're launching a letter-writing campaign to get the legislators to oppose it. I think that's rotten.

   Ralph: What do you mean?

   Merv: I mean these right-wing religious fanatics have no business forcing their views on the rest of us. First they opposed abortion, and when they were proved wrong on that issue, they started opposing mercy killing.

   Ralph: I don't know, Merv. After all, it's called mercy *killing*. And killing is wrong. It's always been wrong. The Bible says its wrong. And who are we to question the Bible?

Merv: I've always wondered about you, man. Now I know—you're weird.

3. *Reggie:* Hey, Barbara, what's happening? How'd you like to take in a flick tonight?

   Barbara: What's playing?

   Reggie: I think *The Watchdog Caper.* S'posed to be good.

   Barbara: What's it rated?

   Reggie: I think R. I'm not really sure.

   Barbara: R? That gets me. Everything's R or X these days. Aren't they making any decent films anymore? This country's really in trouble with its sick fascination with sex and violence.

4. *Claude* (standing on line in the cafeteria): Hi, are you a freshman?

   Agnes: Yeah. Are you?

   Claude: Yeah. What are you taking? I mean, what's your major?

   Agnes: Business. What's yours?

   Claude: Biology.... How're your courses? Pretty good so far?

   Agnes: Too early to say, really. But the first couple of classes have been OK ... in everything but English. I don't know why I have to take it to begin with. I did real good in high school English. I mean, if you learned a subject, why should you have to repeat it?

   Claude: Hey, that's the way I feel too. Like my major is biology. So why do I have to waste time reading poetry and writing papers? I'd be better off taking just science courses.

   Agnes: Yeah. And these English teachers are just like my high school teachers. Mine wears glasses and always has a tie on and sits at his desk for the whole period. Just like old Mr. Penrod in high school. I just know it's going to be the dullest course.

   Claude: Yeah. It's unreal.

5. *Bertha* (at a midterm conference with her English teacher): I can't understand why you gave me a D for midterm.

   Mr. Santello: Because you did C work and were missing several papers, which reduced your grade.

   Bertha: I didn't know you had to hand in all the work. I mean, you never said so in class.

Mr. Santello: It said so very plainly on the course information sheet I gave out the first day of class.

Bertha: Did it? I don't remember seeing it there. Anyway, it just doesn't seem fair to get such a low grade when I try so hard. My roommate gets B every time and she doesn't spend half the time on her writing that I do on mine. I don't really understand it, either. My high school teacher said I was a fine writer. I never did this bad in her course. I guess I just didn't give you what you want.

Mr. Santello: If I remember correctly, you were absent from both composition clinics I held. I gave extra help then to students who were having trouble with their writing.

Bertha: That wasn't my fault. I had cheerleading practice.

Raising Important Questions

Developing the three characteristics just discussed will do a great deal to enhance your critical thinking. But you can do more than that. You can raise specific questions about the ideas you intend to use in your composition, particularly about your controlling idea. The following questions are especially helpful because they address the most common problems that occur in writing.

Which of My Ideas Are Judgments?

There is nothing wrong with judgments. They are your only means of dealing with facts—sorting them out, combining them, learning from them, and putting them to use. But errors in thinking do not occur with facts*; nor do they occur with expressions of taste (as long as such expressions are not substituted for judgments). They occur with judgments. Identifying your judgments will help you focus on the places where errors are most likely to occur and where you will need to defend your statements to your reader.

If it were always easy to distinguish among facts, expressions of taste, and judgments, then you could simply look at your notes and decide which are which. Unfortunately, they sometimes look

---

*Even cases where what is accepted as fact at one time is later discredited are best classified as errors in judgment.

alike. Let's examine a variety of ideas and see how they are best classified:

> I hate Professor Mentor's class. He is an unbelievably boring lecturer. Any normal person falls asleep the moment Mentor opens his mouth.
>
> Henry David Thoreau was born in 1817 and died in 1862. He was a naturalist and author. Two of his best known works are *A Week on the Concord and Merrimack Rivers* and *Walden.*
>
> Henry David Thoreau's best work is *Walden.*
>
> *Walden* is one of the most interesting books I have ever read.
>
> Afghanistan occupies an area of 251,773 square miles. Its population, according to a 1981 estimate by the International Demographic Data Center, is 15,400,000. Its capital is Kabul and its monetary unit, the afghani.
>
> Russia's invasion of Afghanistan in 1979 was an act of aggression.
>
> The word *Afghanistan* has an unpleasant sound.

Sentence 1 is an expression of taste. Sentence 2 is ambiguous as stated. (If it means, "I dislike his style," it is an expression of taste. If it means, "He violates the rules of public speaking," it is a judgment.) Sentence 3 is a judgment.

All facts. (Provided, of course, they are not misstated.)

Judgment.

Expression of taste.

All facts. (Provided, of course, they are not misstated.)

Judgment.

Expression of taste.

The more common, and therefore more familiar, your judgments are, the more they are likely to seem indisputable. For this reason, it is important to examine every idea carefully, taking nothing for granted. Any idea that can be disputed by honest and intelligent people is best considered a judgment that needs defending, not a fact, no matter how strongly you feel about it.

To What Extent Are My Judgments Influenced by Preconceived Notions?

Preconceived notions are firm convictions about people, places, and things that we form before we encounter them. Most of us succumb to at least a few such notions. They save mental effort and spare us the confusion of dealing with complex decisions. They are convenient. But they are also harmful, because they prevent us from seeing reality, substituting in its place a prefabricated conception of what reality must be like.

Some common preconceived notions are that people of the same race, religion, ethnic group, or social class have the same traits; that familiar ideas are more valuable than unfamiliar ideas; that whatever the majority of people, or people in authority, say is true must be true. We'll examine each in turn.

The notion that people of the same group have the same traits is a kind of verbal averaging. It is as illogical as the idea that because the average of the numbers 3, 5, 8, 11, and 13 is 8, each of the numbers must therefore be 8. Whatever similarities there may be among members of a group, they are never *necessary* similarities. And they exist side by side with numerous differences. No two flowers, rocks, animals, or people are ever exactly alike. Even identical twins are individuals. For this reason, any neat description you have for Poles or Italians or Jews or homosexuals or atheists or Democrats or college students or construction workers or feminists will corrupt rather than enhance your thinking.

The notion that familiar ideas are more valuable than unfamiliar ideas is probably rooted in insecurity. The new and the different pose a threat to our peace of mind. They demand that we reconsider our old ways of viewing things, ways we have become comfortable with, and entertain new, strange ways. Yet every creative breakthrough, every discovery, every invention, every fresh insight is by definition new and unfamiliar. Thus if you accept only those ideas you are comfortable with, you will shut out many of the best and most valuable ideas.

Next we come to the notion that the majority must be right, a notion that makes us blind and passive, mindless followers of others whose ability to judge is often no greater than our own. After all, in various cultures at various times, the majority have approved of infanticide, human sacrifice, and cannibalism. In our own culture, the majority at one time believed that animals should be held legally responsible for their actions (trials, and even executions, were held for dogs and cats and bulls and wild animals), and that maggots and other vermin spring into existence spontaneously from rotten meat, without any reproductive activity. To accept the majority view because you believe it is the best view is sensible; to accept it simply because it *is* the majority view is an insult to your intelligence.

Similarly, it is a mistake to endorse the notion that people in authority must be right. The wisest and most honorable authority is still human and therefore subject to error. And if the most expert mind is capable of an inferior thought, consider how much more fallible are the less wise, less honorable, less expert among us. You should always respect honest authorities, but you do no service to them or to yourself by following their thinking slavishly.

If you find that your ideas are influenced by a preconceived notion, be sure to modify those ideas sufficiently to remove any trace of the notion. And remember that since preconceptions often penetrate deeply into your ideas, cosmetic changes may not be enough. You may have to change the substance of your ideas.

To What Extent Is My Reasoning Self-Serving?

Most people want to be open-minded and objective about issues. But intending to be so is easier than being so. William J. Reilly tells the story of a boy who went fishing with three friends. They all agreed when they started out that the catch would be split four ways. Then as the day wore on and the boy began reeling in more fish than the others, his attitude toward splitting began to change. By the end of the day, when his catch was far greater than theirs, he had become violently opposed to splitting at all. He couldn't understand why a good fisherman should be penalized for the incompetence and bad luck of others.[4] As his perspective changed, so did his judgment.

Like the boy in the story, you may tend to judge issues and ideas narrowly, in a way that serves your own interests. Perhaps you want to believe what is flattering to you and compatible with your habitual way of seeing things. Where more than one view of an issue is possible, you may tend to embrace the one that is closest to your view, selecting those facts that support your view and ignoring those that challenge it. You may see the tiniest flaw in the argument of someone who disagrees with you, while overlooking far greater flaws in the arguments of those who agree with you. And whenever your pride and ego are at stake, perhaps you get defensive, frantically seeking excuses for yourself and your views.

Is this to say that you are any different from other people? Not at all. Everyone suffers from these tendencies. They are part of the human condition. As James Harvey Robinson accurately observed, "Most of our so-called reasoning consists in finding arguments for going on believing as we already do."[5] To be a critical thinker, you must realize your tendency to be self-serving in your thinking and make your ideas fit the facts rather than selecting the facts to support your ideas.

Have I Judged Too Hastily?

A judgment arrived at quickly is not necessarily an inferior judgment. The judgment that flashes to mind almost at the instant you begin addressing the issue may prove to be the most sensible judgment. Yet the odds are against its being so, especially when you are dealing with a complex issue. To be sure, there is no virtue in spending more time than is needed in making a judgment. But just how much time is enough?

You can be reasonably sure your judgments are not made too hastily if two conditions are met. The first condition is that you have obtained a fair sampling of the facts and interpreted them carefully. The second condition is that you have examined the arguments on both sides of the issue and honestly considered a number of possible judgments before settling on any one judgment.

Have I Assumed Too Much?

To assume is to take for granted, usually without even consciously thinking about it. When you attend a class each day, you seldom wonder whether your instructor will be there, unless she has missed a number of classes in the past. You merely assume that she will be there. In this case, your assumption is warranted by the fact that the institution is a reputable one, the class has been formally scheduled at that hour, the instructor has always been there before, and she has made no announcement to the contrary for today. (Even if she is absent today, your assumption, though proved incorrect, will have been justified.)

But to assume that middle-aged people do not understand the problems of young people, or that the rating of a movie is an index of its quality, or that a person who attends church is more honest than one who doesn't, is unwarranted. What makes each of these assumptions unwarranted is that in each case the reverse is as likely to be true. There is no special probability supporting the assumed idea.

To avoid assuming too much, examine your judgments and ask what assumptions they reveal. Then decide if those assumptions are warranted by the facts or by past experience.

Have I Overlooked Important Distinctions?

To make distinctions is to realize that differences exist. Whenever you fail to make distinctions, you confuse things that should not be confused. For example, when you look unfavorably on the ideas of people you dislike and favorably on the ideas of people you like, you are confusing the idea with the person. Critical thinking demands that you separate the idea from the person and consider the idea on its own merits.

Similarly, when you evaluate the soundness of an idea by speculating about the motives of the person who expresses it, you are confusing what is said with why it is said. At a town meeting, for instance, a person may propose that land owned by the town be leased or sold to a developer for a new shopping center. Now he may stand to gain personally from such a development. (He may have a business that would prosper from being located there.) But the possibility that he is making the proposal entirely for personal reasons does not make it a bad proposal. Critical thinking demands that the proposal be separated from the maker's motives.

There are other kinds of distinctions that must be made as well. Consider the negative attitude many people have toward homosexuals. Often such people fail to distinguish between those homosexuals who (like most of their heterosexual neighbors) keep their sexual lives private and separate from their jobs and those who are more blatant or let their sexual preference affect their jobs. And then there is the issue of disciplining children. Many who oppose all discipline do not distinguish between physical punishment and other forms, such as taking away privileges.

The key to making necessary distinctions is to examine your judgments for any elements that seem confused, and then to separate them appropriately.

Are My Judgments Reasonable?

The most reasonable judgment is the one that fits the facts better than all other possible judgments. To be sure your judgments are reasonable, make them meet the exacting standards given here.

When the facts will not support any firm or final judgment, make your judgment appropriately tentative. Many writers do almost the opposite. The slimmer their evidence, the more forceful and final their judgments. They actually believe that extravagance of expression will hide the weakness of their position. It may from the undiscerning reader, but not from anyone else.

If you cannot speak with certainty, then don't. Make it clear that you are merely speculating, stating what seems to be so, or indicating what is probable. No sensible reader will think less of you for saying "This evidence suggests," instead of "This evidence proves," or "I find this persuasive," instead of "This is the only answer that makes any sense." You may think this means you should "ride the fence" on issues. It does not. Riding the fence is refusing to take a stand that the facts permit you to take. That is very different from recognizing when the facts will not permit a conclusive stand.

When the facts will not support a generalized judgment, particularize your judgment. All but the most disciplined writers have a tendency to overgeneralize. If you have a 1985 Ford Mustang and are pleased with its performance, you might easily think and write, "Ford Mustangs are the best small cars on the market today," when your facts cover only a single Ford Mustang. Similarly, if you know eight Chinese people, you may be tempted to write about "the Chinese." Yet eight is hardly a representative sampling of one billion.*

You are justified in extending a judgment about a small number of things to all members of that class only when you have good reason to believe that the small sample you are familiar with—people or anything else—is typical of all others. Otherwise, make your judgment no more general than your facts will support.

When the issue is complex, be sure your judgment does not oversimplify. Whenever those who know a great deal about a complex subject speak to (or write for) those who know little or nothing about it, they must reduce the subject to a less complicated form. In other words, they must simplify. The most common example of simplification is seen in education. The teacher devises explanations and lessons that make the subject accessible to the students.

There is nothing wrong with simplification so long as it does not twist and distort the reality it describes. When it does this, it is *over*simplification. Oversimplification is an obstacle to effective thinking because it presents partial truths as truths. (What is partly true, of course, is also partly false.) Thus it makes your thinking and writing shallow.

Take, for example, the subject of divorce. To say that divorce is a social evil or divorce is a social good, and leave it at that, is to oversimplify. It would be an oversimplification even if you wrote a long scholarly article on the subject complete with a hundred footnotes. This is so because the truth about divorce is that it is not merely a social evil or a social good. It is a complex phenomenon that in some ways causes pain and harm and in other ways brings relief from pain and harm.

---

*Of course, it is also true that you do not have to know all one billion Chinese to make a fair generalization about them.

Evaluating Your Ideas

The most common cause of oversimplification is the tendency to see everything as black or white, to demand a world of absolutes. Thus communism must be all bad and capitalism all good (or vice versa), and abortion must be right in all cases or wrong in all cases. In the real world, however, the choice is not always between best and worst. In fact, with most dilemmas we must decide which is the lesser of two evils or the greater of two goods: "Shall I tell my child the truth—that she is dying of cancer—and add fear to her burden of suffering, or shall I lie to her and bring her a measure of comfort?" "Is it better to continue in a well-paying, secure job that I strongly dislike or to risk my family's welfare by entering a new field I might not succeed in?" Such choices are never clear-cut.

To avoid oversimplifying, consider the possibility that the best judgment is neither an absolute "Yes" nor an absolute "No," but rather a balanced answer that rejects extremes and matches the complex nature of the issue.

Even when the facts support a firm judgment, use moderation and understatement. There is nothing really wrong about writing in superlatives when the facts warrant doing so. Yet the frequent use of superlatives can become a handicap. Once you say something is the "most significant" or the "greatest," what can you call something else that is even more significant or greater? But there is an even better reason to avoid superlatives. The opposite tendency in expression, *understatement*, shows the sense of restraint and caution that has traditionally been associated with good thinking. It takes discipline to write, "We mustn't underestimate the dangers of inflation," when you really want to say, "Sound the alarm—inflation is killing us!" And it is precisely that discipline that will make your judgments impressive to the critical reader.

Asking the right questions is only the start of evaluating your ideas. You must then answer them honestly and, where appropriate, modify your ideas to eliminate any shallowness, narrow-mindedness, or illogical thinking. If you put off these steps until the writing process, you run the risk of neglecting them. It is far safer to act now, while your ideas are in the note stage.

Exercises

Read each of the following statements carefully to decide whether you agree or disagree with it. If you agree with a statement, let it stand as your own. If you disagree, modify it to reflect your position. (You may change it as drastically as you wish.) Then select the four statements you feel most strongly about and analyze each in light of the questions on pages 72–77.

1. Homosexuals should not be granted equal rights because homosexuality is abnormal and represents a danger to society.
2. Most of us are brought up to be concerned for our neighbors and to help those in need. But that idea makes poor people dependent and indulges laziness. A better idea is to let everyone look out for himself. Then if people are poor, they have only themselves to blame.
3. If we were really serious about solving the crime problem in this country, we'd get rid of laws that tie the hands of the police. The police should be allowed any means they wish to deal with suspects. They are close to the problem of crime and know what must be done.
4. Prostitution should be legalized. People should be able to use their bodies as they wish as long as they don't injure anyone else.
5. When parents teach a child their religious and political views and their values, they take away the child's individuality.
6. It is hypocritical for states to have laws against drunken driving and continue to license bars that can be reached only by car. Liquor licenses should be granted only to those bars that are within village or city limits (and presumably within walking distance of patrons' homes).
7. Doctors, lawyers, and dentists should be prohibited from advertising their services in newspapers and magazines and on radio and television. Such advertising is unprofessional.
8. Anyone who fails to achieve a twelfth-grade level of reading and writing proficiency should be denied a high school diploma.
9. Girls should not be allowed to play on boys' varsity teams because they are not equal to boys athletically and they cannot handle the strenuous training required to be a varsity athlete.

Composition Assignment

Write a composition on one of the following topics. (Unless your instructor specifies a different length, make it between 300 and 500 words.) Don't skimp on the writing and revising stages, but pay particular attention to planning, especially to evaluating your ideas.

1. Should suicide be condemned as immoral?
2. Should parents be granted the right to decide whether their retarded child should be sterilized?

3. Should teachers be held legally liable (for malpractice) if their students do not learn?
4. Should a person who has lived with someone for several years but never married be granted alimony when they break up?
5. Should parents be allowed to keep their children out of school if they believe they can educate them better at home?
6. Are pornographic books and movies harmful?
7. Should the drinking age in your state be raised, lowered, or left as it is?
8. Should Congress pass a gun-control law restricting the right to own handguns, or rifles and shotguns, or both?
9. Should it be required that the theory of creation (that God created the world and everything in it) be taught in biology classrooms along with the theory of evolution?
10. Should students on your campus be allowed to miss classes without penalty as long as they are responsible for all work covered?

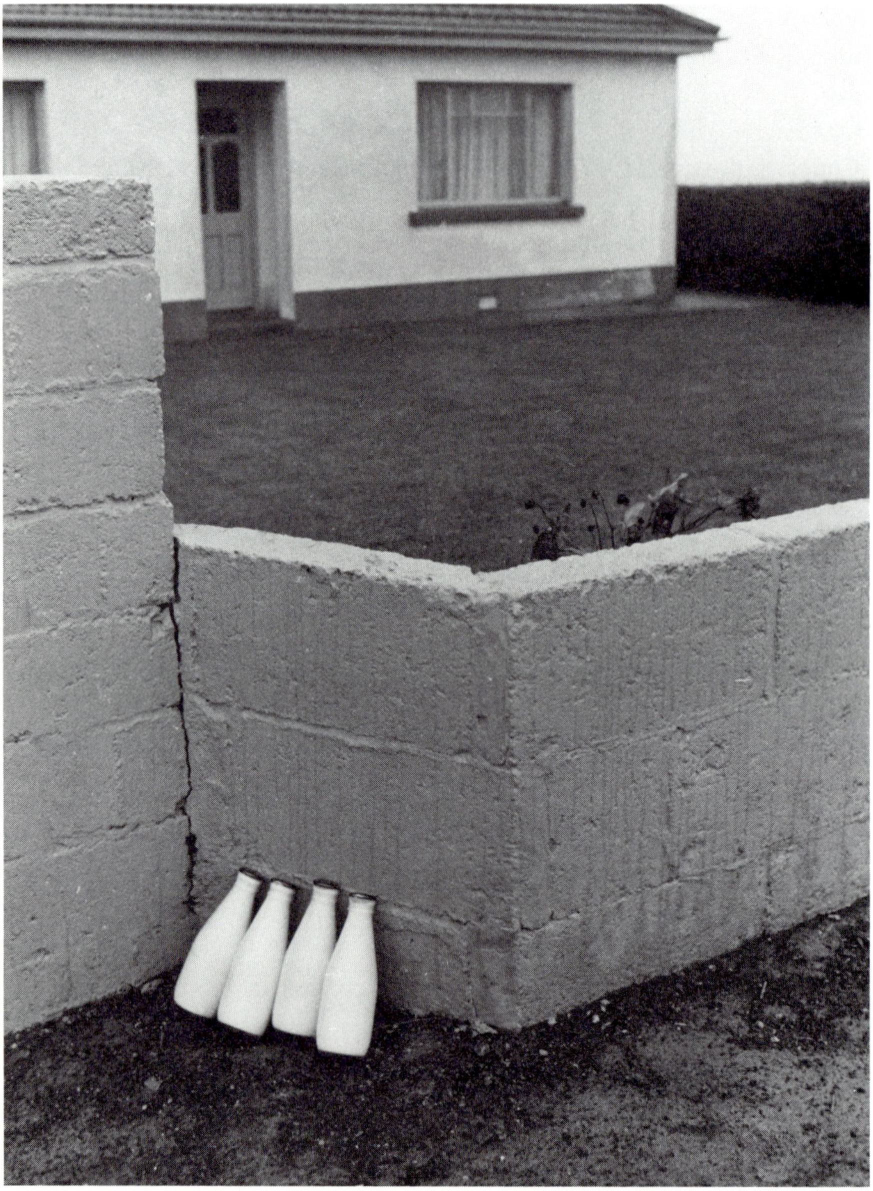

Chapter 5

Considering Your Readers

This chapter explains the importance of considering your readers and offers you ways to anticipate their knowledge and points of view about issues. It also details the principles of persuasion and demonstrates how to apply them in planning your composition.

It is possible to write a composition without ever considering the readers. Many writers, in fact, write just that way. They are their own audience and all they demand of their writing is that it give them satisfaction. They reason that if they are impressed with the substance and form of their expression, others will be too. Such a view is at best naive.

In informative and narrative writing, where success depends on the readers' understanding the message or feeling the experience vicariously, consideration of audience is important enough. But in persuasive writing, where the readers often disagree with you at the outset, it is crucial. Not to consider your readers in such a situation is like shooting an arrow at a target blindfolded. It offers little chance of success.

Writing *to* Versus Writing *for* Readers

Before proceeding further with our discussion of audience, it is important to make the distinction between writing *to* your readers and writing *for* them. Letters are written to someone. So are memorandums and many reports and proposals. In other words, they are addressed to one or more individuals by name. But most other forms of writing are not addressed to anyone in particular. Take, for example, the examination essay and the term paper. They are not written to anyone. Nevertheless, they are written *for* someone, usually a professor. And their success or failure (as measured by the grade they receive) will depend on that person's reaction to them.

A letter to the editor of a newspaper or magazine, though formally addressed to that person, is often written for someone else, often someone who wrote an earlier letter to the editor. Or it may be written for a particular segment of that publication's readers. A letter about the need for a traffic light at a dangerous intersection might, for example, be written for members of the city council.

In many writing situations the audience will be larger and more complex. The audience of a news article, an opinion column, or an editorial will usually be all the subscribers of the newspaper or magazine. They may number in the tens of thousands or more. The audiences of most film and book reviews are often similarly complex.

Yet whether the audience is being addressed directly or indirectly, and whether it is one person or many people, the basic questions you must consider are the same: *What do they know about the subject or issue?* and *Where and to what extent are they likely to disagree with your view?*

First let's consider the question of what your readers know. If they are well informed, you can usually dispense with background material and get right to the point. You can also dispense with many of the explanations, definitions, and analogies that might be necessary for the less informed reader. On the other hand, if the readers are ill-informed or if the subject is new to them, a great deal of background information and explanation may be necessary. Of course, the exact kind and amount of explanation required will vary from person to person. Different readers may be confused about different points. Clearly, before you can decide what to explain, define, or illustrate, you must have some idea of what your readers know about the subject.

Now let's examine the question of reader disagreement. If your readers agree with you, they will tend to be less critical; therefore, it will take less complete and less impressive evidence to reach them. If they disagree, however, they will tend to be more critical, and the evidence required to win their favor will have to be both thorough and compelling. It is no great feat to win student approval for a proposal to reduce the number of students housed in a dormitory room from three to two. But to win the approval of the college administration may be very difficult.

Whenever the audience is likely to disagree with your idea, you should determine the exact points of disagreement. Even more important, you should identify the reasons for disagreement. In the case of the housing proposal, that would mean finding out whether the administrators believe that three in a room is a desirable condition or just a necessary one. It would also mean learning their reasons for thinking as they do. This kind of inquiry will make it possible to focus on the arguments that will be most effective with your audience, arguments designed to answer their most serious objections and to appeal to their interests.

As you can see, the effectiveness of your writing will depend in great measure on how well you answer the questions concerning your readers' knowledge and possible disagreement with your views. Of course, since you can never know another human being completely, and since people's reactions are not always predictable, your answers are bound to be imperfect. The best you can do is speculate on the basis of your knowledge of the people themselves and the issue. Where you cannot find an answer that is certain, you must look for one that is probable. Exactly how you proceed will depend on whether or not the audience is familiar to you.

Familiar Audiences

At times you will write to or for an audience you know personally. For example, you may write a letter to your brother disagreeing with his assessment of a particular high school teacher. Or you may write a composition on a controversial subject for a teacher who has made her (opposing) point of view very clear in class. In such cases, even though you will be unable to predict the reader's thinking exactly, you will at least be relatively sure of most of his or her ideas. Here's how to proceed:

1. *Try to recall any previous exchanges of ideas you've had with your readers about the subject at hand or related subjects.* Consider what they said on those occasions and what those statements suggest they would say in response to your ideas.

2. *Consider how your readers characteristically react.* (You can do this even if you have never actually discussed the subject at hand with them before.) Are they calm and rational in their approach to issues, or are they highly emotional? Do they grasp ideas quickly, or are they slow to comprehend? Have they a fairly long attention span, or do their minds tend to wander? Are they impatient with detail? Do they tend to jump to conclusions? Do they tend to be slaves to intellectual fashion? Have they a strong regard for authority (and therefore for statements by authorities)? Do certain subjects or approaches bore them? How easily confused are they by complexity? What kinds of examples and analogies are most likely to be meaningful to them?

Unfamiliar Audiences

More often than not, your audience will be composed of people you have never met. They will be a crowd without names, faces, or personalities. In such cases, it is more difficult to determine what they know about the subject and where they are most likely to disagree with your views. But it is not impossible. And you do not have to limit your approach to blind guessing.

Consider, for example, this textbook. I wrote it for you, the readers, without ever having met you. Yet I was able to form a fairly accurate picture of you (most of you, at any rate) despite that. I speculated that you would be a mixed audience, most of you between eighteen and twenty years old, but a fair number over twenty-five and some over forty; that you would have had some training in writing but no comprehensive instruction in rhetorical techniques and principles; that many of you would feel apprehensive about writing compositions for English teachers; and that you would, as the content of earlier chapters suggests, have some difficulty selecting your topics, thinking critically, avoiding tangents, and finding enough to say without resorting to padding.

The key to effective speculation about audiences you are unfamiliar with is understanding that most of what people think and say and believe is not fresh and original at all. It is a reflection of what they have heard others say. And since you have access to the most commonly expressed views on issues, you can predict with reasonable accuracy how most audiences will react to various ideas. You must simply be alert to what you see and hear. Here's how to put this understanding to use in considering your audience:

1. *Reflect on your experience with the subject or issue, and on the experiences you know or have read about or have seen on television.* Note those that are common to you and others; they are likely to be common to your audience as well.
2. *Recall the views you have heard expressed: not just those in conversation, but also those in books, magazines, and newspapers, in soap opera dialogue, and so on.* The more frequently an idea or argument is expressed, the more likely it is that your readers have been influenced by it.

Let's consider how this works in an actual situation. Suppose you are writing about the issue of abortion. If you have heard and read even a little about the debate that has raged over this issue in recent years, then you know that those who approve of abortion usually argue that a woman has a right over her own body and that this right extends to the decision of whether or not to end a pregnancy. You also know that those who disapprove of abortion tend to argue that a fetus is a person and that the law ought to protect his or her rights. In your consideration of audience, therefore, you can be reasonably sure how those who oppose your view will react to your position and what kind of argument will be most effective with them.

Speculation, of course, carries with it some risk of error. (In the case of abortion, some readers might oppose or favor it for other than the commonly presented reasons.) Thus, if you can determine your readers' thinking through discussion or some other means, do so. But where you have no way to determine what your readers think, speculation is the next best approach.

Exercises

For each of the following ideas, decide how well the specified audience is likely to understand the issue and where and to what extent they are likely to disagree with the point of view. (If you know people who could be classified as members of the audience, consider what attitudes and habits might affect their view of the issue.)

1. *Idea:* A part-time or summer job can help a teenager prepare for adulthood. *Audience:* A group of young teenagers who have never had a job.
2. *Idea:* Jobs are available to teenagers if they know how to seek them out and present themselves to employers. *Audience:* A group of older teenagers who, because of their appearance or manner, have never been able to get a job.

3. *Idea:* In many American schools, teachers have difficulty maintaining discipline and creating an atmosphere conducive to learning. *Audience:* People from a foreign country where teachers, indeed all adults, are treated with respect and where rules are obeyed.
4. *Idea:* Violence in schools is best handled by expelling those who terrorize others. *Audience:* A group of idealists who believe that "there is no such thing as a bad boy" and that understanding and kindness can solve all problems.

How to Be Persuasive

Consideration of audience is crucial in persuasive writing. Such writing presents your evaluations of issues that to some degree are open to dispute. Because your judgments are not the only possible ones, the effectiveness of your writing depends on how well you dispose your readers to prefer your view to other views.

The five principles of persuasion discussed in this chapter are the most fundamental. If applied carefully to every persuasive situation, they can guide you to more effective presentation of your arguments.

Principle 1: Understand the Opposing Side of the Issue

As we have noted, it is important to be observant of the positions people take about issues and the support they offer for those positions. Yet it is even more important that you go beyond mere observation, that you achieve real understanding of their views. Your objective in noticing everything you can about an issue is to make your own presentation more effective. You must know how your readers think before you can hope to reach them with your argument.

There's More than One Side to an Issue

It's a good idea to approach any issue with the attitude that there is more than one side to it. This attitude is especially helpful in dealing with highly controversial issues. A controversy, after all, is by definition a matter on which intelligent and perceptive people are divided. It is highly unlikely that one side is totally right or totally wrong. Yet, ironically, the greater the controversy, the more each side is likely to think so. In such situations, there is a greater need for rationality and open-mindedness.

Your best hope for persuasiveness, then, is to notice what has been said about the issue, study it thoughtfully, and reflect on it before committing your own position to words. The uttered word carries the ego with it. Once we express something, we seem to feel we must stand by that expression and defend it at all costs, lest we lose face. By keeping your idea tentative until you have weighed it against the opposing view, you will be lessening the chance of embarrassment and the need for face-saving.

Show that You Understand the Other Side

When you do express your position, your words should show your understanding of the opposing view. And you should be especially careful not to misrepresent or oversimplify that view or to resort to ridicule. If, for example, you are writing an essay against literary censorship, you may understand that those who favor it have some substantive arguments (that pornography does give a distorted view of the role of sex in life and encourages immature and unrealistic expectations; that it often degrades women by portraying them as instruments of male pleasure and not as full human beings). And yet you may be tempted to forget that understanding in the heat of presenting your own view and write as if the only opposing arguments were based on squeamishness about sex and resistance to unfamiliar ideas and values. Whenever you fail to show your understanding, your readers will infer that you do not understand.

Principle 2: Respect Your Readers

You will never be persuasive unless you respect your readers. If you are hostile and sarcastic toward them, they will likely feel that way toward you. If you are too aggressive in attacking their position, they will be defensive. If you are narrow-minded and unwilling to consider the possibility that their side of the argument has even the slightest merit, they will be disinclined to be open-minded and reasonable in assessing your position. If you dismiss their position lightly or ridicule or misrepresent it, they will be tempted to respond in kind.

On the other hand, if you are respectful, rational, open-minded, and more interested in discovering the truth about an issue than in releasing your emotions or "scoring points," your readers may be prompted to similar behavior. There is no guarantee of this, naturally. There are small-minded, insecure, egotistical readers as well as writers. The point is that in matters of understanding and respect, you will seldom get more than you give. But the more you give, the more you are likely to get in return.

Of course, *intending* to respect your readers is much easier than actually respecting them. In situations where you feel strongly about your position, you will probably tend to interpret other people's disagreement as a personal attack and to regard them with suspicion and hostility. Overcoming such reactions takes effort.

Separate the Person from the Idea

There are two ways to avoid such negative feelings toward your readers. The first is to keep in mind the distinction between the person and the idea. They are two different things entirely. A good person (in the moral sense) may have a bad idea. A bad person may have a good idea. The wise person will occasionally say something foolish. And the dullest of dolts will at times achieve a real insight. There is simply no guarantee that the source of an idea will determine its quality. Nor is personal regard for someone a reasonable basis for accepting his or her idea. Surely you know numerous people whom you respect and admire yet whom you disagree with strongly on some matter or other. Undoubtedly you also know people whom you have little regard for yet whom you agree with on some matter. Others have had the same experiences. And their disagreement with you is not necessarily a sign of disrespect or hostility toward you. So you needn't react with disrespect or hostility.

This distinction between the person and the idea can help you give your readers the benefit of the doubt. If you can't tell from a single issue whether people are wise or foolish, sensitive or insensitive, honorable or dishonorable, why not be generous and regard them as the more favorable in each case. Doing so will help you avoid negative feelings. And the implied compliment will surely not displease your readers.

Write When You Are Calm

The second way to avoid negative feelings toward your readers is to write when your emotions are cool and your mind is clear. Feeling angry or resentful about an issue is nothing to be ashamed of. Strong emotions are what prompt most people to express their views in controversial situations. But such emotions must not be allowed to dominate. They must be harnessed to reason. If you want to take notes when you are "hot," that's fine. But don't try to compose a persuasive piece of writing in that state. Give your sense of outrage, and the inevitable hostility that accompanies it, a chance to pass, and you will reduce the chance that you will think or say things that will offend your readers and undermine your objective.

A qualification is necessary about the principle of respecting your readers. Although you must convey a feeling of respect for your readers, you should not proclaim that feeling. Saying explicitly that you respect someone, particularly while you are disagreeing with his view, can sound a bit insincere, as if you were buttering him up. Be content to feel that respect, and avoid saying or implying anything that might suggest you do not.

Principle 3: Build a Balanced Case

A good "blast" at some real or imagined enemy is very satisfying. It gives you not only a sense of emotional release but also a perversely pleasurable feeling of power. So it is understandably tempting to want to "put people in their place," to "tell people off." If you happen to get a couple of bad meals in a row in your dining hall, for example, you may want to write a blast to the dining hall manager. And your first impulse will be to recall every bad experience you ever had in the dining hall and every complaint you ever heard anyone else voice, from slow service and cold food to foreign objects (flies, hair, yecch!) in the mashed potatoes, dirty silverware, under- and overcooking, inferior quality food, warm milk, rancid butter, and watery ice cream. Next you'll want to add some sarcastic remarks—"I guess the workers must come in early to achieve such total ineptitude"—as well as the charge that the meal ticket fee is exorbitant. And you'll probably want to close with a personal insult to the manager—"Do I really think you'll do something about this rip-off? Hell, no. I'm sure you're too busy closing your eyes to it."

Satisfying? Indeed. And if satisfaction is your purpose in writing, then you'll have written successfully. But if your purpose in writing is to persuade the manager to improve his operation, you'll have failed dismally.

Limit the Number of Arguments

A persuasive case is a balanced case. It is forceful but never overwhelming. That is, it omits none of the important points the writer wants to make, no matter how delicate the issues being raised, but it does not include a lot of unnecessary secondary points that beat the readers down and make them feel the writer is rejecting them and their position totally.

Use Understatement

There are several approaches you can take in addition to limiting the number of your arguments. One is to use understatement to express points you feel the reader will be especially sensitive about. For example, instead of saying, "That was positively the worst meal I have ever eaten," you might say, "That was a bad meal," or, even more understated, "I was not entirely pleased with that meal." Understatement has two benefits: it softens the effect of your criticism or disagreement, and (as we noted in chapter 3) it suggests that you have a sense of restraint, one of the marks of a good mind.

Concede a Point or Two

Another approach is to concede whenever the opposing side of the argument has a point, and to do so generously. In the case of the dining hall complaint, this would mean admitting that there are some good features of the dining hall operation. (It would be a rare dining hall that was without a single redeeming quality.) Perhaps the employees are usually cheerful, or the cashiers are quick and efficient. Perhaps certain meals—breakfast, for instance—are generally well prepared. Keep in mind that the more generous your concessions, the more open your readers will be to your argument. (If your only concession about the dining hall is that the napkin holders are kept filled, you should not expect the dining hall manager to feel very complimented.)

There may, on occasion, be little you can honestly concede. In that case, you will surely have some difficulty thinking of something favorable to say. But even then you will find something if you make a sincere effort. If your dining hall is truly the worst place you have ever eaten—a veritable ptomaine palace—you can still admit that it is no easy job to feed hundreds of people three times a day and do it well; that tastes in food being so varied, it is virtually impossible to please everyone; and that some people will complain no matter how good the food and service are. And such admissions, though modest, will help demonstrate that you are at least trying to be fair and balanced in your assessment.

Begin on a Point of Agreement

Still another approach to building a balanced case is to begin on a point of agreement. The value of this approach is difficult to overstate. When you launch right into disagreement with your readers, you put them on the defensive. This often makes it difficult for them to respond favorably to your later points, no matter how reasonable those points may be. On the other hand, when you begin on a point of agreement, you establish at the outset that you are attempting a balanced presentation and that the readers need not be defensive. This approach invites the readers to give your views a fair hearing. And most honest, open-minded readers will respond that way.

Principle 4: Support Your Judgments with Appropriate Evidence, Carefully Interpreted

In the broadest sense, *evidence* is anything that serves to support a judgment. A sufficient amount of evidence can constitute *proof,* but the two terms are not synonymous. The term *proof* suggests finality, certainty, the elimination of all doubt. Because few important issues can be closed to further inquiry, it is usually more appropriate to speak of evidence than of proof.

Evidence reveals to others the validity of your judgments. Even though a good deal of experience is common to all people, no two people have precisely the same perceptions. Even identical twins differ in what they perceive, for it is impossible for them to occupy the same place at the same time. Moreover, since their moods and their degree of interest and attention will differ, they will not interpret things in the same way. If such differences exist between identical twins, how much more so do they exist among the rest of us!

When you present evidence to support your views, you provide a guide for other people through unfamiliar territory, the domain of your impressions, feelings, thoughts, and understandings. You recreate for them what you have experienced and observed and learned. Thus you provide a basis for them to accept your judgments.

It is as foolish to offer conclusions without evidence as it is to say to someone, "I have added up a dozen numbers and arrived at a total of 32,456. Please endorse it as the right answer." The person would very likely respond, "If you want me to endorse it as the right answer, give me the dozen numbers and let *me* see if they add up to your total." To expect others to accept your unsupported calculations of reality is to expect them to consider you incapable of error. It is not a reasonable expectation.

Kinds of Evidence

There are four broad categories of evidence, and they differ in their effectiveness with a discerning audience. A close look at each category will help you to understand its particular importance and enable you to support your judgments accurately and effectively.

Confirmed Details or Statistics

How many drug-related deaths were there in the United States last year? What percentage of our taxes is spent on defense? What is the present rate of illiteracy in New York State? What does the eighteenth amendment to the U.S. Constitution concern? The answers to these questions, which can be found with ease in any library, are examples of confirmed details or statistics.* This kind of evidence is usually most effective because it is least subject to error or the distortion of individual perception.

Your Own Experience and Observation

This includes anything that has happened to you and anything you have witnessed happening to others. It is the one kind of evidence about which you can

---

*For a more complete discussion of such sources of evidence and how to use them, see Part V The Research Paper.

speak with authority regardless of your lack of scholarly credentials. And the fact that it is first-hand testimony gives it special force with your readers. This does not mean, however, that your experience and observation are necessarily of the highest quality. It is possible to misconstrue the meaning or importance of a particular experience; and your observation can be careless and inaccurate. (Perceptions and recollections can be unconsciously twisted to conform to your own attitudes, needs, and wishes.) Therefore, in selecting the experiences and observations you use to support your judgments, be sure they actually apply to the situation and report them accurately.

The Judgments of Authorities   *Authority* is expert knowledge. A person who has authority is not only familiar with a subject but also in command of it. He or she has gotten beyond superficial knowledge, penetrated the complexities of the subject, and come to terms with its intricacies. This, of course, does not place a person above error. Even the most respected experts can be wrong. What, then, is the difference between experts and amateurs? Experts are less likely to err than amateurs. And when they do err, their errors are seldom gross or common; rather, they occur in a framework of valid ideas. Therefore, their testimony—and their judgments—are more trustworthy than those of others.

This is not to say that experts always agree. No field is without its areas of dispute, and it is not uncommon to find several competing theories or interpretations, each with a sizable number of advocates. Therefore, the effectiveness of this kind of evidence depends on the number of authorities who accept it and their eminence in the field. A judgment shared by virtually all respected people in the field would be more persuasive than one shared by a small number of relatively unknown persons.

The effectiveness of this kind of evidence rivals that of personal experience and observation (and at times surpasses it) because it has the force of expertise.

Other People's Experience and Observation   This differs from your own experience and observation in that you do not know it first-hand, but only from the reports of others. They may have told you directly or indirectly (for example, through a third party or through a medium such as magazines or television). Obviously, this kind of evidence is riskier than the other kinds in that it leaves more opportunity for rumor and error to creep in. Any time you use it you should be reasonably sure of the veracity of your sources and the accuracy of the report. You would naturally put more trust in a reliable person than an unreliable one, a careful reporter than one given to exaggeration, a critical-minded person than a rumor-monger. Similarly, you should be more skeptical of second-hand and third-hand reports than of first-hand observation.

Although it is at times very effective, this kind of evidence has a limitation the others do not: it is at best a second-hand report and therefore more subject to error.

When Is Your Evidence Adequate?

"Have I enough evidence? Is it the right kind of evidence?" There is no easy formula for answering these questions. The adequacy of your evidence depends on the particular audience, the degree of controversy involved, the scope of the issue under discussion, and the number and kind of judgments being made. If, for example, you were arguing that a particular administrator in the student affairs division of your college was incompetent, you would obviously need examples of what she had not done that she should have done or what she had done that she shouldn't have done. But to make an effective case, you would also need some documentation that her action or inaction really constituted incompetency. Your simply saying it did would probably not be persuasive. Even quoting her co-workers' judgments might not be sufficient: after all, professionals can disagree about the best course of action without one of them being incompetent. You would have to cite the official description of her job (if it specified what she should or should not do in such matters) or the judgments of authorities, such as would be found in articles or books dealing with the subject.

In general, you may consider your evidence adequate when you have addressed and eliminated all reasonable doubts that are likely to occur to your readers. In any case, it is not so much the *quantity* of evidence that matters, but rather the *quality* of that evidence.

Interpreting Evidence

As important as the evidence itself is your interpretation of it. In fact, evidence and interpretation sometimes become so intermingled that they seem to be the same thing. This is because of the ease and naturalness with which people move back and forth from what they have seen or heard or read to their conclusions about it. In many cases, the emphasis is more on interpretation of the evidence than on the evidence itself. This is especially true when the discussion concerns not what *is* but what *should be*. For instance, you may wish to argue that the system of tenure (permanent appointment) for teachers should be replaced by a system of term appointments. In this case, you would surely include such evidence as details of the history of tenure, actual cases in which poor or incompetent teachers remained in the classroom because they had tenure, and the statements of some educational authorities who have spoken out against tenure. But much of your argument would probably be your own interpretation of how tenure has failed to live up to its promise and why it should be changed.

> In my high school a tenured science teacher managed to resist repeated efforts of parents to remove him from the faculty. I had him myself, so I know first-hand of the shabbiness of his teaching. He spent at least half of every period talking about his experiences in the service during the Second World War or talking about his wife, his dog, and his hobbies. He never went over the reading assignments in class, let students do what they wanted in lab while he talked to whoever happened to be passing by in the hall, and gave everyone a B at the end of the term.
>
> Every time an irate parent complained to the principal, he got the same answer: "We can't touch him—he has tenure." My parents took the matter to the school board, and their answer, though more detailed, was no less discouraging. The board acknowledged they might remove him, but the amount of documentation that would be required to make a case against him would be formidable, and a good union lawyer might be successful in defending him anyway. It would be better, they added, to wait until he retired in a few years.
>
> This situation, in my view, is intolerable. I appreciate the difficulty of the principal's and school board's situation. But something is seriously wrong when a procedure that was originally designed to improve the quality of education—tenure—has become an obstacle to quality education. I simply can't accept the answer that preserving the rights of teachers requires that students suffer at the hands of incompetents. There must be a way to protect teachers *and* students from injustice. . . .

The first two paragraphs of this excerpt from a composition present evidence. The third provides the writer's comment about it, her interpretation of it. That paragraph contributes significantly to the effectiveness of the passage by suggesting the meaning the writer finds in the evidence.

Because interpretation is so important, you must be careful not only in your selection of evidence but also in the reasoning you do about it. It does little good to assemble an impressive array of details, examples of first-hand experience and observation, and judgments of authorities, if you then make careless and illogical comments about your data.

Principle 5: Anticipate Your Readers' Reactions

As we have seen, the persuasiveness of a presentation depends on the readers' reaction. It stands to reason, therefore, that your focus in writing such a paper must be on presenting the argument (or arguments) best calculated to persuade the readers. However, that argument will not always be the one you feel most strongly about, and that is a source of difficulty for many writers. You must get beyond your own perspective and build your argument to reach your readers' perspective—without, of course, compromising your integrity by adopting an argument you do not believe.

Let's say you are arguing that capital punishment ought to be used in certain cases and you are writing for an audience that disapproves of capital punishment in any case. Let's say, further, that the basis of your position is a practical consideration—that the cost of housing criminals for life is too high to make their victims pay (through taxes)—and that your readers reject capital punishment on moral and religious grounds. Your argument of practicality is not likely to persuade them. It would be more effective to construct an argument with more appeal to them—for example, that it is sometimes more humane (hence, more moral) to take a prisoner's life than to imprison him for the rest of his days without hope of parole.

If you do not believe that argument, of course, then honesty would demand that you not pretend you do. But if you do accept it as a secondary argument, there is nothing dishonest about giving it more prominence in your presentation than you give the practical argument, as long as you do not present it as the argument you yourself find most compelling.

In addition to aiming your presentation toward the readers' perspective, you should also consider their likely reaction to every point you make and the way you make it. More specifically, you should ask: Which of my points will they regard as weakest? Which as strongest? What objections will they have to the points they consider weak? How can I best construct my points to avoid their objections? Where are they most likely to misunderstand my argument? How can I best clarify those parts so as to reduce the chance of misunderstanding? Have I used any words that might offend them unnecessarily and undermine persuasion? If so, what words might I substitute without altering my meaning? Are they likely to conclude that I understand their position and have dealt with it fairly? If not, what might I add to my presentation to get a more favorable reaction?

Two Sample Papers

The five principles of persuasion presented in this chapter are not to be taken as token nods to propriety, a kind of etiquette for writers. They are the absolute demands of the psychology of argument, based on what is known about human intellectual reaction to controversial issues. And what recommends them to any writer is the simple fact that *they work.*

The best way to see how these principles work is to examine people's attempts at persuasion and note how they succeed or fail. We will now consider two such attempts. First, some background. A columnist for a campus newspaper wrote an article that was critical of fraternities. In brief, he complained that on more than one occasion, men whom he had considered friends had snubbed him when they were with their fraternity brothers. He observed that the same thing happened to other people as well. Something seems to happen to men when they join a fraternity, he reasoned: they become clannish and snobbish, rejecting former friends and even roommates. Moreover, he argued, though many men claim to join fraternities to make lasting friendships and learn to live in harmony with others, the real reason is in many cases to gain social or economic advantages after graduation and access to examination files before graduation. He concluded that the actions of fraternity men give little evidence of concern for brotherhood, because brotherhood means more than "secret handshakes, Greek letters, mumbo-jumbo, 'Rah! Rah!' songs, and fancy jackets with emblems"; it means accepting all men as brothers.

The columnist's criticism, predictably, caused a furor on campus, especially among fraternity men. A number of people wrote letters to the editor. Here are two such letters. Read each one carefully, and consider how persuasive it would be with the columnist and those who tend to agree with him.

Dear Editor:

I cannot let Jim Pepper's attack on fraternities go unanswered. It is true that fraternity men take separate tables when they are together. They are proud to be frat men—and for the best of reasons. They have achieved brotherhood in the truest sense of the word. Living in a college dormitory does not permit a person to develop brotherhood. In fact, it exposes him to pettiness, selfishness, irresponsibility, lack of dedication, and a thousand other human frailties. Living in a fraternity means rising above these frailties. When a young man joins a fraternity he becomes a truly dedicated person. He is willing to put aside former ways and former relationships, because he has found something higher and nobler.

"One for all and all for one" is the fraternity motto. If one fraternity brother is in trouble, all the others rush to his assistance. If he needs a job, he knows that there are hundreds of other members, brothers who graduated years before him, who are ready to employ him. If he finds himself in a strange city, he is assured that if a single brother lives there, he will be welcome in that brother's home. No fraternity man ever denies a brother anything it is in his power to give.

It is true that fraternity men are concerned with wild parties and drinking. This is because they place high value on good living. Warmth and good cheer are an expression of the joy that comes from brotherly association. Wild parties and drinking are a basic part of growing up. (Besides, a fellow has to have some stories to tell his children.)

I realize that it is impossible for an "independent" to understand fraternity life, for it can only be understood from the inside. Whether that lack of understanding is joined with envy and resentment or just honest wondering, it never results in valid criticism. Ideally, an outsider will simply admit that there are some profound and mysterious situations in life that are closed to him. Such situations his mind can't penetrate, no matter how powerful it may be. And one of them is the brotherhood of fraternity men.

Sincerely,
Benjamin Boister

Dear Editor:

I am writing in response to Jim Pepper's article on fraternities. I am a fraternity member myself, and can verify that much of what Mr. Pepper says is true. The charge that fraternities tend to make men clannish and snobbish can be documented on this campus at any time of the day—in the library, the snack bar, the athletic fields, the classrooms. Something does seem to happen to many men when they join fraternities. They do often ignore their former friends. It is understandable and right that such behavior makes nonfraternity observers angry and resentful. For that matter, it doesn't please everyone in fraternities.

The idea that some men join fraternities for economic or social advantage, or even for the advantage of using fraternity files of exams and assignments, is also true. It's not easy for a fraternity man to admit that some of his brothers are hypocritical, and outsiders shouldn't be surprised if they don't hear any quarrels about such hypocrisy among fraternity men. But they shouldn't conclude from that silence that there are no quarrels inside the fraternity house. And they shouldn't conclude, either, that everyone in a fraternity uses the exam files. Not every fraternity man sets aside all his convictions and values when he joins a fraternity.

Mr. Pepper's comments about brotherhood cut deep. The temptation is strong for a fraternity man to deny them and attack him for making them. I know more than a few fraternity men who have already responded that way in private discussions. "Jim Pepper is just jealous," "he's filled with bitterness because he didn't get a bid to pledge a frat," "he's just a stupid punk liar" are just a few of the (more printable) comments his remarks about brotherhood prompted. But the fact is, what he says is *true*. And many of us in fraternities tend to forget it.

If I feel this way, why don't I quit my fraternity? Aren't such admissions the mark of a traitor? The questions are sure to arise. Well, I won't quit, and I don't consider myself a traitor. I believe with Jim Pepper that there should be the larger type of brotherhood in the world. I believe that fraternities often unknowingly work against it. But I do believe they *can* work toward it. We can't behave right toward the world until we learn to behave right toward those around us, the little worlds of our everyday associations. A fraternity with the right emphases can develop the idea of brotherhood and prepare its members to be brothers to all men. Because it is a close-knit association, it can do so better than dorm life can. There are, I think, more than a few fraternity members who are trying to make it do so.

Sincerely,
Marvin Mindful

The difference between these two letters should be fairly obvious. The first violates all five principles of persuasion. It shows little real understanding of the columnist's position, suggesting instead that he had no substantive arguments and that he was not entitled even to judge from his own experience because fraternity life is too "profound and mysterious" to be judged from the outside. Ironically, this comment (and others) displays the same quality of snobbishness the columnist was attacking. Further, the first letter offers a very unbalanced, biased case—to the point of ludicrousness. It actually characterizes wild parties and drinking as almost noble activities. (The writer would have done better not to mention them at all.) And the author clearly never bothered to wonder what his readers' reactions would be. Or perhaps he didn't care. For though his formal intention seems to have been to persuade others, his approach shows he was really only stroking his ego.

The second letter is very different. It shows admirable openness of mind and willingness to acknowledge the truth, even when it is unpleasant. It piles concession upon concession, and not at all grudgingly, but generously and in a cordial manner. Throughout the letter, the author's sensitivity to his readers and awareness of their probable reactions is shown. The best example of this awareness is the question that begins the last paragraph. The fact that it is precisely the question that would occur to most readers at that point demonstrates the writer's attention to audience. Yet despite all the concessions and the cordial manner, this letter is by no means weak. Where it expresses a point that opposes the columnist's position, it does so directly and forcefully and reasonably, as all persuasive writing must; for thoughtful readers are not persuaded by a tepid, apologetic style any more than by an offensively aggressive style. They expect forceful argument to be tempered by open-minded civility.

What to Expect from Your Readers

Whatever the subject of your persuasive composition, whatever the kind of disagreement you may have with your readers, and whatever the extent of your personal knowledge of your readers, you can be fairly sure of one thing—few of them will roll over and play dead no matter how well you state your case. Few people who have thought about an issue and have formed at least a tentative opinion are apt to say, upon reading someone's opposing viewpoint, "Oh yes, you're absolutely right; how could I have been so mistaken? I concede on every point and accept your position completely." So if you expect to get people to renounce their views completely and embrace yours, you had better prepare to be disappointed, because people seldom behave that way. It's far better to keep your expectations more modest. Aim to get your readers to reopen the issue, to reflect on their views in light of what you have said, and to modify their opinions to some extent. More than that the most persuasive writers do not often achieve.

Exercises

1. In a sentence or two, state your tentative judgment of each of the following cases. Then state (1) the kind and amount of

evidence you would need to support that judgment for a critical audience and (2) how and where you might obtain that evidence. Be as specific as you can in your answer.

   a. Should bartenders be held legally responsible for automobile accidents caused by people to whom they have served alcohol?
   b. Should the rules of the Olympics be changed to permit the participation of professional athletes?
   c. Does television have a more negative influence or positive influence on children?
   d. Is there a monster in Loch Ness, Scotland?
   e. Does your favorite team (any sport) have a better chance for a winning season this year than last?

2. For each of the following problems select the point of view closer to your own. Then, after reflecting on the idea and the audience, answer these questions: What arguments and evidence would *your readers* most likely offer to support *their* view? Which of those arguments and which parts of that evidence would any reasonable person have to accept? What arguments and evidence would *you* offer in support of *your* position? Which of those arguments and which parts of that evidence would be least appropriate for your readers? Which most appropriate?

   a. (1) When fixtures and furniture on a particular dormitory floor are damaged and the person responsible is not identified, *everyone* on the floor should be charged for the repairs. (Readers: a group of commuting students who believe that the charging of innocent students would be unjust.)

      (2) When fixtures and furniture on a particular dormitory floor are damaged and the person responsible is not identified, *no one* on the floor should be charged for the repairs. (Readers: several college administrators who, knowing that someone must pay for the damages—if not students, then parents through higher tuition, or taxpayers in the case of a state college—believe that there is no reasonable alternative to charging residents of the floor.)

   b. (1) Growing up today is easier than it was thirty years ago. (Readers: students who believe that the pressures on them today are greater than the pressures their parents felt.)

(2) Growing up today is more difficult than it was thirty years ago. (Readers: a group of men and women, age forty-five to fifty, who feel that the pressures were much greater when they were teenagers.)

c. (1) Students who fail out of this college should be permitted to apply for readmission. (Readers: a group of professors who believe that students would be more conscientious if they knew there would be no second chance.)

(2) Students who fail out of this college should not be permitted to apply for readmission. (Readers: a group of honor students who believe that every student deserves a second chance.)

d. (1) Marijuana should be legalized. (Readers: a group of former drug addicts who are opposed to the legalization of marijuana because they believe their early use of it helped dispose them to the use of hard drugs.)

(2) Marijuana should not be legalized. (Readers: several college professors who have been using marijuana in place of liquor at social gatherings for several years and have found themselves neither addicted to it nor prompted to try hard drugs.)

e. (1) Extremist political groups (for example, Nazis) should be allowed to hold rallies on public property. (Readers: a group of survivors of Nazi concentration camps who believe that there are grave dangers in letting such groups preach their propaganda.)

(2) Extremist political groups (for example, Nazis) should not be allowed to hold rallies on public property. (Readers: a group of civil rights lawyers who believe that a democracy must guarantee everyone's freedom of speech, even that of people who preach hatred and insurrection.)

Composition Assignment

Select one of the composition possibilities that follow, then write a brief composition on it. (Unless your instructor specifies a different length, make it between 300 and 500 words.) Don't skimp on the writing and revising stages, but pay particular attention to planning, especially to considering your readers.

1. Select one of the topics from exercise 2. Building on the analysis you did there, compose a persuasive presentation of your position for the audience specified. Be sure to apply all the principles and approaches detailed in the chapter.

2. Think of a current controversy on your campus, one that has been the subject of considerable discussion among students. Briefly state the idea you wish to defend and the reader or readers you will be writing for (in the manner described in exercise 2). Keep this information apart from your actual composition. Plan and write a persuasive composition for that audience. (Be sure you select an audience that disagrees with you.)

3. Think of an incident that occurred within the past year, something you felt strongly about at the time (for example, getting a traffic ticket). In your view, it might have been a case of bad judgment, indiscretion, tactlessness, and so on. It might have affected you directly, indirectly, or not at all. Your readers will be others who saw the incident but disagree with your reaction to it, or, if you wish, the very people whose actions you are speaking against. Plan and write a persuasive composition for those readers.

4. Think of a statement that you disagree with that was made in one of your textbooks or by one of your instructors. Be sure you do not consider it out of the original context, and be sure it is controversial, not factual. Compose a persuasive composition expressing your disagreement with the statement. Your reader will be the textbook author or instructor who made the statement. (Attach a copy of the statement to your finished paper.)

5. Find in a newspaper (campus, local, or other) or magazine an article or letter to the editor that you disagree with. Study it carefully, applying what you learned in the chapter. Then compose a persuasive response with that author as your reader. Attach to your paper either the original piece itself, a photocopy, or a brief summary.

Part III

Writing the Composition

In the writing stage of the composition process you carry out your plan for the composition and complete the rough draft. If you have attended carefully to the considerations detailed in Chapters 2 through 5, when you begin writing you will already know not only your topic but also what you will say about it. Moreover, you will have decided on a controlling idea and a particular composition form, and you will have considered your audience. If the composition will include one or more of your judgments, you will also have tested their reasonableness.

Your focus in the writing stage is the arrangement and development of your ideas into a meaningful presentation. It would be a mistake to spend time now reviewing your reasoning,* or finely crafting your sentences and paragraphs, or checking your spelling or grammar. Those activities are sure to distract you and may even cause writer's block. The time for revision and editing is after you have completed the rough draft.

The chapters in Part III build upon the brief introduction to basic composition forms included in Chapter 3. There we noted that there are three such forms—narrative, informative, and persuasive—and examined their essential distinguishing features. Here we will devote a chapter to each form, identifying the techniques and strategies professional writers use in their work.

As you study the chapters in this section, keep in mind that what many people call writing talent is often no more than creative application of writing

---

*One exception should be noted. If in writing you discover that the judgment your paper is based on is invalid, you should stop writing and return to the planning stage. If you plan properly, however, this will seldom happen.

techniques, and there is no magic in that. By diligently practicing the approaches detailed in these chapters and combining them in ways that effectively serve your purpose and controlling idea, you too can achieve excellence in your writing.

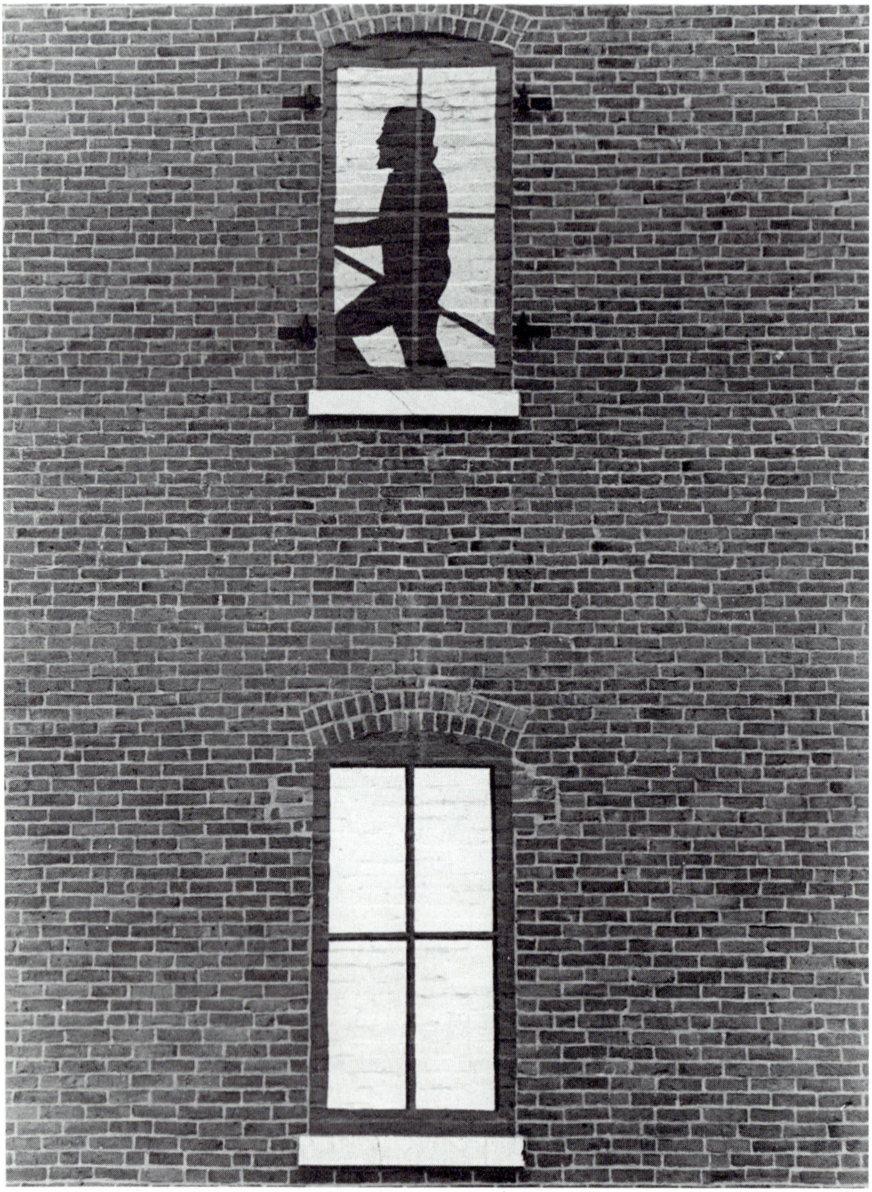

Chapter 6

Writing a Narrative Composition

This chapter details the characteristics of an effective narrative composition and the techniques of development most closely associated with narrative writing. It demonstrates how to use those techniques both singly and in combination and offers four helpful writing strategies.

A narrative composition, as we noted in Chapter 3, recounts actual experience, aiming not merely to tell the readers what happened but to show them, so that they can participate in the experience vicariously. This often involves recreating the experience in considerable detail and with considerable dramatic intensity to make the readers feel that they are experiencing the situation themselves, with all the emotional reactions of the person or persons to whom it happened. This dramatic quality of the narrative composition is its most distinguishing feature.

Characteristics of a Narrative Composition

An effective narrative composition has several significant characteristics, which you may use as standards to guide your writing, and which your instructor will undoubtedly use as criteria for evaluating it. The characteristics are as follows:

An effective narrative composition presents a single meaningful incident. It is possible to write a narrative that deals with more than one incident, but single-incident narratives are both more common and less risky. (Narrating two or more incidents in the same composition increases the chance that the composition will degenerate into summary and thus lose its dramatic quality.) Further, the incident that is presented must be worthy of meaningful dramatic treatment. In other words, it must be one that resulted in the resolution of some external or inner conflict or in an appreciable increase in understanding. Trivial occurrences do not qualify for narrative treatment.

An effective narrative composition is factual rather than fictional. This statement in no way derogates fictional narratives. It merely reflects the fact that fiction is a highly specialized kind of writing that depends not only on careful observation but also on a more particular application of creative imagination than that which can be taught in a general composition course. Limiting your topics to real events needn't be confining. The list of possibilities is virtually endless. If you are a history major, for example, you may wish to write a narrative account of General Custer's last stand at the Little Big Horn, or of the bombing of Hiroshima. If you are a science major, you may prefer a narrative account of Harvey's discovery of the circulation of the blood, or Pasteur's arduous effort to cure rabies. The narratives on which you will be able to speak with the greatest authority, of course, and that require no research, are the incidents you have experienced firsthand, the significant events in your own life.

An effective narrative composition makes the order of events clear. The dominant organizational pattern in narrative compositions is *time order*—first this happened, then that, and finally something else. The readers' ability to follow the narrative, therefore, depends on the clarity of the ordering of events. Generally, the ordering should be strictly chronological, with each stage of the incident presented in the order in which it actually took place. Professional writers sometimes break chronological order in their narratives with *flashbacks*—movements backward in time. Such moves, however, depend for their effectiveness on how well the writer signals the flashback and later resumes the narrative's forward progression. If you use flashbacks, take special care not to confuse your readers.

An effective narrative composition contains no superfluous details. The inclusion of superfluous details is one of the most common errors in narrative writing. It is an understandable error because the effort to re-create experience dramatically is directed at the inclusion of details, and the more observant the writer is, the more details he or she is aware of. Yet not every detail is worthy of inclusion. It is a writer's responsibility to select details judiciously, omitting all those that do not contribute to the intended effect.

An effective narrative composition includes a climactic moment. The climactic moment or "high point" in a narrative composition is the moment when conflict is resolved or understanding is reached. Since the composition builds toward this moment and reaches its fulfillment in it, the composition should end shortly after it is reached.

Basic Narrative Techniques

The four techniques most closely associated with narrative writing are narrating, describing, defining figuratively, and dialogue. Let's examine each one closely and see its particular contribution to the narrative composition.

Narrating

This is the principal technique in narrative writing. Its purpose is to move the story through time. Though it may be interrupted so that another technique (description, for example) can make its contribution, narrating provides the composition with its essential structure. Here are two examples of narrating.*

> The genial, courteous attitude of the late John B. Stanchfield toward everyone he came in contact with in the trial of his cases was one of the secrets of his success. Shortly before he died he told me of his experiences in Washington when he was retained by some of the leaders of the Washington Bar to conduct, with them, the defense of the president of the Riggs Bank. Immediately upon his arrival in Washington, Mr. Stanchfield was summoned to a meeting of all the lawyers in the case and was told that he had been selected to assume the burden of the trial. He was warned, however, that the feeling

Close examination of this narrative will reveal several places where the author was selective about what he included. For example, in sentence 3 he moves directly to Stanchfield's meeting with the other lawyers. The circumstances of how he was retained in the case are

---

*Because our purpose here is merely to illustrate the basic form narrative takes, the examples shown are briefer than the typical narrative composition.

omitted because they are not relevant to the story.

against the bank official was so intense, and the bias of the judge who was to preside at the trial was so marked that there was little hope of a successful defense, unless Mr. Stanchfield could so irritate the trial judge that he would not only display his prejudice to the jury and thus arouse their sympathy, but also make erroneous rulings that might upset the verdict upon appeal. It was apparent to Mr. Stanchfield that he had been called from New York to undertake a task none of the local attorneys was willing to assume. He promptly refused to depart from his usual method or conduct the trial upon any such lines as were laid down by the Washington lawyers. He would try the case in his own way or not at all.

Throughout the trial Mr. Stanchfield's attitude toward the court was one of extreme courtesy and respect. At the end of a week the issue was narrowed down practically to the single question of *reasonable doubt*. Was the defendant guilty "beyond all reasonable doubt"?—otherwise he should be acquitted. Mr. Stanchfield devoted practically his entire summing up to the jury to this question. He cited authorities and explained with great minuteness all the intricacies of this perplexing rule of law—to such good effect that when the judge came to charge the jury, he complimented the courteous gentleman from New York upon the clearness and accuracy with which he had stated the law to the jury and ended by saying he could think of nothing he could add to or subtract from Mr. Stanchfield's statement. The result was a prompt acquittal. When the jury had rendered their verdict, the judge invited Mr. Stanchfield into his private chambers and then remarked: "Mr. Stanchfield, when I heard that you had been called from New York to try this case before me, I could almost see you arriving in the city and almost hear the instructions that were given you as to how to conduct yourself during the trial. I just want to say this one thing to you: *it pays to be a gentleman.*"[1]

This narrative, taken from an anthropologist's study of a primitive tribe, is more dramatic than the previous one. Note the author's attention to detail and the vivid language he uses to re-create the experience.

Manyalibo's wife picked up the banja and beat them, sharply and decisively, and the girls began the song. The men followed in obedient chorus. Once again, as the song grew faster, the old woman began to twitch until her whole body was alive with movement. Then she sprang up and came into the center of the kumamolimo alone. For an instant she stood there, and her head moved sharply from side to side. It was like the movement of a bird, keeping a wary eye open for possible foes. As she began to dance she seemed to sink slowly into the ground, her knees folding up like a concertina, her body bending at the waist; but always her head stuck out in front, jerking from side to side, eyes staring and expressionless.

She circled the fire three times, looking out and upward into the night, but unseeing; then as if satisfied that she was alone and unobserved she flung her head and her whole body around and faced the fire directly. She was about seven or eight feet away from it. She advanced slowly and cautiously, two steps forward, one step back, her attention riveted on the flames. The singing was louder and faster, but she refused to be hurried. At her own pace she approached closer and closer until it seemed impossible that she could stand the heat. She hesitated at the brink of the fire, her frail body gleaming with sweat, her face glowing and trembling. She made as if she was going to pounce on the fire, but whirled around at the last moment and danced quickly back to where the women were singing, watching her, eagerly and anxiously. She sat down on her haunches and accepted a steaming bowl of liko.

The singing did not stop this time but went on quietly at a slower tempo. The men made no attempt to move back closer to the fire. After about ten minutes the old lady, apparently refreshed and as full of vigor as ever, danced back into the men's circle, with Kondabate at her side. Their movements were perfectly co-ordinated, even to the twitching of their heads; as they sank down close to the ground they might have been one person. But as they neared the fire, again having circled it several times, the old woman sprang to her feet and ran swiftly around to the far side and crouched there, staring at Kondabate through the flames. They started circling once more, each keeping her eyes on the other, moving from side to side so that they were always opposite each other. But now they were closer to the fire than they had ever been and on their hands and knees they passed through the hot ashes, as though trying to reach each other through the flames.

Finally Kondabate retreated and squatted down at the edge of the circle, her body twitching just as the old woman's had done, her eyes staring and empty as she gazed at the molimo fire. The men heaped more wood on the flames, which were beginning to die down. Now they were singing as loudly as the women, stamping on the ground with their feet and dancing with their arms and bodies, but never moving from where they stood. The old woman grew taller and more upright. Her bent old frame straightened out and she stood proudly, arms at her side, bent at the elbows so that her hands were out in front. Those hands had a life of their own, pointing and gesticulating and dancing with infinite grace at the end of motionless arms. The old woman no longer looked from side to side. She knew she had nothing to fear now, that she was the victor. And when she stooped once more to approach the fire she did not stoop so low, and each step was a step forward. As the singing quickened so did her steps, until with a burst of frenzied shouting she was driven right into the flames.

She seemed to hover there an instant, that skinny old crone who should have been burned to a cinder in a flash. Then she whirled around and kicked out with her feet, scattering the sacred molimo fire in all directions. Blazing logs and glowing embers alike she scattered, right among the circle of men surrounding her. And then she danced away, erect and proud.[2]

Describing

Description is useful when you wish to create a sensory impression for your readers—to enable them to see, hear, taste, smell, or touch something you have experienced. It may also be used to convey thoughts, feelings, impressions, and states of mind. The heart of description is *concrete detail*—that is, detail that can be known through sensory experience and that produces images in your readers' minds.

The more detail you provide, the sharper the picture you create for your readers. A sense of proportion is necessary, of course. Too much description, or description for its own sake, can be counterproductive. But this will not be a problem so long as your descriptions serve your controlling idea and so long as important matters are given more space than less important ones.

Here are some examples of effective description.

Describing People

This example describes a person as she usually appeared. Sometimes it is useful to describe someone as she appeared on a particular occasion.

She was about 5'9" tall and must have weighed at least 195 pounds. Her eyes were beady and very suspicious, her nose absurdly tiny for such a broad face. The corners of her mouth dipped in a perpetual frown, and her normal speaking voice was a low hiss. Her figure resembled a German tank on stilts—large and shapeless, with skinny, stick-shaped legs and big, long, flat feet.

Describing Places

Place description often depends for its effectiveness on how well we handle direction. Expressions like "below," "to the right," and "at the very top" help the reader see each detail in exact relation to other details.

Directly below my window a sidewalk stretches up to the parking lot behind the dormitory. To the right of the sidewalk a hill rises gradually to a broad plateau, bare except for an old barn made of rough-sawn lumber, its tin roof pitted with rust. To the left of the sidewalk, perhaps a half-mile up a gently sloping hill, is a large white frame farm house with a matching white barn. At the very top of the hill are dense woods.

His 12′ by 5′ room was originally planned to be a closet. The furniture consists of a sofa with three pillows and a 12″ portable TV that refuses to work. Two hundred sixty beer cans are piled on top of one another to form a pyramid running the entire width of the room. A dozen mobiles made from popsicle sticks and empty six-pack cartons hang from the ceiling.

Here direction is not so important. The focus is not on the arrangement of the furnishings but on their bizarre character.

Some [old statues in the Colombian Andes] consist of huge slabs with bas-relief carvings on the flat front and back surfaces; others are simple cylindrical shapes on which a human or animal figure is outlined only superficially. Still others, carved in the round and using various planes, give proof of highly skilled workmanship and true mastery of form and material. Varying in body proportions and height—the tallest statues are about twelve feet—these stone carvings show a wide array of human and animal shapes or monstrous combinations of both. Squat human bodies with short, stiff limbs carry disproportionally large heads with feline features. Pointed fangs protrude from snarling jaws. There are warriors with helmets and clubs with secondary figures crouching on their heads, as if climbing over the backs of the statues. Others show females with elaborate headdresses, squatting animals, and a bird of prey holding in its beak and claws a writhing snake.[3]

Describing Things

Here the writer can assume that the reader is familiar with characteristics of statues in general and focus on the special features of these statues. Note that it is not a single statue that is described but a whole class of statues.

Describing Impressions

Here accuracy of description demands not the differentiation of faces and clothing but the blurring of them, for that is what was seen.

The train sped through the station. There were some people on the platform, perhaps a dozen. They all seemed mesmerized by the motion of the train. The speed at which we were moving blurred their features and transformed their clothing into a multicolored ribbon.

Describing Thoughts

The writer used this description because it was an inaccurate depiction of college life—that is, because it permitted her to show (later) how mistaken she had been.

Before I entered college, my thoughts of college life were rather stereotyped—cobblestone paths; tall, dark, suave, handsome men speeding about in little red sports cars; distinguished professors graying at the temples, dressed in tweed, puffing on pipes, and speaking polysyllabically.

Describing Feelings

To the other patients the writer may have appeared calm as he sat in the dentist's waiting room. But he didn't feel calm, and it is his feelings he is describing here.

I had managed to forget my fear—until I heard the low moan from behind the door to the dentist's office. Then I grew tense. My stomach ached. I felt very cold, yet perspiration was running down my forehead. "Make an excuse to the receptionist," I thought. "Just get out." I wanted to run. For the next twenty minutes I sat fixed to my chair, heart pounding, legs trembling.

Defining Figuratively

Figurative definition differs from literal definition in that it is not literal but *literary*; that is, it deals with subjective, rather than objective, meaning. For example, the literal meaning of the term *concentration camp* is "a prisonlike place where people are incarcerated, usually without due process of law." But the meaning of the term to people who lost their loved ones in such a camp goes far beyond such a matter-of-fact definition. To such people, a concentration camp is a diabolical place, the product of insane minds filled with blind, irrational malice, a place where every vestige of human decency is forgotten in an orgy of senseless pain and persecution, a place of supreme insult to God and humanity alike. As this definition suggests, where the thing being defined arouses powerful emotions in people, literal definition cannot convey ideas adequately. In such cases, you should consider using figurative definition.

This definition cannot be found in a dictionary yet it is no less valid for that fact. It expresses the meaning of the word "rape" in terms of its effect on the victim, adding intensity to the idea.

To Sally the rape meant many things. At first it meant helplessness and utter terror. Next it meant the violation not only of her body but of her whole being as well. Her mind was invaded, her emotions assaulted, her spirit grievously wounded. It meant, too, a sense of outrage mingled with a feeling of loathing, revulsion, nausea; an acute awareness that a beautiful, tender human act had in a moment been made ugly, coarse, bestial, obscene. Then it meant a profound sense of shame and embarrassment bordering on paranoia—"Everyone is watching me; they know what happened." Sometimes it also meant an unaccountable feeling of guilt—"Maybe I could have anticipated the attack and avoided it; perhaps I should have died rather than submit"—and thus a loss of self-respect. But the most tragic meaning of rape to Sally lay in the more remote effects: a permanent distrust of others, a perpetual fear of dark places and ambiguous glances and little noises that startle, a recurring sense of wretchedness.

Here the figurative definition of student protest, in terms of the associations it had for "many Americans," is divided into the initial reaction and the later one.

To many Americans in the mid-1960s student protest was a frivolity, a prank, the modern equivalent of flagpole sitting and goldfish eating. Lines of students picketing an administration building to demand a voice in curriculum planning and campus regulations were to them cause more for laughter than for alarm. But as the lines grew longer and less orderly, the voices louder and accompanied by rocks and torches, to those same Americans student protest came to mean a threat to society, to civilization itself. As protest escalated, so did their response, until anyone of college age who spoke of any grievance—no matter how reasonable the person nor how obvious the grievance—seemed to represent the forces of willful chaos.

To Joe, college means working out in the gym, speeding around town in his car, girl-watching in the student union, dancing and drinking every evening. It means spending his parents' money and all the change he can beg or borrow to gratify whatever urge happens to be shouting loudest at the moment. An exception, of course, is the urge to achieve academically, which he shows admirable skill in controlling, acknowledging it only by an occasional visit to class or the library, which more often than not is given less to learning than to snoozing or to dreaming about his future success in business.

Here the meaning of college for one individual is presented as a list of his activities.

A common error in figurative definition is lack of clarity as to whose viewpoint the definition represents and what times, places, or conditions, if any, it is limited to. Another common error is unnecessary repetition of the definition "formula"—"it is" or "it means." It is not necessary to avoid this formula completely; just avoid using it to the point of distraction.

Dialogue

Dialogue is the technique used to recreate conversation in a composition. It is an especially effective way of conveying a sense of reality and immediacy. Nevertheless, it should be used sparingly, because it takes up more space than other narrative techniques and because it can wear on readers' patience if it is extended unreasonably or includes material that is not relevant to the narrative. Be sure to use dialogue in your compositions only when it will make a positive contribution to the narrative. In addition, be sure to compress it as much as you can by eliminating unessential comments or relegating them to brief explanatory passages.

It is conventional to begin a new paragraph with every change of speaker in dialogue. This approach enables you to eliminate unnecessary designations of speaker. In using it, however, remember that your readers will expect a change of paragraph in the dialogue to signal a change of speaker, and any lapse of consistency on your part will confuse them and undermine the effectiveness of your narrative. Here are two examples of effective dialogue:

The secretary gave me a vacant half-smile and said, "The dean will not be able to see you now."

"But I had an appointment."

"Something important came up. I'll reschedule you for tomorrow."

I decided to try the forceful approach. "Look, I've been waiting to see him for a week. That's long enough. I want to see him *today*."

She gave me a long, withering look and then said, matter-of-factly, "He's free at 11 A.M. and 2 P.M. tomorrow. Which time shall I put you down for?"

"I guess 2 P.M. will be OK."

As I rode down on the elevator, I decided that my forceful approach still needed work.

We had been arguing about the value of education for more than ten minutes, the exchange growing increasingly heated. Then Jim said something that turned heat to light.

"It's not necessary to go to college to become an educated person," he said.

"Obviously," I replied, irritated.

"How can you say 'obviously' now, after you've been arguing against the idea all this time?"

"I haven't been arguing that going to college is important. I've been arguing that some form of education after high school is important."

"Well, I never disagreed with that idea. I was only saying that people can become educated without going to college."

"If you had made that clear, we wouldn't have been arguing."

"Wrong. It was *your* responsibility to make your view clear."

There was a pause, and then we both broke out laughing, realizing that we were now arguing over why we had been arguing.

Exercises

Choose one assignment from each of the following groups and write one or more paragraphs on it, following the guidelines and examples of narrative techniques in the preceding pages.

1. Narrating
   a. Write a narrative account of the strangest experience you've ever had.
   b. Write a narrative account of the first fight you had as a child.
   c. Write a narrative account of the first time you were admitted to a hospital.

2. Describing
   a. Describe an interesting place you have visited.
   b. Describe an interesting person you know (for example, a friend, member of your family, or roommate).
   c. Describe a place of unusual activity and confusion (for example, the team locker room after an important win, or the dressing room between acts of the college play).
   d. Describe how you feel when you have to go to the doctor or dentist. (You may speak about how you always feel or how you felt on a particular occasion.)
3. Defining Figuratively
   a. Define what home means to a student who has been away at college for a semester.
   b. Define what freedom means to a person who was just released from prison after many years.
   c. Define what Mother's Day means to someone whose mother has just died.
   d. Define what a job means to an unemployed man or woman with a large family.
4. Dialogue
   a. Write a brief dialogue re-creating a disagreement you had with someone.
   b. Write a brief dialogue re-creating a conversation in which someone revealed a secret to you.
   c. Write a brief dialogue re-creating an unusual or otherwise interesting conversation you heard two other people engage in.

Combining Narrative Techniques

So far we have examined narrative techniques as they are used singly. More commonly, however, they are used in combination. In other words, the writer will pause in her narrative long enough to complete a figurative definition or a description of a person, place, thing, or emotion, and then continue with the narrative. Many times she will also weave description into the fabric of the narrative itself, so that the readers receive vivid sensory impressions while the narrative continues. In addition, the writer may turn from narrative to dialogue and then back to the narrative. (Since dialogue is a form of action, this change does not constitute a pause in the action.)

Here are some examples of effective combinations of narrative techniques:

The writer begins with a lead-in explanation specifying his reason for offering the narrative. Then he explains the particulars of the assignment.

When Henry Brooke Carter died recently, the news stories in all the media included highlights from his long and distinguished career in journalism. But for those of us who studied journalism with him, the anecdote that will perhaps be longest remembered is the following one, which I offer here as a personal footnote to the record.

The assignment was to be done during the semester break and would serve as our lead-in to the second semester. There was almost a month to complete it—nevertheless it was difficult. We were to obtain an interview with someone who had just made the front page of a daily newspaper and write a lively account of the person's reactions to being in the spotlight. The instructor explained that the person's story needn't have been glamorous—it could have been just a slender human interest affair. What was important was the person's reactions and how well we could commit them to words.

Here he recounts what happened after the semester break.

For most of us the vacation passed swiftly. When we returned to campus, a single question was on everyone's lips—"What did you get?"

The answers drew varying responses, from polite nods and ho-hum expressions to excited requests to explain every detail.

"What did you get?"

"Queen of the County Fair."

"Uh huh."

"How about you?"

"A man attacked by a pig."

"Really? Attacked? By a *pig*?"

And so on through a small catalog of events, many predictable, a few bizarre. But the one that earned the admiration and awe of all of us was Henry Carter's. For it revealed a preview of that rare combination of good fortune, nerve, and ingenuity that mark the superlative newsman. And we didn't have to ask him about it. We'd read about it in the papers.

Note the use of broken time order (flashback) here. The writer takes Henry's experience out of the natural sequence of events and places it at the end to give it emphasis.

Henry had spent the first three weeks of the semester break enjoying himself—skiing, dancing, playing ball. Only at the beginning of the fourth week did he begin to develop the slightest concern about the assignment, reading the newspapers every day but finding nothing that interested him. Then one day he was talking to a friend on a downtown corner of his city when a masked man ran out of a nearby bank and bumped into Henry. Reacting quickly, Henry grabbed the

Writing a Narrative Composition

bandit's arm and twisted it, wrestling him to the ground and immobilizing him. The driver of a car that had apparently been waiting for the robber paused only long enough to survey the situation. Then he sped away. A moment later the police arrived.

When the man was identified as a well-known bank robber, wanted in several states, Henry's face and story made national headlines. And Henry completed the journalism assignment by interviewing *himself*.

It was Burma, a sodden morning of the rains. A sickly light, like yellow tinfoil, was slanting over the high walls into the jail yard. We were waiting outside the condemned cells, a row of sheds fronted with double bars, like small animal cages. Each cell measured about ten feet by ten and was quite bare except for a plank bed and a pot for drinking water. In some of them brown, silent men were squatting at the inner bars, with their blankets draped round them. These were the condemned men, due to be hanged within the next week or two.

One prisoner had been brought out of his cell. He was a Hindu, a puny wisp of a man, with a shaven head and vague liquid eyes. He had a thick sprouting moustache, absurdly too big for his body, rather like the moustache of a comic man in the films. Six tall Indian warders were guarding him and getting him ready for the gallows. Two of them stood by with rifles and fixed bayonets, while the others handcuffed him, passed a chain through his handcuffs and fixed it to their belts, and lashed his arms tight to his sides. They crowded very close about him, with their hands always on him in a careful, caressing grip, as though all the while feeling him to make sure he was there. It was like men handling a fish which is still alive and may jump back into the water. But he stood quite unresisting, yielding his arms limply to the ropes, as though he hardly noticed what was happening.[4]

This is a composite description. It lets the readers feel the day, picture the cells, the prisoners, and the guards, and see the events that took place. Not everything is described in detail, of course. The day is described in one short, quick stroke. Similarly, only a few details are given about the condemned men in general. The focus is on the one prisoner to be hanged that day. The author is directing the readers' attention to what he feels is important.

... Michael lurched over and peered in. Against the window he could see Thomas' face plastered for an instant of fixed, grinning agony. It was a horrible picture, a Bosch nightmare come alive.

Long, quickly lashing tongues of flame were licking at Thomas' temples, neck, and hair. Through the hissing and crackling of the fire, Michael could hear Thomas laughing, but very dimly, almost lost to the ear. Between the flames he could see the shelves with their gray-white load of corpses. Some were melting. Some were burning. Eyes oozing out of sockets like broken eggs. Hair burning in little tufts. First, fingers and toes and noses and ears, then whole limbs and torsos melting and blackening. And the smell. God! That smell!

This passage combines narrating and describing. It illustrates how vivid description can intensify a narrative's dramatic effect. (A note of caution: such vividness is not necessarily appropriate for every narrative, nor for every part of a dramatic narrative.)

Then the fixity of Thomas' grin broke; his face seemed to be replaced by another face with a similar grin. At the top speed of a kaleidoscope, a long succession of faces came and went, one flickering after the other. All grinning. All with "Cain's thumbprint on the chin," as Michael described the mark that haunted him for the rest of his life. Every pair of lips was rounded into the grinning shape of Thomas' last word: "*one!*" Faces and expressions Michael never had known. Some he imagined he knew. Some he knew he imagined. Some he had seen in history books, in paintings, in churches, in newspapers, in nightmares. Japanese, Chinese, Burmese, Korean, British, Slavic. Old, young, bearded, clean-shaven. Black, white, yellow. Male, female. Faster. Faster. All grinning with the same grin. More and more and more. Michael felt himself hurtling down an unending lane of faces, decades and centuries and millennia ticking by him, until the speed slowed finally, and the last grinning face appeared, wreathed in hate, its chin just one big thumbprint.

Now the window was completely black. Michael could see nothing. "Cain . . ." he began to say weakly to himself. But a stablike realization stopped the word in his throat, just as if someone had hissed into his inner ear: "Wrong again, fool! Cain's father. I. The cosmic Father of Lies and the cosmic Lord of Death. From the beginning of the beginning. I . . . I . . . I . . . I . . . I. . . ."

Michael felt a sharp pain in his chest. A strong hand was around his heart stifling its movement, and an unbearable weight lay on his chest, bending him over. He heard the blood thumping in his head and then loud, roaring winds. A dazzling flash of light burst across his eyes. He slumped to the ground.[5]

Exercises

1. Photocopy a factual narrative you recently read and found effective. In the margins or on a separate sheet of paper, identify the individual narrative techniques and combinations of techniques the writer used.
2. Write a narrative treatment of several paragraphs on one of the following topics. Use a combination of at least three of the four narrative techniques.
    a. Your first (or most significant) encounter with prejudice.
    b. The most impressive act of sportsmanship you ever witnessed.
    c. An experience in which you made an important discovery about a friend.
    d. An experience in which you made an important discovery about yourself.

Writing a Narrative Composition

Four Helpful Strategies

The best way to make your narrative compositions effective is to develop skill in using the narrative techniques we have discussed. Yet there are other ways as well. Here are four helpful strategies that many professional writers use in their work.

Get into the narrative quickly. Uncertain where to start, beginning writers often start their narratives at a point well before the incident they wish to write about and spend the first few paragraphs leading up to the logical starting point of the action. Professional writers, on the other hand, waste no time getting the narrative under way. An amateur writing about the time he was on a small pleasure craft and got caught in an ocean storm, for example, might begin telling about how the trip was planned two weeks earlier and then proceed to recount the preparations for the trip. By the time he'd get around to the experience of riding out the storm, he'd be several hundred words into the composition.

A professional, in contrast, might begin as follows: "The sky had suddenly grown ominous and the swells began to toss the boat maliciously...." If prior events were worth including, he would work them in later in a flashback sentence like this: "When we had planned the trip two weeks earlier, we'd never realized the danger of a summer storm, so we were unprepared for what was about to happen." That's how you should start your narrative compositions. You needn't worry about having enough to say. If you use dialogue effectively and pause at appropriate places for description and figurative definition, you will have no difficulty meeting the length requirements for the composition.

Expand more important moments, compress less important ones. A good narrative composition is well proportioned: each part of the experience is given the space it deserves, no more and no less. It is not unusual in an effective narrative treatment of, say, seven paragraphs to find one paragraph skimming the events of several days, and two or three paragraphs detailing the events of *a single hour*. This expansion and compression is achieved simply by reserving the techniques of dialogue, description, and figurative definition for the most significant moments in the narrative.

End the narrative quickly and naturally. Once you have presented the climactic moment of the experience or situation, you will be writing on borrowed time. Your readers will know that the story is essentially over and will therefore be expecting you to end the composition quickly. Beginning writers are often insensitive to this fact and proceed to add several paragraphs of interpretation and comment. The effect of such additions is to bore the readers and undo whatever positive effect the narrative achieved. When you write a narrative composition, remember that if you do your job properly there will be no need for extended remarks at the end; and that if you do not do it properly, such remarks will not redeem the composition. Just devise a brief and graceful closing. In a narrative about the final sickness of a loved one, that closing might be as simple as "Early on the morning of July 24 her suffering ended." If you feel it important to include the significance of her death to you, you might add another sentence, such as "I wondered then, as I have continued to wonder since, why we so often come to appreciate our loved ones only after they are gone."

Choose an appealing title. This strategy is mentioned last because you should select your title last, when you have your rough draft before you and can reach a more informed decision about the best title for it. Don't settle for the first, or for that matter the tenth, title that comes to mind. Brainstorm the possibilities, listing at least a couple of dozen before deciding. And never use a topic as your title. That is as foolish as calling your paper "A Narrative Composition" (and almost as foolish as naming a child "Boy" or "Girl"). If that narrative about being caught in an ocean storm were yours, for example, you might choose an understated descriptive title, such as "A Summer Squall," or use a thought that ran through your mind during the experience, such as "My God, I'm Drowning," or even a line of actual dialogue, such as "Help! Man Overboard." Whatever title you select for your narrative composition, be sure it reflects the uniqueness of your treatment and, if possible, stimulates your readers' interest.

A Sample Composition

My Racing Debut

The writer gets into the narrative quickly, working in necessary background information skillfully.

More than 2,500 auto-racing fans had gathered on that warm June evening in 1983. Mid-State racetrack had never had a bigger crowd on opening night. I had a special reason for being there—I was about to drive my first professional race.

Even in grade school my friend Charlie and I had been interested in cars and racing. We read racing magazines, watched mechanics work, and went to the racetrack whenever we could. Then when we were a little older and learned to drive, we entered some local

Writing a Narrative Composition

amateur racing competitions. It wasn't surprising, then, that we decided in the summer of '83 to buy a 1975 Chevy, rebuild it to racing specifications, and apply to race at Mid-State.

The opening night festivities seemed to take forever. The local high school band marched to the infield playing a John Philip Sousa classic. Next an overweight soprano sang the "Star Spangled Banner" slightly off key but with great enthusiasm. And then came the speakers—the mayor, followed by the president of the racing association. Finally, we were ready to race.

Here and elsewhere the writer presents descriptive details not merely for their own sake but to re-create the experience as he wants the readers to see it.

The call came for the drivers to take the track and warm up. The announcer introduced us one at a time. "Boswick ... Shaver ... Reilly ... Seaver...." I grew nervous, wondering if my name had been left off the list. "Edwards...." That was it. As I drove onto the track a big cheer went up from the crowd. I smiled, realizing that I had a lot of friends out there, and a lot of family—my Mom, Dad, and sisters, and even my aunt and uncle who had always thought me lacking in ability. "Tonight I'll not only make my family proud," I thought, "but I'll make believers out of my aunt and uncle too."

Note the description of his thoughts and feelings.

Completing my warm-up laps, I left the track for a few last-minute adjustments to the engine and one last strategy session. As Charlie and I talked I could see he had the jitters, and I wondered if he could see that I did too.

"Remember, you've got the pole position, so that gives you a big advantage," Charlie reminded me.

Note the use of dialogue.

"I know, I know, all I've got to do is get the jump on them."

"Right. Get the quick start and then just let 'er out. You've got the horses to hold the lead, and...."

"Gentlemen, take your positions," the announcer interrupted.

I gave Charlie the thumbs-up sign and eased out on to the track. As I sat at the pole revving my engine and waiting for the flag, I glanced around the stands. People were waving and shouting. Though I couldn't hear my name, I knew my buddies were chanting "Edwards, Edwards, Edwards" as they had said they would. I'd soon give them something to cheer about.

Here the details are carefully selected to make the climax more effective.

Now I kept my eyes on the starter. "Vroom, vroom," I revved the car again and again. There it was, the green flag. All in one smooth motion I let the clutch up and jammed the gas pedal down, bracing myself against the seat for the car to surge forward. Instead, the car lurched ahead a few feet, and then the engine sputtered and died. Ram! Bam! Crash! The car behind me rammed into me and several other cars rammed the cars in front of them.

The climactic moment is not merely stated but dramatized.

I couldn't believe it. I wanted to die. I had stalled the car in my first professional race. It turned out that no real harm had been done,

Because the readers will have questions about sub-

sequent events, the writer provides answers, but ends the composition as quickly and naturally as possible.

though, so the starter lined us up again. That time I started all right, and though I lost the race, I won a nickname that will probably last a lifetime: "Stall."

Suggested Topics for a Narrative Composition

Topics from Your Own Experience and Observation

Your most unforgettable experience

Your worst failure

The experience that humbled you most

Your greatest achievement

Your biggest disappointment

The worst example of face-saving you ever encountered

Your first encounter with hate

The most harmful rumor you ever heard

Your first encounter with death

Your happiest occasion

The funniest experience you ever had

Your most costly mistake

Your first case of puppy love

Your most embarrassing moment

Your most valuable lesson

The day your hero disillusioned you

The experience that contributed most to your maturing

The most courageous act you ever witnessed

The greatest act of kindness you ever witnessed

Topics Requiring Investigation

Note: For a discussion of helpful strategies for researching a topic, see pp. 301–308.

A great discovery in science (for example, Einstein's theory of relativity, Halley's discovery of the comet that bears his name)

A great discovery in medicine (for example, Pasteur's development of the cure for rabies or Harvey's discovery of the circulation of the blood)

Writing a Narrative Composition

A famous disaster (for example, the sinking of the Titanic, or the great Chicago fire, or the destruction of the ancient city of Pompeii)

The story of an important invention (for example, the printing press, umbrella, typewriter, telephone, or airplane)

The story of a famous battle (for example, the Battle of Saratoga during the Revolutionary War or the Battle of the Bulge during World War II)

A dramatic moment in history (for example, Martin Luther's posting of his famous 95 theses on the cathedral door, the signing of the Declaration of Independence, the surrender of General Robert E. Lee, the finding of the tomb of Tutankhamen)

A Checklist for Your Narrative Composition

After completing the rough draft of your narrative composition, examine it carefully, asking the following questions. If the answer to any question is "No," your composition may contain a weakness that will affect your grade. Reread the appropriate section of the chapter to determine whether there is a weakness and, if so, how to overcome it.

1. Does the composition present a single meaningful incident?
2. Is the narrative factual rather than fictional?
3. Is the order of events clear?
4. Are all superfluous details omitted?
5. Does the composition include a climactic moment?
6. Does the composition make effective use of the appropriate narrative techniques (narrating, describing, defining figuratively, and dialogue)?
7. Does the narrative begin quickly?
8. Are more important moments expanded and less important ones compressed?
9. Does the composition end quickly and naturally?
10. Are your readers likely to find the title appealing?

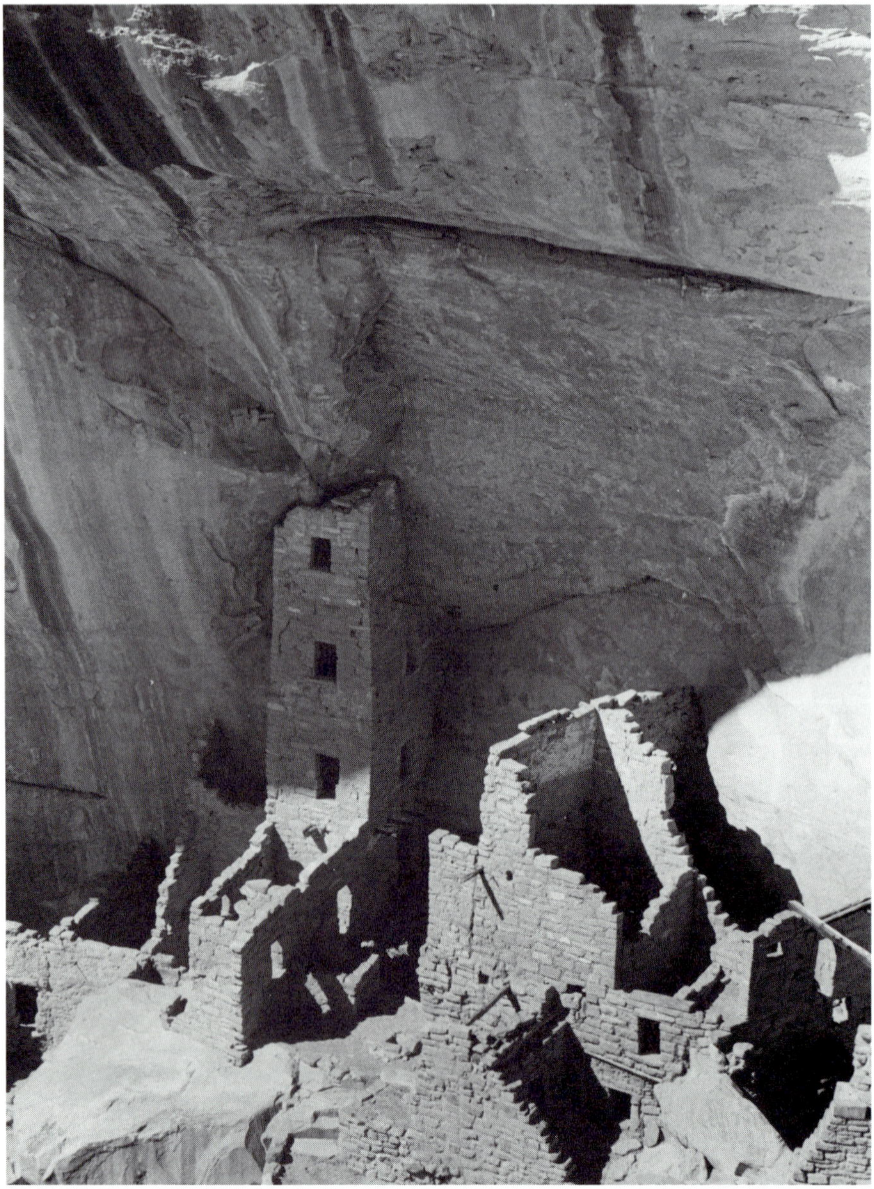

Chapter 7

Writing an Informative Composition

🍎 *This chapter details the characteristics of an effective informative composition and the techniques of development most closely associated with informative writing. It demonstrates how to use those techniques both singly and in combination and offers four helpful writing strategies.*

An informative composition, as we noted in Chapter 3, presents factual data in an impersonal way, aiming to improve readers' understanding of the topic rather than persuade them of something. Informative writing has more applications than either narrative or persuasive writing. For example, business reports, encyclopedia articles, textbooks, and many trade books are informative. And so are news articles in newspapers and many magazine articles. You may use informative writing in a variety of composition situations, from presenting a person's biography to explaining how to do something, discussing the points of interest in a particular city or state, or detailing new and interesting developments in science, law, or technology. In short, you may use informative writing whenever your focus is on facts.

Characteristics of an Informative Composition

An effective informative composition has several significant characteristics, which you may use as standards to guide your writing, and which your instructor will undoubtedly use as criteria in evaluating it. Those characteristics are as follows:

An effective informative composition never takes sides. Unlike a persuasive composition, in which you present your judgment about an issue, an informative composition is limited to factual material. This is not to suggest that judgment is unimportant. Quite the reverse, in fact—it is so important, and the job of supporting it and presenting it effectively so demanding, that wherever it is present, it should receive the writer's undivided attention. If you find that you have such strong views about a subject that you cannot write about it without taking a stand, then you should not attempt to write an informative composition. You should instead write a persuasive composition.

It is possible, of course, to write informatively about the most controversial subject. You may, for example, write a lengthy composition about capital punishment and even detail the arguments offered on each side of the issue and the criticisms each side has for the opposing arguments—all this without ever stating, or even implying, which view is in your judgment more reasonable. To do this, however, you must be genuinely more concerned about presenting facts than about advancing a particular viewpoint.

An effective informative composition focuses on the new. There is nothing more calculated to bore your readers than a lengthy recitation of what they already know. When a writer makes the mistake of focusing on common knowledge, the problem may seem to lie with the topic, but it seldom does. There are little-known facts about every subject. Moreover, few fields of knowledge remain untouched by progress for long—new research findings and new interpretations of old phenomena are continually being published. So even if your topic is as old as motherhood or taxation, there is no need to focus on what your readers already know. You can treat them to something new.

An effective informative composition devotes more space to the particular than to the general. If you are like most writers, you tend to generalize and summarize more than you should. Therefore, to write an effective informative composition you will have to make a special effort to include the particulars of your topic.

If you are writing about the increase in the crime rate, concentrate on presenting the specific data that add up to that fact—the then-and-now statistics, examples of actual cases, quotations from authorities about the extent and characteristics of the increase. If you are writing about the nationwide effort to include instruction in critical thinking at all levels of education, don't merely add one general statement to another and call the result an informative composition. Instead, allow some space between your generalizations and fill that space with particulars. For example, after saying "It's an important development in education," provide the details that demonstrate its importance; similarly, after saying "Critical thinking was neglected during the 1960s and 1970s," give some details that show how and why it was neglected. (The techniques presented later in this chapter illustrate a variety of ways to present specific details in your composition.)

An effective informative composition is arranged clearly. Because the number of facts in an informative composition is often large, readers can easily become confused. That confusion is avoided only by clear arrangement—that is, by your using a sensible, systematic pattern of organization. Four such patterns are commonly used in informative writing:

Time order. Arranges facts in the order in which they occur in time. This pattern is useful in presenting historical information or presenting a process (such as how to change a flat tire or how to hang glide).

Space order. Arranges facts in the order in which they are found in space (left to right, up to down, east to west). This pattern is useful in presenting geographical information.

Order of complexity. Arranges facts from the simple to the complex. This pattern is useful for any subject whose complexity could pose a barrier to the readers' understanding, such as the moral and legal foundations of the insanity defense in capital crimes.

Order of interest. Arranges material in the order that will most effectively arouse and sustain readers' interest. This order is generally reserved for compositions in which the material does not require order of time, space, or complexity. It places the most interesting facts or groups of facts last, the next most interesting facts or groups of facts first, and the others in between. This arrangement ensures that the composition will gain maximum interest in the two most crucial places. (*Note:* there is no special formula for determining what facts will most interest readers, but a good guide is what is least widely known or most recently learned.)

Basic Informative Techniques

There are eight writing techniques most closely associated with informative writing. They are presenting factual data, citing examples, making analogies, defining literally, presenting a process, tracing, summarizing, and quoting and paraphrasing. Let us examine each closely.

Presenting Factual Data

Presenting factual data is the simplest of all techniques—so simple, in fact, that many writing texts do not consider it a technique at all. Yet it deserves close attention because it is so central to informative writing that it might well be considered the mortar that bonds together other informative techniques and gives them structure.

Facts by themselves are not interesting. They are made interesting by the way the writer handles them. To present your facts in an interesting way, arrange them in groupings that show their relative importance. In other words, give prominence to more important facts by reducing lesser facts to short phrases and clauses and, where possible, by tucking them into the middle of sentences. Remember, though, to keep the sequence of your facts clear and easy for your readers to follow.

Note how the facts that the hotel is seventy-one years old, that it holds a position of eminence, that it is in New York City, and that it has hired its first female bellhop are combined in a single paragraph with emphasis given to the last fact (second sentence of first paragraph).

Although the union classification of the job is still "bellman," the Plaza Hotel has officially switched to "bellperson." The reason is that the 71-year-old grande dame of New York City hotels has hired its first female bellhop.

Kathleen Shearer, 25, got the job, not because of any affirmative-action pressure, but because, according to Tom Mylonas, who is her supervisor, she has, among other things, a firm handshake.

A firm handshake, Mr. Mylonas said, "is a good indication of hand and arm strength," prerequisites for carrying luggage.

Miss Shearer had been a waitress at the hotel's Palm Court restaurant. "It was the nicest waitressing job I ever had," she said with a laugh, "but I wanted to see what the rooms at the Plaza looked like."

As a Palm Court waitress, Miss Shearer earned $91.40 plus tips for a five-day week; union scale for a bellperson is $93.75 plus tips. The number of hours she works each day (seven and a half) is the same; it's the tips that will, she hopes, make the difference. Since she started the job during the holiday season—"It's always slow then"—she has not yet been able to determine how big the difference will be.

Her biggest tip so far has been $7. The smallest, for handling two pieces of luggage was, would you believe it, 20 cents? . . .[1]

In little more than 20 years, the population of U.S. mental hospitals has been cut from 560,000 to 170,000, and a million or more patients have been restored to bearable, often productive lives. This mental-health revolution was brought about by a group of drugs, mostly phenothiazines (best-known: Thorazine). But like all potent medications, these have severe long-term side effects in some patients (for example: muscular spasms of the tongue, mouth or limbs).

Two of the men who introduced drug treatment for mental illness into North America, Dr. Nathan S. Kline, director of New York's Rockland Research Institute, and Dr. Heinz Lehmann of Montreal's McGill University, now report highly promising results with a substance that occurs naturally in the human body.

The substance is beta-endorphin, classed as a hormone, tested by medical researchers as a pain killer, and hailed as "the brain's own opiate." Actually it originates in the pituitary gland but seems to exert its effects in the brain. Because camels have a notoriously high tolerance for pain, the University of California's master hormonologist, Choh Hao Li, imported more than 500 camel pituitaries from Iraq and identified and synthesized the active segment—beta-endorphin—of a larger molecule he had identified in 1965.

Kline and Lehmann first thought beta-endorphin might be most effective against depression, but tried it on schizophrenics with auditory hallucinations and victims of severe neuroses. So far, they have treated only 14 patients with a total of 40 injections because the cost is forbidding: $3,000 for one 10 mg dose. But the effects in treatment-resistant patients have been startlingly good, sometimes lasting for weeks. Schizophrenics have stopped hearing voices, and most patients were, at least temporarily, partially restored to their pre-illness personalities.

Beta-endorphin works best when patients are taken off phenothiazines. But the average dose of phenothiazines and similar medications costs only a few dollars a week, so these will probably remain the primary treatment until an inexpensive synthesis of beta-endorphin or a comparable substance is achieved.[2]

The facts here range from background information about mental illness and its treatment to information about the researchers, to details about the drug they experimented with, all effectively grouped and arranged.

Citing Examples

The technique of citing examples is more basic to informative writing than any other technique except presenting factual data. It is the technique through which you make your general informative statements specific and therefore meaningful to your readers. Consider the following passage: "In addition to having everyday benign uses, cyanide has its sinister uses. History has recorded many cases where it has been the instrument of murder." By the time a reader has finished reading this, she is not only ready to be offered one or more examples—she *expects* them. And if you do not offer them, she will be disappointed. That is the case whenever you write a passage about which the readers may reasonably ask, "Do you have an example of this?" Whenever that question may arise, unless you have compelling reason to move to another point, you should answer it with one or more examples. They needn't be dwelled on at length unless they are important enough to warrant extended treatment, but they should be adequate in number and detail to satisfy the readers' expectation. Here are two illustrations of the technique of citing examples.

This passage contains a number of vivid examples offered in support of the assertion made in the first sentence. Because the assertion is so strong and sweeping, both the number of examples and their vividness were required for adequate support. (Had the author been unable to provide such support, honesty would have demanded that he temper his assertion.)

There was hardly any limit to the tale of indignities to which the Jew was subjected, especially in the Papal States. Many famous communities, such as that of Venice, existed down to the eighteenth century on a precarious tenure under an agreement lasting for only a short period of years, continually modified and sometimes not renewed. Each year, the leaders of the down-trodden *Universita degli Ebrei* of Rome had to pay homage to the Pope by the presentation of a Scroll of the Law, which the Vicar of God would return contemptuously over his left shoulder, with a derogatory remark. Contributions were exacted for the upkeep of the House of Converts, to which their children might be snatched away for baptism at any moment, under the flimsiest pretext. . . .

To prevent any semblance of authority, the Jew was forbidden to ride in a carriage, or to employ a Christian servant, or even have some kindly neighbor perform for him the service of kindling a fire upon the Sabbath day. Throughout Germany the Jews, like cattle, had to pay a special toll or *Leibzoll* when they crossed the frontiers of the innumerable petty states, or entered any city. From place after place they were excluded, or admitted only during the day. When they appeared in the law-courts, the oath had to be taken *more judaico*, according to a special, degrading formula, and to the accompaniment of an obnoxious ceremonial. War was even waged upon their books which were confiscated, censored, or burned, without compunction. In a large part of Italy, indeed, the possession of the Talmud was a criminal offense, and early specimens of Hebrew printing are frequently disfigured by unsightly expurgations made by some friar better endowed with zeal than with a sense of proportion. During the whole of Eastertide, from Holy Thursday onward, the gates of the Ghetto were kept rigorously closed, and no Jew dared to show his face in the streets. Each year, at the Carnival season, especially fattened Jews, stripped almost naked, had to run a race down the Corso at Rome for the delight of the populace—a privilege shared with the women of the town. At the slightest pretext, the race was declared null, and had to be repeated on another day. This supreme indignity was abolished only in 1668, though the special tribute instituted to compensate for it continued to be paid for nearly two hundred years after. Worst of all (in obedience to Nicholas III's Bull of 1278, confirmed by Gregory VIII in 1577 and 1584), the Jews were forced at regular intervals to attend conversionist sermons, at which their ears were examined lest they should have been plugged with cotton wool, and officials armed with canes effectively prevented the obvious expedient of slumber.[3]

Making Analogies

An *analogy* is a reference to a point of similarity between two things of different classes. This technique is used whenever you want the reader to see something clearly and the complexity of the matter makes it difficult for you to use simple explanation. It can be very vivid and can be useful in situations where exactness is not necessary. But because it ignores the differences between things, it should not be used carelessly or as a substitute for more exact techniques.

> Most of the common snakes of field and woodland use a method of *lateral undulations* to move along. In this method the snake lays out its long body in a series of S-shaped curves that hug the ground. By pressing backward and outward against the rough ground surface, the snake is pushed forward on its glass-slick ventrals, or *belly scutes*. Lateral pressure to produce forward movement is somewhat like "squirting" a slick prune seed through your fingers by pressing on the sides.[4]

Here the analogy with the slippery seed is employed to help the reader understand a difficult point—the method by which the snake slides.

> An observant eye soon notices, however, that [Pelé], although average in size, is a giant in skill. He glides through and around the thickets of opponents with the effortless power of a jaguar. He turns up first here, then there, all over the field, often reaching a critical spot just before the action does—perpetually poised to spring with catlike grace in any direction. When the ball comes near, there is a good chance that he will suddenly erupt in an explosive series of gymnastic maneuvers, sometimes too quick to follow. The flurry may merely lead to a

The analogy here is between the movement of a great soccer player and the movement of a jaguar. Note that though the analogy is made in the second sentence, it is reinforced later in the phrase "perpetually poised . . . catlike grace. . . ."

perfectly placed pass to a teammate. Or Pelé may sense the chance for a breakaway dribble through some nearly imperceptible opening in a swarm of defenders.[5]

At times you may be tempted to use two or more analogies in the same passage. This temptation is best resisted. It is extremely difficult to multiply analogies without having them clash. For example, combining the analogy of the jaguar in the previous passage with, let's say, the analogy of a steamroller (rolling over opponents) would obscure rather than illuminate the point being made.

Defining Literally

Literal definition is used when you have reason to believe that a term may be new to your readers, when you are using a word in an unusual way, or when the purpose of your writing suggests the need for definition.* To define literally, identify first the general class to which the term belongs and then the special features that differentiate it from other members of that class. Thus *soccer* might be defined as a team sport (general class) in which the object is to kick a round leather ball into the opposing team's goal while preventing them from kicking the ball into your goal (special features).

The first sentence identifies the general class to which the word belongs. The other sentences identify its special features.

Conscience, as the word indicates, is consciousness. It is a specific kind of consciousness—moral awareness, an inner sense of right and wrong. And it is an awareness that has compelling power. We feel bound by it. It commands us. If we disobey it, we feel remorse or anxiety.[6]

This definition differs slightly from the usual type. It identifies two senses in which the term may be understood and differentiates between them.

In common usage, the term *immortality* possesses both a broad and a narrow sense. In the former, it denotes the state of being in eternity—that is, in a dimension of existence that transcends physical life and therefore also physical death. In the latter, it is simply a synonym for afterlife or, by extension, for posthumous fame (as when Shakespeare and Dante are said to be immortal). The term itself is somewhat unfortunate, for it focuses attention on what is secondary

---

*Remember that words have no meaning in themselves. They acquire meaning through the way they are used. And since the way they are used changes over a period of time, meanings change.

instead of on what is primary. The essence of the concept of immortality is transcendence of life rather than escape from death.[7]

When he speaks of religion, he does not mean membership in a particular church or temple. Nor does he mean acceptance of a particular creed or doctrine or a special set of notions about God. Rather, he means a belief that man is not the be-all and end-all of his own existence, a sense of gratitude for the gift of life, and an attendant sense of obligation for what he does with that life.

Though this definition can be found in the dictionary, it is a restrictive definition—a special, limited meaning that includes certain aspects of the common definition but excludes others. (Note how in the first two sentences the definition is sharpened by the writer's stating what he does not mean.)

Presenting a Process

The technique of presenting a process is used to state how something works or happens; how it is done or how to do it. Its application is diverse. It can, for example, be used to detail a scientific phenomenon such as the way mountains are formed, or a cultural or religious ritual, or the changing of an automobile tire. As a rule, each step in the process should be presented in the exact order in which it occurs, and no step should be omitted. However, where the writer's purpose is more to interest the readers than to instruct them, this rule is sometimes violated.

So the two necessary conditions for the formation of black holes are: a truly huge mass, concentrated within a truly small distance. Giant stars provide the mass. When they grow old and begin to burn out, their internal, thermonuclear fires no longer can withstand the inward gravitational crush of the outer layers. Consequently, these outer layers begin to fall toward the center, packing atoms together, shrinking the star. Then Newton's inverse square law begins to run wild. As the atoms jam closer and closer, the force of gravity grows much more rapidly, accelerating the collapse inward. The process feeds on itself. More shrinkage means closer atoms, hence more gravity. More shrinkage . . . more gravity . . . more shrinkage. . . . At a critical point, the imploding star may be held in check: A small star lacking the gravitational wallop to jam its electrons any closer together ends up as a tremendously dense, hot cinder called a "white dwarf"; a somewhat larger star collapses to an even denser "neutron star," a star in which all the electrons have been squeezed into the protons of atomic nuclei, forming neutrons. Or the star undergoes final collapse to a single point of infinite density. The speed of this final cave-in approaches the velocity of light, and can happen in less

Notice that each step is presented in the order in which it occurs and that no steps are omitted. (Notice, too, how effectively the author highlights the key point of the process—"More shrinkage . . . more gravity . . . more shrinkage. . . .")

than a second. The star disappears; it literally "winks out," and a black hole is born.[8]

This passage details how something is done rather than how to do it. If the purpose had been to explain how to define a word one's self (as a dictionary editor would), the author would have used the imperative mood—"First do this, then do that."

To define a word . . . the dictionary-editor places before him the stack of cards illustrating that word; each of the cards represents an actual use of the word by a writer of some literary or historical importance. He reads the cards carefully, discards some, rereads the rest, and divides up the stack according to what he thinks are the several senses of the word. Finally, he writes his definitions, following the hard-and-fast rule that each definition *must* be based on what the quotations in front of him reveal about the meaning of the word. The editor cannot be influenced by what *he* thinks a given word *ought* to mean. He must work according to the cards or not at all.[9]

Tracing

Tracing is used to show the history (that is, the growth and development) of something—for example, the history of the essay, of the American secondary school, or of the idea of free enterprise—where space limitations do not permit detailed treatment. It is characteristic of this technique for the writer to make great leaps in time and space in moving from one important point to another. But the movement is almost always chronological, thus avoiding any distracting jumps back and forth in time.

This passage includes jumps of two centuries and one century and rapid shifts from England to Germany to France to the United States. Yet it is not at all confusing. As its form makes clear, it is telescoping a long and complex development.

The principle of poker is very ancient. One of its precursor games, *primero*, appears in literature at least as early as 1526. Around 1700 the betting and bluffing aspect produced the games of brag in England and *pochen* (to bluff) in Germany. The French borrowed from the Germans and created *poche*, which they brought to New Orleans in 1803. During the next several years English-speaking settlers in the Louisiana Territory anglicized *poche* to poker, altered the rules slightly, and created the essential game played today.[10]

This passage illustrates a slightly different type of tracing. Because it is employed here to show the typical patterns of a child's education, it confines itself

Besides the occasional admonitions and weekly catechisings of his parents, the Puritan child was subjected to instruction in school and in church. Most of the training which he received at school was of a secular nature providing him tools for acquiring religious knowledge itself. Before he was five years old he might be learning to read at a "Reading School" or "Dame School." After he had mastered his hornbook and speller and perhaps a first reader, like the New England Primer, he went on to a writing school, and thence, if he was a boy, to grammar school. Here he studied the classics. If his father was wealthy enough and he himself intelligent enough, he might next attend Harvard College to study the seven liberal arts. If he chose to, he might continue his education by the study of theology, with a view to entering the ministry, but the degree in liberal arts did not of itself qualify him as a minister. The narrowness of the catechising method was thus in a way offset by the school program.[11]

to the years of formal education. Yet even though its leaps in time are more modest than those of the previous example, it still covers all major steps in the education process in a single paragraph.

Summarizing

Summarizing is restating something more concisely than it was originally stated. This technique is often used at the beginning of scientific and technical articles to give the reader an overview of the content of the articles. But its use is not confined to such writing. Summaries are useful in any relatively long piece of writing (i.e., at least several thousand words) when an important idea needs reinforcing.

Summaries are especially valuable when you are citing research data. A single essay, for example, may join data from several different studies. And each of the works referred to may be ten times longer than the essay. The problem is to present the data without assigning it too much space and thereby allowing it to steal the focus from your main idea. Summarizing can be the solution to this problem. The shorter the summary, of course, the greater the risk of distortion and oversimplification. Nevertheless, if approached with care, even long and complex material can be effectively summarized.

> Other discoveries made by the survey are that, regardless of income, family life gives people the greatest satisfaction, and that the majority of North Americans and Western Europeans generally enjoy their jobs, while people from the developing nations overwhelmingly do not. Sociability, too, appears to be related to income. In advanced nations, most of those interviewed claim to have five or more close friends. But, as income and literacy fall, the number of close friends drops proportionately to two, one, or none at all.[12]
>
> In past ages, philosophers such as Aristotle, Aquinas, Descartes, and Kant upheld free will, while Hobbes, Spinoza, Hume, and J. S. Mill opposed it. In our own day, Jean Paul Sartre, the French existentialist philosopher, is perhaps the most extreme protagonist of man's power to determine for himself what he will become. Sartre says man

All data supporting this passage—the specific questions that yielded these facts, the number of people asked, the range of response, the exact statistics included—are omitted. Though possibly interesting, they were not necessary; so summarizing was considered the appropriate technique.

Though each of the dozen or so philosophers referred

to here probably wrote more than a volume on the perplexing subject of free will, the author sums up all their views in less than a page without distorting or oversimplifying.

is absolutely free of all conditions, including the influence of his own past. We are only what we choose to be. We have to be free in order to *be* at all. Human existence is freedom. The unfree is the inhuman. Says Sartre:

> Human freedom precedes essence in man and makes it possible.... Man does not exist *first* in order to be free *subsequently;* there is no difference between the *being* of man and his *being-free.*

Other modern thinkers, such as A. N. Whitehead, Henri Bergson, Paul Weiss, and Charles Hartshorne, agree with Sartre in affirming freedom of choice. However, they differ from him in ascribing some influence to an individual's past and in extending freedom of choice to the nonhuman world.[13]

Quoting and Paraphrasing

To quote is to express another person's idea *in exactly his or her words*; to paraphrase is to express another person's idea in *your* words. These techniques are not an indication of slavishness or mindlessness, but of maturity. They show your recognition that other people's ideas and experiences are valuable and can aid in your efforts to understand and communicate. It is possible, of course, to overdo these techniques. But you needn't fear this if you remember to use other people's thoughts to complement and support your own and not to *substitute* for them.*

When should you quote and when should you paraphrase? Professional writers follow this rule: *Quote whenever the source's wording is so concise or appropriate that a paraphrase would do the idea an injustice; paraphrase at all other times.*

You may quote a single word, a phrase or clause, or a paragraph or more. But however brief or long your quote, you should take care to maintain the context—that is, to preserve the meaning of the quoted passage as conveyed in the original material. In addition, you should follow these conventions to ensure correct reading:

1. Since the readers will assume that anything within quotation marks is exactly as it appeared in the original, be sure not to change any wording or punctuation inadvertently. If the mate-

---

*Remember, too, that using other people's ideas entails the obligation of acknowledgment. Presenting other people's ideas as if they were your own is dishonest. (In certain circumstances, it is also criminal.)

rial contains archaic spelling or errors, copy them exactly as they are, followed immediately by *sic* (Latin for "thus it is") in brackets. This will indicate that the error occurred in the original material. Similarly, if you are quoting part of a sentence, try to select your sentence structure to fit that of the quoted passage. If for some reason you cannot do so, use brackets to indicate any changes you make. For example, if the verb in the quoted passage was "keep" and you must change it to "keeping" to fit your sentence structure, write "keep[ing]" so the reader will see where you have altered the quote.

2. If you omit any words in the quoted material, mark the omission with three spaced periods (four if the omission occurs at the end of a sentence). This punctuation is called an *ellipsis*.
3. If you wish to underline any words that were not underlined in the original version, in order to create emphasis for your own purpose, you may do so provided you say "emphasis added" in parentheses immediately after the end of the quoted material.
4. If the quotation runs more than several lines, set it off in a separate, indented paragraph. (In such cases, many writers also change to single-spacing and drop the quotation marks.)

In seventeenth-century New England no respectable person questioned that woman's place was in the home. By the laws of Massachusetts as by those of England a married woman could hold no property of her own. When she became a wife, she gave up everything to her husband and devoted herself exclusively to managing his household. Henceforth her duty was to "keep at home, educating of her children, keeping and improving what is got by the industry of the man." She was "to see that nothing be *wasted*, or *prodigally spent;* that all have what is suitable in due season." What the husband provided she distributed and transformed to supply the everyday necessities of the family. She turned flour into bread and wool into cloth and stretched the pennies to purchase what she could not make. Sometimes she even took care of the family finances. Samuel Sewall, the famous Puritan diarist, recorded on January 24, 1703/4, that he had turned over the cash account to his wife, relying upon her superior financial judgment:

> I paid Capt. Belchar £8-15-0 Took 24s in my pocket, and gave my Wife the rest of my cash £4-3-8, and tell her she shall now keep the Cash; if I want I will borrow of her. She has a better faculty than I at managing Affairs: I will assist her; and will endeavor to live upon my Salary; will see what it will doe. The Lord give his Blessing.[14]

This passage contains examples of both partial quoting (sentences 4 and 5) and full quoting (the single-spaced, indented paragraph). Note that the original author footnoted the full quotation though the reference is omitted here.

Note the reference to the speaker (Kayaba) in the next-to-last sentence. The author included this because without it the readers might have been confused about who was speaking.

All Japanese wardens began as guards. Their experiences have given them both "hands on" time with prisoners and philosophical depth. Yokosuka's Warden Kayaba affirms the good of man. "All human beings are 98 percent good and 2 percent bad," he says. "The men who end up in prison are not more evil than others in our society. They are weaker. With the proper education, we can make even the worst offenders as calm as the others." Guards do this not through force, but through intense counseling and physical denial. A difficult prisoner is removed from the collective environment and placed in an even more austere "punishment cell," where counseling continues. "We make them think," says Kayaba. "We talk to them again and again about why they were sent to prison, until gradually they understand."[15]

Note the quotation marks around "improper." These indicate that it was exactly that word that Chancellor Holcomb used. Given the criticism that follows, the reader might well wonder whether that was the actual word used if that fact were not made clear. Note, too, the use of ellipses and underlining.

When Chancellor Holcomb addressed the faculty of this college last May, he was asked for his view of the dismissal of Professor Nicoletti from the biology department. He said it would be "improper" for him to comment, explaining his position as follows: "Until such a case has gone through the grievance procedure on the local campus . . . and has been formally referred to me, I will *not* offer an opinion. That has been and will continue to be my policy" (emphasis added). Yet less than a month after he made that statement, he publicly supported the dismissal of Professor Nicoletti not once, but three times, the last in a prepared statement at a news conference. Following that conference the secretary of the professors' union commented that the chancellor's policies appear to be "subject to suspiciously rapid revision."

Whenever there is no good reason to quote, paraphrase. Paraphrasing is used more often than quoting because, like summarizing, it can reduce long passages to fit briefer treatments. Remember, though, that no two words have precisely the same meaning and that any time you translate another person's words into your own, you run the risk of distortion. Choose your paraphrases with care.

Had there been no special advantage to quoting, our three earlier passages might have been paraphrased as follows.

This passage is identical to that on page 143 with one exception—the quotations have been changed to paraphrases. Note that the paraphrases are accurate. The date on which Samuel Sewall wrote in his diary is

In seventeenth-century New England no respectable person questioned that woman's place was in the home. By the laws of Massachusetts as by those of England a married woman could hold no property of her own. When she became a wife, she gave up everything to her husband and devoted herself exclusively to managing his household. Henceforth her duty was to stay home, teach her children, practice thrift, and watch over the things her husband obtained.

Writing an Informative Composition

What the husband provided she distributed and transformed to supply the everyday necessities of the family. She turned flour into bread and wool into cloth and stretched the pennies to purchase what she could not make. Sometimes she even took care of the family finances. Samuel Sewall, the famous Puritan diarist, recorded that he had turned over the cash account to his wife, relying upon her superior financial judgment.

omitted here because without the actual quotation it would serve no purpose.

All Japanese wardens began as guards. Their experiences have given them both "hands on" time with prisoners and philosophical depth. Yokosuka's Warden Kayaba affirms the good of man, claiming that the great majority of human beings are good and that those who go to prison are simply weaker than others. Education, he believes, can reform them. Guards do this not through force, but through intense counseling and physical denial. Difficult prisoners are removed from the collective environment and placed in even more austere "punishment cells," where counseling continues and prison officials help them understand why they were sent to prison.

Note how this paraphrase expresses the meaning of the original statements but avoids using the phrasing of those statements.

When Chancellor Holcomb addressed the faculty of this college last May, he was asked for his view of the dismissal of Professor Nicoletti from the biology department. He said it would be wrong for him to offer his opinion until the case was officially forwarded to him. That, he stated, was his policy, and it would not be changed. Yet less than a month after he made that statement he publicly supported the dismissal of Professor Nicoletti not once, but three times, the last in a prepared statement at a news conference. Following that conference the secretary of the professors' union criticized the chancellor's rapid change in policy.

Though this paraphrase lacks the exactness of the corresponding passage with quotations, it is accurate and somewhat more concise than the original. (Though the saving in space is negligible here, it could be appreciable in a longer passage.)

Following the guidelines and examples of informative techniques, choose one assignment for each of the following techniques specified by your instructor and write one or more paragraphs on it.

Exercises

1. Presenting Factual Data
    a. Consult the current issue of an almanac for information about a country you know little about (population, geography, form of government, economy, and so on). Arrange the information in complete sentences and in paragraph form.
    b. Consult the current issue of an almanac for statistical information on one of the following topics: crime, traffic fatalities, disease (maybe a particular disease), marriage and divorce. Arrange the information in complete sentences and in paragraph form.

c. Think of a topic you are interested in but know little about (perhaps an exotic topic like headhunting or cannibalism). Look it up in a good encyclopedia. Present the information in your own words and sentence structure. (To ensure that you do not inadvertently borrow the phrasing and structure of the encyclopedia article, jot down the pertinent information in fragmentary form while you are reading. Then close the encyclopedia before beginning to write.)

2. Citing Examples
   a. Give examples of pranks or practical jokes you've played or seen played.
   b. Give examples of embarrassing moments you've experienced.
   c. Give examples of things you're afraid of.
   d. Give examples of television commercials that offend or aggravate you.
   e. Give examples of well-known people you think have charisma.

3. Making Analogies
   Complete the following. Make the analogy effective by saying not merely what the thing is like but also *how it is like it:*
   a. The taxi driver made his way through traffic like _____.
   b. Listening to Professor X lecture is like _____.
   c. The sun shining on the lake looked like _____.
   d. Waiting in line for dinner in the college cafeteria is like _____.

4. Defining Literally
   Present the literal definition of one of the following: education, democracy, patriotism, male chauvinism. You may look in the dictionary if you wish, but be sure to present your definition in complete sentences and to make it reflect the range of use and the subtlety of the term.

5. Presenting a Process
   a. Explain how to cook your favorite dish.
   b. Explain how to change a flat tire.
   c. Explain how to "psych" out a teacher.
   d. Explain how to prepare for an examination.
   e. Explain how to get rid of an unwanted suitor without offending the person.

6. Tracing
   a. Trace the history of bathing. (If you use the encyclopedia or some other source, be sure you take care not to borrow the

Writing an Informative Composition

phrasing or structure of your source. A good way to do this is to jot down the pertinent information in fragmentary form while you are reading, then close the encyclopedia before beginning to write.)
   b. Trace the history of a particular sport.
   c. Trace the development of dogs or of a particular breed of dog.
   d. Trace your formal education to date.

7. Summarizing

   Summarize an encyclopedia article on a subject of special interest to you or on one of the following subjects: brainwashing, volcanoes, asthma, cancer, photography, superstition, human intelligence, creation.

8. Quoting

   Select one of the following quotations. Then write a short paragraph, working the quotation in smoothly.
   a. "Fanaticism consists in redoubling your effort when you have forgotten your aim." (Santayana)
   b. "A cathedral, a wave of a storm, a dancer's leap, never turn out to be as high as we had hoped." (Proust)
   c. "The greatest of faults, I should say, is to be conscious of none." (Carlyle)
   d. "People hate those who make them feel their own inferiority." (Chesterfield)
   e. "Men are not punished for their sins, but by them." (Hubbard)
   f. "The magic of first love is our ignorance that it can ever end." (Disraeli)

9. Paraphrasing

   Select one of the following quotations. Then rewrite it in your own words, being careful to avoid distorting the idea.
   a. "Chins are exclusively a human feature, not to be found among the beasts. If they had chins, most animals would look like each other. Man was given a chin to prevent the personality of his mouth and eyes from overwhelming the rest of his face, to prevent each individual from becoming a species unto himself." (Chazal)
   b. "To suppose, as we all suppose, that we could be rich and not behave the way the rich behave, is like supposing that we could drink all day and stay sober." (L. P. Smith)
   c. "The value of philosophy is to be sought largely in its very uncertainty. He who has no tincture of philosophy goes

through life imprisoned in the prejudices derived from common sense, from the habitual beliefs of his age or his nation, and from convictions which have grown up in his mind without the cooperation or consent of his deliberate reason. As soon as we begin to philosophize, on the contrary, we find that even the most everyday things lead to problems to which only very incomplete answers can be given. Philosophy, though unable to tell us with certainty what is the true answer to the doubts which it raises, is able to suggest many possibilities which enlarge our thoughts and free them from the tyranny of custom." (Russell)

d. "In learning to write, a good student often passes through three stages. The first is the inarticulate. He has little to say and words elude him. Then suddenly he discovers the joy of playing with words as a kitten romps with a ball. His writing becomes frothy, extravagant and ridiculous. A good teacher must be alert for this development, which should be encouraged, not repressed prematurely, for it is a natural stage of adolescent growth in the art. After a time exuberance subsides into controlled expression as ideas and experience mature. Shakespeare himself went through these stages from the stiffness of *Two Gentlemen of Verona* to the bubbling brilliance of *Love's Labor's Lost*, which was a necessary prelude to the perfect poise of *Twelfth Night*." (G. B. Harrison)

Combining Informative Techniques

Like narrative techniques, informative techniques may be used in combination as well as singly. Moreover, they may be combined *with* narrative techniques to achieve a more dramatic effect and thereby make a composition more interesting.* Combinations of informative or informative and narrative techniques are not difficult to select. Often one technique will suggest another. Literal definition, for example, may suggest tracing. The presentation of factual data may suggest the citing of examples, one of which may be significant enough to handle descriptively, perhaps even as a brief narrative. Here are some examples of effective combinations of techniques.

*The only requirement is that the material used in the narrative techniques be *factual*. Fictional material would not, of course, be appropriate in an informative composition.

Writing an Informative Composition

Defining Literally and Tracing

The Enlightenment, sometimes called the Age of Reason or the *Aufklärung*, refers to a profound intellectual revolution in world history which rejected theology as the final arbiter and sought instead to interpret the universe in terms of logical analysis. It was a rational movement, extending from about 1650 to 1800, in which faith in science and human reason was substituted for dogma based on religious belief and supernatural revelation. During this period philosophers began to view mankind's problems in a different light, discarding many preconceived ideas founded on doctrine. Believing mathematics to be the ultimate key to universal problems, these men adopted a mechanical approach to their surroundings and built a new world view to explain the secrets of nature. Medieval theologians and philosophers had interpreted man and the universe in terms of the Scriptures; for the new philosophers the path to understanding was mathematics, logic, and human reason. With historical roots deep in the Middle Ages, the Enlightenment was one of the few movements which led to such a fundamental change in human thought, freeing the minds of men from centuries of dogma and myth and preparing the way for a dynamic world perspective. This new spirit of inquiry led to great scientific advances which had important implications for education at every level.[16]

The principal technique in this passage is literal definition. *But this is blended with a* tracing of the history of the period.

Presenting Factual Data and Describing

Outside West Berlin's Zoo-Palast Cinema, near the bombed-out shell of the Kaiser Wilhelm Memorial Church, as well as at scores of theaters in the rest of West Germany, long lines of Germans have been lining up to see a new hit. The central figure—his black hair combed flat across his forehead, his impassioned voice exhorting his followers to build a thousand-year *Reich*—is *der Führer* himself. The 2½-hour documentary movie about him, *Hitler—A Career*, is the smash of the summer, drawing thousands to the box offices and spurring a nationwide reexamination of the Nazi past.[17]

Here the emphasis is on presenting factual information. *Yet a brief* description *of Hitler is included in the second sentence.*

A Combination of Several Techniques

Agoraphobia? Fifteen years ago the word meant nothing to most people. Certainly it meant nothing to the college girl about to sled down the hill in Vermont. As a cold wind hit the hill, she stood

This passage begins in figurative definition *and then turns quickly to* narra-

tion filled with descriptive detail. In the second paragraph, after the first sentence (factual *details), the author presents a* literal definition of "agoraphobia," which includes *brief examples of places the agoraphobe fears ("elevators, bridges," and so on).*

holding her chin, looking back at the house in the distance. Her friends heard her mutter something—that she had snow in her boot, or needed the bathroom—some such lie. Then she began to run, looking down at the snow. She couldn't look at the house, it seemed too far away. She started to sweat and her legs went soft. She could not feel her feet, but they were running. Her heart was pounding, her face flushed. She began to pant. She felt as though she were coming apart, as if she had been running forever through the syrupy snow of a nightmare. Six Miltowns rattled against four Valiums in her pocket. The sweat on her body tripped triggers in her brain; the adrenaline signaled the nerves to further panic. "What if I die?" she thought. "Oh, my God, I'm going crazy." Then she was at the house, the "safe" place. But she had added more fears to an already long list. She was afraid of snow. She was afraid of hills. And, above all, she was afraid of ever again feeling the way she did running from that snowy hill in Vermont.

This attack might have happened anywhere because the girl was an agoraphobe. Agoraphobia once meant "fear of the marketplace," but it has come to mean fear of the marketplace of life. It includes the fear of both open and closed spaces—elevators, bridges, ball parks, bank lines—as well as a sort of floating dread that travels as far as the imagination can reach. The agoraphobe fears unfamiliar situations, being alone and separated from a "safe" place or person, and losing control in front of others. The agoraphobe avoids or runs away from situations, and has panic attacks even when he or she is at home, seemingly relaxed.[18]

A Combination of Several Techniques

This passage is a blend of many techniques. The first paragraph cites three brief examples. *The third example is given slightly expanded treatment, including (in the next-to-last sentence) an* explanation.

Paper towels were reportedly first developed when a manufacturer got a load of paper too thick for toilet tissue and had to decide what to do with it. The forklift truck was invented when a man saw donuts being lifted out of a bakery oven on steel "fingers." Similarly, Gutenberg, the inventor of the printing press, had long pondered how to achieve quicker book production than carving words laboriously on blocks and rubbing paper against the blocks. Watching a wine-press one day gave him the necessary insight—that the same process could be used in printing. That is, the image could be transferred to paper by pressing an inked lead seal against the paper. Gutenberg, like the inventor of paper towels and the forklift, was being resourceful.

Resourcefulness is the ability to see the connections between things, to improvise, to make new applications. This, research has shown, involves a disposition to search out and try a variety of solutions to a problem, even those that seem irrelevant, to combine things previously uncombined. Edison's success in inventing the phonograph reveals this disposition. Instead of trying to copy the human anatomy of sound production, as others did, he devised a new method. (Incidentally, in the 1860s a man named Faber invented a crude talking machine that *did* imitate the human speech mechanism.) Similarly, successful airplane inventors such as the Wright brothers got beyond imitating birds flapping their wings.

At the heart of resourcefulness is another characteristic of creative people—playfulness. It is playfulness that allows a person to arrange and rearrange the elements of a problem and its possible solutions much as a child arranges his building blocks, now in one combination, then in another, taking his delight in finding ever new and unexpected combinations. In fact, it may well be that this seemingly frivolous characteristic is one of the most important in the creative process. Einstein thought it was. He once remarked that "combinatory play seems to be the essential feature in productive thought."

It is to this quality of resourcefulness that we owe one of the greatest breakthroughs in the history of medicine, the development of penicillin. Countless lives have been saved over the past three decades by that development, which began when Alexander Fleming noticed what other researchers observed but remained incurious about—the inhibiting effect of molds on staphylococcus colony growth. (At least one of those other researchers regarded what he saw as a mere *nuisance!*) Fleming was not only unusually observant and curious, but resourceful as well. For he worked out the connection between that action of the molds and the conquering of disease.

The second paragraph begins in literal definition, *then presents* factual information *(the reporting of research findings), and finally cites two* brief examples. *The third paragraph begins with* factual assertion, *followed by (in the second sentence)* explanation *and* analogy. *The next sentence is a speculation, and it is followed by a supporting* quotation *from Einstein. The final paragraph is a blend of* factual assertion *and* brief examples.

Exercises

1. Identify the various techniques used in the following passages. Remember that narrative techniques may be combined with informative techniques.
    a. It is morning at Morris High School, a gothic fortress rising above the ruins of New York City's scarred South Bronx. All but the main entrance is sealed; in front of it is a security guard, ready to turn back anybody who tries to enter without proper identification. Inside, five more guards equipped with walkie-talkies patrol the halls and cafeteria in the 60% Hispanic, 39% black school. Most classroom doors are locked after classes begin, and study halls, once a favorite spot for fights, have been shut down. The dingy lockers that formerly lined the corridors have been removed. Explains Principal

Chester Wiggan: "The kids used to store drugs in them and set fires." Four trailers equipped as classrooms, in which pupils who are disciplinary problems study in isolation from the rest of the student body, are parked outside.

The military-camp atmosphere of Morris High is extreme. But increasingly, schools from Memphis to Los Angeles are adopting similar methods—as well as closed-circuit TVs, guards, emergency phones in the classrooms—to combat a violence that was once unheard of.[19]

b. The word on the street was that Weird Reggie was bad news. A strong-arm for a policy operation, he had a fondness for neon suits and sawed-off shotguns. A real whacko. Facing a felony charge for reckless endangerment, he had jumped his $5,000 bail and disappeared into the uptown wilderness. He had been "in the wind" for over a month. Word along the jungle telegraph was that Reggie was not to be taken alive.

The cops on the warrant squad were looking for Reggie, but not very hard and in all the wrong places. In the course of a year, the NYPD handles over 100,000 arrest warrants, a significant number of them bail jumpers. But there are just not enough cops to go around looking for everybody. Reggie had good reason then to fancy his chances of staying loose. On certain days he even jumped around right in front of the cops' faces as he went about his uptown business. Today was going to be one of those days. He had no way of knowing there was another man out looking for him on the streets.

The man was not a cop, but he had a license to bring in Weird Reggie.... The man was not The Lone Ranger. His name was Stan Rivkin. To him Weird Reggie was not just another freefloating felon, but money in the bank. Reggie was worth $1,000 to him.

Stan Rivkin is a bounty hunter....[20]

c. When I learned that I had business appointments in Liechtenstein four days apart—on a Friday and the following Tuesday—I didn't know what to do with myself, so I decided to import my family from Vienna for company.

All month, my wife, Valerie, kept telling people she was "going to Luxembourg," which I begged her not to tell the conductor—for Luxembourg and Liechtenstein are more than 200 miles apart and the former is 16 times the size of the latter.

Monica, just turning 14, knew exactly where she was going and was remarkably enthusiastic for her age. It turned out she wanted "to meet the Prince of Liechtenstein," at 71 the

Writing an Informative Composition

last reigning Hapsburg monarch in the world and possessor of its greatest private collection of art, conservatively valued at $300 million. Asked why, Monica said, "For personal reasons," and clammed up.

Erika, 12 going on 13, took it as lightly as kids her age take everything until, when I left on Thursday, I said: "See you Saturday morning in Vaduz."

"Vaduz?" she said. "What's Vaduz?"

"The capital of Liechtenstein."

"I didn't know Liechtenstein had a capital! I thought it was only one meter square."

The principality of Liechtenstein is 61 square miles. Postage-stamp sized it isn't, though 10 percent of its income stems from stamp sales. By the time my family arrived at breakfast time Saturday on the Wiener Walzer express from Vienna, 350 miles away, I had news for them: There was so much to do in Liechtenstein that they would be on the go from that moment until their Sunday night return trip. . . .[21]

2. Select a piece of informative writing you recently read and found interesting. It may be any type of writing—a book, an article, a letter to a newspaper editor. Photocopy a passage from it (at least several paragraphs), noting in the margin the techniques of development the author used.

3. Using one of the following quotations as a springboard for ideas, write a two- or three-paragraph informative treatment that includes one or more combinations of techniques. (Identify the combinations in the margin.)
   a. "The wise man does at once what the fool does finally." (Gracian)
   b. "The unexamined life is not worth living." (Socrates)
   c. "The cruelest lies are often told in silence." (Stevenson)
   d. "How glorious it is—and how painful—to be an exception." (Musset)
   e. "Conscience is, in most men, an anticipation of the opinion of others."

Four Helpful Writing Strategies

The main way to achieve excellence in your informative composition is to use appropriate techniques and combinations of techniques. However, you can enhance the effectiveness of your work by applying the strategies professionals use in their writing. Here are four such strategies.

Use the journalist's 5W formula. The 5W formula is the questions *who, what, when, where,* and *why.* Journalists use this when they write to be sure they have included all the important facts in their news stories. Since the informative composition is essentially the same rhetorical form as the news story, you can use the same formula to guide your writing. When using it, keep in mind that effective informative writing devotes more space to particular details than to general statements of fact.

Decide whether you will address the readers directly and be consistent in carrying out your decision. In some compositions direct address—*you*—is appropriate. For example, in a composition detailing the process of preparing a car for winter, you might include as important ideas "Have your battery checked," "Replace your summer tires with snow treads," and "Be sure your radiator has the proper mixture of antifreeze." Each of these ideas addresses the readers directly with an implied "you." A similar approach might be appropriate for a composition on choosing a vacation place. You might even use direct address in the title (for example, "Planning Your Budget Vacation").

In the majority of informative writing, however, direct address is not appropriate. In a composition on the Civil War, or on the Andes Mountains, for example, there would be little if any reason to address the readers personally. The best approach would be the impersonal approach. Whatever you decide is the best way to address your readers, though, be sure to follow that decision consistently throughout the composition. Switching back and forth carelessly will distract your readers.

Credit your sources briefly within the text of your composition and provide a bibliography at the end. It is not necessary to use footnotes in your informative composition, but you should mention the sources of any information you use other than information you get from an encyclopedia. There are two reasons for doing so—because you owe your sources an acknowledgment for the specific help their work provided you, and because you owe your readers clarification of which statements you are making on your own authority and which on the authority of others. These references should be brief, generally including no more than the person's name and his or her position. (See "Quoting and Paraphrasing" earlier in this chapter for ways to express such credits.) In addition to crediting your sources within your composition, you should provide a bibliography at the end, listing all the relevant

Writing an Informative Composition

information about the sources you referred to in the body of your paper.

Choose a lively title and introduction and an effective conclusion. As we noted in our discussion of the narrative composition, you should select a title only after you have completed your composition, and you should aim to have it reflect the uniqueness of your treatment and arouse your readers' curiosity. Before selecting a title for your informative composition, be sure to consider a number of possibilities.

There is no special technique to be used for the introduction or conclusion to an informative composition. Any of the techniques we have discussed in this chapter may be used, as long as they achieve the required purpose. The purpose of an introduction is to further stimulate the readers' interest and lead them to the controlling idea of the composition. The purpose of a conclusion is to provide a sense of completion. To illustrate these points, here are several examples of an effective title, introduction, and conclusion.

When Fat Was in Fashion

Somewhere in the first fifteen minutes of *North by Northwest*, Cary Grant pats his stomach, frowns, and tells his secretary to make a note: "Think thin!" Everybody in the audience laughs in instant sympathy—we are all patting our stomachs and thinking thin as hard as we can. One glance at the art of Rubens, however, shows that this was not always so—obviously, thinking fat used to be the thing. The opulent fleshy beauty of Rubens' women probably made the leaner ladies of his day frown when they patted their own meager stomachs, and wish they could compete in the big leagues.

Yet today the very name of Rubens is apt to produce a reaction of disgust. Those puffy knees, those bumps and hills of flesh have never had less fashionable appeal than right now, in the very year of Rubens' 400th anniversary. . . .

. . . .

Recent movie images, mostly imported from Italy, may foster a new change in visual taste. The enormously ample women in Fellini and Wertmüller films could create a new standard of sexual desirability. Just as perverse taste for scrawny, hollow-cheeked, morbid images during the Romantic era gradually generated a new ideal image, so the perversely fascinating fatties in the new movies may start an underground vogue which will surface in the future as an acknowledged ideal. In fact, at this present thin-conscious moment, fat beauty has all the more edge—all the more chance to be the newest, most outrageous avant-garde trend in erotic taste. We have

The occasion of this article was Flemish artist Rubens' four-hundredth anniversary. The article is both a discussion of Rubens' art and a comment on changing tastes in body size and shape. The conclusion speculates about future tastes in figures, at the same time referring to the article's focus on Rubens' art.

already had some models to admire: Mama Cass in the '60s, Barbara Cook in the '70s. It may even be that the memory of Zero Mostel's vast grace will bring about the epoch of the desirable fat man. Other big figures, such as James Coco and Robert Morley, have already expressed personal pleasure in their own size. One of these days, the bulk of us may be on the way to Fat City—just in time, and in better shape for the next celebration of the art of Rubens.[22]

From Con to Pro

The title provides an interesting play on words. The introduction is an appropriate quote from the man the story is about. The conclusion makes creative use of the con/pro contrast referred to in the title.

"I was hiding out in Philadelphia's Germantown while the FBI turned the country on end looking for me. I needed an occupation that would explain why I seldom left my apartment except for food and an occasional fresh supply of hair dye, so I told everyone I was a freelance writer." Albert F. Nussbaum is explaining how he became a "writer" before starting to write.

In reality, Nussbaum had been pursuing an entirely different—but eminently successful—career as a notorious bank robber whose "business earnings" made John Dillinger's look puny by comparison....

. . . .

In the first edition of *The People's Almanac*, the name Albert F. Nussbaum appears in Chapter Nine: "Disasters and Violence," under the heading, "The FBI's All-time Ten Most Wanted Fugitives List." In Volume Two of the almanac, you will find Nussbaum's name again—as the contributor of a number of learned articles. At the rate he is going, it isn't at all difficult to imagine that, by the time Volume Three comes out, Al Nussbaum may have moved from the "Ten Most Wanted" list to the "Ten Bestsellers" list. And you may be certain that his success as a writer is already being celebrated—with sighs of relief from bank presidents all over the country.[23]

The Mystery of the Missing Bones

This informative article begins with a narrative, pauses to report some background facts, then resumes the narrative. The conclusion first heightens the sense of mystery by reminding the readers of the unanswered questions and then emphasizes the unusual interest the case continues to generate.

At 9:30 a.m. on June 9, 1972, the phone rang in Christopher Janus' room at New York's Harvard Club. When the 62-year-old millionaire businessman picked it up, a husky-voiced woman with a foreign accent was on the line: "Mr. Janus, I am not an eccentric," she began. "I'm the widow of a U.S. marine who was serving in North China when World War II broke out, and I have the bones."

Janus had just returned from Peking, where the director of the Peking Man Museum and officials of the People's Republic of China had asked him to help recover the more than 500,000-year-old fossilized remains of Peking man—China's most precious anthropological treasure, which vanished some time after December 8, 1941. Janus

Writing an Informative Composition

was offering a $5,000, no-questions-asked reward for information leading to recovery of the bones.

The caller declined Janus' invitation to come to see him. . . .

. . . .

Does the woman in black hold the missing piece to the puzzle? Why has she not contacted Janus again? Why did the Chinese select him as their intermediary? And what about the bones themselves? Buried for half a million years, exposed for less than 20, they still grip men's imaginations by their absence as strongly as they did by their presence.[24]

There's No Madness Like Nomadness

They are named *Phantom Flasher, Lazarus, The Red Onion, Chiquita Vananna, Vandal,* and such. They ride high and graceless, as always, but now their boxy bodies cry out for attention with garish designs and obstreperous Pop art: frontier scenes, Hawaii schlock, seascapes, erotic mush. Even one—the specimen, say, that flashes nude girls in and out of view with Op-artful magic—can pop the eyeballs. When large numbers heave into sight, zooming along the road in a spaced-out phantasmagoria of a caravan, they can set the innocent motorist to gaping and muttering, "What *is* going on here?"

The short answer is that vanning has become an American craze. *Vanning?* To van once meant to ship freight in a certain way. Today it also means to personalize a common van and build a life-style around it. . . .

. . . .

. . . Surely the vanners have also fulfilled Boorstin's unsettling vision of a people who "prefer to be no place in particular—in limbo, en route."

Vanners, to be sure, see themselves in a simpler light. They think of themselves, as one of their songs puts it, as "freewheeling and easy . . . livin' our lives while we can." Such a romantic view is no doubt harmless. Yet it offers less insight into the new nomads than can be found in the remarkably prophetic first chapter of the *Book of Ecclesiastes*: "Vanity of vanities, saith the Preacher. . . . All is vanity."[25]

Both the title and the conclusion here use clever plays on words. The introduction presents interesting factual details.

"Hey, You Ought to Sue the Doctor"

Only the most misanthropic doctor could be pleased by the news that teachers, as well as physicians, are now being sued for malpractice. I am not the most misanthropic of physicians (had I been sued a couple of times, especially by educators, I might be) and therefore am

Notice the way the title, introduction, and conclusion are connected to create coherence and reinforce the controlling idea.

(The title is in quotation marks only because it is a statement people often make.)

saddened by this new development. As a member of a profession which has just begun to work its way out of a genuine malpractice crisis, I can, however, give my friends in teaching some advice. . . .

. . . .

. . . There is one final consolation for teachers as they face potential malpractice suits, and that is my mordant observation that in twentieth-century America you know that people take your work seriously only when they are willing to sue you about it.[26]

A Sample Composition

Poison from the Skies

Note that the title foreshadows the controlling idea expressed in the final sentence of the first paragraph and that the introduction stimulates readers' interest by dramatically contrasting traditional associations with the present reality.

The warm spring rain falls gently on the forest, spilling from leaf to leaf and then to the forest floor, where it seeps into the ground or runs in quiet rivulets into a nearby creek or lake. The scene has traditionally held only pleasant, poetic associations—nature renewing itself. Yet today scientists warn that rain can be a poison that harms virtually everything it touches.

The second paragraph, like most paragraphs in the composition, presents factual data, arranged for clarity and interest.

The harmful phenomenon is known as acid rain. Rainwater, like any chemical, is measured on the pH scale, which measures hydrogen ion concentration. The scale extends from 0 to 14, with the lower end representing extreme acidity. Distilled water measures 7; normal rainwater, 5.6. Since the scale is logarithmic, a small change in the pH reading reflects a significant change in acidity. For example, rainfall that measures 5.5 is ten times more acidic than normal rainfall. To appreciate the extent of the danger posed by acid rain, we need only consider that pH values of *less than 4.0* have been recorded from water samples taken from certain Adirondack Mountain ponds.

Note the brief presentation of the process by which acid rain is formed.

Acid rain results from the release of sulfur oxide and nitrogen oxide into the upper atmosphere. Though automobile exhaust fumes contribute to the formation of acid rain, its main source is smoke from coal-burning or electric power plants, which rises into the upper atmosphere, where its pollutants combine with water vapor and are carried hundreds and even thousands of miles, eventually falling to earth as rain or snow.

Note the brief example cited here.

The damage caused by acid rain is staggering. Though this damage is centered in the northeastern United States and Canada, an area of at least 2¼ million square miles, its effects are felt throughout those countries and far beyond them to the outermost reaches of prevailing winds. In Eastern Europe, for example, acid rain has endangered an estimated 2½ million acres of forest.

Although some plants thrive on high acidity, many others cannot tolerate it. The Argonne National Laboratory estimates that 5% of the nation's soybean crop has been lost to acid rain. Moreover, acid rain sterilizes the seeds of hardwood trees. In the period from 1956 to 1965, tree growth in the White Mountains declined by 18%. Nor is the harm done to plants alone. Acid rain pollutes rivers and streams and poses a double danger to fish by increasing the acidity of the water and causing soil reactions that release large quantities of aluminum. Thus the fish either die from a lack of oxygen at lower depths or from high acidity or aluminum poisoning near the surface.

The writer here cites examples of the harm acid rain causes to the environment.

Buildings, monuments, bridges, and outdoor sculpture also suffer ill effects. The rain leaves a crusty deposit on them, which in time washes off, taking layers of stone with it. But none of the damage done to buildings, nor even that to lakes, forests, crops, and such industries as lumber, paper, and tourism is as ominous as one effect whose extent is as yet undetermined—the leeching of acid rain into ground water and the resulting contamination of drinking water.

Here the writer turns to the effects of acid rain on people. (Note also the brief presentation of the process by which objects are harmed.)

Public concern about the acid rain problem has understandably mounted over the past decade. Among the suggested remedies that have been proposed are strengthening the U.S. Clean Air Act by setting emissions limits for sulfur dioxide from coal-fired power plants and closely monitoring actual emissions; a program requiring high-sulfur coal to be cleaned before burning; and installation of low-nitrogen-oxide burners on existing power plants to cut down emissions. A number of bills have been presented before Congress to reduce acid rain, and a number of agreements have been signed between northeastern states and Canadian provinces to help standardize research methods and coordinate clean-up efforts.

This paragraph presents factual data.

Despite such efforts to solve the problem, complications remain. The dramatic rise in oil prices over the past dozen years has driven many industries to convert from oil to coal, thus adding to the acid rain problem. In addition, because there are at least three groups involved with the problem—coal-burning factories and plants, the Environmental Protection Agency (EPA), and the affected downwind areas—resolution is often slow and difficult. Sometimes one party is forced to go to court to get action. Such was the case in Jefferson County, Kentucky, when the Air Pollution Control District filed suit against the EPA for failing to reduce sulfur emission from an Indiana power plant.

The writer here presents general and specific examples of the complications that arise.

Not everyone agrees about the seriousness of the problem or the course of action that should be taken. Anne M. Burford, former head of the EPA, argues that more research data is needed. "The current question before us," she argues, "is will the basis for future measures

Here the writer uses the techniques of quotation and paraphrase. Note that the

writer presents each side objectively without taking sides.

to control acid deposition be blind groping in response to media and political emotionalism, or the result of rigorous scientific analysis that can define some kind of significant benefit?"

John Roberts, Canada's Minister of Environment, disagrees, calling acid rain "cancer of the biosphere" and arguing that since more than 3,000 research studies have demonstrated that it is a "clear and present danger," immediate and decisive action is necessary. "I say we do have enough information to act," he says. "It's not a matter of science any longer; it's a matter of political will."

Even though the conclusion speculates about the future, the statement is so moderate and so in keeping with the facts that it is not likely to prompt any readers to disagree.

The one point everyone seems agreed on is that the problem of acid rain is likely to continue challenging our ingenuity throughout the 1980s and perhaps much longer.

Bibliography

"Acid Rain." *New York State Environment*, 10 Feb. 1981: 6–8.

Burford, Anne McGill, and John Roberts. "Acid Rain: International Irritant." Debate. *American Forests*, May 1983: 12–13.

"Flacke Charges EPA Indifferent to Acid Rain." *New York State Environment*, 24 Dec. 1981: 8–9.

"New York and Ontario Sign Acid Rain Agreement." *New York State Environment*, 18 May 1983: 7.

"Three Proposed Amendments: Acid Rain." *New York State Environment*, 29 March 1982: 7–8.

Suggested Topics for an Informative Composition

Famous People   Who they were, when and where they lived, important details of their lives, especially why they are famous.

Examples: Albert Einstein, Napoleon, Adolph Hitler, Carrie Nation, Florence Nightingale, Benjamin Franklin, Socrates, Confucius, Thomas Jefferson, Vlad Tepes (the original Count Dracula)

Unusual Places   Their location, history, and what makes them unusual.

Examples: the Amazon River, Niagara Falls, Mammoth Cave, the Golden Gate Bridge, Atlantis, the Bay of Fundy, jungles, deserts, a place in your county, state, or region

Interesting Animals   Their history, habitat, and distinguishing characteristics.

Examples: the cow, the wombat, the wolf, the piranha, the shark, the ostrich, the domestic cat, the rhinoceros, the dog

Writing an Informative Composition 161

Interesting Inventions or Creations Who invented them, where, when and how, how they were first received, to what extent they have changed over the years.

Examples: the Mona Lisa, the pyramids of Egypt, the circus, the game of backgammon, the Statue of Liberty, graffiti, the comic strip, the ghetto, the Democratic party, the Republican party, the nudist colony, karate, the concept of childhood, the IQ test

Important Phenomena or Concepts When they first occurred or were conceptualized, by whom, how human understanding or acceptance of them has changed over the years.

Examples: Insanity, the "dirty" joke, habit, the inferiority complex, failure, prejudice, dreams, cannibalism, time, guilt, scalping, headhunting, discipline, creativity, intelligence

Important Historical Events When, how, and to whom they occurred, how people reacted to them then, why they are important.

Examples: The American Revolution, the French Revolution, the Lewis and Clark expedition, child labor laws, the women's suffrage movement

Little Understood Processes The stages by which the process occurs, the characteristics of each stage, the causes and effects, how knowledge of the process has increased; or, in the case of a *directed* process, its origin and development, present criteria, and techniques.

Examples: Aging, the decline of a civilization, physical maturation, emotional maturation, learning to reason, kidney dialysis, film criticism, adoption

A Checklist for Your Informative Composition

After completing the rough draft of your informative composition, examine it carefully, asking the following questions. If the answer to any question is "No," your composition may contain a weakness that will affect your grade. Reread the appropriate section of the chapter to determine whether there is a weakness and, if so, how to overcome it.

1. Does the composition avoid taking sides?
2. Does the composition focus on the new?

3. Does the composition give more space to the particular than to the general?
4. Is the composition arranged clearly?
5. Does the composition make effective use of the informative techniques discussed in the chapter (presenting factual data, citing examples, making analogies, defining literally, presenting a process, tracing, summarizing, and quoting and paraphrasing) and, where appropriate, the narrative techniques discussed in Chapter 6?
6. Does the composition adequately answer the 5Ws (who, what, when, where, why)?
7. Is the composition consistent in the way it addresses the readers?
8. Are your sources credited briefly within the text and is a bibliography provided at the end of the composition?
9. Are the title and introduction lively? Is the conclusion effective?

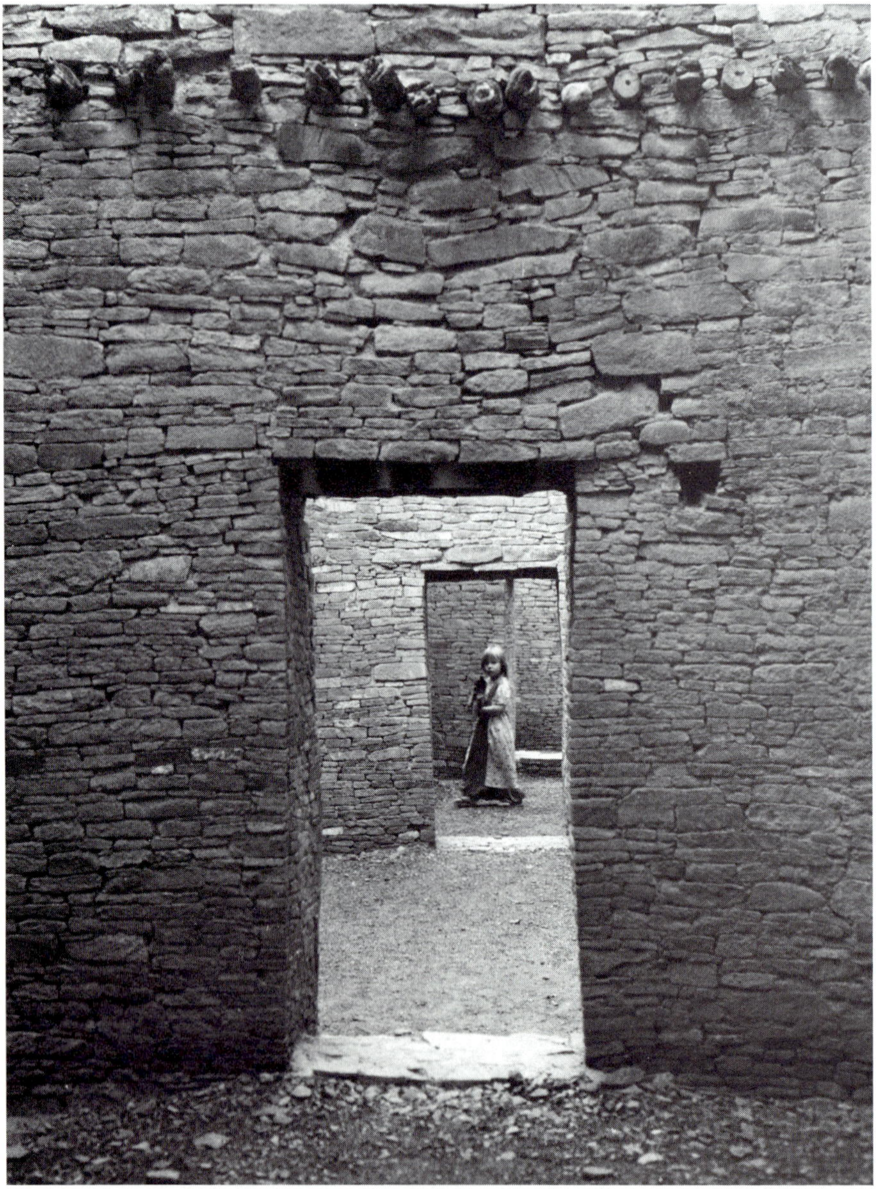

Chapter 8

Writing a Persuasive Composition

❦ *This chapter details the characteristics of an effective persuasive composition and the techniques of development most closely associated with persuasive writing. It demonstrates how to use those techniques both singly and in combination and offers four helpful writing strategies.*

A persuasive composition, as we noted in Chapter 3, evaluates issues by presenting the writer's judgments and the evidence that supports them. It often presents information, as does an informative composition, but its purpose is never merely to improve the readers' understanding of the topic. Rather, it is *to persuade the readers of the reasonableness of the writer's views*. Sometimes it also aims to move the reader to some specific action, such as voting against a proposal.

Characteristics of a Persuasive Composition

An effective persuasive composition has several significant characteristics, which you may use as standards to guide your writing, and which your instructor will undoubtedly use as criteria in evaluating it. The characteristics are as follows.

An effective persuasive composition focuses on judgment. The subject of a persuasive composition is always an issue that is to some degree controversial—that is, an issue about which informed people find reason to disagree. (In situations where everyone completely agrees, there would be no one to persuade.) A persuasive composition is expected to contribute a point of view about—and, if possible, a resolution to—the dispute. Accordingly, the very element that a writer should strive to keep out of an informative composition, his or her judgment, must be the central focus of a persuasive composition.

A persuasive composition that straddles the fence or avoids judgment for politeness' sake is doomed to be ineffective. This, of course, does not mean that you must present an *extreme* view in your persuasive composition. (Such a view is usually one-sided and contributes little to the resolution of the issue.) There is nothing wrong with making the judgment that no responsible decision is possible about the issue because the available evidence is insufficient, as long as you realize that such a judgment clearly implies that those who have already decided the issue have done so mistakenly, and as long as you support your judgment. The error of straddling the fence does not lie in being moderate—it lies in refusing to offer a judgment where a judgment is possible. If you are confused or uncertain about which side of an issue is the best one, then you should consider writing an informative composition rather than a persuasive one.

An effective persuasive composition demonstrates the writer's fairness and reasonableness. One of the reasons that persuasive writing is generally considered the most difficult kind of writing is that the very forcefulness and directness of statement necessary for it to be effective can easily be misinterpreted as stubbornness and unreasonableness. The way to avoid such misinterpretation is to demonstrate that you arrived at your judgments fairly and reasonably. The key word here is *demonstrate*. It means presenting the evidence you considered and the way you interpreted and evaluated that evidence. In short, it means not merely stating your case, but documenting it.

An effective persuasive composition is persuasively arranged. A persuasive composition may employ one or more of the patterns of organization common to narrative or informative compositions (time order, for example), but the dominant pattern is usually one of the following:

Conclusion-to-Evidence (Evidence-to-Conclusion) Order   In conclusion-to-evidence order, the conclusion is presented first, and then the evidence that supports it. Evidence-to-conclusion order is the reverse, with the evidence coming first, followed by the conclusion drawn from it. Conclusion-to-evidence order is more common because it is clearer. But wherever the readers are likely to respond to the conclusion with disbelief or resistance, evidence-to-conclusion order is preferable. By presenting the evidence first, you can lead them to the conclusion gradually and thereby increase the chances that they will respond to it favorably. Thus if a newspaper editor wished to endorse a particular candidate for office and anticipated disagreement from her readers, she would present her reasons first and end with the statement of her endorsement.

Cause-to-Effect (Effect-to-Cause) Order   In cause-to-effect order, a phenomenon is identified and then its effects are identified. For example, an economics course examination question on the effects of the Great Depression would be effectively answered by identifying the Great Depression (what it was and when it occurred) and then discussing the various effects it had on different segments of the population, on business and industry, on government and world affairs. If, however, the question called for a discussion of the *causes* of the Great Depression, then effect-to-cause order would be used—that is, the Great Depression would be identified and then the various causes that led to it would be discussed.

Order of Importance   In order of importance, details or arguments are presented in ascending order, from the least important to the most important. This arrangement subtly suggests that the writer's case is gaining strength as the presentation progresses. In addition, this order places the writer's best point in the final position, the position of greatest emphasis. (The reverse order—the most important point first, the least important last—is used only when the author's intention is ironic or humorous.)

In many writing situations, particularly those in which the issue is controversial, it is beneficial to modify order of importance slightly and to begin not with the least important argument, but with the *second most important*. This arrangement is designed to give the reader both a good first impression and a good final impression.

Basic Persuasive Techniques

There are six techniques most closely associated with persuasive writing. They are as follows: presenting reasons, explaining, classifying, comparing, interpreting and evaluating, and speculating. Let us examine each closely.

Presenting Reasons

This is the most basic of the techniques of persuasive writing because it answers the questions critical readers are most likely to ask about the writer's judgment—"Why does the writer take this view rather than one of the other possible views? What are the writer's reasons for concluding it is the best view?" Presenting your reasons is one of the most effective ways of demonstrating that your judgments are not arbitrary. Here are two examples of this technique.

> I oppose increases in military spending not because I believe the Russians pose no threat to our nation's security, nor because I believe our military might is invincible, but because the defense budget has never been purged of waste, inefficiency, and unnecessary duplication of equipment and services. Thus the Administration should be able to make a significant cut in the defense budget without reducing our defense capability.

> There are three good reasons for not allowing young children to watch MTV (also known as Video Jukebox). First, the scenarios often depict bizarre dress and behavior, sometimes with a strongly sexual or violent message. In addition, whereas music by itself stimulates the child's own imagination, MTV provides ready-made images. Finally, and most important, by presenting a new dramatization every three or four minutes, MTV prevents the natural advancement of the child's attention span.

Explaining

An explanation is useful whenever simple assertion of an idea, even when done with great care, is not sufficient to convey the meaning—that is, whenever the idea or some part of it is apt to confuse the readers or lead them to misinterpret. To use this tech-

Writing a Persuasive Composition 169

nique effectively, you must be sensitive to what is clear without further elaboration and what is not. Putting yourself in the place of your readers and reading your work as if you did not write it can help you achieve such sensitivity.

Here are three examples of effective explanation.

> I . . . should be sorry if any teacher felt incapable of teaching philosophy just because he was not expert in it. Philosophy is not that kind of subject; indeed, it is not a subject in the usual sense at all. It is rather a certain kind of communication, in which both teacher and taught share in a dialogue. In an important sense, we are all students or learners in philosophy: some people are better at it than others, but there are no experts, in the way that there are experts in science or history or mathematics. It is not a matter of taking notes or memorizing facts, but a matter of learning to talk and think in a particular kind of way: to talk and think about *meaning*.[1]

The first two sentences, though clearly expressed, raise questions that the writer must address if he wishes his meaning to be clear—"What kind of subject is this that doesn't require expertise to teach? How can a subject not be a subject?"

> It needs but the simple statement of the nature of cross-examination to demonstrate its indispensable character in all trials of questions of fact. No cause reaches the stage of litigation unless there are two sides to it. If the witnesses on one side deny or qualify the statements made by those on the other, which side is telling the truth? . . . The opinions of which side are warped by prejudice or blinded by ignorance? Which side has had the power or opportunity to correct observation? How shall we tell, how make it apparent to a jury of disinterested men who are to decide between litigants? Obviously, by the means of cross-examination.
>
> If all witnesses had the honesty and intelligence to come forward and scrupulously follow the letter as well as the spirit of the oath, "to tell the truth, the whole truth, and nothing but the truth," and if all advocates on either side had the necessary experience, combined with honesty and intelligence, and were similarly sworn to *develop* the whole truth and nothing but the truth, of course there would be no occasion for cross-examination, and the occupation of the cross-examiner would be gone. But as yet no substitute has ever been found for cross-examination as a means of separating truth from falsehood, and of reducing exaggerated statements to their true dimensions.[2]

This author first explains what he means by "nature of cross-examination," and then, in the second paragraph, why it is "indispensable."

> The old warning "Don't believe everything you read in the newspapers" makes a lot of sense. It's not that newspaper reporters and editors purposely try to deceive anyone. It's rather that in their rush to make deadlines they aren't always able to verify their stories, check their details, study the implications of their headlines. The

This passage illustrates the importance of the writer's sensitivity to what is clear without further explanation and what is not. The author realizes that it is not enough to answer the implicit question "Why does it make a lot of sense?" by saying that reporters and editors don't try to deceive, but that she must explain how deception can occur despite their good intentions.

inevitable errors and unintentional distortions such rushing causes are not always discovered, and even when they are, the corrections are usually printed days or weeks later and seldom in the most prominent place in the newspaper. So cautious readers, while avoiding outright skepticism, maintain a certain mental reservation about the "news."

Classifying

Classification is useful whenever you wish to show how you believe individual members of a group should, in your judgment, be grouped according to some organizing principle. You might, for example, classify people according to how chauvinistic they are, or foreign countries according to their relative political stability. Here is an example of classification.

Notice the consistency of structure here—the dashes and parenthetical comments used in each part of the classification. This aids the reader in understanding the writer's meaning.

> There are three kinds of book owners. The first has all the standard sets and best-sellers—unread, untouched. (This deluded individual owns woodpulp and ink, not books.) The second has a great many books—a few of them read through, most of them dipped into, but all of them as clean and shiny as the day they were bought. (This person would probably like to make books his own, but is restrained by a false respect for their physical appearance.) The third has a few books or many—every one of them dog-eared and dilapidated, shaken and loosened by continual use, marked and scribbled in from front to back. (This man owns books.)[3]

It is not necessary, however, for classification to be handled all at once in a single paragraph. Where each of the things classified is to be dealt with in some detail, the classification may be broken into several parts. Thus the author of the above passage might have chosen to write, "There are three kinds of book owners. The first . . . ," and then present a paragraph or more of specification, perhaps accompanied by some examples. Then he might have turned to the second type, writing, "The second kind of book owner has. . . ." And finally, one or more paragraphs later, he might have written, "The third kind. . . ." In cases where the complexity of the material increases the chance for misunderstanding or confusion, another alternative for organizing the classification is to present the classification as the author did above and then, in the course of the development, use the "first," "second," and "third" (or similar) references to reinforce the classification.

Comparing

Comparison is useful when you wish to show the similarities or differences (contrasts) between two or more important things of the same class. (Note the word "important." To use comparison indiscriminately will detract from your controlling idea.) Similarities are relatively easy to deal with. You can say, for example, "Both boys were well over six feet tall, both were talented athletes, and both were intellectually superior." Contrasts, however, are somewhat more difficult. You must choose between an opposing pattern of organization and an alternating pattern. In an opposing pattern, all the characteristics of one boy are presented before turning to the other boy. In an alternating pattern, each contrast is completed within a sentence or a pair of sentences: "Joe was mild-mannered and easy-going, whereas Bill was aggressive and hot-tempered."

Here is an example of the opposing pattern of comparison.

> The casual visitor to a classroom would have difficulty separating the mature students from the immature. At a glance, they may look very much alike in many respects. Both may be tall or short, slender or heavy-set, fair or dark, fashionably or shabbily dressed, shy and reserved or bold and bubbly. The visitor would have to know them a little better to recognize the differences.
>
> To begin with, mature students want to get as much from the course as they can, even if it is not one they are intensely interested in. And they expect the burden of the course to fall on them, so their thoughts and conversation tend to focus on what they can do for themselves to improve their performance and grades.
>
> From the moment a course begins, when the professor explains something, mature students listen attentively; when directions are given, they make certain they understand them, and they follow them exactly. Moreover, they never ask favors, but expect to be treated like everyone else: if they fail to hand in an assignment or miss an important exam and no makeup is permitted, they accept the penalty without complaining. Before protesting a grade or criticizing the professor for it, they ask themselves honestly whether they deserved the grade. They are considerate of their teachers and fellow students, too, paying attention when they speak and avoiding any kind of distracting behavior.
>
> Most important, mature students exercise discretion: they are not afraid to raise questions and speak their minds, but they do so at the right time and in the right way. Far from stifling their creativity, they

In this passage, the similarities are disposed of quickly ("Both may be tall or short . . .") since the more significant matter is the differences. Those are presented in the opposing pattern, the mature students' characteristics given first, and then the immature students'.

Notice that the sequence of points in each case is the same—that is, attitude toward learning is discussed first in each case, then attention in class, and so on.

give it full expression—but always within the framework of the course.

Immature students, on the other hand, are not so much interested in what they can get from a course as what they can get away with in it. They are more concerned with a grade than with learning. In their minds the burden of the course falls on the professor, so they think and talk a lot about what's wrong with the course and how the professor should try to make it more interesting. When explanations or directions are given, they listen absent-mindedly at best, so they frequently do their work in a different way than they are supposed to.

Immature students are always looking for some special consideration or some loophole in the rules. When they miss an assignment or an exam, they expect to be allowed to make it up, even if the class rule is "no makeups." If this privilege is denied them, they grumble and pout and curse the professor to all their friends. Any grade they are dissatisfied with they automatically blame on the professor. And though they expect others to listen when they speak in class, they regularly interrupt others and distract those around them. Where mature students exercise discretion, immature students specialize in ill-timed and tactless questions. They confuse creativity with attention getting.

The alternating pattern, as we have noted, would complete each contrast within a sentence or pair of sentences. This pattern poses one problem for the writer—how to keep the sentence structure varied enough to avoid monotony. Here is how the first part of the preceding comparison might be expressed in the alternating pattern.

Note how the structure maintains the mature student versus immature student pattern without repeating that phrasing over and over as a kind of formula.

The casual visitor to a classroom would have difficulty separating the mature students from the immature. At a glance, they may look very much alike in many respects. Both may be tall or short, slender or heavy-set, fair or dark, fashionably or shabbily dressed, shy and reserved or bold and bubbly. The visitor would have to know them a little better to recognize the differences.

To begin with, mature students want to get as much from the course as they can, even if it is not one they are intensely interested in. Immature students, on the other hand, are not so much interested in what they can get as what they can get away with. They are more concerned with grades than with learning. Mature students expect the burden of the course to fall on them, so their thoughts and conversation tend to focus on what they can do for themselves to improve their performance and grades. Immature students believe the burden of the course falls on the professor, so they think and talk a lot about what's wrong with the course and how the professor should try to make it more interesting.

When explanations are given, mature students listen attentively and make sure they understand; immature students listen absent-mindedly at best. When directions are given, mature students follow them exactly, whereas immature students frequently ignore them. . . .

Interpreting and Evaluating

To *interpret* is to examine an idea or statement, or even a longer work (such as a literary work), to probe its significance, the assumptions on which it rests, the attitudes it suggests, or its relation to other ideas, statements, or works. In analyzing a work of literature, interpretation may also be used to explore how the work creates its meaning. For example, in analyzing a short story or novel, you might study how a character's behavior throughout the events of the story reveals his personality traits.

> This leaves us with Fowler's second rule: "Prefer the concrete word to the abstract." Very good. Plain talk, as we all know, consists of concrete words; that's practically a definition of it. But which words are concrete and which abstract? You think you know? Well, is *apple* a concrete word? Of course, you say: you can look at apples, smell them, touch them, eat them. But how about the concept *apple*? Isn't it true that the word *apple* also stands for what all the apples in the world have in common, for their "appleness"? Isn't that abstract? How can you tell about any word whether it is abstract or concrete?
>
> Actually, it is a question of meaning and of degree. Some words, like *democracy*, can safely be called abstract since they are used chiefly with abstract meaning; others, like *apple*, are felt to be concrete because they usually apply to concrete objects.[4]

This interpretation focuses on the terms concrete *and* abstract. *Its purpose is to reveal that they are more complex than the quotation suggests and to help the reader understand them more fully. So the author identifies the problem they pose and then shows how to solve it.*

Evaluation is similar to interpretation. It, too, is used to analyze, but your analysis will involve an added component—*judgment*. To *evaluate* is to engage in a critical examination of something, pointing out its strengths and weaknesses, or its advantages and disadvantages, and sometimes suggesting alternatives or solutions.

> It is customary to speak of the bustle and strenuousness of our epoch. But in truth the chief mark of our epoch is a profound laziness and fatigue; and the fact is that the real laziness is the cause of the

This passage evaluates the notion (then common) that modern living is character-

ized by great physical and intellectual "bustle and strenuousness." The author rejects the notion and suggests that the truth is quite the opposite. Note the care with which he develops his argument. This is important in matters of judgment, in which effectiveness depends on how persuasively the case is made.

apparent bustle. . . . Our world would be more silent if it were more strenuous. And this which is true of the apparent physical bustle is true also of the apparent bustle of the intellect. Most of the machinery of modern language is labour-saving machinery; and it saves mental labour very much more than it ought. Scientific phrases are used like scientific wheels and piston-rods to make swifter and smoother yet the path of the comfortable. Long words go rattling by us like long railway trains. We know they are carrying thousands who are too tired or too indolent to walk and think for themselves. It is a good exercise to try . . . to express any opinion one holds in words of one syllable. If you say, "The social utility of the indeterminate sentence is recognized by all criminologists as a part of our sociological evolution towards a more humane and scientific view of punishment," you can go on talking like that for hours with hardly a movement of the gray matter inside your skull. But if you begin, "I wish Jones to go to gaol and Brown to say when Jones shall come out," you will discover, with a thrill of horror, that you are obliged to think. The long words are not the hard words, it is the short words that are hard. There is much more metaphysical subtlety in the word "damn" than in the word "degeneration."[5]

The author made his position clear enough in the first two or three sentences. But had he stopped there, or even after the fifth or sixth sentences, the critical reader would not be so inclined to accept his judgment. For this reason, wise writers take additional time and special care with their evaluations.

Telling us to obey instinct is like telling us to obey "people." People say different things: so do instincts. Our instincts are at war. If it is held that the instinct for preserving the species should always be obeyed at the expense of other instincts, whence do we derive this rule of precedence? To listen to that instinct speaking in its own cause and deciding in its own favour would be rather simple minded. Each instinct, if you listen to it, will claim to be gratified at the expense of all the rest. By the very act of listening to one rather than to others we have already prejudged the case. If we did not bring to the examination of our instincts a knowledge of their comparative dignity we could never learn it from them. And that knowledge cannot itself be instinctive: the judge cannot be one of the parties judged: or, if he is, the decision is worthless and there is no ground for placing the preservation of the species above self-preservation or sexual appetite.[6]

Speculating

Speculation is the technique to use when you wish to project the outcome of a present situation, to make an educated guess about future events. It is, of course, not the same kind of prediction that a

Writing a Persuasive Composition

seer makes. Rather, it is a suggestion about probabilities; that is, possibilities that prevailing conditions indicate are most likely or predictable. When you use this technique, keep in mind that you are speaking about the future, a matter that is closed to all but the clairvoyant and subject to variables too numerous to be accounted for. Avoid any pretense of certainty. Instead, be tentative.

> Occultism, then, is doomed to obsolescence as the enlightenment of scientific research spreads to the dark corners wherein mystery still lurks. Just as the occult practices of astrology gave way to a science of astronomy, occult alchemy turned into scientific chemistry, magical cures were supplanted by sound medicine, witchcraft and fortune telling yielded to parapsychology, so in time will a more reliable foundation supplant the remaining occult systems. An extended psychology and psychiatry, for example, will take over the still flourishing practice of exorcizing devils and will offer something better. Probably many of the more morbid and unsavory derivatives of our religious primitivism that still survive as occult orgies, even in the more sophisticated centers of population, can be converted to more hygienic modes of emotional release. Purporting, as it does, to deal with hidden matters, occultism becomes a challenge to the inquiring mind.[7]

Here the author is speaking of the future of occultism, speculating that it will not survive the continued growth of psychology and psychiatry. Though the first three sentences seem dangerously positive they are saved from being irresponsible by the fact that no date is given for this projected development.

Exercises

Following the guidelines and examples of persuasive techniques, choose one assignment for each of the following techniques specified by your instructor and write one or more paragraphs on it.

1. Presenting Reasons
   a. Do you believe that the death penalty should be abolished? State your judgment and your reasons for making it.
   b. Should a student who cheats on an examination receive a grade of F in the course? State your judgment and your reasons for making it.
   c. Do you believe that women are equal to men in athletic ability? State your judgment and your reasons for making it.
   d. Do you believe in life after death? State your judgment and your reasons for making it.
2. Explaining
   a. Explain your idea of an educated person.
   b. Think of a habit you find annoying and explain why it bothers you.

c. Explain your views on religion.
  d. Do you plan to marry some day? Explain why or why not.
  e. Do you plan to have children some day? Explain why or why not.
3. Classifying
  a. Classify the students of your college according to their table manners.
  b. Classify modern movies according to your degree of interest in them.
  c. Classify parents according to their relative success in raising children.
  d. Classify women according to their degree of liberation.
  e. Classify the students in your school according to their dominant interests (for example, athletes, musicians).
4. Comparing
  a. Compare a wise person you know with a foolish person.
  b. Compare two teachers who made a special impression on you (good or bad).
  c. Compare your two closest friends.
  d. Compare your home town with your college town.
  e. Compare love and infatuation.
5. Interpreting
  a. Interpret Heraclitus' assertion, "We never step into the same river twice."
  b. Interpret the Yiddish proverb, "The girl who can't dance says the band can't play."
  c. Interpret the expression, "God is dead."
  d. Interpret Thomas Fuller's assertion, "Travel makes a wise man better but a fool worse."
6. Evaluating
  a. Evaluate a particular course you are now taking.
  b. Evaluate an English course you took in high school.
  c. Evaluate a particular television program you like or dislike (or current television programming in general).
  d. Evaluate a proposal for change currently being discussed by students on your campus.
7. Speculating
  a. Speculate about how your favorite team (any sport) will do next season.
  b. Speculate about the future of coeducational varsity sports.
  c. Speculate about the possibility that some day people may live forever.

d. Speculate about the possibility of life on other planets.
e. Speculate about the social changes that will come about in the next fifty years.

Combining Persuasive Techniques

Like informative and narrative techniques, persuasive techniques may be used in combination as well as singly. Moreover, they are often combined with informative or narrative techniques or both. You might, for example, present factual information, trace a historical development, summarize a research study, and quote an authority—all to provide factual support for your judgment about a controversial issue. And if your evidence included a particularly significant experience of your own or someone else's, you might present it as a narrative, complete with description and figurative definition, to add dramatic effect and make your composition more persuasive.

The most common combination of techniques used in persuasive writing involves citing examples to support a judgment. Here is an example of this technique. (The judgments are italicized.)

> *There are enough policemen, prosecutors, and judges on various payrolls in New York to produce justice for a hemisphere.* We have city cops chasing pimps and prostitutes, transit cops chasing turnstile jumpers, immigration agents tracing Chinese waiters, the largest contingent of FBI agents in the nation, about 1,000 of them, who fly in planes and live in taxicabs as they chase airport robbers. There are prosecutors and clerks and judges and law secretaries and Secret Service agents and narcotics agents and Internal Revenue accountants and all get paid and all do nothing for the public at a time when the public feels it is a daily victim of theft.
>
> "Why is this man not in jail?" Carter the President said one day as he looked at a picture of Nicky Barnes, the Harlem drug merchant.
>
> The agents working on Barnes were doubled and trebled and the head U.S. attorney, Fiske, prosecuted the case himself. At the end, Barnes, coat over his arm, walked from the courtroom through the door that took him to the detention pens and the start of a sentence of life.
>
> *That's how it can be done when it is deemed important. I have seen it all through the years.* Three hundred FBI agents tracking down one of the Berrigan brothers for his anti-Vietnam activity. There was the

The first paragraph simply lists a number of examples to support the judgment. The second and third paragraphs present a noteworthy example in somewhat greater detail.

Here the author presents four examples in a single paragraph. Note that the careful phrasing of each example makes it possible to include a number of specific details in a brief space.

night they took Angela Davis out of the city in chains, surrounded by agents with automatic weapons, rushed in a convoy to a military air base, flown to California, where more agents waited. Over the past couple of years, there have been as many as 1,000 agents across the country working on the case of Anthony Scotto, the Brooklyn dock union chief. They tapped his phone and bugged his office and steamed open letters and developed stool pigeons. Louis Werner, who helped rob Lufthansa, was around so many FBI agents that he wanted to ask for a badge.[8]

In the following passage the examples are not contained in separate sentences but blended into the sentences used for another technique, evaluation. (The judgment is italicized.)

The dominant technique here is evaluation, but mixed with it are numerous brief examples—virtually every sentence has at least one such example aptly chosen to clarify and support the evaluation. Note that the final sentence contains both the judgment and the author's reason for believing it to be reasonable.

For many people, being creative seems to imply nothing more than releasing impulses or relaxing tensions. They take one part of this extraordinarily complex phenomenon and identify it with the whole. Yet an uninhibited swiveling of the hips is hardly creative dancing, nor is hurling colors at a canvas creative painting. Moreover, too many people confuse creativity with such attributes as verbal skills, quickness of mind, and a sense of order, which are pointers to creativity rather than the thing itself. Others mistakenly equate the creative with the unconventional. They seem to forget that there is no one more unconventional than the lunatic. All too often a child in the first grade is called creative simply because he has produced a finger painting that is a little different from those of his classmates. *Such misuse of language can do the child more harm than good, for it deludes him into believing that creativity can be achieved without hard work.*[9]

The next example of a combination of techniques in persuasive writing also cites numerous examples but includes several other techniques as well. (The judgments are italicized.)

The pattern used in the first three paragraphs is the statement of a judgment followed by a number of examples. Note that four or five times as much space is given to the examples as to the statement of the judgment.

No one could argue that American English is under siege from linguistic falsehood, but euphemisms today have the nagging persistence of a headache. Despite the increasing use of nudity and sexual innuendo in advertising, Madison Avenue is still the great exponent of talking to "the average person of good upbringing"—as one TV executive has euphemistically described the ordinary American—in ways that won't offend him. Although this is like fooling half the people none of the time, it has produced a handsome bouquet of roses by other names. Thus there is "facial-quality tissue" that is not intended for use on faces, and "rinses" or "tints" for women who might be unsettled to think they dye their hair. In the world of deodorants, people never sweat or smell; they simply "offend." False teeth sound truer when known as "dentures."

Admen and packagers, of course, are not the only euphemizers. Almost any way of earning a salary above the level of ditch digging is known as a profession rather than a job. Janitors for several years have been elevated by image-conscious unions to the status of "custodians"; nowadays, a teenage rock guitarist with three chords to his credit can class himself with Horowitz as a "recording artist." Cadillac dealers refer to autos as "preowned" rather than "second-hand." Government researchers concerned with old people call them "senior citizens." Ads for bank credit cards and department stores refer to "convenient terms"—meaning 18% annual interest rates payable at the convenience of the creditor.

Jargon, the sublanguage peculiar to any trade, contributes to euphemism when its terms seep into general use. The student New Left, which shares a taste for six-syllable words with government bureaucracy, has concocted a collection of substitute terms for use in politics. To "liberate," in the context of campus uproars, means to capture and occupy. Four people in agreement form a "coalition." In addition to "participatory democracy," which in practice is often a description of anarchy, the university radicals have half seriously given the world "anticipatory communism," which means to steal. The New Left, though, still has a long way to go before it can equal the euphemism-creating ability of government officials. Who else but a Washington economist would invent the phrase "negative saver" to describe someone who spends more money than he makes?

A persistent source of modern euphemisms is the feeling, inspired by the prestige of science, that certain words contain implicit subjective judgments, and thus ought to be replaced with more "objective" terms. To speak of "morals" sounds both superior and arbitrary, as though the speaker were indirectly questioning those of the listener. By substituting "values," the concept is miraculously turned into a condition, like humidity or mass, that can be safely measured from a distance. To call someone "poor," in the modern way of thinking, is to speak pejoratively of his condition, while the substitution of "disadvantaged" or "underprivileged" indicates that poverty wasn't his fault. Indeed, says linguist Mario Pei, by using "underprivileged," we are "made to feel that it is all our fault." The modern reluctance to judge makes it more offensive than ever to call a man a liar; thus there is a "credibility gap" instead.

The liberalization of language in regard to sex involves the use of perhaps a dozen words. The fact of their currency in what was once

Here an example (speaking of morals) is followed by an explanation.

A brief quotation from an authority is added.

Sensitive to the likelihood that the reader will ask "What 'unanswered questions'?" the author provides some examples.	known as polite conversation raises some unanswered questions. Which, really, is the rose, and which the other name? Are the old forbidden obscenities really the crude bedrock on which softer and shier expressions have been built? Or are they simply coarser ways of expressing physical actions and parts of the human anatomy that are more accurately described in less explicit terms? It remains to be seen whether the so-called forbidden words will contribute anything to the honesty and openness of sexual discussion. Perhaps their real value lies in the power of shock, which is inevitably diminished by
The technique used here is speculation.	overexposure. Perhaps the Victorians, who preferred these words unspoken and unprinted, will prove to have had a point after all.
More examples are added.	*For all their prudery, the Victorians were considerably more willing than modern men to discuss ideas—such as social distinctions, morality, and death—that have become almost unmentionable.* Nineteenth-century gentlewomen whose daughters had "limbs" instead of suggestive "legs" did not find it necessary to call their maids "housekeepers," nor did they bridle at referring to "upper" or "lower" classes within society. Rightly or wrongly, the Victorian could talk without embarrassment about "sin," a word that today few but clerics use with frequency or ease. It is even becoming difficult to find a doctor, clergyman, or undertaker (known as a "mortician") who will admit that a man has died rather than "expired" or "passed away." *Death has not lost its sting; the words for it have.*[10]

The following example analyzes its subject more deeply than do the preceding passages—that is, it presents fewer judgments and provides more thorough development of each. Therefore it employs a somewhat different combination of techniques. (The judgments are italicized.)

The author states his judgment.	*... As public institutions, schools reflect the public. If ... that public has stopped short of full psychological maturity, it is to be expected that the educational system will likewise have stopped short.*
He begins his analysis by stating and explaining the first important way the system will have "stopped short."	In the first place, schools are governed by school boards. These boards are made up of average adults brought up on the average interpretations of our culture. They are not likely to be happy in the thought of turning the schools into experimental stations or into places where the young will learn to look with measuring eyes at the *status quo.* Most board members have relatively fixed attitudes in economic, political, and social matters. These attitudes seem to them, not only reasonable, but the only ones that are reasonable—and this in spite of the fact that they may be far from mature. All attitudes

Writing a Persuasive Composition

that have antedated their own in history are proved unreasonable by the fact that they have become outmoded. All that are contemporary with their own, but representative of other cultures, are "backward." All that look to a different future—unless couched as remote ideals for which the time is not yet ripe—offer, somehow, a threat to their own habits and prestige-pattern, and seem therefore to be either foolish or dangerous. In all sincerity, they come to the conclusion that those schools will best perform their rightful task which turn out students with attitudes like their own.

Few kings in history have willingly abdicated to make way for a system different from their own. The psychological principle back of this fact can be broadly applied: few people who have come to any position of authority and prestige, however small it may be, willingly abdicate in favor of a new regime; and the vast majority of those who tenaciously hold on to positions of power do so believing that they are defending the right and the reasonable. There has been nothing in their own experience of success—and therefore their experience of satisfaction—to make them see as inadequate that by which they have succeeded. School board members, by and large, are among the many human beings who demonstrate the workings of this psychological principle. To the extent that they are mentally, emotionally, and socially immature in a culture where they can find ample support for their immaturity, the schools will tend to be immature in like fashion. This is almost a foregone conclusion.

In the second place, schools are staffed by teachers and administrators who, in large numbers, have come out of immature homes, schools, and colleges. Also, these teachers and administrators—like the rest of us—are daily and hourly played upon by all the various institutions, economic, political, journalistic, and otherwise, that have become arrested short of full social maturity. The fact that these individuals are "educators" neither makes them immune to the pressures to which the rest of us variously yield nor effects in them any sudden transformation from what they have been made by past pressures. For the most part, they remain as much the products of cultural conditioning as the rest of us and they proceed to pass on the immature factors of their conditioning not one whit less honestly and industriously than the mature factors.

It is not surprising, then, that in the average school, students are insidiously led to believe that the mature art of thinking for themselves is "dangerous." It is dangerous so far as their own prospects are concerned: for who is going to want to hire a young person who is known to be "different" or "radical"? It is dangerous, also, they are

Next he adds a classification of attitudes according to a school board's reaction to them.

He continues the example with a brief analogy to the kings in history and then presents historical/psychological information and adds explanation of how it applies to school boards.

Here the author introduces a second example and explains how it fits his original judgment.

Here he presents the reasons that teachers and administrators regard thinking as dangerous.

persuaded, so far as the future of our American way of life is concerned: for how can it be other than dangerous to tamper with the excellent, or to substitute the untried for the tried?

Next he describes the effects of the teachers' and administrators' reluctance to encourage thinking.

Students, naturally, are taught to think *within limits.* The outstanding characteristic of average education is that these limits to thought are not talked about; they are fixed *by the lessons assigned.* Students are required to know what their textbooks and teachers tell them. They are not exposed to other materials that might move them to new doubts and curiosities. If they did happen upon these materials, there would be no scholastic profit to be derived from studying them; there would be no occasion for handing them back to the teacher. They belong to some order of being that is not that of the curriculum. When students know enough of what their textbooks and teachers have told them, they are supposedly ready to go forth into life.

Finally he offers his evaluation and judgment.

This is indeed one way of passing on the traditions of a culture and preparing a student for an adult role—if that role is conceived as one of simply "fitting in." *But if the adult role is more maturely conceived as one of confronting the culture and creatively helping it to grow into its future stages, then the schools, for the most part, prepare badly for this role.* Right preparation for it would require, from the outset, a different attitude. It would require an exploratory and creative attitude toward life. It would ask that children be encouraged to develop inquiring minds rather than merely acceptive and reproducing minds; critical minds rather than merely passive and credulous.[11]

Because the author of our final example desired a more dramatic effect than did the other authors, she employs mostly narrative techniques, notably figurative definition. (The judgments are italicized.)

The author first defines the term according to the general associations it holds for many people.

Appalachia is a beautiful word. It trips off the tongue like the music of a murmuring primeval stream, full of peace and freshness. It evokes (in technicolor) an instant word-association montage of mountain mist and trails worn sleek by long-ago Indians, cherry blossoms, old women smoking pipes, and the family still out back.

Next she expands the definition to the vague geographical reference the word triggers.

Unless you've very recently been helping kids with their geography homework, you may not know exactly just what or where Appalachia is. Naturally it must be connected with the Appalachian Mountains—down south, isn't it, a little to the west, or is it the east? The name seems to keep cropping up in the papers and magazines, and you recall a TV documentary recently with Walter Cronkite talking about depressed areas in Appalachia, but you didn't listen very carefully because it was suppertime and the kids were making a racket.

Writing a Persuasive Composition

Even if you *have* been reading the papers and know that it is the section between the Appalachian Mountain ranges, stretching north to Pennsylvania down through Maryland, Virginia, Kentucky, the Carolinas, and northern Georgia, and that between nine and sixteen million people live there, perhaps the word has a more cultural than statistical meaning for you.

Here she moves from figurative to literal definition.

To you Appalachia may be that part of the country where dwell those beautiful characters of Jesse Stuart's fiction (what a master he is, he makes those people so believable!). Or maybe it is Martha Graham interpreting the Greek drama of an Appalachian spring in barefoot nuance to Copland Dissonance. Or if you're a folk-song buff, maybe it means the carols of John Jacob Niles or those music festivals held in the hill country, in which the natives (called Dovie and Cora and Sister Della) sing their hearts out in sad songs of Elizabethan origin, and which will be taped and sold as collector's items to city folk who will exude admiration for these people's clinging to traditions and their stubborn pride in living as they please. (That's where the true strength of America lies, in its blue-grass roots!)

Returning to figurative definition, she introduces the vivid artistic associations the term has for many people.

But to the people living in Appalachia, the word means tragedy more than poetry. It is a synonym for depressed area—despair, lethargy, and not just poverty but destitution. For one who has grown up believing that the U.S. is the best of all countries in its abundance of physical goods, its gregarious principles (in concept if not always in practice), its concern for its children, its pride in its almost luxurious standard of living, the realization of what life is like right now in Appalachia is like an icy, hard slap in the face. It is running smack into Tennessee Williams when you're thinking Meredith Willson.[12]

Finally, the movement of the previous paragraphs climaxes in the figurative definition of what Appalachia means to those who live there, ending with a brief but vivid analogy.

Exercises

1. Identify the various techniques used in the following passages. Remember that narrative and informative techniques may be combined with persuasive techniques.
    a. [Stereotypes] are an ordered, more or less consistent picture of the world, to which our habits, our tastes, our capacities, our comforts, and our hopes have adjusted themselves. They may not be a complete picture of the world, but they are a picture of a possible world to which we are adapted. In that world, people and things have their well-known places, and do certain expected things. We feel at home there. We fit in. We are members. We know the way around. There we find the charm of the familiar, the normal, the dependable; its grooves and shapes are where we are accustomed to find them. And though we have abandoned much that might have

tempted us before we creased ourselves into that mould, once we are firmly in, it fits as snugly as an old shoe.[13]

b. The other day I was in a restaurant and I overheard two young men talking. The conversation just happened to turn to virgins. They were discussing how they thought any girl saving herself for marriage was dumb. After rattling on for a while in that vein, one of them declared, "I know one thing for sure—the girl I marry will have to be a virgin." In one breath he managed to contradict everything he had said earlier.

How can a man fail to see the inconsistency of such views? And what can make him demand that the girl he marries measure up to a special standard that he *expects* other girls to violate? Maybe beneath the "big man" exterior there's a lot of fear—fear that if his bride has any previous sexual experience, she'll compare him with some other man . . . and *find him wanting.*

c. Early in life many people develop the habit of justifying whatever they do, no matter how offensive it may be. This justifying may take a number of forms. They may say "he deserved it," reasoning that retaliation is a right that absolves them of wrongdoing. Or they may say "she is too thin-skinned," suggesting that the fault lies with the offended rather than with the offender. Or "I couldn't help it," implying that they had no control over the action, that circumstances were somehow to blame. But whatever form this excusing of self takes, it has the same pathetic effect— self-deception.

d. From birth, black people are told a set of lies about themselves. We are told that we are lazy—yet I drive through the Delta area of Mississippi and watch black people picking cotton in the hot sun for fourteen hours. We are told, "If you work hard, you'll succeed"—but if that were true, black people would own this country. We are oppressed because we are black—not because we are ignorant, not because we are lazy, not because we're stupid (and got good rhythm), but because we're black.

I remember that when I was a boy, I used to go to see Tarzan movies on Saturday. White Tarzan used to beat up the black natives. I would sit there yelling, "Kill the beasts, kill the savages, kill 'em!" I was saying: Kill *me*. It was as if a Jewish boy watched Nazis taking Jews off to concentration camps and cheered them on. Today, I want the chief to beat hell out of Tarzan and send him back to Europe. But it takes time to become free of the lies and their shaming effect on black minds. It takes time to reject the most important lie: that black people inherently can't do the same things white people can do, unless white people help them.[14]

2. Select a piece of persuasive writing you recently read and found interesting. It may be any type of writing—a book, an article, a letter to a newspaper editor. Photocopy a passage from it (at least several paragraphs), noting in the margin the techniques of development the author used.

3. Write a two- or three-paragraph persuasive treatment containing one or more combinations of techniques on one of the following topics. Identify the combinations in the margin.
    a. The following sayings clash: "Look before you leap" and "He who hesitates is lost." Which do you think is better advice? Why?
    b. The following sayings clash: "Don't be afraid to speak out for your principles" and "Blessed are the meek, for they shall inherit the earth." Which do you find more acceptable? Why?
    c. The traditional philosophy of sports, "It's not whether you win or lose, but how you play the game," is today challenged by Vince Lombardi's philosophy, "Winning isn't everything—it's the *only* thing." Which philosophy do you endorse?
    d. The following sayings clash: "Absence makes the heart grow fonder" and "Out of sight, out of mind." Which do you believe is more accurate? Why?
    e. The Golden Rule ("Do unto others as you would have them do unto you") is challenged by the common notion that "nice guys finish last." Which do you believe is the better rule to live by? Does the one you choose work better in all situations?

Four Helpful Strategies

The main way to achieve excellence in your persuasive composition is to use appropriate techniques and combinations of techniques. However, you can enhance the effectiveness of your work by applying the strategies professionals use in their writing. Here are four such strategies.

Keep your analysis of audience in mind when you write. In Chapter 5 we dealt in detail with the important considerations you must make in deciding who your readers are and how best to persuade them. By the time you write your persuasive composition you should be sure of the following:

Whether you will write to or for your readers.

That you understand the opposing side of the issue and that you respect your readers.

That the case you will present is a balanced one and that you have appropriate evidence and careful interpretations to offer.

That you have anticipated your readers' objections to your arguments and will include answers to those objections in your paper.

Be sure that you refer to that earlier analysis as you write the composition.

Use a pyramid presentation for your judgments. The pyramid makes an excellent symbol for the relationship between your judgment and your reasons and between your reasons and your evidence, as the following diagrams and comments illustrate. Naturally, the reasons that underlie your judgment will vary in number. Nevertheless, the case you present in your persuasive composition should generally be broader in the middle than at the top and always be broadest at the base.

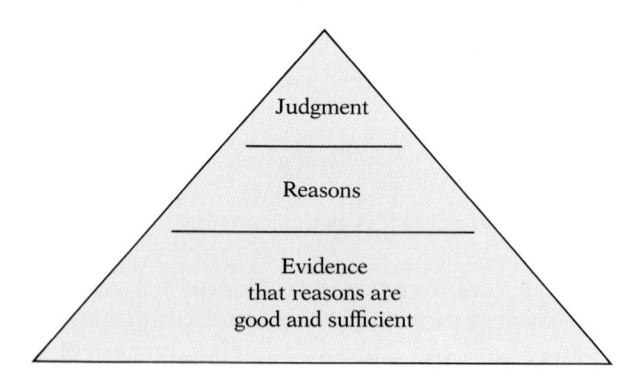

```
         /\
        /  \
       /Judgment\
      /----------\
     /  Reasons   \
    /--------------\
   /   Evidence     \
  /  that reasons are \
 / good and sufficient \
/_____\
```

I oppose
capital punishment

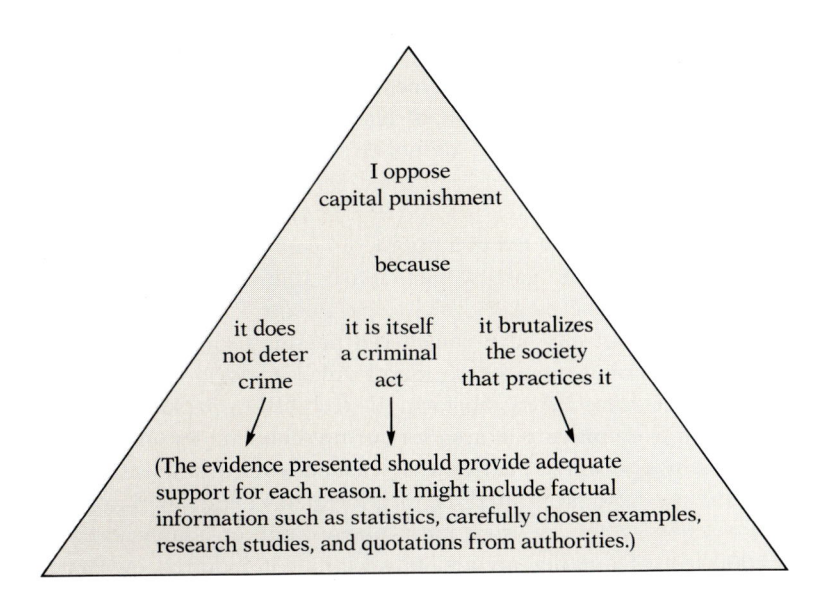

because

it does not deter crime | it is itself a criminal act | it brutalizes the society that practices it

(The evidence presented should provide adequate support for each reason. It might include factual information such as statistics, carefully chosen examples, research studies, and quotations from authorities.)

Credit your sources briefly within the text of your composition and provide a bibliography at the end. The same guidelines given for an informative composition (page 154) apply here.

Choose a lively title and introduction and an effective conclusion. The same guidelines given for an informative composition (page 155) apply here. However, since the readers of a persuasive composition will often disagree with you, the potential for offending them is much greater than in an informative composition. Be sensitive to this fact in choosing your title, introduction, and conclusion.

A Sample Composition

Pac-Man: More Hero Than Villain

Video games have generated considerable controversy in recent years. Numerous individuals have levelled serious charges against them, notably that their emphasis on destruction increases aggressiveness and hostility in young people, that they undermine education, and that they weaken family life. The critics have included people in responsible positions. For example, U.S. Surgeon General C. Everett Koop has charged that video games produce "aberrations in childhood behavior" and concludes that there is "nothing con-

The writer begins by presenting factual details.

Here the writer cites examples of critics in responsible positions and presents their criticisms in quotation and paraphrase, then cites an example of a formal study.

structive in the games." Frank Withrow of the U.S. Department of Education believes that the games may dull a child's enthusiasm for serious computer work. And at least one university study (at the University of Pittsburgh) demonstrated that increased levels of aggression occur in children when they play war-oriented video games.

Next she cites examples of communities that took action and describes the provisions of the ordinances.

Such charges have led to a number of community actions to check the spread of video games, particularly those available in arcades. Cities around the country, including Toledo, Portland (Me.), Pittsburgh, and Detroit, have considered passing ordinances curtailing the establishment and operation of video arcades. Generally these ordinances have taken the form of prohibiting persons under age eighteen from playing in arcades during school hours unless accompanied by a parent or guardian. At least one such ordinance (Toledo's) would have also prohibited the location of any arcade within 500 feet of a school, public library, park, playground, or church, or within 1,000 feet of another arcade. In addition, it required owners and operators to have no criminal record and to demonstrate "good moral character."

This paragraph contains the author's judgment.

Yet despite the widespread public concern about the possible dangers of video games, the preponderance of available evidence suggests that the games are not only harmless, but in many respects beneficial.

The writer begins supporting her judgment by citing two examples of beneficial effects. Note the use of quotation in the first.

William O. Barrett, for example, dean of the Corcoran School of Art, believes that "the creation and playing of video games require, like many art forms, the manipulation of form and color in time and space" and therefore video games have "the potential to create a legitimate and exciting means of artistic expression." The Veteran's Administration Brain Injury Rehabilitation Unit in Palo Alto, California, uses video games for treatment of patients suffering from head injuries, strokes, and brain disease. William Lynch, director of the unit, claims that video games help patients recover by providing positive feedback when they succeed.

Here she cites a third example, dealing with it in greater detail because of its greater importance. The second sentence of this paragraph demonstrates the writer's fairness and reasonableness by presenting factual details that weaken the force of the example.

The most dramatic evidence to date that video games pose no real threat came from a three-day conference held at Harvard University in May 1983 and attended by psychologists, educators, and computer designers from around the country. The fact that the conference was suggested and financed by Atari, and that it excluded experts who believe that video games are harmful, suggests that the conference conclusions should be regarded as less than definitive. Nevertheless, the consensus of the experts in attendance was that video games have a positive effect on children's learning by developing eye–hand coordination and teaching the use of observation and experience to solve problems. In addition, the experts suggested that video games do not lead students to truancy or antisocial behavior, and that, far from decreasing family togetherness, they often increase it.

Much of this data will have to be validated by independent research. Yet at this time it seems reasonable to regard it as persuasive: not just because it represents the best thinking of the experts, but because everyday experience confirms it. A person watching a TV game show or a soap opera—or for that matter even an exciting sports event—is essentially a spectator, and often a very passive one. The same person playing a video game, however, cannot help being active. To evade those racing ghosts, to rescue the maiden in distress, to repel the invaders from outer space, a person must concentrate deeply, be both alert and agile, and at least aim for (if often falling short of) ingenuity in responding to the challenges. Most important, a person must take charge and exert as much control as his or her skill level allows. All these behaviors are an important part of life outside the arcade.

Here the writer offers her evaluation of the evidence, contrasting playing a video game with watching television.

Video games, like any good thing, particularly any entertainment, can be abused and can cause people to neglect their responsibilities. But it is unreasonable to regard them as a threat to social order, education, or family life. From any fair assessment, Pac-Man emerges more hero than villain.

Finally, the writer reinforces her earlier judgment. Note her effort to achieve a balanced view that avoids one-sidedness and oversimplification. Note too how the final line gives direct expression to the idea implicit in the title.

Bibliography

Editorials on File, 14, No. 18 (Sept. 16–30, 1983), pp. 1118–25.

Suggested Topics for a Persuasive Composition

1. Beauty pageants have become a familiar ritual of our culture. Some people regard them as a tribute to women, others as an insult. What is your view of them?
2. Polygamy (being married to more than two spouses at a time) is illegal in the United States, even when it is an expression of a religious belief, as in the case of the Mormons. Should it be illegal?
3. Professors have always condemned the practice of students submitting other people's work as their own. Yet term papers continue to be "borrowed" and even purchased on many campuses. How widespread is this practice on your campus? Do you approve of it?
4. In divorce cases, the courts have traditionally awarded the custody of children to the mother. In recent years, however, there have been exceptions. What guidelines do you believe the courts should follow in deciding the question of custody?

5. Many professional athletes receive salaries in the hundreds of thousands of dollars. And each season the salaries seem to increase. Some people believe there should be some restrictions on athletes' salaries; others argue that athletes are entitled to whatever salaries they can negotiate. What is your view?

6. The question of whether criminals should be made to give up all privileges when they enter prison has been the subject of considerable debate. Many believe that the purpose of imprisonment is to punish offenders and that the granting of any privileges defeats this purpose. Many others disagree, arguing that the purpose of imprisonment is to rehabilitate and that the granting of such privileges as attendance at college, working for pay inside (and even outside) prison walls, and weekend furloughs helps prepare inmates to return to society. What is your view of privileges for prisoners?

7. Reportedly, the "sport" of dog fighting is spreading in the United States. It consists of pitting dog against dog in a contest that may last as long as three hours, ending only when one of the dogs will not or cannot continue. The animals are especially trained for combat and are matched according to weight. This sport dates to the Middle Ages but has long been outlawed in this country. Should it continue to be outlawed?

8. One of the stock jokes comedians used to rely on concerned women drivers. It was based on the notion that women are not as suited for driving as men, that they lack the attentiveness, coordination, reflexes, and calmness of response in a crisis that men display. Is there any truth to this notion?

9. Do colleges have any obligation to close down programs for which the employment outlook is poor? Do they have any moral obligation to inform prospective students that when they complete the programs they are not likely to find jobs?

10. Should teachers be required to perform classroom duties that violate their beliefs? For example, should a Jehovah's Witness be required to teach kindergarten pupils the pledge of allegiance and patriotic songs if she objects to them on religious grounds?

11. Should students who fail out of a particular college be permitted to apply for readmission to that college? Explain your reasoning, specifying any qualifications or restrictions you believe should apply.

Writing a Persuasive Composition

12. The idea of foreign aid is based, at least in part, on the idea that rich nations have an obligation to assist poor nations. Do you accept this idea? Why or why not?
13. Boxing is considered to be one of the most "manly" of sports. It has a rich and colorful history and still has many devoted fans and defenders. But its many critics suggest that it is not a true sport at all, but a form of violence that ought to be outlawed. What is your position and why do you hold it?
14. It has been suggested that cemeteries open their gates to leisure-time activities for the living. Appropriate activities might include cycling, jogging, fishing, hiking, and, space permitting, team sports. Would you favor such a use of cemeteries? Why or why not?
15. Many resident colleges today use "tripling" in at least some of their dormitory rooms. ("Tripling" is housing three students in a room designed for two.) Is this practice ever justifiable? Explain your reasoning.
16. "Hire the handicapped" is a popular slogan, aimed to encourage employers not to discriminate against the handicapped in their hiring practices. Do you think employers are ever justified in refusing to consider a handicapped person?
17. The idea that underlies the public welfare system in our country is that society has a moral obligation to help support those who cannot support themselves. Do you accept this idea?
18. There are many different views of how much freedom and how much responsibility are appropriate for teenagers. What, in your judgment, is the most sensible view?
19. Some people believe that no rape case should be prosecuted unless there is clear evidence that the victim offered "earnest resistance." Do you agree?
20. In the past most people in this country believed in life after death. Today many people do not so believe. What is your position?

A Checklist for Your Persuasive Composition

After completing the rough draft of your persuasive composition, examine it carefully, asking the following questions. If the answer to any question is "No," your composition may contain a weakness that will affect your grade. Reread the appropriate section of the chapter to determine whether there is a weakness and, if so, how to overcome it.

1. Does the composition focus on your judgment of an issue rather than merely presenting information about an issue?
2. Does the composition demonstrate your fairness and reasonableness?
3. Is the composition persuasively arranged?
4. Does the composition make effective use of the persuasive techniques discussed in the chapter (presenting reasons, explaining, classifying, comparing, interpreting and evaluating, and speculating) and, where appropriate, the narrative and informative techniques discussed in chapters 7 and 8?
5. Does the composition reflect the analysis you made of your audience?
6. Does the composition give more space to the reasons and evidence underlying your judgment than to the mere expression of the judgment?
7. Does the composition credit your sources briefly within the text and provide a bibliography at the end?
8. Did you choose a lively title and introduction and an effective conclusion?

Part IV

Revising the Composition

For many amateur writers revising means little more than running their eyes over the composition admiringly and perhaps crossing an occasional *t* or dotting an *i*. That approach to revising serves only to prepare them for a feeling of outrage when someone else finds flaws in their work. As used here, *revising* means scrutinizing the composition for imperfections in logic, sentence style, and paragraph effectiveness and making whatever changes are necessary to eliminate every imperfection that is found. This kind of revising often involves adding, deleting, changing, and rearranging the material in the rough draft.

Far from being the dull, uncreative activity it is sometimes considered, revising can be as creative as you are willing to make it. Every imperfection in logic, sentence style, or paragraph effectiveness you identify in your composition is a challenge to your ingenuity. And though the chapters that follow provide you with the framework in which to make your choices, they do not tell you what choices to make in the particular situations you will encounter in your writing. The only real limits to your choices are the limits of your imagination.

Your motive for revising your work should be to present your thoughts and expression at their best. That is the motive of the sculptor, artist, and skilled craftsperson, and it is matched by their willingness to exert whatever effort is necessary to refine and perfect their work. They realize the truth of Thomas Edison's famous pronouncement: "Genius is one percent inspiration and ninety-nine percent perspiration."

The key to effective revising is *awareness of the imperfection of your work.* You cannot really look for flaws unless you believe they may exist. That is why so many amateur writers never seem able to find the flaws in their writing—they never really admit that they are capable of error. Then, when someone else points out a flaw in their work, they are surprised and often offended. And they quickly fall into the habit of attacking those who point out their flaws and even of justifying the flaws. They never seem to realize that if they simply admitted their own human imperfection and spent some time revising their work before others saw it, they wouldn't have to stoop to face-saving maneuvers later.

Two Approaches to Revising

There are two approaches that can be used in revising a composition. The first is to read through it as a good reader might, not looking for specific weaknesses, but expecting that it will contain weaknesses and being alert to them. This approach works best when you are able to put aside the composition for a time before revising it. Objectivity depends on detachment—when you are too close to something, particularly something as personal as your writing, your ego will be wrapped up in it and you will want to view it favorably and overlook its weaknesses.

In using this approach, make careful note of your reactions as you read. If you find yourself saying, "This is a little confusing," or "Is this the best explanation?" or "What's the connection here?" write that reaction in the margin so you can go back and deal with the problem later. If possible, do this first reading aloud and listen to the sound of the phrasing as you are reading. Many lapses in writing are more easily heard than seen (awkward phrasing, for example). Besides, having two senses working for you instead of one increases your chances of finding flaws.

This approach will provide you with a helpful overview of the composition and will usually reveal some imperfections. Yet it cannot be counted on to reveal all imperfections. The potential problems that may arise in a composition are too numerous for that. Thus the first approach to revising must be followed by a second, in which you look for specific problems that commonly arise in logic, sentence style, and paragraph effectiveness. The three chapters that follow will provide you with both an understanding of those problems and the skills to solve them.

As you read the following chapters and apply their lessons in your writing, keep one important fact in mind: Not every writing occasion will afford you as much revision time as you might wish or need. Because of this, when you are writing an in-class composition or taking an essay examination, you might be tempted to write until the bell sounds and allow no time for revision. That would be a mistake. On such occasions, the potential for error is even greater than usual, so revision (and, for that matter, planning) is no less important.

If your time is limited to a fifty-minute period, you will generally produce a better piece of writing by allowing five minutes for planning, thirty-five minutes for writing, and ten minutes for revising than by spending the entire fifty minutes writing.

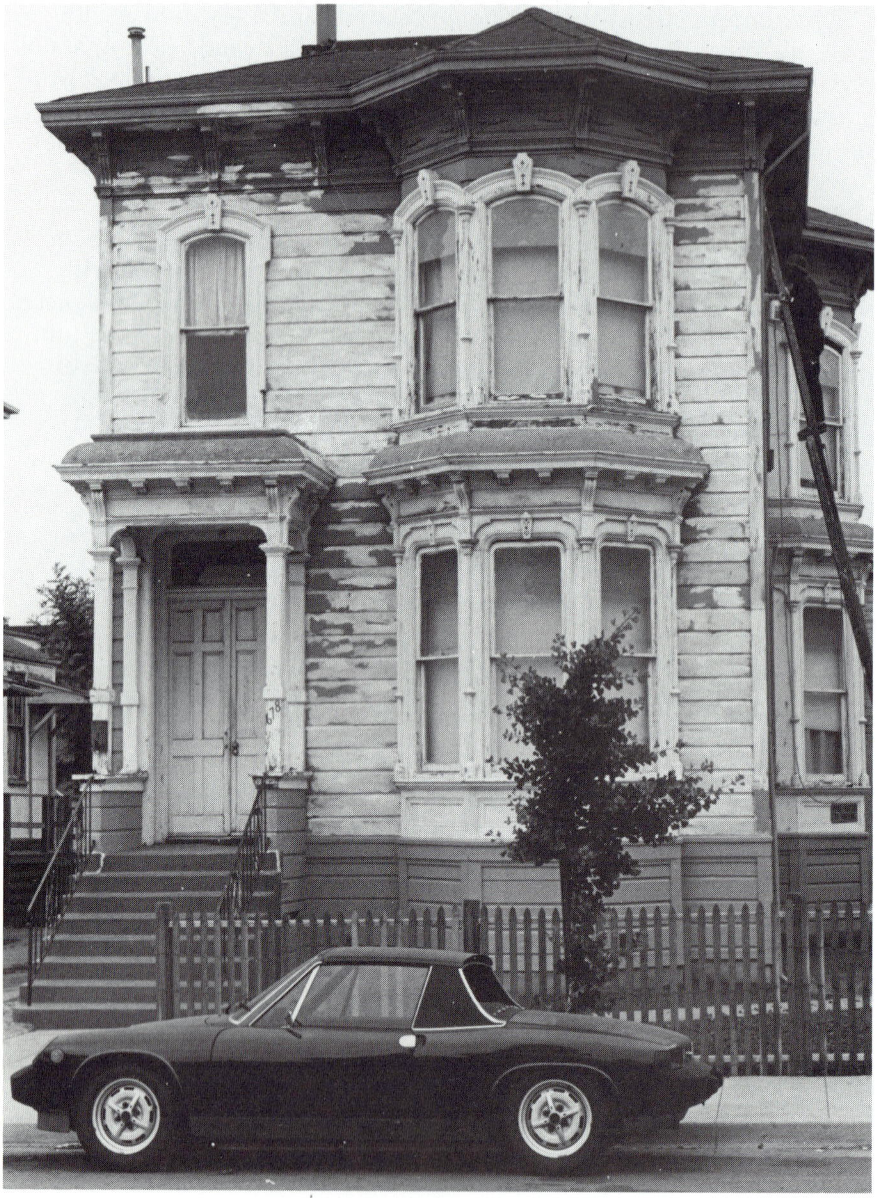

Chapter 9

Revising for Logic

This chapter identifies the ten most common fallacies in writing and explains how to find and overcome them in your writing.

In Chapter 3 we discussed the importance of evaluating ideas during the planning stage of the writing process. More specifically, we noted the value of maintaining a questioning attitude, of separating fact from opinion and taste from judgment, and of being sensitive to the connections between ideas. In addition, we detailed the questions you should ask about your judgments and the reasoning that underlies them. These considerations are crucial in any composition in which you are expressing your judgment of an issue—that is, in any persuasive composition.

Errors in thinking, however, are not limited to the planning stage of the composition process. They can also occur while you write the paper. Therefore, the revision of any composition that expresses one or more judgments must include an examination of the logic of those judgments.

Ten Common Fallacies

The ten most common fallacies that follow are not the only ones that occur in thinking, but they are the most common ones. Learning to recognize each one and eliminate it from your compositions will help ensure that your judgments are reasonable.

Either–Or Thinking

This error consists of viewing a particular reality solely in terms of opposing extremes when in fact other views are possible. It is often accompanied by the demand that people choose between the two extremes and the clear if often unstated suggestion that no third choice is possible. Here is an example of either–or thinking:

Original Passage

The Soviet Union and the United States are engaged in a titanic power struggle. Which one will emerge victorious is uncertain, but one fact can hardly be doubted. Whichever triumphs, the other will be destroyed.

Analysis

Destruction of one or the other is certainly a possible outcome of the struggle. But it is not the only possibility. Perhaps both will be destroyed. Or perhaps the struggle will be one day transformed into cooperation and neither will be destroyed.

Revised Passage

The Soviet Union and the United States are engaged in a titanic power struggle. Perhaps one will emerge victorious over the other. It is impossible to say. But one thing is certain. The situation is extremely dangerous to both.

Comment

This revision is not the only possible one. The controlling idea of the composition may suggest another one. Nevertheless, this revision eliminates the either–or error.

Whenever you encounter either–or thinking in your composition, ask "Why must it be one or the other? Why not both (or neither)?" and revise your composition accordingly.

Stereotyping

Stereotyping is ignoring someone's or something's individuality and focusing instead on some preconceived notion about the person or thing. (It is one of the central features of prejudice.) There are stereotypes about Jews and blacks and atheists and political parties—in short, about almost everything and everyone. Here is an example:

Original Passage

I oppose minority quotas in employment because they translate to giving special advantages to blacks and Hispanics, people who are known to be lazy and irresponsible.

Analysis

Blacks and Hispanics are "known to be lazy and irresponsible" only in the sense that they have been assigned that stereotype. No racial or ethnic group can be so neatly categorized. In addition, because individuals, not races or ethnic groups, apply for jobs, it is unreasonable to discuss any employment practice in such sweeping terms.

Revised Passage

I oppose minority quotas in employment because they result in job decisions being made on a basis other than qualifications. A person should be hired or disqualified on the basis of job qualifications only.

Comment

Whether this is the most reasonable position to take may be debatable. Nevertheless, it is a fair and responsible position, unlike the original one.

Whenever you find yourself expressing a prefabricated assessment of an entire class of people or things, ask "What evidence do I have that the assessment is fair or that it fits all the individual members of that class?" If you have no such evidence, regard the idea as a stereotype and revise it.

Attacking the Person

This error consists of disposing of an argument by attacking the person who advances it. It is not a reasonable approach because an argument's validity does not depend on the character of its advocates. A scoundrel may, on occasion, support a valid argument, and a saint, an invalid one. Here is an example of attacking the person:

Original Passage

Richard Nixon has suggested that the President of the United States and the Soviet Premier should name special individuals to meet regularly and focus exclusively on the relationship between the two countries. I think the President should reject any idea that came from a man who disgraced the presidency and showed himself to be without honor.

Revised Passage

Richard Nixon has suggested that the President of the United States and the Soviet Premier should name special individuals to meet regularly and focus exclusively on the relationship between the two countries. I think the idea should be rejected, not because that relationship is unimportant, but because it is too important to be entrusted to anyone but the heads of state themselves.

Analysis

However disgraceful Richard Nixon's behavior may have been in office, and however lacking he may be in qualities the writer regards as admirable, it is unreasonable to reject his idea on that account. In fact, when it comes to matters such as the one in question, his ideas should be carefully considered because he is an expert in those matters.

Comment

Whatever value this argument may prove to have, it at least has the virtue of focusing on the issue rather than attacking the person.

Whenever you find that you have used arguments for or against the person in place of (or in addition to) assessment of his or her idea, ask yourself "Is what I have said about the *person* sufficient to assess the *idea*?" If it is not, revise your composition accordingly.

Contradiction

Contradiction occurs when a person makes two assertions that are logically inconsistent with each other. It is an error that occurs

Revising for Logic

more often in long compositions than in short ones, and is more difficult to detect than other errors because the conflicting assertions seldom appear together. To detect contradiction you must compare early assertions with later assertions. Here is an example of a contradiction:

Original Passage

Morally our nation is in big trouble. Let's consider a typical example. For centuries, the taking of a human life was regarded as wrong. That's as it should be. No one is ever justified in taking a human life. Yet today books are written defending so-called mercy killing and giving directions on how to commit suicide.

(Then, later in the composition, the following passage appears.)

I say we've grown too casual about human life. The only situation in which the taking of a life is ever justified is self-defense.

Analysis

First the writer says the taking of a human life is never justified; then, later, she says that there is a situation in which it is justified. That is a contradiction. (Revision in this case is easy. All that is necessary is to change the fifth sentence to "No one is ever justified in taking a human life, except in the case of self-defense.")

Whenever you encounter a contradiction in your composition, ask "Does the contradiction invalidate my entire argument or only a part of it? And if a part, which part?" Then revise accordingly.

Faulty Analogy

Analogy is a line of reasoning suggesting that things alike in one respect are also alike in other respects. Analogy is a common kind of reasoning and there is nothing wrong with it, *as long as the similarities that are claimed are real.* An analogy is faulty when the similarities are not real. Here is an example of faulty analogy:

Original Passage	Analysis
The government is reportedly requiring that stronger warnings be placed on cigarette packages and in advertisements. I think it's ridiculous to have even the present warnings. The practice makes no more sense than putting "Warning! Eating too much of this product may make you a fat slob" on packages of spaghetti or "Warning! Careless use of this instrument may smash your fingers" on hammers.	The analogies are vivid, but faulty. Eating spaghetti is good for people if done in moderation—it provides nutrition. Smoking cigarettes does no comparable good. Similarly, the hammer can do harm if used carelessly. But cigarettes have been shown to do harm no matter how carefully they are used.

In this case the writer should either replace the original analogy with one that is not faulty or, preferably, explain why the warnings on cigarette labels are ridiculous. If he cannot do either, he should omit the judgment from his composition.

Whenever you review any analogy in your compositions, say "These two things may be similar in certain respects, but are there any significant respects in which they are dissimilar?" If there are, the analogy is probably faulty and should be changed or eliminated.

Faulty Causation

Faulty causation may take either of two forms. The first is concluding that one thing caused another merely because of their proximity in time or space. For example, shortly after a black cat crosses someone's path, an accident befalls her, so she concludes that the cat's crossing her path caused her misfortune. This error occurs not only in everyday reasoning but in formal reasoning as well. For many years the prevailing medical opinion was that damp night air caused malaria, simply because the onset of the disease occurred after exposure to night air. (The real cause, the bite of infected mosquitoes, was discovered much later.)

The other form of faulty causation is concluding that learning why a person is interested in an issue is the same as evaluating his or her thinking about the issue. "Find the motivation," goes this reasoning, "and you have determined whether the argument is valid." This line of thinking, which resembles attacking the person, is erroneous for a similar reason. A person's motivation for advancing an argument is never sufficient reason for approving or rejecting the argument. Noble motives may underlie bad arguments and ignoble motives, good ones. Here is an example of this form of faulty causation.

Original Passage

One of my professors told the class that he believes the way student evaluations are used on this campus doesn't provide effective evaluations of the quality of teaching. He said the questions themselves are OK, but the evaluation should be made at the end of the semester instead of during the tenth week. He sharply criticized the administration, saying that they are more concerned with suiting their schedules than with getting meaningful input from students.

How reasonable are these arguments? We needn't look far to answer. A secretary in the administrative affairs office revealed that the professor himself received a terrible rating on the student evaluations. His argument is clearly self-serving and therefore unreasonable.

Analysis

Perhaps what the secretary allegedly said about the professor's rating is true. And perhaps that is what prompted him to take a critical look at the evaluation procedure. But so what? That would be a normal enough reaction. More important, it has no bearing on the issue. The validity of his argument can be determined only by evaluating the evidence that supports or challenges it, not by speculating about his motivation in advancing it.

Whenever you have said in your composition that one thing has caused another, ask "Is the proximity in time or space evidence of a true cause-and-effect relationship or merely a coincidence?" Whenever you have approved or rejected a person's view because of his or her motivation, ask "What bearing does the person's motivation have on the quality of the idea?"

Irrational Appeal

There are four common kinds of irrational appeal—appeals to emotion, to tradition or faith, to moderation, and to authority. Each of these is a misuse of a rational appeal and may be identified as follows:

> An *appeal to emotion* is rational when it accompanies thought and analysis and irrational when it substitutes for them.
>
> An *appeal to tradition or faith* is rational when the particular practice or belief is regarded in light of present circumstances and irrational when it means "Let's continue to do (believe) as we have done merely because we have always done so."
>
> An *appeal to moderation* is rational when the moderate approach is offered as the best solution to the problem or issue and irrational when moderation is merely a convenient way to avoid offending someone or to evade the responsibility of judging.
>
> An *appeal to authority* is rational when it acknowledges the fallibility of people and their institutions and the possibility of differing interpretations; it is irrational when it disallows reasonable questions and challenges. (As used here, *authority* means not only eminent people but also eminent books and documents, such as the Bible and the U.S. Constitution, and eminent agencies, such as the Supreme Court.)

Here is an example of irrational appeal:

Original Passage	Analysis
Recent court decisions that permit teenagers to receive birth control prescriptions from clinics without their parents' knowledge should be vigorously opposed. Our society, indeed the larger European civilization in which it is rooted, has always regarded the family as the essential so-	There is nothing necessarily wrong with detailing the historical background to an issue or with making a spirited appeal on behalf of a point of view or principle. But here they are used as a substitute for analysis. The writer says, in effect, "We should oppose the decisions because

Original Passage	Analysis
cial unit. Moreover, the Judeo-Christian tradition has always accorded the family a preeminent place in the hierarchy of human institutions. All right-thinking people will recognize such court decisions as an assault on our heritage and lend their support to the movement to resist those decisions.	our ancestors would have opposed them," and never offers a rational argument for opposing them.

Revised Passage	Comment
Recent court decisions that permit teenagers to receive birth control prescriptions from clinics without their parents' knowledge should be vigorously opposed for two reasons. The first reason is that those decisions undermine the role of parents in the upbringing of children at a time when that role has already been weakened by popular culture. The second and more important reason is that it is unfair for the law to hold parents responsible for their teenagers and yet treat the teenagers as independent in medical matters.	The view expressed in this passage may, of course, be debated. Nevertheless, its essential appeal is rational rather than irrational—that is, to logic rather than to a feeling of respect for our ancestors.

Hasty Conclusion

A hasty conclusion is one that is drawn without appropriate evidence. In other words, it is a conclusion chosen without sufficient reason from two or more possible conclusions. Hasty conclusions are especially tempting in situations where prior opinions compromise objectivity. Those opinions make a person wish for a particular conclusion to be so, and wishing leads to uncritical acceptance. Here is an example of a hasty conclusion:

Original Passage	Analysis
We had a great deal in common. We both played in the band, we belonged to the same church, and we both preferred reading books to watching television. Yet despite all that, and despite the fact that I asked her out numerous times, she always refused me. Instead, she went out with Burton Ogilvy, the star athlete in our class. Looking back on that painful experience, I realize that she was a hypocrite, choosing Burton over me not because she cared for him but because he was the "big man" in the class.	There are actually two conclusions here and both are hasty. The first is that the girl chose Burton because he was a "big man" rather than because she cared for him more than she cared for the author. The second is that choosing Burton, even for the reason stated, makes her a hypocrite. Nothing the writer offers here demonstrates that either conclusion is the most reasonable interpretation of her behavior.

If the writer has more evidence than presented above, evidence that is adequate to support the conclusions, then he should present it. If he lacks such evidence, he should omit the conclusions from his composition. (To do so, he would only have to change the final sentence to read, "Looking back on that painful experience, I will always wonder whether she really cared for Burton more than for me or whether she went out with him because he was the 'big man' in the class.")

When checking your compositions for logic, note every conclusion and ask "What evidence do I have that this is the most reasonable conclusion?" If you lack sufficient evidence to support your choice, revise the conclusion or eliminate it.

Overgeneralization

A *generalization* is a judgment about a class of people or things made after observation of a number of members of that class. *Over*generalization is generalization based upon insufficient observation. One of the most common errors in argument, overgeneralization may be explained by the natural human tendency to classify sensory data tidily and by the difficulty of determining how much data is necessary to support a generalization. Accordingly, writers often make careless assertions about whole groups of people and things. Here is one example:

Original Passage	Analysis
I have been at this college a month now and am glad I chose it over other colleges I was considering. The professors here are very helpful and encouraging, and all the professional and service staff go out of their way to help students. The townspeople, however, are not very friendly at all. They seem to resent the college students for some reason. Perhaps some ongoing town-versus-gown conflict is responsible for their behavior, but whatever its cause, I find it disturbing.	This writer speaks of the professors, the professional and service staff, and the townspeople in sweeping terms. In order to make such generalizations, she ought to have had many more contacts than a month's stay on a campus could possibly have provided. This passage, therefore, overgeneralizes.

In revising this passage, the writer should change the level of generalization to fit the amount of experience it is based on. That change may be accomplished by using such words as "some" and "certain." For example, the writer could refer to "some professors" and "certain townspeople." But a more substantive change is also desirable. The writer should provide one or more examples of helpfulness, friendliness, and encouragement, so that the passage not only tells but *shows* the readers her experiences. (Writers who recognize the effectiveness of demonstration and who take care to limit their topics effectively seldom have a problem with overgeneralization.)

Whenever you check your composition for logic and find generalizations, ask "Is the level of generalization here appropriate, given the amount of data I have?" Be particularly suspicious of generalizations for which you have provided little or no evidence.

Oversimplification

It is natural to want to simplify matters—simplification aids understanding and communication. For that reason, simplification is legitimate, as long as it does not distort the reality it describes. When it does, it becomes *over*simplification. The most frequent kind of oversimplification that occurs in compositions is the presentation of only one side of a two-sided (or three- or four-sided) reality. Here is an example of such oversimplification:

Original Passage	Analysis
There's been a great deal written recently about the need to improve high school education in this country. One of the ways that has been proposed to do so is to raise the salaries of teachers. The reasoning is that, given the years of preparation required to become a teacher, teachers' salaries should be comparable to salaries in the private sector. The flaw in this argument lies in the fact that it ignores the time teachers spend working. They only work nine months of the year to begin with, and their work day ends at three o'clock. The truth is they are paid less because they work less.	There is some truth in what this writer says. The high school class schedule usually ends at three o'clock and the official work year, with holidays and vacations considered, is nine months long. But that is only part of the complex reality of high school teaching. Many teachers are responsible for five different classes each day, each of which requires preparation for lectures and discussions, as well as for the grading of homework. All that work must be done after school. In addition, teachers are often expected to chaperone after-school activities and advise clubs and organizations. Finally, they are generally required to extend their knowledge of their subjects by pursuing graduate degrees in the summer. To ignore all these duties is to oversimplify the reality of high school teaching.

The above analysis should not be taken to mean that the writer is necessarily wrong in arguing against general salary increases for high school teachers. His position may be the most reasonable one. The point is that he should make whatever case he has without oversimplifying—that is, without distorting the facts or being selective in presenting them. (In addition, his paper would be more persuasive if he did a little research and presented actual salary data in place of supposition.)

There is no easy formula for detecting oversimplification. Your best approach is to be suspicious of any neat description of a complex reality. When you encounter one, ask "Is the truth really this neat and simple? Is there another side to it that is not represented here?" If there is, revise your composition to acknowledge it.

A Brief Revision Guide

To help you apply the approaches discussed in this chapter when you revise your compositions for logic, here is a brief summary.

> *Either–Or Thinking.* Seeing a particular reality only in terms of one extreme or the other. Ask "Why must it be one or the other? Why not both (or neither)?"
>
> *Stereotyping.* Ignoring reality in favor of a preconceived notion. Ask "What evidence do I have that the assessment is fair or that it fits all the individual members of that class?"
>
> *Attacking the Person.* Disposing of an argument by attacking the person who holds it. Ask "Is what I have said about the *person* sufficient to assess the *idea*?"
>
> *Contradiction.* Making two assertions that are logically inconsistent with each other. Ask "Does the contradiction invalidate my entire argument or only a part of it?"
>
> *Faulty Analogy.* Suggesting that things alike in one respect are also alike in other respects when, in fact, they are not. Say "These two things may be similar in certain respects, but are there any significant respects in which they are different?"
>
> *Faulty Causation.* Concluding that one thing caused another merely because of their proximity in time or space. Or concluding that learning why a person is interested in an issue is the same as evaluating his or her thinking about the issue. Ask "Is the proximity in time or space evidence of a true cause-and-effect relationship or merely a coincidence?" or "What

bearing does the person's motivation have on the quality of the idea?"

Irrational Appeal. Appealing unreasonably to emotion, tradition or faith, moderation, or authority. Ask whether the appeal is offered in a context of reasoning or as a substitute for reasoning.

Hasty Conclusion. Selecting one conclusion out of two or more possible ones without good reason for doing so. Ask "What evidence do I have that this is the most reasonable conclusion?"

Overgeneralization. Making a judgment about a class of people or things based upon insufficient observation. Ask "Is the level of generalization here appropriate given the amount of data I have?"

Oversimplification. Presenting only one side of a two-sided (or three- or four-sided) reality. Ask "Is the truth really this neat and simple? Is there another side to it that is not represented here?"

One final note. In revising your compositions for logic, it is possible to adopt two erroneous views. The first is that if you find one or more errors, your entire composition is necessarily ruined. The other, perhaps more common view, is that if you find no errors, the argument your composition presents is necessarily the best one. To avoid both errors, keep these principles in mind:

The presence of an error does not necessarily invalidate an argument. Although errors always weaken an argument, not all errors are equally serious. And even the best argument may contain numerous errors when presented by a careless thinker.

The absence of error is no guarantee that an argument is the best possible one. It merely establishes the argument's candidacy for that distinction.

Exercises

Each of the following passages contains at least one of the fallacies discussed in the chapter. Identify each error and revise each passage, if possible, to eliminate it. You may change the idea as much as you wish, even reversing it if that is appropriate. If you are unable to make a judgment, explain what knowledge you would need to do so. (Caution: Make sure your choices are based on reasonableness and not just your preference for one idea over another.)

Revising for Logic

1. It is true that physical education instructors often claim that vigorous exercise can eliminate the tension caused by stress. However, physical education instructors have a reputation for being unintelligent, so their testimony is suspect.

2. The idea that smoking cigarettes affects athletic performance is a lot of nonsense. I've smoked since fifth grade and I've always been able to outrun any kid in the school. Even now, in college, I can outrun my roommate, who's the fastest guy on the track team.

3. I know that nudists are the butt of a lot of jokes, but joking aside, they're sick creatures. I have an uncle who is a member of a nudist colony and when he's visited my home (fully clothed, I might add), he's always ogled my sisters and talked about sex most of the time. Now I'm generally tolerant, but I confess I have little use for perverts. Nudists should be made to undergo psychiatric care.

4. Many people believe that astrology is not a science, but they are wrong. Anyone who will take the time to set aside preconceived notions and investigate the subject will come to the same conclusion. I used to be an unbeliever myself, and then I took the time to read the characteristics of my astrological sign, Gemini, and I was amazed at what I discovered. Geminis are described as mercurial types, with a great range of emotional response. They are two-sided in their natures, capable of both very logical and very creative activity. (A great many artists and writers are Geminis.) That description fit me so perfectly that I knew astrology has to be scientific.

5. I never cease to be amazed at the opinions of some of my classmates. For example, we were discussing sex in my psychology class recently and one student was arguing in favor of virginity before marriage. At first I thought she was joking and would break down and laugh in a minute or two. Then I realized she was serious. She really believes that people should not engage in sex before marriage. The idea is absurd—it's like having a beautiful wardrobe and leaving it to rot in the closet or having a fine automobile and letting it stand until it rusts. Since that day I've wondered what made that girl accept such a foolish idea. I'm convinced it can only be prudishness and fear of sex.

6. The international fashion industry is dominated by homosexuals. In a way this is understandable because gays are more artistic than normal people and therefore find the designing of

clothes a good outlet for their talent. Yet there is a sinister element in the homosexual domination—clothing styles in the past decade or so have become more and more unisex, demonstrating that gay designers are either mocking traditional sexual roles or trying to change those roles.

7. Parents are continually pressuring teenagers to accept their values and conform to traditional ways of behaving. They never seem to realize that each generation has its own unique view of life and its own approach to living, and that by honoring the new perspective, their sons and daughters are showing their individuality. What was right twenty years ago is not necessarily right now. If only parents were less anxious over the differences, they would realize that they are only an expression of the age and that in time, perhaps in their grandchildren's day, a cycle will have been completed and the values and standards they believe in will once again return.

8. Television commercials are a gigantic insult to viewers' intelligence. They blare out their deceitful messages every ten or fifteen minutes all day and night, urging us to rush out and purchase some overpriced item that we don't need or that will fall far short of the advertising claim. And the biggest insult of all is that you and I pay for those commercials because their cost is passed on in the price of the product or service. No one has anything good to say about commercials, and yet they survive and even grow in absurdity. How they manage to do so is a mystery to me.

9. For years liberal politicians in this country have deceived us into believing that the welfare system is necessary to combat poverty. The truth is almost exactly the opposite—welfare *creates* poverty. It does so by making people dependent on government handouts and therefore content to be idle instead of working and being self-sufficient. The proof of this is evident in every community across the nation. Look at the people cashing welfare checks or using food stamps to buy cigarettes and beer, able-bodied people who could hold a job but don't. And if that isn't proof enough for you, reflect on this fact—during the last ten years, when there were more people on welfare than ever, unemployment *increased*.

10. In the 1970s television movies explored subjects previously considered taboo for the media, subjects like homosexuality and rape. Some critics protested that those subjects were not fit for viewing. I disagreed because I opposed censorship in any

form, believing that no subject should be closed to writers or filmmakers. But developments of recent years have caused me to change my mind. In 1983 NBC presented *Princess Daisy*, a film that explored the issue of brother–sister incest; then in 1984 ABC presented *Something About Amelia*, the subject of which was father–daughter incest. Since such films can only serve to stimulate interest in this reprehensible behavior, and thereby lead to an increase in crimes against children, I believe they should be banned from the air.

Composition Assignment

Select one of the following issues and write a 500-word composition on it. Don't skimp on the planning and writing stages, but pay particular attention to revising, especially to revising for logic.

1. Is there a significant difference between male and female athletes in strength, speed, or agility? Explain and support your position and discuss its implications for coeducational sports.
2. What changes do you think are most needed in the fight against crime? In addressing this question, be sure to consider changes in all areas—police work, the courts, probation and parole, and the prison system.
3. In the late 1970s and early 1980s, the world was plagued by a number of incidents (notably the Iranian incident) in which terrorist or revolutionary groups seized innocent hostages and demanded ransoms or certain actions by governments. What should our government's policy be in dealing with such incidents?
4. The following sayings clash: "The squeaky wheel gets the grease" and "Silence is golden." Which do you believe is better to live by? Why?
5. The following sayings clash: "Clothes make the man" and "Don't judge a book by its cover." Which do you believe makes more sense? Why?
6. Should gay couples be permitted to adopt children?
7. Many students complain that the workload in college is so heavy they cannot keep up with their assignments. Is this true at your college? How heavy is the workload at your college?
8. It is standard practice in medical research to perform experimental surgery on animals. Some people strongly protest this practice, known as vivisection. Do you approve of it?

9. Is it reasonable to require citizens to pass a literacy test before allowing them to vote?
10. Since the nineteenth century the theory of creation (the earth and everything on it was created at one time) has been challenged by evolution (higher forms of life developed out of lower ones over millions and millions of years). Which theory do you accept? Why?
11. Conformity is a very common trait in people. What, in your judgment, causes people to conform? (Be sure to explain the *process* by which conformity occurs.)

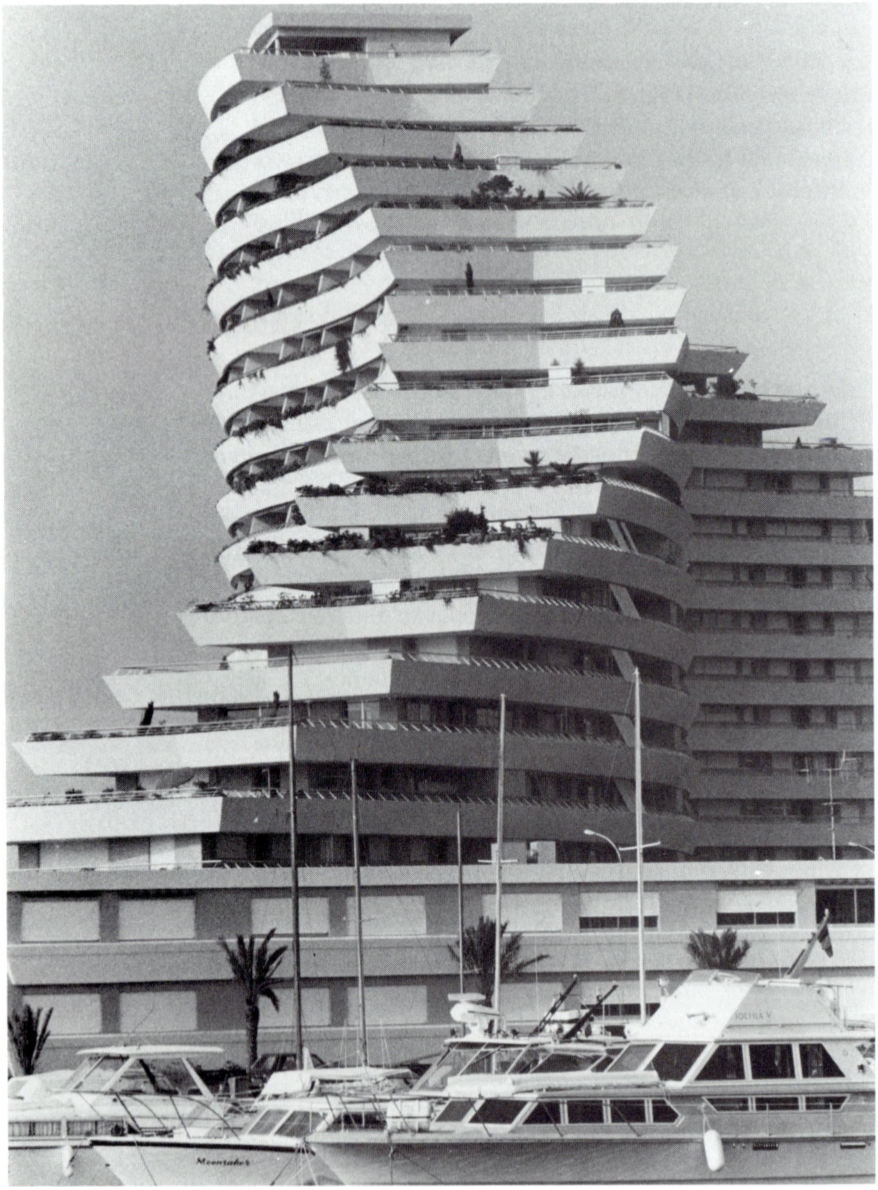

Chapter 10

Revising for Sentence Style

This chapter explains the fundamentals of sentence style, including coordination and subordination, combining and expanding sentences, maintaining clarity, and varying word order. In addition, it shows you how to revise your sentences to achieve exactness, economy, and liveliness.

Effective sentences do not just happen. You must design them. There is little opportunity to do this while writing the composition because at that time you must devote your attention to organizing and developing your thoughts. The time for designing sentences, for employing the traditional rhetorical strategies in your own creative way, is in the revising stage. We will begin by discussing the fundamentals of sentence style and then turn to specific strategies for solving common sentence problems.

The Simple Sentence

There are five basic sentence patterns for the simple English sentence. Although you may have forgotten the terms traditionally assigned to these patterns, you will surely find the patterns themselves familiar.

They are as follows:

Subject/Verb/Object
Seat belts save lives.
George chomps his food.

Subject/Verb/Indirect Object/Direct Object
Bill owes the store a thousand dollars.
Insensitive people cause others embarrassment.

Subject/Verb/Direct Object/Objective Complement
The team elected Jasper captain.
Arthur had his nose broken.

Subject/Linking Verb/Noun
Time is money.
College can be a grind.

Subject/Linking Verb/Adjective
Jan is beautiful.
Taxes are eternal.

The basic patterns are very useful. Without them, you couldn't express your thoughts at all. Nevertheless, if you limit your expression to the basic patterns, your writing will become monotonous. And if your readers are not kept interested, the act of reading will become a chore, or worse, a torture. To keep your readers' attention, you must add art to function and make your sentences pleasing to read. Consider, for example, the following passage. It is made up entirely of basic patterns of the simple sentence.

> The Greco-Roman civilization was efficient. It was productive. It was intelligent. It was tasteful. It was literate. Except in bad reigns, it was filled with spiritual and personal liberties. It was in most ways the greatest success in social living that our Western world has seen. Far more people could read and write in A.D. 150 than in 1550. Perhaps more people could read and write in A.D. 150 than in 1750 and 1850. Schools were nearly everywhere. Europe was filled with books and libraries. So was northern Africa. So was Egypt. The Near East was, too. There was free movement of thought. Over thousands of square miles the travelling teachers moved. They went from city to city. So did the philosophers and orators. The religious and social propagandists did, too. They were all freely explaining. And they were eloquently disputing.

Now that passage is technically correct, and it contains a great deal of significant detail. Yet it leaves much to be desired. Something is missing in it. It is a chore to read. Compare that passage with the following.

> Efficient, productive, intelligent, tasteful, literate, and, except in bad reigns, filled with spiritual and personal liberties, [the Greco-Roman] civilization was in most ways the greatest success in social living that our Western world has seen. Far more people could read and write in A.D. 150 than in 1550, or perhaps in 1750 and 1850. Schools were nearly everywhere. Europe and northern Africa and Egypt and the Near East were filled with books and libraries. There was free movement of thought. Over thousands of square miles, from city to city, moved the travelling teachers, the philosophers and orators, the religious and social propagandists—all freely explaining and eloquently disputing.[1]

This passage has the same material as the first and essentially the same order of ideas. Yet it is more enjoyable to read because it is written in a more mature style. Such a style, as you will see, is not difficult to learn.

Coordination and Subordination

Coordination and subordination are methods of combining two or more simple sentences into a single sentence unit. Coordination leaves each of the original sentence units grammatically independent of the others. That is, it leaves each capable of standing alone as a complete thought. Subordination, on the other hand, makes one or more of the original sentence units dependent on one or more of the others. The following examples further clarify this distinction:

Simple Sentences

The United States should not permit itself to be treated as a doormat by other nations. Also, it should not stand idly by while the Soviet Union nibbles away at the rest of the world.

Revisions

The United States should not permit itself to be treated as a doormat by other nations, nor should it stand idly by while the Soviet Union nibbles away at the rest of the world. (*Coordination*—each of the two sentence units could stand alone as a complete thought.)

Simple Sentences	Revisions
He didn't get the job. He made a very poor impression on the interviewer.	He didn't get the job because he made a very poor impression on the interviewer. (*Subordination*—the word *because* makes the second clause incapable of standing alone as a complete thought.)
I've wasted enough time this term. From here on I'm going to be a model student.	I've wasted enough time this term; from here on I'm going to be a model student. (*Coordination*)
The twins were sleeping soundly. Meanwhile their brother Tim got up, tiptoed to the kitchen, and ate the rest of the cake.	While the twins were sleeping soundly, their brother Tim got up, tiptoed to the kitchen, and ate the rest of the cake. (*Subordination*)

Sometimes a group of sentences may be combined in two or more ways. For example, you may have to choose between coordination and subordination. Your choice in such cases should reflect both the meaning you intend your words to convey and the need for variety at that point in your composition. Here is an example of a group of sentences offering such choices:

Simple Sentences	Revisions
The game seemed out of reach for the visiting team. Then in the final minute and a half they scored six unanswered baskets to win by a single point.	The game seemed out of reach for the visiting team, but then in the final minute and a half they scored six unanswered baskets to win by a single point. (*Coordination*) **or** Although the game seemed out of reach for the visiting team, in the final minute and a half they scored six unanswered baskets to win by a single point. (*Subordination*)

In addition to being used individually, coordination and subordination may also be used together, as the following examples illustrate:

Simple Sentences	Revisions
A teacher sometimes praises a student for a job well done. This builds the student's confidence. It also motivates other students to do their best.	When a teacher praises a student for a job well done, it not only builds the student's confidence; it also motivates other students to do their best. (The *when* clause is subordinate; the other clauses are coordinate.)
Some people do all their own car repairs. I don't do any. I can't tell a fan belt from a fuel pump.	Some people do all their own car repairs, but I don't do any because I can't tell a fan belt from a fuel pump. (The first two clauses are coordinate; the one beginning with *because* is subordinate.)

Exercises

Combine each of the following groups of sentences using coordination and/or subordination.

1. We must address the problem and at least make an effort to solve it. Otherwise it will grow in size and complexity. In time it will do irreparable harm.
2. I've had my fill of listening to him boast about his accomplishments. I've also had my fill of seeing him misuse other people. From now on I'm avoiding him.
3. Calling long-distance is a good cure for loneliness. However, it isn't recommended for those on a budget. Time, as the saying goes, is money.
4. My sister bought a new car last year. She paid as much for it as my parents paid for their house. They bought the house twenty years ago.
5. A series of short sentences seems choppy. A series of long sentences, on the other hand, can seem formidable. Writers who wish to be read avoid both extremes. They strive for variety of sentence length.

Expanding Your Sentences

The second important skill in composing sentences is the skill of expanding basic sentence patterns. This is done by adding words to them. Let's begin our consideration of this process by clarifying three important terms: base clause, free modifiers, and texture.

The *base clause* is the main unit of a sentence. It appears in any of the five forms detailed at the beginning of this chapter (page 220). *Free modifiers* are any words, phrases, or clauses that can be set off from the base clause by punctuation. They are sometimes related to the subject of the base clause and sometimes to the verb. *Texture* refers to the number of free modifiers present in a sentence. If relatively few free modifiers are present, the texture is said to be *thin*; if many, *dense*.

Let's now examine several sentences and see how these terms apply.

Base Clause	*The old man wheezed each breath laboriously.*
Base Clause with one free modifier; texture, thin	*The old man wheezed each breath laboriously, a rattling noise providing rhythmic accompaniment.*
Base Clause with numerous free modifiers; texture, dense	*His body frail, gray, and lifeless, his head barely denting the mattress,* the old man wheezed each breath laboriously, *a rattling noise providing rhythmic accompaniment and signalling that the end was near.*

Free modifiers may be added to any one of three places—before the base clause, within the base clause, or after the base clause. In sentences with a very rich texture they are frequently found in all three places. Here are some examples of the modification that can be used in each place. (The base clause in each case is italicized.)

Modification before the Base Clause

Suddenly, before anyone in the car realized what was happening, *the driver slumped over the wheel and veered off the road into the ditch.*

With heart pounding and eyes darting nervously from left to right, *Jennifer entered the darkened hallway.*

Intent on impressing the girl, *he sucked in his stomach and flexed his muscles.*

The moment he was handed the letter, *he knew the news was bad.*

Modification within the Base Clause

He thought to himself, tentatively at first, and then with increasing conviction, *that she had cheated him.*

The economy, which every candidate for high office has a plan to control, *may very well be uncontrollable.*

Professional tennis players, whose media coverage (like their earnings) has increased dramatically during the last decade, *enjoy a celebrity once reserved for rock stars.*

The party, unless I am mistaken, *is closed to everyone but dormitory residents.*

Modification after the Base Clause

The three sisters left home at the same time—Jane to get married, Agnes to join the Navy, and Marie to study law.

He dribbled the basketball the length of the wet concrete court, water splashing up with every bounce.

He wore a blue three-piece suit that looked as if it had come from a charity bin.

Some say the signs of our society's demise are already clear—the failure of education to provide basic intellectual skills; the lack of regard for craftsmanship among workers in business and industry; and the inability of government to find real solutions to the problems of unemployment, inflation, and Latin American unrest.

Down the block from my house is a park with an Olympic-size swimming pool, eight tennis courts, and twelve acres of picnic area with tree-lined walks, fireplaces, and picnic tables.

On that evening she began her relationship with cocaine, a relationship that would cost her tens of thousands of dollars, a career, two marriages, and her self-respect, a relationship from which she is only now, a decade later, beginning to escape.

Although free modifiers may be placed in any or all of the three positions in a sentence, they are most frequently placed at the end. The typical base clause used by professional writers is general or abstract and is followed by free modifiers that add specific, concrete detail. The resulting sentence is called a *cumulative sentence.*

A Strategy for Expanding Sentences

An effective way to decide when and how to expand your sentences is to ask appropriate questions about them, the kinds of questions an interested person might ask to obtain more information. Here are some examples of this questioning strategy:

Base Clause	*The left fielder caught the fly ball.*
Appropriate Questions	How deep was he in left field? Did he have to move to the ball? How exactly did he catch it? What did he do after he caught it?
Resulting Sentence	After racing back almost to the left center-field wall and leaping high in the air, *the left fielder caught the fly ball* with a stabbing motion, then rifled the ball to second base to catch the runner for a double play.
Base Clause	*Sally could be a world-class runner.*
Appropriate Questions	What talents does she have that suggest this conclusion? Are there any conditions she will have to meet in order to realize her potential?
Resulting Sentence	A gifted performer with a long, loping stride, unusual stamina, and a formidable finishing kick, *Sally could be a world-class runner* if she would accept the difficult regimen required for successful competition at that level.
Base Clause	*Three deer walked into the open meadow.*
Appropriate Questions	How exactly did they walk? Were they bucks or does? Did they seem afraid? If so, why?
Resulting Sentence	*Three deer*, a buck and two does, *walked* noiselessly *into the open meadow*, listening and sniffing cautiously, their senses sharpened by a week of shotgun blasts, ready to dart for the safety of the woods at the first hint of danger.

Exercises

Select five of the following sentences and expand each using the strategy explained in the preceding pages. You may insert modification before, within, or after the base clause, or (if appropriate) in all three places. Read the resulting sentences aloud to be sure they are neither awkward nor confusing.

> The divorce was bitter.
> We walked quietly along the deserted beach.
> Hockey is a violent sport.
> The arms race between the United States and Russia frightens me.
> He sat in the church and prayed.
> We argued about whether the drinking age should be raised.
> They met under unusual circumstances.
> He sat thinking of his wedding vows.
> She promised her mother she would study medicine.
> "A fool and his money are soon parted."
> I love to ski.
> The race was disappointing.
> Being alone can be painful.
> Agnes gave Charlie her pen.
> Betty dyed her hair brown.
> The food tasted awful.
> Peace of mind must be earned.
> Few dentists work painlessly.
> Swimming is an excellent form of exercise.
> I hate losing.
> Rationalizing is a sign of insecurity.
> The best part of being in love is the sharing.
> Failing is no fun.
> She jogs five miles every day.
> My car stopped.
> The sign said "10% discount for cash."
> Blind dates are risky.
> We mustn't forget the persecuted people of the world.
> The two boys were led to the principal's office.

Maintaining Clarity

As you move beyond basic sentence patterns to combined and expanded patterns, many of your sentences will become longer. Moreover, the relationships between the parts of those sentences will grow more complicated. This will increase the danger of lapses in coherence and will necessitate your taking steps to maintain clarity. Parallel structure is an invaluable aid in such situations.

Parallel structure is a kind of repetition. However, it is not repetition of words, but repetition of grammatical form. The kinds of parallelism range from the simple pairing of two or more adjectives, nouns, verbs, or adverbs to the more complex repetition of phrase or clause structure. Here are just a few examples of parallel structure:

Parallel Adjectives	The creative person is not only *imaginative and flexible* but *conscientious and persevering*.
Parallel Nouns and Past-tense Verbs	Whenever she entered a room, *conversation stopped*, *heads turned*, and *eyes followed* her every movement.
Parallel Gerund Phrases	*Getting up late in the morning, relaxing on the beach in the forenoon, playing tennis in the afternoon,* and *dancing until late at night*—that's my idea of a vacation.
Parallel Adjective Clauses	This is the roommate *who uses my aftershave lotion and never replaces it, who gets my clothes dirty and never cleans them, who borrows my money and never repays it*.

Parallel structure helps you maintain sentence clarity in two ways. First, its consistency of form provides the reader with signposts that show the relationships among the parts of the sentence. Here are two examples of this effect.

The main elements of parallel structure here are "staggering," "bending," "slogging," and "driving." But there are other elements, too—"blue-lipped," "covered," and "chilled"; "from

As I listened to those songs of the glee club, in memory's eye I could see those staggering columns of the First World War, bending under soggy packs, on many a weary march from dripping dusk to drizzling dawn, slogging ankle deep through the mire of shell-shocked roads to form grimly for the attack, blue-lipped, covered with sludge and mud, chilled by the wind and rain; driving home to their objective, and for many, to the judgment seat of God.[2]

Let the word go forth from this time and place, to friend and foe alike, that the torch has been passed to a new generation of Americans, born in this century, tempered by war, disciplined by a hard and bitter peace, proud of our ancient heritage, and unwilling to witness or permit the slow undoing of those human rights to which this nation has always been committed, and to which we are committed today, at home and around the world.[3]

dripping dusk to drizzling dawn"; and "to their objective," "to the judgment seat of God."

The main elements of parallelism here are "born," "tempered," "disciplined," "proud," and "unwilling." Minor elements include "friend and foe," "witness or permit," and "at home and around the world."

Second, parallel structure permits the expression of ideas in balanced form, as these examples illustrate:

The more I watch him humiliate his wife, *the more I appreciate* the importance of respect in marriage.

The greater the Russians' success in interfering in the affairs of other countries, *the more formidable the threat* to peace and stability in the world.

It's naive to expect to experience *the thrill of victory* without ever tasting *the agony of defeat*.

Either she'll begin living up to her end of the agreement we made at the beginning of the semester, *or I'll stop living up to mine*.

Arthur is *not only the handsomest and best dressed* boy I've ever dated *but also the most considerate*.

Here is a passage that demonstrates both effects of parallel structure; that is, it makes clear the relationships among the ideas and presents the ideas in balanced form.

The tragedy of life is not *in the hurt* to a man's name or even *in the fact* of death itself. The tragedy of life is *in what dies* inside a man while he lives—the death *of genuine feeling*, the death *of inspired response*, the death *of* the *awareness* that makes it possible to feel *the pain* or *the glory* of other men in oneself. [Albert] Schweitzer's aim was not *to dazzle an age* but *to awaken it, to make it comprehend that moral splendor is* part of the gift of life, and *that each man has* unlimited strength *to feel human oneness* and *to act upon it*. He proved that although a man *may have no jurisdiction over the fact* of his existence, he *can hold supreme command over the meaning* of existence for him. Thus, no man need fear death; he need fear only that he may die without having known his greatest power—the power of his free will to give his life for others.[4]

Exercises

Each of the statements below expresses an idea that can be more effectively expressed using parallel structure. Rewrite each, making it more effective. (Where two or more sentences are present, consider combining them.)

1. If you can't let me be free, then you might as well kill me.
2. When you have a cold, you should eat more than you usually do, but with a fever you're better off not eating at all.
3. If you don't try to do things, you have no chance of succeeding.
4. I'd rather you do what I tell you to do than have you imitate me.
5. If you don't like the deal I'm offering you, you don't have to accept it.
6. He left town a villain, but when he returned he was considered to be heroic.
7. She was born in Chicago but spent her childhood and teenage years in New York and went to England to attend college.
8. That family survived poverty; they also had to overcome prejudice; and personal tragedy was another obstacle they met successfully.
9. An educated person should be able to get beyond his personal feelings and make decisions objectively. Deferring judgment until he has considered evidence and choosing the course of action that is most beneficial or least harmful are also important qualities he should have.
10. A teacher's greatest reward is to see students learn that hardships can be overcome, it is worthwhile to put forth effort, and they can make succeeding a habit.

Varying Word Order

We have seen how you can relieve monotony in your sentences and make them more interesting by combining and expanding the basic sentence patterns. A third way to ensure that your writing is enjoyable to read is by adding variety to your word order. Not every word order, of course, is acceptable, because not every word order makes sense. Consider the sentence "I will miss her when she's gone." It can also be written, "When she's gone, I will miss her." But "Gone her I will when miss she's" is absurd, and "Miss her I will when she's gone" would only work in certain contexts. So effective variation of word order demands great sensitivity to language.*

The list of all possible pattern variations would be too long to include here. Nevertheless, we can identify some of the most common variations on the basic patterns.

Invert Subject–Verb Order

Original	Revision
The stranger came softly.	Softly came the stranger.
The security of the world depends on the restraint of a handful of political leaders.	On the restraint of a handful of political leaders depends the security of the world.
The team charged onto the field chanting "We're number one."	Onto the field charged the team chanting "We're number one."

Open with a Prepositional Phrase

Original	Revision
Few teachers in my high school gave regular homework assignments.	In my high school few teachers gave regular homework assignments.
He tried with all his strength to resist the muggers.	With all his strength he tried to resist the muggers.
I really believed, for one brief moment, that she cared for me.	For one brief moment, I really believed that she cared for me.

Open with an Adjective

Original	Revision
The girl was dejected and sat in the corner by herself all evening.	Dejected, the girl sat in the corner by herself all evening.

---

*For a discussion of the errors caused by insensitivity to language, see "Faulty Modification" in the handbook.

Original

The driver, weak from his accident, crawled out of the car and stumbled across the highway.

The challenger, taller and more muscular than the champion, seemed a good bet to take the title.

Revision

Weak from his accident, the driver crawled out of the car and stumbled across the highway.

Taller and more muscular than the champion, the challenger seemed a good bet to take the title.

Open with an Adverb

Original

My grandfather usually visits us for the holidays.

The best time to begin saving money is now.

We entered the haunted house cautiously, looking quickly from side to side and listening intently.

Revision

Usually my grandfather visits us for the holidays.

Now is the best time to begin saving money.

Cautiously we entered the house, looking quickly from side to side and listening intently.

Open with a Participle

Original

Mrs. Murphy, outraged at the implicit insult, shouted an obscenity.

The big dog edged toward me threateningly, its head lowered and teeth bared.

Agnes, dazzling in her floor-length sequined gown, drew the attention of every man in the room.

Revision

Outraged at the implicit insult, Mrs. Murphy shouted an obscenity.

Head lowered and teeth bared, the big dog edged toward me threateningly.

Dazzling in her floor-length sequined gown, Agnes drew the attention of every man in the room.

Open with an Infinitive Phrase

Original

He scaled the side of a five-story building to prove his courage to his roommates.

Her dream is to become president of the United States.

It is both foolish and dangerous to try to lose all that weight in just a few weeks.

Revision

To prove his courage to his roommates, he scaled the side of a five-story building.

To become president of the United States is her dream.

To try to lose all that weight in just a few weeks is both foolish and dangerous.

Change the Order of Clauses in a Complex Sentence

Original

We plan to travel to Europe this summer, if we can afford to go.

She did well in that course, even though she lacked the background for it.

Try studying when all else fails.

Revision

If we can afford to go, we plan to travel to Europe this summer.

Even though she lacked the background for that course, she did well in it.

When all else fails, try studying.

Exercises

1. Each of the following sentences is acceptable as written. But the word order could be varied to relieve monotony and create additional interest. Rewrite each sentence using a different word order.
    a. The city of Oneonta, New York, sits in a scenic valley in the Catskill Mountains midway between Albany and Binghamton.
    b. The bright sunlight made her hair shine as she stood before the class with her head tilted toward the window.
    c. Just like the three famous monkeys, they heard no evil, saw no evil, and spoke no evil.
    d. She would have had a 4.0 index last semester if she hadn't gotten a B in Health.
    e. His thoughts were filled with memories of her.

f. Agatha, confused about the purpose of the assignment, asked the teacher to explain further.
g. He called his girlfriend every night to be sure she wasn't out with someone else.
h. He was elated over his acceptance into graduate school and treated himself to filet mignon and a bottle of champagne.
i. She approached her father fearfully, expecting to be punished for borrowing the car without permission.

2. Using the techniques of sentence composition you learned in this chapter, rewrite any five of the following passages, making them effective and pleasurable to read.

    a. Jupiter has four moons. Their names are Io, Europa, Ganymede, and Callisto. Galileo discovered them. This happened in 1610. They were the first bodies in the solar system to be discovered by telescope.

    b. The little old man lies in bed. He is propped up by pillows. His face is pale. Wrinkles etch his cheeks. His arms are as thin as vines. They extend precariously from his body. His lips are trembling. He speaks to the nurse. His voice is barely audible. "May I have some orange juice?"

    c. John F. Kennedy was riding in a motorcade. He was heading for a speaking engagement. Lee Harvey Oswald shot and killed him. This occurred in Dallas, Texas, on November 22, 1963.

    d. Polar bears are huge and powerful. They have a keen sense of smell. They are much faster-moving than they appear. They are agile in and out of the water. They are excellent predators.

    e. Charles Atlas' real name was Angelo Siciliano. He was a ninety-seven-pound weakling in real life. He was beaten up by another boy. Then he became obsessed with physical strength. He watched a tiger in a zoo. He marveled at its sleek power. He decided that its conditioning was achieved by pitting muscle against muscle. Thus Atlas developed his body-building method. He called it dynamic tension. Its present, more scientific name is isometrics.

    f. The most likable kids aren't always the best looking. They aren't always the most intelligent. They aren't always the best dressed. They aren't always the wealthiest. They are not too self-absorbed. They have some concern for others. They try to give at least as much as they demand from others. They practice understanding. They respect others and forgive others' faults and offenses. They're honest and

Revising for Sentence Style 235

forthright. Yet they're tactful too. They aren't two-faced. They try to be positive and constructive in their outlook. They make others feel good.

g. Power over words gives a person a sense of confidence. That sense of confidence projects to others. It projects as competency. Power over words helps a person overcome tension and frustration, too. It does this by allowing an adequate outlet for thoughts and feelings. It also aids the person's understanding. It does this by providing a means of dealing with complexity and confusion.

h. On summer days my brothers and I played cowboys and Indians. We played from breakfast until bedtime. We stalked one another around the house. We also stalked one another through neighboring fields. We tried desperately to watch in every direction at once. We wanted to prevent being caught unaware. We exulted when we caught someone else. For then we could fire our guns. And we could shout "Bang! Bang! You're dead."

i. Yesterday I was in biology lab for what seemed an eternity. I peered into my microscope. I was trying desperately to see a group of cells. They were intent on hiding from me. I turned the knobs one way and then another. That only worsened the image. The instructor came around and asked, "Does everyone see them now?" I nodded my head dishonestly. I felt foolish. I assumed all my classmates saw the cells. Later I found out most of them had seen no more than I.

j. The gang approached the intruder. They moved slowly. They encircled him. They menaced him. Some were swinging clubs. Others fingered switchblades. All hurled taunts at him. Suddenly the leader shouted "Now!" Then they descended on him. They pummeled him. They slashed at him. His screams filled the night air. Then the screams stopped abruptly.

k. The price of gasoline rose dramatically from 1978 to 1980. It more than doubled. Every driver felt the strain. But it was especially punishing to older people on fixed incomes. It was also especially punishing to the poor. The oil companies, however, prospered. They showed record profits during the period.

l. My psychology professor is a spellbinder. To look at him, though, you'd never guess that he was. He is quite short. He stands about five feet seven. He seems very shy. He dresses like a banker. He wears conservative three-piece suits. And he always has a white handkerchief in his jacket pocket. But all that changes in the classroom. He sheds the jacket. He rolls up his sleeves. He loosens his tie. His voice seems to deepen. It also gets louder and more dramatic. His dark eyes flash with enthusiasm. A torrent of words bursts forth from him. The words are precise and vivid. He enunciates them flawlessly. He never once refers to his notes. And fifty minutes pass in an instant.

m. The clock showed seven seconds. Our team trailed 62 to 63. The referee waved in the substitute. It was Splinters O'Hara. He hadn't played a minute all year. Now the league championship was at stake. The opposing player stood on the foul line. He bounced the ball again and again. He raised it above his head and shot. It bounced off the rim and into the hands of our center. He tossed the ball to one of the guards. The guard dribbled once. Then he spotted a teammate alone up court. It was Splinters. The crowd screamed wildly. The ball whizzed the length of the court. Splinters caught it. Two seconds remained on the clock. He bent his knees. He jumped up. He released the ball. It went up and up and . . . over the backboard.

n. Sex discrimination means unfairness to individuals. It also means a denial of Constitutional guarantees. But it means more. It means a loss of half the talents our society possesses. It means the loss of half the wisdom. It means the loss of half the ingenuity. It means the loss of half the creativity. It means the loss of half the leadership. All of industry is impoverished by that loss. So is all of government. And so are all of the arts and sciences. Each of us is victimized. The old and the young are victimized. The rich and the poor are victimized. Men and women are victimized.

Revising Sentences for Exactness

Exactness means precision in choosing words that will convey your thought with complete accuracy. To be exact would not be a difficult task if language were fixed and stable. But it is not. As long as it continues to be used, it changes. That is, some words die and others are born. And between their birth and death most words undergo constant, though often subtle, shifts in meaning. Over a long period of time such shifts can be significant. The English language of a thousand years ago must be studied as a foreign language. It is impossible for a modern reader to understand even Shakespeare's works fully without the aid of numerous footnotes to explain the different meanings many words and expressions had in the late sixteenth and early seventeenth centuries. And words we take for granted today—words like *elevator, penicillin, television, movies*—would have been meaningless to Shakespeare and his contemporaries.

Invention and discovery are two obvious causes of changes in language. But there are other causes as well. Terms like *moon shot, nuclear reactor, cold war,* and *McCarthyism* owe their existence to particular historical events. Still another cause is the shift in people's awareness and knowledge and interest and attitude toward things. The word *heretic* used to say something negative about the person it referred to. Now it says something worse about the person who uses it to describe someone else. Our modern tendency to place the individual's right of choice above any doctrine is responsible for this change. *Pink* used to be just a color; now it is a reference to socialist or communist beliefs. A *gay* person was once a happy, carefree individual; a *gay* person today is a homosexual.

Two Kinds of Meaning

In revising your sentences for exactness, you must be sensitive to the meaning of your words. There are two kinds of meaning: denotative meaning and connotative meaning. *Denotative* meaning is the direct, explicit, literal meaning of a word. Many words have similar meanings, but few, if any, have exactly the same denotative meaning. For example, *conscious, aware,* and *cognizant* are often used interchangeably. Yet there are subtle differences among them. *Conscious* refers to an inner realization, *aware* to sensory realization, and *cognizant* to reasoning about sensory realization. Similarly, the words *unbelief* and *disbelief* both signify not believing. But *unbelief* refers to simple absence of belief, and *disbelief* to refusal to believe.

Connotative meaning is implied or associative meaning, the favorable or unfavorable aura that surrounds denotative meaning. For example, *thrifty* and *stingy* have similar denotative meanings. But *thrifty* implies a positive kind of frugality and *stingy* a negative kind. This is true to such an extent that thrift is regarded as a virtue, stinginess a vice! Similarly, to say someone *planned* what she did is a compliment, whereas to say she *schemed* is an insult. Though the denotative meanings are quite similar, the connotative meanings differ greatly. A *statesman* and a *politician* are both engaged in the same line of work, but the former term is more favorable.

Not all terms have strong connotations, however. Sometimes a term has a relatively neutral one. Consider, for instance, these sentences:

George *manages* the records at Hillman's Department Store.

George *manipulates* the records at Hillman's Department Store.

George *handles* the records at Hillman's Department Store.

The word *manage* has a slightly favorable connotation, suggesting competency. The word *manipulate* is strongly negative, to the point of implying some criminal activity. But the word *handle* is almost neutral.

How Inexactness Occurs

Your revision for exactness is likely to be most effective if you are alert to the common enemies of exactness—words that sound alike, empty expressions, and vogue expressions. Let's examine each more closely.

The first great enemy of exactness is confusion between words that look or sound alike but have widely different meanings. The writer who uses *censer* (a vessel containing incense, used in worship) or *censure* (to disapprove or condemn) when she means *censor* (to suppress something believed to be objectionable) is not likely to impress educated readers. If she says *home wrecker* (one who breaks up others' marriages) instead of *house wrecker* (one who demolishes houses), she may cause considerable misunderstanding. And if she makes more than a few such mistakes—say, for example, confusing *ingenious* and *ingenuous*, or *counsel* and *council*—she will not only jar her readers' sensibilities, break their concentration, and distract them; she will probably lose any confidence they may have had in her and kill their interest in her idea. (See the handbook for a glossary of commonly confused words.)

The second enemy of exactness is the *overworked* or *empty expression.* Some examples of overworked expressions (commonly called clichés) are *couldn't care less, burn the midnight oil, a crying shame, last but not least, sink or swim, toe the line, make your mark, low man on the totem pole, sneaking suspicion, the other side of the coin, truth is stranger than fiction, a fight to the finish,* and *up for it* (as in "The Bloomville Bombers are really up for today's game against the Bovina Bonzos"). Originally such expressions were fresh and vivid. The problem is that most people have heard them so often in so many contexts that they have lost their power to illuminate any particular context.

Empty expressions are substitutes for exactness. Whenever you say something is *cute* or *great* or *good* or *pretty good* or *really good* or *bad* or *lovely* or *beautiful* or *wonderful* or *fine*, you have not described anything. You have merely pretended to describe, given a broad clue to a description you might have given. Now there are occasions when that is enough, when time or space do not allow more precise and meaningful statement. But usually it is not enough and is the result of laziness rather than necessity. Similarly, when you speak of *stuff* and *things*, you are identifying only in the broadest and least helpful sense. Writing that is filled with such generalities cheats readers and, not infrequently, bores them.

A special kind of overworked and frequently empty expression is the *vogue expression*. There is a fashion in words and it works much like fashion in clothing. That is, once it appears and becomes "in," unthinking people immediately adopt it. Some expressions that have recently been in vogue are *go with the flow, I hear you* (meaning "I more or less agree with you"), *ego trip, mellow, in touch with yourself, wasted, getting your head together, unreal* (as in "That movie was unreal"), *I know where you're coming from, up front* (as in "Be real up front with me about our relationship"), *put it all together, hang-up, relevant, meaningful, turns me on, uptight, the name of the game, laid back, right on, dig it, I can't relate to it, into* (as in "I'm heavily into dominoes lately"), and *bottom line.* Writers who use such expressions in their writing risk anesthetizing their readers.

Three Important Choices

The three basic choices you must make to achieve exactness in your sentences concern level of diction, degree of clarity, and degree of concreteness and specificity.

Level of Diction   There are three broad levels of diction: *standard written*, *standard conversational*, and *colloquial*, or *slang*.* All three have their place and are appropriate when used there. The line between the first two was until recently quite sharply drawn. But the lessening of formality in all areas of modern living has brought a tendency toward coversational diction in writing. The result has been a blurring of the traditional distinction. Many respected writers today use a very loose, casual, informal style. Yet there remain occasions in which formality is preferred. Let's consider some examples of each style:

Standard Written	Standard Conversational
purchase	buy ("I plan to buy a car.")
demonstrate	show ("She will show you how.")
approximately	about ("It has been about a year.")
inquire	ask ("Tell him to ask in a letter.")
complete	finish ("We will finish the job.")
assist	help ("Can you help us?")
difficult	hard ("The course was hard.")
prepare	do ("I will do my tax return.")
obtain	get ("Did you get permission?")
forward	send ("Please send me a copy.")
contribute	give ("She gives a lot to charity.")
sufficient	enough ("Enough time has elapsed.")
initial	first ("The first application is easy.")
do not	don't ("Please don't be late.")
cannot	can't ("They can't help us.")
should not	shouldn't ("We shouldn't go.")

There is no absolute rule as to when conversational diction is permissible in writing. The best guide is this approach—when the piece of writing is formal (a scholarly article, a business letter to someone you don't know), use standard written diction; at most other times prefer the simpler and more economical conversational diction.

---

*Since colloquialisms and slang are seldom appropriate in writing, except in dialogue, they are not covered here.

The diction in each of the following examples is appropriate to the occasion and audience. Notice that the first is formal without being stuffy or inflated, and the second is informal without being chummy or impolite.

> Because I have had some difficulty obtaining the information necessary to complete form 32986S, as you requested, I will be unable to submit it by November 30. I therefore request a one-month extension of the deadline.
>
> —from a letter to the Internal Revenue Service

> I've had some trouble getting the information necessary to finish the form you asked for, so I won't be able to send it by November 30. I'd appreciate your giving me an extra month to do it.
>
> —from a letter to a business colleague

Degree of Clarity   Normally you will want your writing to be as clear as possible. In most situations *ambiguity* (openness to more than one interpretation) is a fault. Yet there are situations where ambiguity is intended. And where this is so, you should choose wording that retains just the degree of ambiguity you wish. For example, in the sentence "Bertha did not at that time show malice," the key words are "at that time." The sentence is open to the interpretation that at other times, perhaps usually, Bertha does show malice. In other words, the sentence is ambiguous. (Whether this ambiguity is desirable depends on the writer's intention.)

Let's consider another example. Suppose you are asked to supply a reference for someone who has worked for you. You find little good to say about him, and yet you want to be as charitable as possible, consistent with honesty. One of the questions you have to answer concerns his competency, a quality you did not associate with his work. You might write something like this: "I have never found Blair to be incompetent." Now that speaks to the question. But it speaks ambiguously. What exactly does it mean? That Blair is competent? Perhaps. But not necessarily. It could mean, instead, "I have never *found* him to be incompetent, but I've strongly suspected him of being so. His work certainly leaves a lot to be desired."

A caution is necessary here. The careful reader will recognize ambiguity and realize you are consciously or unconsciously avoiding an issue. So unless you have good reason to be ambiguous, strive to be clear.

Degree of Concreteness and Specificity *Concrete* and *specific* words are often more precise and vivid than are *abstract* and *general* words. Abstract words deal with large concepts that cannot be touched, seen, or heard. For example, *liberty* is an abstract term; *freedom of speech as expressed in the U.S. Constitution* is a concrete phrase. General words embrace all the members of a class or group rather than particular ones. Thus *human beings* is a general term; *Americans*, a more specific one; *Irish-Americans*, still more specific; and *James Murphy*, very specific.

There are many times when you will want to speak about abstract and general matters. If that is your purpose, there is certainly nothing wrong with it.* The problem is that most of us tend to speak more abstractly than we really need to or intend to. It's often easier to use abstract terms than to think of exactly what we want to say. Careful writers, however, are aware of this tendency and try to check it. They strive to get just the right degree of concreteness and specificity in their writing. Here are some examples of varying degrees of concreteness and specificity:

> From the General and Abstract ... to the Specific and Concrete
>
> animal > domestic animal > house pet > dog > collie > seven-year-old female collie
>
> man > Oriental man > Chinese man > young Chinese man > twenty-year-old Chinese man
>
> city > New York City > Queens County > Jackson Heights > the corner of 82nd St. and Roosevelt Ave.
>
> car > General Motors car > Chevrolet > 1977 Chevrolet Nova > dark blue 1977 Chevrolet Nova with a cream vinyl top

It should be obvious that in each of the above cases the more specific and concrete reference makes it easier for the readers to visualize what you are speaking of. Such references, then, make your writing more real to them. This is true not only of the nouns you use but also of the verbs. For even the smallest, most mundane of activities there are numerous verbs. You don't have to say someone *put* food into her mouth. You can say she *shoveled* or *crammed* or *stuffed* or *slopped* it in (assuming the movement was unmannerly). Nor need you be limited to saying a baseball player *hit* the ball. You can say he *slapped* it, *punched* it, *slugged* it,

---

*It is quite common to move back and forth between levels of generality and abstractness—to move, for example, from the concept *liberty* to specific cases that demonstrate it and then back to the abstract concept again.

swatted it, *clouted* it, *stroked* it, *belted* it, *pounded* it, *whacked* it, *walloped* it, or *tapped* it.

The same principle applies to adjectives and adverbs. There is a rich choice of precise words to select from. With a little effort and imagination, you can transform *funny* into *droll, farcical, amusing, ludicrous, laughable, comical, rollicking, hilarious, diverting, jocular, witty, humorous, entertaining,* or, if delicacy is not important, *gut-busting.* Similarly, *hot* can become *blistering, boiling, sweltering, sultry, muggy, suffocating, steamy, wilting,* or *scorching.* And *slowly* can become *ploddingly, deliberately, leisurely, laggardly, haltingly, stumblingly.* And so on.

Your word choice should, of course, depend on the context of your writing. You cannot base your selection merely on the appeal of the word itself. Rather, the word must fit the composition form, the controlling idea, and the audience. Obviously these are complex considerations, and successful handling of them will depend on your skill in writing. But that skill will come to you if you make your choices with care.

Exercises

1. Look up each word in each of the following sets of words in a good dictionary. Note and explain any significant differences in denotation or connotation.

    reserved, secretive, aloof
    loquacious, garrulous, talkative, verbose
    clever, crafty, wily, astute
    persevering, stubborn, adamant, inflexible
    eccentric, weird, strange, uncommon
    comrade, colleague, collaborator, accomplice
    obedient, servile, slavish, fawning
    develop, invent, create, discover, find
    stupid, ignorant, unschooled, dense

2. The following sets of words are often confused with each other. Look up each word as necessary. Then explain the differences in meaning.

    misplaced, displaced
    practical, practicable
    phase, faze

raze, raise

complement, compliment

misdirected, undirected

ascent, assent

misinformed, uninformed

dissent, descent

dying, dyeing

respectfully, respectively

credible, creditable

3. Each of the following sentences is written in standard written English. Each would be appropriate in relatively formal writing, but not in informal writing. Rewrite each, making it suitable for informal prose. Be sure to avoid chumminess.
   a. Senator Smith's aversion to debate may be prompted more by his ignorance of the issue than by his busy schedule.
   b. Should you fail to respond by July 15, I shall be forced to turn the matter over to my attorney.
   c. I am pleased to recommend John E. Begood for this position without reservation.

4. Each of the following sentences is written in standard conversational English. Each would be appropriate in relatively informal writing, but not in formal writing. Rewrite each, making it suitable for formal prose. Be sure to avoid stuffiness.
   a. I heard you got the promotion you've been hoping for. Congratulations. You really deserve it. And I know you'll be the best regional manager in the company.
   b. I'd like to thank your foundation for the scholarship you gave me. I'm sure I couldn't have attended Splendor University without that $2,000 a year. I'm going to work my hardest to show my appreciation.
   c. We're having a few couples over for dinner next Friday. We hope you and Carol will be able to make it. The time will be 7 P.M.; the dress, casual. Please let us know if you're coming.

5. Each of the following words is rather general and/or abstract. Think of as many more specific/concrete substitutes as you can for each.

walked

ran

sat

Revising for Sentence Style

went

heavy

dirty

said

happily

beautifully

6. Consult the sports pages of a newspaper. Find as many terms as you can that mean either *win* or *beat*. Add any others you can think of to the list.
7. Revise the following passage, making it more interesting by substituting more concrete and/or specific words for the italicized words. You may add or omit words if you wish.

> The night club was *crowded*, the air *hot* and *stale*. *A large* man *entered* the room from the bar. The lights *went off*. Then a spotlight *went on*. The man *walked over* to the stage, *went up* the steps, *picked up* a banjo lying next to a chair, and *sat down hard* on the chair. The *noise* of the crowd *stopped*. Everyone *was watching* the man. He *picked casually* at the banjo a few times, his eyes *looking* around the room, his mouth *closed tightly around* a *well-chewed cigar*. Then he *took* the cigar from his mouth, *placed it gently* on the floor beside him, *took a long breath*, and *began playing* in earnest.

Revising Sentences for Economy

Economy and its related quality, simplicity, have always been recognized as two of the best indicators of competency, excellence, and eloquence in writing. "The language of truth," said Marcellinus Ammianus, fourth-century Roman historian, "is unadorned and always simple." In our own time the message is the same. G. K. Chesterton noted that "long words go rattling by us like long railway trains. We know they are carrying thousands who are too tired or too indolent to walk and think for themselves." Sir Winston Churchill had little patience with linguistic barbarism. On one occasion he delivered this attack on it:

> I hope you have all mastered the official Socialist jargon which our masters, as they call themselves, wish us to learn. You must not use

the word "poor"; they are described as "the lower income group." When it comes to a question of freezing a workman's wages the Chancellor of the Exchequer speaks of "arresting increases in personal income." . . . Sir Stafford Cripps does not like to mention the word "wages," but that is what he means. There is a lovely one about houses and homes. They are in future to be called "accommodation units." I don't know how we are to sing our old song "Home, Sweet Home." [He then began singing.] "Accommodation unit, sweet accommodation unit, there's no place like our accommodation unit." I hope to live to see the British democracy spit all this rubbish from their lips.[5]

H. L. Mencken once wrote this criticism of a well-known economist's writing:

And so it goes, alas, alas, in all his other volumes—a cent's worth of information wrapped in a bale of polysyllables. . . . Words are flung upon words until all recollection that there must be a meaning in them, a ground and excuse for them, is lost. One wanders in a labyrinth of nouns, adjectives, verbs, pronouns, adverbs, prepositions, conjunctions, and participles, most of them swollen and nearly all of them unable to walk. It is difficult to imagine worse English, within the limits of intelligible grammar. It is clumsy, affected, opaque, bombastic, windy, empty. It is without grace or distinction and it is often without the most elementary order. The learned professor gets himself enmeshed in his gnarled sentences like a bull trapped by barbed wire, and his efforts to extricate himself are quite as furious and quite as spectacular. He heaves, he leaps, he writhes; at times he seems to be at the point of yelling for the police. It is a picture to bemuse the vulgar and to give the judicious grief.[6]

Such reactions to inflated and pretentious writing are almost universal (except among those who commit it). The reason for this is not difficult to grasp. Simplicity and economy make writing easier to understand, more accessible to the readers. They save them time and effort in finding the writer's meaning. Moreover, they make it easier for readers to retain the ideas. Memorable writing is always simple, always brief: "The only thing we have to fear is fear itself"; "Ask not what your country can do for you; ask what you can do for your country"; "Brevity is the soul of wit." The Gettysburg Address contains a total of 267 words. Of those, 217—or 81 percent—are words of *one syllable!* And another 32 are two-syllable words.

The Basic Principles

You should not infer from what was said above that words of more than one or two syllables are always to be avoided. Often the word that exactly expresses the thought is a long word—and in such cases it would be foolish to substitute a shorter, less accurate word. But you should, in the words of George Orwell, "never use a long word where a short word will do." If the idea, the audience, or the occasion demands the long word, then go ahead and use it. But prefer the short word wherever it will fit.

Moreover (again quoting Orwell), "Never use a foreign phrase, a scientific word, or a jargon word if you can think of an everyday English equivalent." If you can't think of an equivalent, if the foreign or scientific or jargon word is the only one that fits, then by all means use it. But first look for the simple word.

Similarly, honoring the quality of economy does not require you to write only short sentences or compositions of no more than a paragraph or two. Length by itself is no index of economy. A relatively short piece of writing can be very bloated, whereas an entire volume on so limited a topic as the courtship practices of the earthworm can be admirably brief, given the amount and complexity of information it conveys. You achieve economy by saying whatever you have to say—however much or little—in as few words as possible consistent with your purpose. To do this, eliminate unnecessary words and, wherever possible without sacrificing effectiveness, reduce a clause to a phrase, a phrase to a word.

But what, you may wonder, about the element of flair in your writing? Doesn't a preference for the simple and the brief rule out richness of texture, vividness of description, and the dramatic power that comes from the use of metaphorical language? The answer is no! By trimming off excessive words and bloated phrasing you don't prevent the development of an exciting writing style. Rather, you make such development possible. It is very much like developing your body. Getting rid of the extra pounds you may have acquired is not an obstacle to the development of a stronger and more attractive body—it is one of the necessary first steps in that development.

Three Kinds of Inflatedness

Now let's examine some inflated passages and see how they can be improved by applying the basic principles of simplicity and economy. The first is a letter expressing interest in a job opening.

Dear Mr. Wemple:

With the presentation of these lines, I herewith evidence an occupational interest in the accounting department of Wemple Industries. Realizing that your schedule is a crowded one, I shall endeavor to be concise.

I am a graduate of the Southcentral University's School of Business, having earned the bachelor's degree in accounting. Twelve hours of graduate study were completed at the same institution.

Since earning my degree I have been employed at Amalgamated Acme Corporation as a junior assistant accountant. This position has been a source of considerable gratification to me. However, for a considerable number of years I have nurtured the hope of one day securing employment with a large international corporation; hence, the purpose of these lines.

An opportunity to meet and discuss with you the prospect of my joining the Wemple accounting staff would be most appreciated. Thanking you for the consideration I am sure you will render these lines, I am,

Sincerely yours,
Radley Harper

The problem here is *pretentiousness*. The writer may have meant to sound serious and respectful, but he manages to sound only stuffy. In fact, some of his phrasing is so overly formal ("With the presentation of these lines," "Hence, the purpose of these lines") that it almost makes him seem insincere. How much better his letter would have been had he written it like this:

Dear Mr. Wemple:

I would like to be considered for a position in the accounting department of Wemple Industries. Here are my credentials in brief.

I hold a bachelor's degree in accounting from Southcentral University's School of Business. In addition, I completed twelve hours of graduate study at Southcentral.

Since I graduated, I have worked for Amalgamated Acme Corporation as a junior assistant accountant. The work has been interesting, but for many years I have looked forward to working for a large international corporation like Wemple.

I would appreciate the opportunity to meet with you and discuss the possibility of my joining the Wemple accounting staff.

Sincerely,
Radley Harper

Here is another passage to consider.

> For the period of June through August of last year I was employed at an eating establishment called the Surf Inn for the purpose of getting some experience in my field, which is restaurant management. In view of the fact that I had had no experience prior to that time, I was assigned to do the most menial tasks—that is, those in connection with cleaning the kitchen, washing dishes, and scrubbing pots and pans. The manager, however, made me a promise that in the event that I did a good job, he would give consideration to promoting me to waitress. And he made me a further promise that, in the event that I did a good job as a waitress, he would give consideration to letting me work as hostess during the regular host's day off. These promises gave me encouragement. . . .

The problem here is not pretentiousness. It is simple *wordiness*. Many of the expressions that contain three or four words could be replaced by one or two words. And the unnecessary repetition could be removed. The result would be the following.

> Last summer I worked at a restaurant, the Surf Inn, to get some experience in my field, restaurant management. Because I had no previous experience, I was assigned to cleaning the kitchen, washing dishes, and scrubbing pots and pans. The manager, however, promised that if I did a good job, he would consider promoting me to waitress and maybe even to hostess during the regular host's days off. These promises encouraged me. . . .

In addition to pretentiousness and wordiness is a third common problem, *jargon*, which is the technical terminology used in various fields (law, medicine, the social sciences). The problem is usually compounded by the long, involved sentence structure that often accompanies such terminology. Here is an example of jargon:

> There has come to be associated and blended with the traditional objective that the aim of all pedagogical systems is to stimulate the learner's apprehension of factual and theoretical knowledge and develop his or her cognitive processes, the more recent, sociologically prompted objective of personal adjustment to environment and the development of highly individualized value-focuses. The attendant ascendency of the affective dimension of learning has eroded the position of the cognitive sufficiently as to transmogrify the reality of contemporary education and create certain diriment impediments to effective integration of competing goals in the foreseeable future.

Jargon, unlike pretentiousness and wordiness, can seldom be corrected by changing a word here and a phrase there. Because it is not merely inflated but overly abstract, sometimes to the point of obscurity, it must be rewritten entirely. And particular care must be taken to clarify all obscure parts. Here is a revision of the above passage.

> Traditionally the aim of education was to instill knowledge and develop intellectual skills in students. But in recent years other aims have been pursued, notably helping students adjust to the world around them and choose their own values. The emphasis on *feeling*, however, has so weakened the place of *thought* that the two may not be effectively integrated for some time.

Dealing with Profound Ideas

The best writers have always recognized that a simple, economical style is the best way to deal with any subject—and that includes the most complex and the most subtle of ideas. Profound thoughts, in fact, require simplicity and economy even more than others, because they pose greater challenge to understanding. The more difficult and elusive the thought, the more help the reader needs to capture it. Here is an example of such a profound issue and of an unusually clear presentation of the writer's idea.

> ... The kind of explanation which explains things away may give us something, though at a heavy cost. But you cannot go on "explaining away" for ever; you will find that you have explained explanation itself away. You cannot go on "seeing through" things for ever. The whole point of seeing through something is to see something through it. It is good that the window should be transparent, because the street or garden beyond it is opaque. How [would it be] if you saw through the garden too? It is no use trying to "see through" first principles. If you see through everything, then everything is transparent. But a wholly transparent world is an invisible world. To "see through" all things is the same as not to see.[7]

When reviewing your compositions for economy, keep in mind that the purpose of writing is to communicate thoughts, not to befuddle your readers or to dazzle them with your vocabulary, and make your revisions accordingly.

Revising for Sentence Style

Exercises

1. Examine each of the following passages carefully. Decide whether it suffers from *pretentiousness*, *wordiness*, or *jargon*. Then rewrite it in a simple, economical style. (Remember that jargon usually requires not just minor changes but complete revision.)
   a. The Efficiency Plus Company has been retained by the university to establish a uniform record and perpetuation system. The system will be designed to meet the requirement standards of the state Division of Audit and Control and to further facilitate funds availability in future years through supportable budget-forecasting techniques. The company's inventory team will commence activity on our campus in April. Their identities can be established from their company identification cards and their name tags signifying their individual names and the name of the company.
   b. For value received, the undersigned jointly and severally promise(s) to pay the sum of five hundred dollars.
   c. Due to the fact that your office experienced a delay in mail service, it is the decision of this committee to extend your allocation of time for the completion of your report one full month from the originally assigned completion date.
   d. All employees are urged to extinguish the illumination in all rooms and facilities not in use so that the maximum benefit of our energy-saving potential may be realized by this company.
   e. Tom is of the opinion that we are not in a position to make contact with any amateur player for the purpose of recruiting him for our professional team without coming into violation of the latest NCAA directive.
2. Each of the following sentences contains an inflated expression (in italics). Rewrite each sentence, substituting a more economical expression. Be sure not to change the meaning of the sentence.
   a. He sent me a check *in the amount of* twenty dollars.
   b. Please call Agnes *in connection with* that overdue loan.
   c. I'd like to meet you sometime next week and speak *with respect to* the proposal you made.
   d. *On the occasion of* his eighteenth birthday, he celebrated for a week.
   e. We'll be able to take a vacation *in the near future*.
   f. *Enclosed you will find* my application form.
   g. He is an expert *in the area of* civil rights.

  h. *I would like to request that* you get here on time.
  i. Judging *on the basis of* the available evidence, I'd say he's guilty.
  j. Henry *made inquiry regarding* the job.
  k. *There are many cases in which* students succeed without trying.
  l. I am not able to do it *at this time*.
  m. See if you can *make contact with* him before Wednesday.
  n. Rainy days *afford me an opportunity to* get my housework done.
  o. The report was *of a confidential nature*.
  p. Maybe we'll be able to *hold a meeting* next week.
  q. My English teacher *offered instruction to* more than 150 students last semester.

3. The words and expressions below are acceptable in many contexts. Yet each has a simpler, more everyday equivalent. Write that equivalent for each.
  a. fracture
  b. undulate
  c. emancipate
  d. rancor
  e. avarice
  f. edifice
  g. veracious
  h. instructional activity
  i. extracurricular activity

4. Revise each of the following passages in light of what you have learned in this chapter so far. Be prepared to explain your revisions.
  a. The thing that makes me most angry with myself is the way I plan my time concerning school work. I have a tendency to be very lazy all through the term. I have a tendency to put everything off until the last minute. I have a tendency not only to do all of my work at the last minute but also to try to learn a whole term's work at the last minute. An example of waiting until the last minute to do something is my recent term paper. My class had a whole term to complete this paper. I did most of the paper the last night. This paper I did in such a hurry that it was very messy and received a grade of only an F. This paper I could have done in an organized manner and received a grade of at least a C, perhaps better.

However, the important point is that I did wait until the last minute, I did receive an F, and I did become angry with myself. Whom can I blame? Only myself.

   b. Generally, movies are thought of as strictly a form of entertainment. This is true also of the form of photography known as home movies. Besides entertainment, though, home movies have several other benefits in that they enhance the pride of the photographer, provide a means of reminiscence, and induce family unity.

      Entertainment, while not the greatest benefit derived from home movies, is nevertheless generated during the viewing of such films. For the most part, home movies present the photographer's family, and in doing so some amusement is obtained. A person always deduces enjoyment from seeing himself or someone close to him in movies. For this reason, we can say that entertainment is beneficial to some extent in the viewing of such cinema.

      Home movies have a beneficial effect upon the photographer's pride. Parents are always pleased in acquiring a chance to boast about their family and in doing so their egos are greatly augmented. Therefore, by having friends participate in the viewing of these movies, photographers are able to sustain ego enhancement and impress visitors and acquaintances. This also gives them the opportunity to display their family's personality.

5. Revise the following letter to make it more effective with its audience. (Don't be afraid to make radical changes if necessary.)

Dear Mr. Fetish:

   Persistence is an admirable trait in, for, and of human beings because it inherently implies a willingness on the part of the individual to pursue his or her obligations with fervor and zeal. I am hopeful that I am the possessor of this quality.

   A year has passed since I had the opportunity to meet with you and discuss the English program offerings. The passing of this year has not dimmed my enthusiasm for and my desire to become a staff member of the department. Certainly I have continued to grow professionally during the past twelve months. These lines would not have been forwarded to you if I did not feel able to make a substantial contribution to the program offerings at Blatchford College. Vital teaching is an end result of professional growth and experience. Good teaching is more than a chronological acquisition of credit hours; my past experience is replete with first-hand experiences and know-how. Teaching is, has been, and always will be my vocation.

I would be most happy to, once again, come to Blatchford to discuss, at your convenience, job possibilities for the forthcoming academic year.

Thanking you for the consideration I am sure you will render these lines, I am,

Yours most cordially,
Parker P. Parker

Revising Sentences for Liveliness

More than a little writing today seems to have been produced by machine. It is flat, stale, mechanical, and therefore tedious to read. There is no hint of a living, breathing human being behind it, no trace of the feeling and animation that are found in real people, and especially in vibrant, vivacious people. If your writing tends to be this way, it is important for you to understand that you can transform it if you take the time to revise for liveliness. Here are six techniques for doing so.

Eliminate the Predictable

No matter how predictable the idea you are expressing may be, there is no need to express it in a predictable way. All you need do is apply your creativity and express the idea imaginatively. Here are two examples of ideas that have been expressed countless times before. Each is presented first in the common, predictable way and then in the imaginative way one professional writer actually used.

Predictable

Since the time of Adam and Eve, new discoveries have surprised humankind. Copernicus found that the earth revolves around the sun. Darwin developed his theory of evolu-

Imaginative

Since the Fall it has been one rude truth after another. Copernicus elbowed us from celestial stage-center with his observation that the earth revolves around the sun. Darwin

Predictable	Imaginative
tion. Freud found out about the important role sex plays in human life.	opened the closet of evolution to introduce family skeletons that further questioned our singular divinity. Under the damp side of civilized behavior, Freud found the perpetually rutting id.[8]
People today must be very gullible to be taken in by advertising. It's really such a big joke, a kind of self-praise, that people in other ages would not have been impressed by. It works with us because our minds are weak; we're sort of hypnotized.	Only a very soft-headed, sentimental, and rather servile generation of men could possibly be affected by advertisements at all. People who are a little more hard-headed, humorous, and intellectually independent see the rather simple joke; and are not impressed by this or any other form of self-praise. Almost any other men in almost any other age would have seen the joke. If you had said to a man in the Stone Age, "Ugg says Ugg makes the best stone hatchets," he would have perceived a lack of detachment and disinterestedness about the testimonial. If you had said to a medieval peasant, "Robert the Bowyer proclaims, with three blasts of a horn, that he makes good bows," the peasant would have said, "Well, of course he does," and thought about something more important. It is only among people whose minds have been weakened by a sort of mesmerism that so transparent a trick as that of advertisement could ever have been tried at all.[9]

Put Yourself in the Background

Many a writer has reasoned that since she finds herself interesting, so will others. That is a mistake. Nothing is more boring to others than when a writer constantly parades herself in her writing. What you have done, seen, heard, thought, felt—these are what you should write about, and not *who you are.* Your presence, in other words, should be kept subordinate to your purpose.

The way to put yourself in the background is to reduce your use of *I, me, mine,* and *myself* to the absolute minimum. The most difficult place to do this is in personal narrative, where references to self are quite natural, even necessary. Yet it can even be done there. The following passages show how.

Self Dominating

I was having a sandwich in the college snack bar when I saw her enter. I was struck by her incredible beauty. I saw that she was about five feet eight inches tall. I also saw that she had a model's figure. I don't mean the flat, emaciated kind, but lean in a healthy way, with gentle curves. I was especially taken by her hair, a deep chestnut brown with natural red highlights. I knew I'd have to meet her that very day.

Self in Background

I was having a sandwich in the college snack bar when she entered. She was incredibly beautiful—about five feet eight inches tall, with a model's figure. Not the flat, emaciated kind, but lean in a healthy way, with gentle curves. Her hair was especially attractive—a deep chestnut brown with natural red highlights. I knew I'd have to meet her that very day.

Substitute Active for Passive Voice

Active voice preserves the natural order of action: "Joe failed the test." Passive voice inverts the natural order: "The test was failed by Joe." There are certain situations where passive voice may be more appropriate than active voice, such as where the focus is on what was done rather than on who did it, and where you either do not know who acted or don't want to say. Thus it would be appropriate to say, "The crime was committed last Thursday," and "The department store was invaded by a horde of bargain hunters." But in most other cases active voice is preferred because it is easier to read and therefore does not slow down the pace of the writing unnecessarily. "Joe failed the test" is immediately clear. It says only one thing to the reader. But "The test was failed by Joe" says two things: that the test was failed and that it was Joe who did the failing. The reader's mind must work a bit harder with passive voice to grasp the meaning. When passive voice dominates your writing, the effect is a loss of liveliness.

Substitute Vivid Words for Bland Words

Vivid words are dramatic. They make an ordinary passage come alive for the readers. You may be inclined to think that most subjects you have to write about could not appropriately be expressed in vivid terms. You think that if you tried to express them that way, you'd feel uneasy, awkward, embarrassed. That reaction is understandable. It takes courage to be dramatic. Even when the words were written by someone else and all you have to do is read them aloud (as, for example, in the recitation of a poem), you'll have a natural tendency to read them blandly, to blunt their vigor. Yet just as all good readers know they must fight that tendency and express the dramatic force of the author's words, so too all good writers know they must conquer their fear of using vivid words. For such words stimulate the readers' imaginations and heighten their interest. To appreciate what they contribute to a piece of writing, you need only compare the following bland and vivid passages. (The vivid words are italicized.)

Bland Version

I listen hard but unsuccessfully for the sound of bugles playing reveille, of drums playing the long roll. In my dreams I hear again the noise of guns and muskets and of people on the battlefield.

Those who are afraid the Democratic party and the White House will be taken over by Southerners need not worry. Behind the Southern

Vivid Version

I listen *vainly*, but with *thirsty ear*, for the *witching melody* of *faint* bugles *blowing* reveille, of far drums *beating* the long roll. In my dreams I hear again the *crash* of guns, the *rattle* of musketry, the *strange, mournful mutter* of the battlefield.[10]

Those who *fear* the Democratic party and the White House will be taken over by a *bunch* of Deep South *corn pone characters* need not *fret*. Behind the

Bland Version	Vivid Version
characteristics is an organization made up of the same kind of people as can be found in the advertising industry.	*sorghum drawl* and *picket fence smile* is an organization made up of the same kind of *video-age, image-shaping, media-manipulating, issue-fuzzing political technicians* and *hustlers* that you can hire all along Madison Avenue.[11]
It was a time when a simple refrain could make successes out of untalented singers.	It was a time when *five dums* and a *doobie-doobie* could make *chart-busters* out of *incompetent hog callers* with a three-note range.[12]

Is it possible to overdo vividness or to use it inappropriately? Of course. But for the beginning writer this is not a serious concern. The opposite problem—not being vivid enough—is much more common. If you keep your audience and purpose in mind, there is little danger that your use of this technique in revising will be excessive.

Substitute Figurative for Literal Language

Figurative language is liter*ary* as opposed to liter*al* expression. It is language that employs the devices of literature, particularly poetry. Here are the more important of those devices.

Simile   A *simile* is an imaginative comparison of one thing to another, very different thing. It can be recognized by the use of the word *like* or *as*. For example, in the sentence "Leonard was like a lion in the office but like a mouse at home," the lion and mouse references are similes. No literal comparison can be made between a man and a lion because they are different species. The sentence means that in the office Leonard displayed the power and dominance we usually associate with lions and that at home he displayed the meekness we usually associate with mice. But it says this more concisely and poetically. Similarly, in "My dorm is as exciting as an amusement park during a power failure," the meaning is that the dorm is dull, but the comparison with a nonfunctioning amusement park expresses it more cleverly.

Metaphor   A metaphor is much like a simile, except that it is more than an imaginative comparison of two different things. It is an imaginative identification of such things. An easy way to remember the difference is this: a metaphor is a simile without *like* or *as*. Thus in "Leonard was a lion in the office, but a mouse at home," the lion and mouse references are metaphors. Here are some other examples of metaphors: "It wasn't much of a baseball game—the other team *slaughtered* us"; "Agatha is the prettiest girl on campus, but she's *an iceberg*"; "The class *roared* their approval of the decision to close school."

Personification   Personification is the assigning of human capabilities or qualities to nonhuman things. For example, in the sentence "The best teacher is a quiet place," a place is spoken of as if it were a person. In the literal sense, of course, a place cannot teach anyone anything. Yet in a figurative sense the statement is meaningful.

Understatement   Understatement, as the term suggests, is the expression of an idea with considerably less force than might be reasonably expected. To say that Julius Erving is a fair basketball player is understatement because Julius Erving is an unusually gifted basketball player. And to say that Aleksandr Solzhenitsyn has had some acquaintance with the forces of repression is understatement because most of his life was spent suffering under those forces.

Metonymy and Synecdoche   The closely related techniques of metonymy and synecdoche are, respectively, using the name of one thing for another closely related thing, and using the part to stand for the whole or the whole for the part. Instead of saying that a judge retired and his judicial responsibilities were assumed by someone else, we might say that "the gavel was passed" from one to the other. Similarly, we might say we wrote to a college concerning admission, meaning we wrote to the admissions director of the college. Here are other examples of these techniques: "*His bat* is as much a threat today as it was ten years ago"; "*The United States* has made its position clear—now it is *Russia's* turn to do likewise"; "Give us this day *our daily bread*."

When used with some originality, all of the devices of figurative language have one thing in common—they are completely unexpected by the reader. It is for this reason that they create interest.

Vary Your Sentence Style or Structure

One of the most common causes of lifelessness in writing is sameness of sentence style or structure. If your sentences tend to be too much alike, use the principles and strategies discussed at length in the first part of this chapter. More specifically, make one or more of these changes:

> If your sentences are all simple, change one or more of them by using coordination or subordination.
>
> If too many of your sentences are short, expand one or more of them.
>
> If too many of your sentences are long, use an occasional short one.
>
> If your sentences all begin alike, vary the word order in some of them.

The following passages show how changes in sentence style and structure can make a monotonous passage lively:

Monotonous

The Great Houdini was born Ehrich Weiss. He was born in Budapest, Hungary. He was born in 1874. He was the fifth of eight children. His father was a poor rabbi. His father immigrated to Wisconsin. At that time Ehrich was still an infant. As a small boy Ehrich sold newspapers. He also shined shoes. And he worked in a Milwaukee luggage shop. Occasionally he had some free time. Then he liked to tinker with the locks on trunks and valises. At 16 he read the autobiography of Robert Houdin. Houdin was a great nineteenth-century French magician and diplomat.

Lively

The Great Houdini was born Ehrich Weiss in Budapest, Hungary, in 1874, the fifth of eight children of a poor rabbi who immigrated to Wisconsin when Ehrich was still an infant. As a small boy, Ehrich sold newspapers, shined shoes, and worked in a Milwaukee luggage shop where, during his free time, he liked to tinker with the locks on trunks and valises. At 16, after reading the autobiography of Robert Houdin, the great nineteenth-century French magician and diplomat, he began to dream of becoming a great magician himself. When he was 17, the family resettled in New York,

Monotonous

Ehrich began to dream of becoming a great magician himself. When Ehrich was 17 his family resettled in New York. By now he called himself Harry Houdini. He became an apprentice cutter in a tie factory during the day. He also became a magician whenever someone would hire him for an evening or weekend show. He performed a spectacular quick-switch trunk escape. He used a friend or his brother Theo as his partner in the escape. With this act Harry played firemen's picnics. He also played boilermakers' soirees. And he played lodge halls.

Lively

and Harry Houdini, as he now called himself, became an apprentice cutter in a tie factory during the day and a magician whenever someone would hire him for an evening or weekend show. Using a friend or his brother Theo as his partner in a spectacular quick-switch trunk escape, Harry played firemen's picnics, boilermakers' soirees, and lodge halls.[13]

Summary of Sentence Strategies

To assist you in applying the approaches to revision discussed in this chapter, here is a brief summary of them.

To Revise for Exactness

Be sensitive to denotative and connotative meaning.

Be careful with words that sound alike but have different meanings, and avoid both overworked or empty expressions and vogue expressions.

Choose your level of diction, degree of clarity, and degree of concreteness and specificity with care.

To Revise for Economy

Check for pretentiousness.

Check for wordiness.

Check for jargon.

To Revise for Liveliness

Eliminate the predictable.

Put yourself in the background.

Substitute active for passive voice whenever possible.

Substitute vivid words for bland words.

Substitute figurative for literal language.

Vary your sentence style or structure.

Exercises

1. Read each of the quoted passages carefully. Then identify the various ways in which the author has made the writing lively.
    a. A convict's paranoia is as thick as the prison wall—and just as necessary. Why should we have faith in anyone? Even our wives and lovers whose beds we have shared, with whom we have shared the tenderest moments and most delicate relations, leave us after a while, put us down, cut us clean aloose and treat us like they hate us, won't even write us a letter, send us a Christmas card every other year, or a quarter for a pack of cigarettes or a tube of toothpaste now and then. All society shows the convict its ass and expects him to kiss it: the convict feels like kicking it or putting a bullet in it. A convict sees man's fangs and claws and learns quickly to bare and unsheath his own, for real and final. To maintain a hold on the ideals and sentiments of civilization in such circumstances is probably impossible.[14]
    b. "The Americans," Walt Whitman wrote in the 1850s, "are going to be the most fluent and melodious-voiced people in the world, and the most perfect users of words." The line was more hopeful than prophetic. Today, many believe that the American language has lost not only its melody but a lot of its meaning. School children and even college students often seem disastrously ignorant of words; they stare, uncomprehending, at simple declarative English. Leon Botstein, president of New York's Bard College, says with glum hyperbole: "The English language is dying, because it is not taught." Others believe that the language is taught badly and learned badly because American culture is awash with clichés, officialese, political bilge, the surreal boobspeak of advertising ("Mr. Whipple, please don't squeeze the cortex"), and the sludge of academic writing. It would be no wonder if children exposed to such discourse grew up with at least an unconscious hostility to language itself.[15]

Revising for Sentence Style 263

    c. On Wednesday morning at a quarter past five came the earthquake. A minute later the flames were leaping upward. In a dozen different quarters south of Market Street, in the working-class ghetto, and in the factories, fires started. There was no opposing the flames. There was no organization, no communication. All the cunning adjustments of a twentieth-century city had been smashed by the earthquake. The streets were humped into ridges and depressions and piled with debris of fallen walls. The steel rails were twisted into perpendicular and horizontal angles. The telephone and telegraph systems were disrupted. And the great water mains had burst. All the shrewd contrivances and safeguards of man had been thrown out of gear by thirty seconds' twitching of the earth's crust.[16]

2. Read each of the following compositions carefully. Note the ways in which it lacks liveliness. Rewrite each, applying what you have learned in the chapter. You may add or delete parts as you deem necessary.

    a. First we must distinguish between a good student and a poor one. A good student is someone who does her work all the time and does it well. She also has her work handed in on time. She is someone who has no trouble when it comes to studying, for it doesn't bother her. A poor student, on the other hand, is someone who dislikes studying, reading, and writing. She probably doesn't like as many classes as a good student does. She often hands in work late or doesn't do it at all.

    To cite my own case, I do my homework and I hand it in on time. But I don't do a good job on it because I dislike homework. I dislike studying because the material is boring. I always take notes during class. I would receive higher marks if I didn't dislike a few of my classes. It's hard to get a good mark in a class that you aren't interested in. And when I study for such a class, after the exam I forget everything that I studied because it doesn't stay in my head.

    So I tend to be a poor student. If I could make boring classes interesting, then I think I could be a good student. I would also have to spend more time on homework, though. I believe that anyone can become a better student by working harder.

    b. It was a Sunday morning, the first week in June. The time was about 10 A.M. I was over at my aunt's house for lunch. I had come over early to help her. She is a nice lady, and is around forty-five years old. She'd just bought a new car for almost $15,000. It had under a hundred miles on it. The car was beautiful. It was a light brown with a dark brown vinyl roof. The interior was beautiful too. It had suede bucket seats and every option available.

I was admiring the car when she asked me to run an errand for her. She also asked me if I wanted to take her car instead of mine. I said I would. By this time it was 11 A.M. and it was raining outdoors. She asked me to pick up the *Sunday News*. In order to get to the store I had to cross the bridge. I drove her car to the store and bought the paper. As I was coming back, it was raining harder and harder. The approach to the bridge is very difficult because it bears to the left and then goes directly to the right at almost a ninety-degree angle.

The rain was falling harder and harder and the windows were beginning to fog and the visibility was very poor. I came up to the approach and it was clear so I went ahead up the approach and on to the bridge just before the two tight curves. As I came up the bridge I started to pass a car crawling along in front. We were both going rather slowly. I spotted something up ahead, but I was too far back to make out what it was. I was right alongside the other car when I saw it was a kid on a bike. Apparently the other car's driver didn't see him because he was picking up speed as we approached the tight right-hand turn. I was less than a hundred yards from the kid, side by side with that car.

The way I saw it I had two choices. I could either put the brake on hard and hope to avoid hitting the bike or the car, but this seemed hard to do because of the conditions of the road. Or I could hit the accelerator hard and try to pass them both. That was my split-second choice. We were still on the curve and I put my foot down and started to pass them, and then the other driver spotted the bike and almost cut me off. I hit the horn and he moved just enough to let me get by. I was picking up speed and almost out of the turn when my back end slid to the left, so I tried to steer it back. But I oversteered it, and the car spun twice before slamming into the guardrails. The car was twisted and bent and cost $3,000 to repair. And I was trembling and ashamed.

3. The following details are from an account of the Wright brothers' historic first flight. Work them into a lively account, applying what you have learned in the chapter.

The place: Kittyhawk, North Carolina

The men: Wilbur Wright—well groomed, 5' 6", 150 lb., straight black hair, blue eyes, long and sharp nose, swarthy complexion; Orville Wright—blonde, shorter but huskier than his brother, black eyes, fair complexion

The beach: Quiet and secluded

Wind: 21 miles per hour

Plane was three years in the making

Brothers financed work themselves

U.S. had spent thousands on rival project by Prof. Langley of Smithsonian Institute

Details of plan: Resembled box kite, had large frame—light timbers 33' wide x 5' deep x 5' across the top; small gas engine in center; also in center large canvas rudder (looked like fan), could move up, down, and side to side; two 6-bladed propellers, one below center of frame to pull plane up, the other partly to the rear to push plane forward

The flight: Engines roared, plane moved forward, then lifted, rose into wind over waves; turned right, left, went back and forth over beach, at 8 miles per hour; total distance covered—3 miles

Small crowds watched (fishermen and coastguardsmen)

Pilot shouted "Eureka" as plane landed

Select one of the following topics, quotations, or issues and write a 500-word composition on it. Don't skimp on the planning and writing stages, but pay particular attention to revising, especially to revising for sentence style. (*Note:* If you choose one of the topics, be sure to narrow it sufficiently before generating ideas; if you choose one of the quotations, you may include it in the composition as a reinforcement for your controlling idea, but not as a substitute for that idea.)

Composition Assignment

Topics

Victory	"Quiet hours" in the dorm
Language	What I'm most ashamed of
Heaven	Sports injuries

Mediocrity	Elementary school
Hair styles	The strangest attitude I've encountered

Quotations

1. "The greater number of men pass through life with souls asleep." (Paul Sabatier)
2. "Misfortune is our greatest master and our best friend. It teaches us the meaning of life." (Anatole France)
3. "The word *love* is used too freely today." (Anonymous)
4. "It is characteristic of human nature to hate the person you have wronged." (Tacitus)
5. "The tremendous skill and the enormous resources available to [the comic book, the radio, the motion picture, the slick-paper magazine, television, and the sensational press] make them more influential in molding the lives of our people than the whole educational process." (Robert Hutchins)

Issues

1. Reincarnation is the belief that after death living things return to earthly life in a different form. Do you accept or reject this belief? Why?
2. Some people believe that if students study faithfully they will succeed in college. Do you agree?
3. Many people believe that the current practices of trying youthful offenders in juvenile rather than adult court, and of keeping their names out of the newspapers, coddle them and retard their growth into mature and responsible citizens. What is your view?
4. The college degree has virtually become *the* basic job requirement in this country. Most businesses and industries are apparently "sold" on its importance—this despite the fact that the degree itself is not an especially good index of a person's capabilities or aptitudes. Should the degree be abolished as a job requirement? If not, why not? If so, what do you think should take its place? Explain carefully.
5. Some people say "You're never too old to learn." Others say "You can't teach an old dog new tricks." Which do you believe and why?

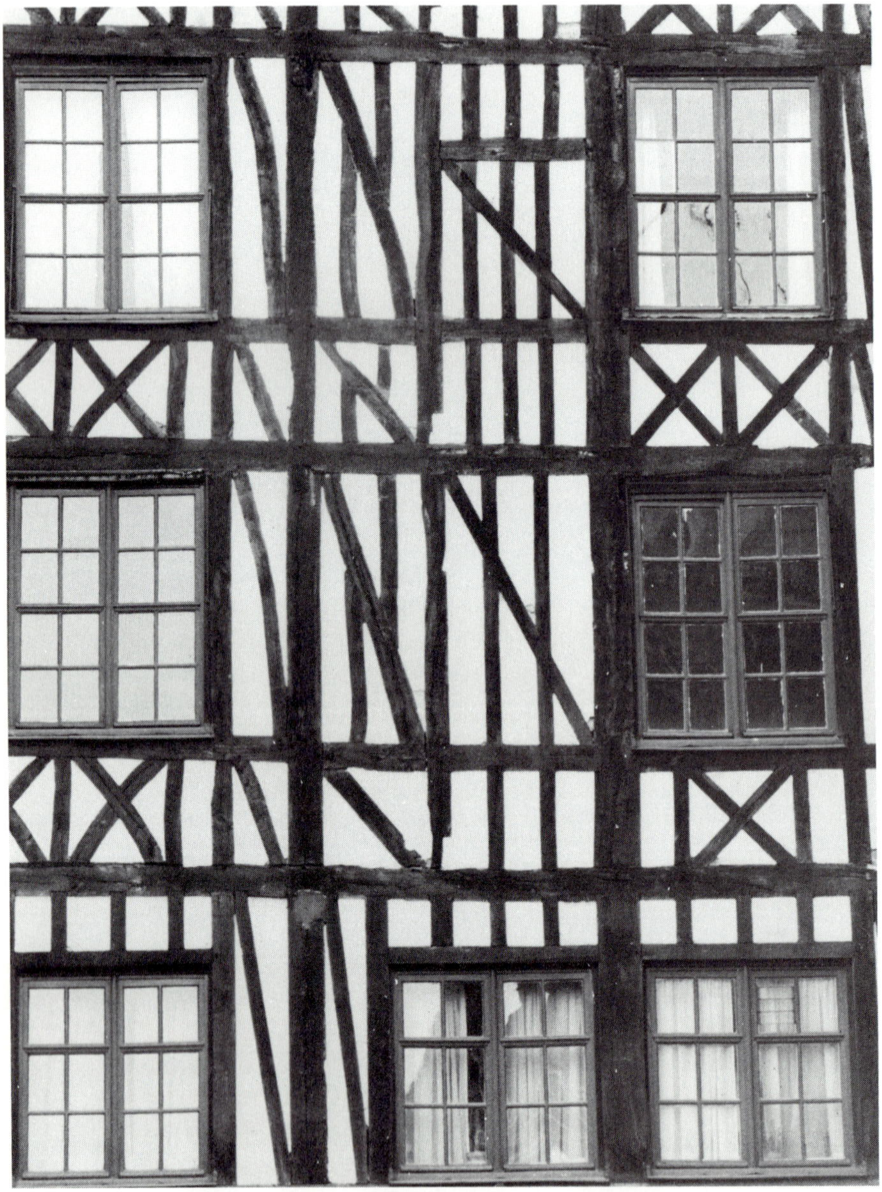

Chapter 11

Revising for Paragraph Effectiveness

This chapter explains the fundamentals of paragraphing. It also demonstrates how to revise your paragraphs for length and coherence.

Like effective sentences, effective paragraphs can seldom be achieved during the writing process. They must be crafted during the revision stage. To accomplish that task you need to understand the dynamics of paragraphing. Let's begin with some background information.

There is no immutable law that messages must be broken into paragraphs. After all, there are no paragraphs in speaking. It is only in writing that the convention of paragraphing has been developed. The reason for this is that the written word lacks some of the advantages of the spoken word. When you speak, you gesture, raise and lower your voice, and pause for shorter or longer periods of time. In addition, you look at the person you are speaking to and read her reaction. The moment you see any sign of confusion or misunderstanding, you restate your point to clarify it.

Such devices are not available to you in writing. Yet your readers can be confused or have difficulty understanding your message. So you must find other ways of making your message clear to them. Paragraphing is one of the best ways to do this. It serves to break down your ideas into easily digestible pieces. It signals how your thoughts are being grouped and marks your turning from one idea to another.

Unfortunately, misunderstanding of paragraphing has led to extreme views of it. Some people believe that the guidelines governing paragraphing are absolute and permit no flexibility. Others believe the exact opposite—that anything goes, and that a writer may approach paragraphing however he or she wishes. Both these views are incorrect.

Two important changes that have occurred over the past hundred or so years are responsible for the confusion. One change is the preference of the reading public. A hundred years ago the pace of living was quite different from today's pace. Life, if more difficult in many respects, was less hurried. There was no television or radio to speed communication. And in the same way that people were prepared to spend hours and hours to travel a relatively short distance, so they were content to take their time reading, proceeding at a very deliberate, relaxed rate of speed. (Speedreading is also a modern invention.) Long paragraphs did not threaten them; they were in no hurry to be finished. Sensitive to that reality, writers of that day wrote paragraphs that ran on for several pages.

Today's readers, however, are more aware of time and less leisurely in their reading habits. They expect their reading to be fast-paced, and modern writers accommodate them. Instead of starting a new paragraph once in several pages, they do so several times per page.

The second important change that has occurred is writing format. With the growth and development of newspapers and magazines have come a greater variety of writing (and printing) formats. In all of these formats the column is considerably narrower than a book page. Therefore the paragraphs are squeezed in at the sides *and extended in length on the page.* Paragraphs that appear distractingly short when typed or handwritten on an 8½-by-11-inch page thus appear to be of reasonable length when printed in a newspaper or magazine.

There is an important inference to be drawn from these facts about the recent history of paragraphing: responsible writers neither worship the conventions of their art nor take those conventions lightly; they apply them thoughtfully to the demands of the writing situation.

Basic Paragraph Patterns

Traditionally, the paragraph has been approached as a mini-composition with a specific purpose (for example, to describe, narrate, or define); a controlling idea, called a *topic sentence*; and systematic development. That approach was the only reasonable one when paragraphs were long and therefore could easily become confusing. Changes in readers' preferences and publishing formats have, of course, prompted different approaches to paragraphing. Nevertheless, since clarity of meaning is as important today as ever, the traditional approach to paragraphing continues to be of fundamental importance. It is an approach that every writer who aspires to excellence should master.

Here is an example of a paragraph developed as a mini-composition. (The topic sentence in this paragraph is italicized.)

> *The search for principle is the essence of the judicial process.* It can never be enough for a court to say, as a legislature properly can, "X wins the case because he has more votes behind him." Especially in the Supreme Court, which must find in the vague words of our fundamental law the guideposts for a nation, every decision should be supported by reasons that appeal to the intellect and to the ethical sense of Americans. The requirement that a court give reasons for its judgments is a basic safeguard, as the country began to realize belatedly during that shameful era when men were labeled "security risks" by boards of quasi-judges who gave no reasons at all and thus avoided responsibility for their conclusions.[1]

Although the topic sentence may be placed anywhere in the paragraph, it is usually placed at the beginning to provide an immediate signal to the readers of what ideas will be developed. For the paragraph to be successful, the rest of it must be purposeful and controlled, not random, so that it can meet the expectations the topic sentence raises. Following are three of the most common patterns with topic sentences italicized. (*Note*: For a more complete presentation of paragraph patterns, see the techniques of development detailed in Chapters 6 through 8. Each of those techniques may be considered a paragraph pattern.)

Generalization Followed by Specific Details

> *Nowhere is the refugee impact more starkly evident than in Dade County, Florida,* which was inundated by 153,000 Cubans and Haitians during an 18-month period in 1980 and 1981. Although most of the Mariel boat-lift refugees from Cuba have been assimilated, they account for 16 percent of the total felony arrests in Dade, and jailing these refugees and other Latin-Caribbean aliens accused of crimes is costing Dade taxpayers more than $6 million a year. Further, the federal government has refused to reimburse the county for the esti-

This topic sentence makes readers wonder "What exactly is that impact?" The rest of the paragraph answers the question.

mated $130 million spent on health, education, police protection and social services for refugees.[2]

Statement of Opinion Followed by Cases-in-point That Support It

Here the examples of Milton, Cellini, and Machiavelli are offered to illustrate the reasonableness of the opinion. Without such development, readers might be inclined to challenge the opinion.

An eventful life exhausts rather than stimulates. Milton, who in 1640 was a poet of great promise, spent twenty sterile years in the eventful atmosphere of the Puritan revolution. He fulfilled his great promise when the revolution was dead, and he in solitary disgrace. Cellini's exciting life kept him from becoming the great artist he could have been. It is legitimate to doubt whether Machiavelli would have written his great books had he been allowed to continue in the diplomatic service of Florence and had he gone on interesting missions. It is usually the mediocre poets, writers, etc., who go in search of stimulating events to release their creative flow.[3]

Here the cases-in-point are necessary not to offset possible challenges to the opinion expressed in the topic sentence but to demonstrate to readers the kind of exaggeration Arabs are noted for.

Of the world's exaggerators, none surpasses the Arabs, whose language is a symphony of poetical excess. A Cairo gas station attendant greets his co-workers in the morning: "May your day be scented with jasmine." Sometimes the exaggerations that are inherent in Arabic can be dangerous. Saudi Arabia's late King Saud once told a visiting group of Palestinian journalists that "the Arabs must be ready to sacrifice a million lives to regain the sacred soil of Palestine." It was rhetoric, a flourish; Arabs hearing it would no more take it literally than would an American football crowd hearing "Rip 'em up, tear 'em up." But the words made headlines all over the world as a statement of bloody Saudi intent.[4]

Personal Perspective Followed by Reasons That Explain It

"What about the automobile gives this author cause for concern?" readers may wonder. In the rest of the paragraph the author presents his reasons for worrying. (Note: this was written years before the oil shortage actually occurred.)

Thirdly, I worry about the private automobile. It is a dirty, noisy, wasteful, and lonely means of travel. It pollutes the air, ruins the safety and sociability of the street, and exercises upon the individual a discipline which takes away far more freedom than it gives him. It causes an enormous amount of land to be unnecessarily abstracted from nature and from plant life and to become devoid of any natural function. It explodes cities, grievously impairs the whole institution of neighborliness, fragmentizes and destroys communities. It has already spelled the end of our cities as real cultural and social communities, and has made impossible the construction of any others in their place. Together with the airplane, it has crowded out other, more civilized and more convenient means of transport, leaving older people, infirm people, poor people and children in a worse situation than they were a hundred years ago. It continues to lend a terrible element of fragility to our civilization, placing us in a situation where our life would break down completely if anything ever interfered with the oil supply.[5]

Exercises

Choose three of the following sentences and let each serve as the topic sentence of a separate paragraph. In composing your paragraphs, be sure that your development is adequate to meet the expectations raised by the topic sentence.

1. You can keep your fine restaurants—I prefer fast-food places.
2. The political process in this country leaves a lot to be desired.
3. The concert was a big disappointment.
4. You're never more alone than when you're out of money.
5. I may not have won any medals for my athletic performance, but I gained a great deal from being on the team.
6. He told himself he wouldn't get too attached to the dog, but deep inside he knew better.
7. When the subject turned to religion, the discussion became heated.
8. Thoreau was right when he called Spring "an experience in immortality."
9. My dormitory has to be seen to be believed.
10. Perhaps might doesn't make right, but it gives a person a powerful advantage.

Revising for Paragraph Length

If during the writing process you developed your important ideas using the appropriate techniques explained in Chapters 6, 7, and 8, your first draft will be arranged in rough paragraph form. In revising that draft for paragraph length, you should apply the following guidelines, which professional writers use in revising their paragraphs. Keep in mind that these guidelines are not a substitute for traditional paragraphing practice but a refinement of it to meet the demands of contemporary writing situations.

Make Your Paragraphs Average About Ten Lines in Length

This, of course, doesn't mean that every paragraph must be ten lines long. Some should be shorter, some longer. Seldom, however, should any paragraph exceed fifteen lines, because at that point a paragraph begins to look formidable.* Remember too that a typed ten-line paragraph that is set in column format will stretch to double its original length. So if you're writing for such a format (say, a letter to a newspaper editor), make your average typed paragraph *five* lines long.

Vary the Length of Your Paragraphs to Avoid Monotony

If all your paragraphs are about the same length, they will look boring to your readers even before they begin reading them. Variety creates interest. This doesn't mean you have to force radical differences in paragraph length. Two or three paragraphs in a row may be eight to ten lines long before you need to be concerned. But at that point you ought to consider making the next one four or twelve lines long. And don't be afraid of the one-sentence paragraph. Too many of them, to be sure, can make your writing choppy and fragmented and can be as distracting as too many long paragraphs. But used sparingly and with care, they can be very effective. Whenever you do use a one-sentence paragraph, keep in mind that since it contrasts sharply with the rest of your paragraphs, it will give added emphasis to whatever idea is placed in it. So be sure to place only important ideas there.

Break Your Paragraphs at the Natural Junctures of Your Ideas

Little is gained by writing paragraphs that appeal to the eye, that seem to be readable, but that on closer inspection are found to group thoughts confusingly, combining things that should be separated and forcing awkward, unnatural interruptions in ideas that belong together. Therefore, it is important not only to control the length of your paragraphs but also to make the paragraph breaks occur in appropriate places, at the natural junctures of the ideas. Those junctures are:

Between Techniques of Development
A natural paragraph break may occur whenever you end a description and begin a compari-

---

*One occasion in which paragraphs may be longer is when you are writing for a scholarly audience. Such an audience is usually accustomed to close reading of complex material and is not intimidated by lengthy presentations.

son, or turn from interpretation to evaluation, or finish an explanation and start a narration. Here is an example.

> A profound transformation took place in costume after the First World War. Initially it was linked to the various consequences of the war, but it continued and became more marked with further changes in people's way of life, with new attitudes of mind and new modes of production.
>
> Whereas before 1914 economic evolution had produced a trend toward internationalism, the war forced the various countries toward economic centralization for their war efforts. State direction of industry not only accelerated centralization—which had already begun in any case—but also helped to transform the social scene. Women contributed to the industrial war effort, and after the war took on an ever widening range of work, gained civil and economic rights, and played a greater role outside their homes. Between 1920–25 costume adapted to suit this new fact of life. What had begun as mere acceptance of wartime conditions became the preferred style, one stripped of all "Belle Epoque" reminiscences.
>
> For a woman leading a freer life, trained to work, enjoying sports and dancing, fashion had to be functional. It ignored the waist and breasts, abbreviated the skirt, abolished the corset in favour of the suspender belt, introduced pyjamas for night wear, and cropped the hair. This was the transformation awaiting men returning from the war to their wives and sweethearts: clean-cut, consciously young forms, surprising but no less attractive for that, foreshadowing the boyish look of the next decade.
>
> This revolution was not immediately accepted by haute couture, which lost its hold over most of its customers. In a few years, houses such as Doucet, Poiret, Doeuillet, and Drecoll were to close, while others reopened and new ones were founded. Among the names that brought back elegance to Paris, in the interwar years, there were a large number of women. This indeed was one of the characteristics of the period: besides Mme Gerber, Mme Paquin, and Jeanne Lanvin, Madeleine Vionnet and Chanel were to occupy star positions for twenty years, later joined by Mme Grès, Mme Schiaparelli, Mlle Carven, and a dozen others.[6]

The first paragraph here presents a factual assertion and an explanation of its cause and later development.

The second paragraph traces that development more closely. The third presents another factual assertion, followed by descriptive examples. The fourth paragraph presents still another (related) assertion and a number of examples.

Here is another example of the breaking of paragraphs between expository techniques.

> Shortly before he died Russell Davenport wrote a friend: "I have worked out my 'philosophy,' have developed a coherent approach to

This passage begins with a quotation, a factual asser-

tion about the book, and an evaluation of the book's quality. The second paragraph moves to factual information about the man and his time. (Notice how, out of the mass of information that could have been included, the information here is carefully selected to create a focus on the writer's particular interest.) The third paragraph moves to a judgment about the man's personal qualities, followed by a paraphrase.

the whole problem of freedom, and rough-drafted about three-quarters of a first book." This volume is that three-quarters, carried as far toward a conclusion as his notes would permit. Even in its unfinished form, it is the best thing Davenport ever wrote. How good that is, and how relevant to current American thinking, can be better appreciated with some knowledge of his life and previous work.

Russell Wheeler Davenport was born July 12, 1899, in South Bethlehem, Pa., and died in New York City April 19, 1954 (the anniversary of "the shot heard round the world"). His mature life, brief as it was, spanned a period of nearly unprecedented change in the patterns of American life and the direction of American national policy. In these changes Davenport participated as an intensely committed citizen, and some of them he directly influenced as a publicist. While America was groping reluctantly for the role of successful world leadership, Davenport was groping for the ideas and policies that would support this role.

The qualities he brought to his search were among the best qualities that America was at the same time bringing to her ordeal. They were qualities that George Santayana once touched on in a classic description of the Yale man. . . .[7]

Within an Expository Technique When There Is a Change in Time, Place, or Focus In a comparison between two people, you might be mentioning their behavior in class, their behavior out of class, and their general attitude toward others. All these characteristics would be part of the same comparison. Yet each is a separate aspect, and each marks an appropriate place for starting a new paragraph.

This entire passage, taken from a current proposal for reforming American education, is explanatory. The paragraphing occurs where the focus changes. That is, the author begins a second paragraph when he turns from discussing the program in general to discussing elective courses, and he begins a third paragraph where he turns from elective courses to the special case of foreign language. (Note: in the original the final paragraph continues on for two more sentences.)

To give the same quality of schooling to all requires a program of study that is both liberal and general, and that is, in several, crucial, overarching respects, one and the same for every child. All sidetracks, specialized courses, or elective choices must be eliminated. Allowing them will always lead a certain number of students to voluntarily downgrade their own education.

Elective choices are appropriate only in a curriculum that is intended for different avenues of specialization or different forms of preparation for the professions or technical careers. Electives and specialization are entirely proper at the level of advanced schooling—in our colleges, universities, and technical schools. They are wholly inappropriate at the level of basic schooling.

The course of study to be followed in the twelve years of basic schooling should, therefore, be completely required, with only one exception. That exception is the choice of a second language. . . .[8]

Revising for Paragraph Effectiveness

Here is another example of breaking paragraphs at an appropriate place within an expository technique.

> Sometimes, watching television helps you learn to think on your feet. Like an old friend of mine named Shakey, who once escaped from the North Dakota State Penitentiary. While he hid in the basement of a private residence, they were putting up roadblocks all around the city of Bismarck. But Shakey was smart. He knew that there had to be some way for him to extricate himself from this mess. Then, all of a sudden it occurred to him: Shakey remembered a caper film he'd seen on television once, in which a fugitive had managed to breach several roadblocks by using an emergency vehicle.
>
> With this basic plan in mind, he proceeded to the Bismarck City Hospital and, pretending to be hysterical, he stammered to the first white-coated attendant he met that his brother was lying trapped beneath an overturned farm tractor about 12 miles or so from town. He then climbed into the back of the ambulance, and with red lights blazing and siren screaming, the vehicle drove right through two roadblocks—and safely out of Bismarck.
>
> Two days or so later, Shakey arrived back on the same ranch in Montana where he'd worked before his jail sentence. The foreman even gave him his job again. But Shakey was so proud of what he'd done that he made one big mistake: he boasted about his escape from the North Dakota state prison, and in the end he was turned over to the authorities, who sent him back to North Dakota—and prison.[9]

The technique used here is a combination of description and narration. The first break occurs when the writer turns from the plan to the action implementing the plan. The second occurs at a significant change in time.

Between Speakers in Dialogue This kind of paragraph break is not distracting to readers even if there is a change of speaker after every few words, because it provides them with a guide to who is speaking without repeating "John said" and "Bill replied" over and over. Here is an example of such paragraphing.

> As they shuffled along the street, eyes cast down as if looking for money, John and Bill grappled with the problem of what to do that night.
> "How about checking out the dance?" John offered.
> "Nah. Bunch of creeps there."
> "Then how about catching a flick?"
> "Nothin' good's playin'."
> "We could go over to the recreation center."
> "No way. Art's always there and I owe him money."
> "I don't know what to do then."
> "Come on. Think of somethin'. I don't want to walk around the street all night."

Notice that after the first speaker is identified ("... John offered"), there is no need for further identification. In a longer dialogue, of course, there might be such a need. And a dialogue in which three or more speakers contributed would require additional identification. How much would be required would vary from situation to situation, depending on how clear the changes in speakers were.

Here is a slightly different variation of the same kind of paragraphing.

Here the same paragraphing rule is used even though technically there is no dialogue (only the headmaster speaks). Nevertheless, the narrator's own unexpressed thoughts are recorded in response to the headmaster's comments as if they were spoken.

> I had better explain that I was a frequent visitor to the headmaster's study, because of the latest thing I had done or left undone. As we now say, I was not integrated. I was, if anything, disintegrated; and I was puzzled. Grown-ups never made sense. Whenever I found myself in a penal position before the headmaster's desk, with the statuettes glimmering whitely above him, I would sink my head, clasp my hands behind my back, and writhe one shoe over the other.
> The headmaster would look opaquely at me through flashing spectacles.
> "What are we going to do with you?"
> Well, what *were* they going to do with me? I would writhe my shoe some more and stare down at the worn rug.
> "Look up, boy! Can't you look up?"
> Then I would look up at the cupboard, where the naked lady was frozen in her panic and the muscular gentleman contemplated the hindquarters of the leopard in endless gloom. I had nothing to say to the headmaster. His spectacles caught the light so that you could see nothing human behind them. There was no possibility of communication.
> "Don't you ever think at all?"
> No, I didn't think, wasn't thinking, couldn't think—I was simply waiting in anguish for the interview to stop.
> "Then you'd better learn—hadn't you?"
> On one occasion the headmaster leaped to his feet, reached up, and plonked Rodin's masterpiece on the desk before me.
> "That's what a man looks like when he's really thinking."
> I surveyed the gentleman without interest or comprehension.
> "Go back to your class."[10]

Although it would be difficult to keep all these guidelines in mind while writing your composition, it is easy to check for them after you have finished your first draft. That is why you should do no more than rough in your paragraphs while writing and leave your final decisions about paragraphing until the revision stage.

Exercises

1. The following two excerpts appeared in *column* format, the first in a newspaper, the second in a magazine. Rewrite each, changing the paragraphing to make it appropriate for *full-page* format (as in a book). Apply the guidelines explained in the chapter.

a. A two-year survey of New York State's mental health system has found that more than a fourth of the 26,000 adult patients in mental hospitals are not ill enough to be kept there.

　　The survey, completed last year, found that 17.5 percent of the mental patients are, in fact, capable of leading relatively independent lives outside the hospital, either by themselves, with families, or in adult homes, halfway houses, or boarding houses. A total of 10.6 percent would require care in nursing homes or health-related facilities that are less restrictive than mental hospitals.

　　The patients cannot now be discharged, mental health officials acknowledged, because there are not enough community facilities to provide services they would still require outside of the hospital environment.[11]

b. From my "balcony" seat atop a barren skyline ridge I watched intently as an ancient drama unfolded in the sprawling Arctic valley below. The scene was Bathurst Inlet in Canada's Northwest Territories, and a great white wolf was making its way over the tundra straight toward a herd of caribou.

　　It was a mixed herd of about a hundred, with bulls in velvet, a high proportion of ragged, shedding cows, and several calves perhaps a month old. They were all passing along a parallel series of animal trails, stopping every few strides to nibble choice pieces of dwarf birch or willow.

　　Then suddenly the herd, sensing the wolf, was drawn together as if by some giant biological magnet. The tightly pressed group flowed quickly forward. Four or five caribou on a nearby slope also sensed the danger and bolted downward to join the dense nucleus of their kind.

　　The white wolf made its decision. Instantly it sprang forward. While the stragglers gravitated toward the herd, the wolf began closing the 200-yard gap.

　　As the wolf pressed closer, the caribou increased their speed. Straight toward them the white wolf shot, with long legs alternately stretching out then pulling together in 15-foot bounds. And directly away from the wolf the caribou sped. The chase covered a quarter of a mile, and the wolf tried its best all the way. Still the wild hunter was unable to come closer than about 200 feet to its intended prey. It chased the caribou at this distance for about fifty yards. Then all of a sudden the wolf slowed, and less than a minute after the chase had begun, it was over.[12]

2. The following excerpt originally appeared in *full-page* format. Rewrite it, changing the paragraphing to make it appropriate

for *column* format. Apply the guidelines explained in the chapter.

Where *are* you aiming your life? This may sound like too broad or moralistic a question. But what life *means* is and always has been the main concern of education. Education, fundamentally, is a *moral* enterprise. Harvard's President Nathan Pusey recently said: "The chief aim of undergraduate education is to discover what it means to be a man. This has always to be done in personal, individual terms." For you to discover the meaning of maturity and the direction of your life is therefore an inclusive aim of your studies.

Presumably you are in college because you want an education. You might well ask the next two logically inevitable questions: *What* is an education? *Why* do I want it?

The first question is, of course, difficult; it has almost as many answers as there are people who try to respond to it. And in the current literature on education, there are literally yards of library shelves taken up with books that discuss the matter. But there are some clear and useful general ideas on the meaning of an education that should help you think about it for yourself in practical and immediate terms.

Obviously, an education is something more than the acquiring of mere information. Pieces of knowledge, no matter how largely accumulated, are dead lumps unless you know what to do with them. As one philosopher put it bluntly, "A merely well-informed man is the most useless bore on God's earth." Yet the culture in which we live seems to put large and often spectacular premiums on the possession of factual knowledge. It would not be surprising, for example, if you have been impressed, and perhaps influenced, by the television and radio quiz programs of the past decade: winners in these fact-derbies have often walked away with fortunes in money and goods. Clearly, at least in this limited activity, the possession of great stores of random facts has a measurable pay-off. Yet actually there is little qualitative difference between the responses of quiz contestants in various categories of "knowledge" and the old-fashioned circus and vaudeville performances of trained animals who can "count," "talk," and perform other feats of "reasoning." Both quiz contestants and trained animals perform under special, limited conditions.

But life is never as tidy or controlled as a quiz program; in real living, the rewards usually go to the person who knows when and how to ask the right questions—not to the person who has sets of answers to predetermined questions. Life never has any predetermined questions either; it has only problems which must be coped with and dilemmas which rarely, if ever, come when they are supposed to, in the form they should.[13]

Revising for Paragraph Effectiveness 281

3. The following passages are unparagraphed. Read them carefully. Then, in light of the guidelines explained in the chapter, decide how they should be paragraphed for a *full-page* format, and write them out providing that paragraphing.

   a. When Arthur was in the first grade, the teacher directed the class to "think." "Now, class," she said, "I know this problem is a little harder than the ones we've been doing, but I'm going to give you a few extra minutes to think about it. OK? Now start thinking." It was not the first time Arthur had heard the word used. He'd heard it many times at home. But never quite this way. The teacher seemed to be asking for some special activity, something he should know how to start and stop. Like his father's car. "Vroom-m-m," he muttered half aloud. Because of his confusion, he was unaware he was making the noise. "Arthur, please stop making noises and start thinking." Embarrassed, and not knowing quite what to do, he looked down at his desk. Then out of the corner of his eye he noticed that the little girl next to him was staring at the ceiling. "Maybe that's the way you start thinking," he guessed. He decided the others had probably learned how to do it last year, that time he was home with the measles. So he stared at the ceiling. As he progressed through grade school and high school, he heard that same direction hundreds of times. "No, that's not the answer, you're not thinking—now think!" And occasionally, from a particularly self-pitying teacher given to talking to himself aloud: "What did I do to deserve this? Don't they teach them anything in the grades anymore? Don't you people care about ideas? Think, dammit, THINK." So Arthur learned to feel somewhat guilty about the whole matter. Obviously this thinking was an important activity that he'd failed to learn. Maybe he lacked the brain power. But he was resourceful enough. He watched the other students and did what they did. Whenever a teacher started in about thinking, he screwed up his face, furrowed his brow, scratched his head, stroked his chin, stared off into space or up at the ceiling, and repeated silently to himself, "Let's see now, I've got to think about that, think, think (I hope he doesn't call on me), think." Though he didn't know it, that's just what the other students were saying to themselves. Since Arthur's situation is not all that uncommon, your experience may have been similar. That is, many people have told you to think, but no one ever explained what thinking is, how many kinds of thinking there are, and what qualities a good thinker has that a poor thinker lacks.[14]

   b. Dying is an integral part of life, as natural and predictable as being born. But whereas birth is cause for celebration, death has become a dreaded and unspeakable issue to be avoided by every means possible in our modern society. Perhaps it is that death reminds us of our human vulnerability in spite of all our technological advances. We may be able to delay it, but we cannot escape it. We, no less than other, nonrational animals, are destined to die at the end of our lives. And death strikes indiscriminately—it cares not at all for the status or position of the ones it chooses; everyone must die, whether rich or poor, famous or unknown. Even good deeds will not excuse their doers from the sentence of death; the good die as often as the bad. It is perhaps this inevitable and unpredictable quality that makes death so frightening to many people. Especially those who put a high value on being in control of their own existence are offended by the thought that they, too, are subject to the forces of death. But other societies have learned to cope better with the reality of death than we seem to have done. It is unlikely that any group has ever welcomed death's intrusion on life, but there are others who have successfully integrated the expectation of death into their understanding of life. Why is it so hard for us to do this? The answer may lie in the question. It is difficult to accept death in this society *because* it is unfamiliar. In spite of the fact that it happens all the time, we never see it. When a person dies in a hospital, he is quickly whisked away; a magical disappearing act does away with the evidence before it could upset anyone. But, as you will read later in various contexts, being part of the dying process, the death, and the burial including seeing and perhaps interacting with the body, is an important part of coming to grips with death—that of the person who has died and your own. We routinely shelter children from death and dying, thinking we are protecting them from harm. But it is clear that we do them a disservice by depriving them of the experience. By making death and dying a taboo subject and keeping children away from people who are dying or who have died, we create fear that need not be there. When a person dies, we "help" his loved ones by doing things for them, being cheerful, and fixing up the body so it looks "natural." Again, our "help" is not helpful; it is destructive. When someone dies, it is important that those close to him participate in the process; it will help them in their grief, and it will help them face their own death more easily.[15]

c. My older sister, Ann, and my younger sister, Martha, always think they are right. They are so stubborn! They fight over the silliest things. I remember hearing them fight last year over the rain. They were watching television with my cousin when he commented that it was raining out. Ann said she knew it was raining, that it had been pouring for a half hour. Martha looked out and said it wasn't pouring, but only sprinkling. In a few minutes they were screaming at each other about how hard or lightly it was raining. My cousin's TV viewing was ruined. Another of their dumb fights occurred last month. Ann had just returned home from staying overnight at a friend's house. Her clothes lay strewn on the couch. Martha saw the clothes and told Ann to pick them up because we were going to have company for dinner. Ann ignored her. About a half hour later, Ann looked on the couch for the clothes, but didn't find them there. She looked all around the room and then happened to glance out the window—there were the clothes, strewn across the yard (where Martha had obviously thrown them). Ann said nothing. She walked upstairs, went into Martha's room, took all her clothes out of the drawers, and threw them out the window. Nor was that enough for Ann. She then went downstairs and began arguing with Martha. The battle raged for more than an hour. Finally, Ann stormed out of the house. When she returned later that evening, Ann found the door locked. (Martha had decided that was a good way to get the last "word.") She was forced to spend the night at a friend's house. But even that was not the most ridiculous fight they ever got into. The most ridiculous one was over a tuna fish sandwich. I was in the living room with my boyfriend at the time. My sisters were in the kitchen. All of a sudden we heard Martha yelling at Ann and calling her a pig. I rushed to the kitchen to see what was going on. Ann was trying to leave the room with her tuna fish sandwich. Martha was holding on to her, shouting that she would let go only when Ann got a plate to put under the sandwich. They both stood there for about fifteen minutes . . . until Martha got tired and let Ann go. Ann walked into the living room, put her sandwich on the coffee table, and turned on the TV set. When she turned around to pick up the sandwich, there was Martha standing in front of her, sandwich in hand. And in a flash she had squashed the sandwich in Ann's surprised face.

Revising for Paragraph Coherence

In Chapters 6, 7, and 8 we discussed the basic way to make your writing coherent—by arranging the ideas in your composition in the most logical and easy to follow order. If you have written your composition carefully, there will be no need to rearrange it during the revision stage. Even the most carefully arranged paper, however, will often need improvement in coherence. Following are four strategies for improving the connections within and between your paragraphs.

Use Pronouns Effectively

Pronouns, words that stand in place of nouns, provide a subtle way of keeping your subject in clear focus without repeating it again and again. They include *I, me, mine, you, yours, it, its, we, us, ours, they, them, theirs, this, that, who, whom, whoever, someone, anyone,* and *no one.* Here is an example of their use:

In the original passage, un-italicized, the pronouns were unobtrusive despite their number.

> I came to marvel at John F. Kennedy's ability to look at *his* own strengths and weaknesses with utter detachment, *his* candid and objective responses to public questions, and *his* insistence on cutting through prevailing bias and myths to the heart of a problem. *He* had a disciplined and analytical mind. Even *his* instincts, which were sound, came from *his* reason rather than *his* hunches. *He* hated no enemy, *he* wept at no adversity. *He* was neither willing nor able to be flamboyant or melodramatic. [Emphasis added.][16]

Repeat Words Skillfully

Undoubtedly you were warned against repetition in high school. Such warnings are justified, for repetition can as easily be a vice as a virtue. The trick is to avoid using it as a cover for poverty of thought, and instead to use it judiciously to reinforce the connections between ideas. Consider this passage.

> Philosophy is the *love of wisdom*. There are many who believe that for a red-blooded man there are better things to *love* than *wisdom*. It seems to be supposed by such persons that *wisdom* is an abstraction that one can best find when he manages to get lost from life. However, one cannot be on good terms with *wisdom* and on bad terms with life, for we would hardly call a man *wise* who did not get along well with life. If one really wishes to understand philosophy, it is not enough to learn to pass formal examinations in this subject; one must also learn to face the tests of living. If one has knowledge of the truth as an intellectual matter but does not live it, then this knowledge is shallow and incomplete; if a philosopher speaks about the truth and yet fails to make it a part of his existence, his words have a hollow ring. [Emphasis added.][17]

In the twenty-odd paragraphs that follow this quoted paragraph, the author discusses various philosophers and holy men from ancient times to the present, pointing out the particular ways in which they manifested their love of wisdom. And every couple of paragraphs or so—whenever he feels the readers could benefit from a reminder of the central focus of his ideas—the author repeats the key phrase "love of wisdom." For example, he writes, "Yet even in this century the love of wisdom has not been entirely eroded and has remained strong in some of our great philosophers, such as the French philosopher Henri Bergson." And later, "Just as Bergson in France managed to love wisdom in this war-torn century, Bertrand Russell in England did so too." And still later, "The love of wisdom embraces the love of peace, and perhaps no human being better exemplified this love than Mahatma Gandhi."

Use Echo Words

Echo words are words that do not exactly repeat what was said, but whose sense is so nearly the same that they *recall* what was said. In the passage about love of wisdom, for example, the author used numerous echo words in the paragraphs following the one quoted above. These included "to know the truth," "love, truth, and justice," "the highest values," and "truth, justice, and virtue."

Use Relationship Words

Relationship words signal that a change of some sort is about to occur in the idea. Such words show exactly how a group of subsequent words relates to a group of preceding words. The following types of relationship words are used for this purpose.

Words for Adding   Whenever another example or case in point is being added, or further details are being provided, or additional development in the same vein as previous development is being presented, there is a potential for misunderstanding. The readers may wonder, "Is this new material more evidence of the same kind or contrasting evidence?" The use of one or more relationship words will answer the question. You may choose from a number of words that show you are adding a point—*also, first (second, third, and so on), in addition, next, further, finally, lastly, besides, another, still another*. However, the most common and simplest adding word is *and*.

From the time you were in grade school, you probably were taught that you should never begin a sentence with *and*. Countless students (and English teachers) have been taught this "rule," although where it originated is uncertain. In any case, there is absolutely no foundation for it in the writing of prose stylists in any period of English literature. The anonymous author of the Old English epic *Beowulf* used *and* as a connective. So did Chaucer in the Middle English period. And virtually every writer of any distinction since that time has also used it. Here are just a few examples from the works of respected twentieth-century writers:

> The music of poetry, then, must be a music latent in the common speech of its time. And that means also that it must be latent in the common speech of the poet's *place*.[18]

> Even supposing that all teachers were willing and able to exact vigilance over written work, there would still be many practical problems of detail. And first, what motive for writing well can the student be made to feel?[19]

> When one watches some tired hack on the platform mechanically repeating the familiar phrases—bestial atrocities, iron heel, blood-stained tyranny, free peoples of the world, stand shoulder to shoulder—one often has a curious feeling that one is not watching a live human being but some kind of dummy: a feeling which suddenly becomes stronger at moments when the light catches the speaker's spectacles and turns them into blank discs which seem to have no eyes behind them. And this is not altogether fanciful.[20]

If these examples are not enough to persuade you that it is perfectly proper to use *and* to begin a sentence, pay a quick visit to your library and check further. And don't look only at books; look at current magazines and newspapers, including *Time* and *Newsweek* and *The New York Times*. You'll find more than enough evidence that *and* is not only acceptable, but one of the most natural and helpful connectives available to you as a writer.

Words for Intensifying   Whenever you are adding something that is more important than preceding points, you need a relationship word that both signals adding and increases the emphasis on what follows, intensifying it. The most common words that achieve both aims are *moreover, more (most) important, more (most) significant, above all, mainly,* and *principally*.

Words for Illustrating   Whenever you turn from an assertion to a point of evidence that supports it, you need words that signal that you are illustrating your idea. You may choose *for example, for instance, to illustrate,* or *a case in point,* to name a few popular phrases.

Words for Changing Time or Place   Whenever you progress or switch from one time or place to another, you need to signal the exact change you are making. Sometimes a simple expression like *afterward, later, then, soon, now, before,* or *eventually* will suffice. At other times a more specific reference will be necessary, such as *at nine o'clock, the following Thursday, in Oakdale,* or *when we finished that.*

Words for Contrasting   Whenever you turn from one idea to an opposing idea, you need a word that signals that opposition or contrast. For example, in "I went to the movie, but I didn't enjoy myself," the *but* alerts the reader that the expected reaction (the writing enjoying himself) did not occur. Some common expressions used to signal contrast are *however, nevertheless, yet, or, on the other hand, in contrast, to be sure, unexpectedly, surprisingly, still.* But the most frequently used is *but.*

Unfortunately, many people have been taught not to begin a sentence with *but.* That prohibition is as unfounded as the prohibition concerning *and.* The word *but* has been used to begin sentences since Anglo-Saxon times. And a check of current books, magazines, and newspapers will reveal that no other connective, with the possible exception of *and,* is used so often in this way. Here are a few examples of its occurrence in the work of respected writers.

> When the churchwardens apply to me at the usual seasons I contribute; and when the hat goes round for special expenses for repairs to the building, I pay my share of what may be necessary to keep it standing. I am on intimate terms with the rector. I am, in short, a local pillar of the Church; and I visit it occasionally. But I have never attended a service there. Whether from defect or excess of intellect, I cannot use the Church of England ritual either as spiritual food or to express and demonstrate my religion. The last time I tried it was when my mother died. She was not a Church of England ritualist; but she had no prejudices nor bigotries. . . . And so the Church of England burial service was read. But I found it morbid and heathenish. It was all wrong for my mother and all wrong for me.[21]

> I have noticed that, as a class, it is the rich who are especially anxious to be loved for themselves alone. The fact is understandable since they are no doubt particularly likely to be imposed upon. But it tends to become an obsession and is one of their less attractive traits.[22]

> There have always been people who devoted their lives to definite regions of thought. In particular, lawyers and the clergy of the Christian churches form obvious examples of such specialism. But the full self-conscious realization of the power of professionalism in knowledge in all its departments, and of the way to produce the professionals, and of the importance of knowledge to the advance of technology, and of the methods by which abstract knowledge can be connected with technology, and of the boundless possibilities of technological advance—the realization of all these things was first completely attained in the nineteenth century; and among the various countries, chiefly in Germany.[23]

Because the point at which a contrast is begun is often the start of a new paragraph, your *but* will often be in an especially prominent position. If you are not used to starting sentences with it, you will undoubtedly be especially reluctant to start a paragraph with it. If such is the case, remind yourself that you are using it to help the reader understand the relationship between your thoughts.

Words for Drawing a Conclusion   Whenever you are pointing out cause-and-effect relationships or drawing a conclusion from the evidence you have presented, you need a word that emphasizes the reasoning you are doing. You may choose from *therefore, so, for this reason, consequently, in conclusion, accordingly, thus, hence, as a result, it follows that, because of this,* and *for* (in the sense of *because*). The last word, *for,* has been subject to the same misunderstanding as *and* and *but*. But, like them, it is completely acceptable at the beginning of a sentence, as these examples demonstrate.

> But the joke is one for the white man to ponder. For it frees him, too: from the need to "love" in order not to lynch.[24]

> Bellamy's utopia now reads so strangely, not through the absurdities of his prophecies, but because of the humane hopes that he attached to their fulfillment. For despite his compassion and his democratic ideals, Bellamy unguardedly embraced, under the rubric of the general welfare, the implacable totalitarian features that Bulwer-Lytton shrank from.[25]

Words for Comparing   Whenever you compare one thing with another, you need a word that signals that a comparison is being made. Choose from *like, as, just as, just like,* and *similarly.*

Words for Summarizing   Whenever you draw a piece of writing to a close and wish to bring together in a concise way some or all of the points you made earlier, use one of these expressions: *to repeat, to sum up, in summary.*

Longer Connectives   Often a single word or a short expression is not adequate to signal the relationship involved. In such cases, longer connectives are necessary. These may be a clause, a whole sentence, or even, in some cases, a paragraph in length. Here are two examples of such longer connectives.

> Another example of Ed's cruelty to his wife, not physical in this case but mental, occurred last week.

> These are the proposals that have been made. All of them, as we have seen, are reasonable. But which of them offers the best prospect of success?

The test for the appropriateness of any connective, even longer ones such as these, is whether it makes clear the relationships among your ideas. To be sure that it is appropriate, put yourself in the place of your readers and consider whether their understanding will be as clear and complete as you intend it to be.

A Sample Passage

How important is it, really, to connect your ideas effectively? Let's look at a brief passage that contains a number of connectives and decide how large their contribution is to its meaning. Each of the italicized words or phrases is a connective of one of the four main types explained earlier in the chapter.

> Something has to be done about the number of violent criminals, many of *them* teenagers (in some cases, *even* children) who prey on law-abiding citizens. *These sociopaths* are seldom imprisoned for any length of time. *Even when they* are caught and convicted of a violent crime, the law seems weighted in their favor, *and because* of *their* youth *or* some legal technicality *or* the judge's leniency, *they* are soon

free to *victimize* others again. *For example,* a convicted felon was recently released in his parents' custody *after being* found guilty of a sex crime. *Within a month* he had raped *and* murdered another young woman. *Moreover,* he was tried on a lesser charge *and, as a result,* got a lighter sentence. *So* in seven or eight years he may be walking the streets again. *Nor* is his situation all that uncommon. Reduced charges, light *or* suspended sentences, *and* early parole seem to be the dominant pattern in today's courts. Something must be done to change *this pattern.* The answer, *of course,* is not a merciless, repressive legal system. *Neither* is it vigilante action. *Those solutions* would be little better than the problem itself. *Surely* our democratic principles demand that the rights of suspects be upheld *and* that humane treatment be given *even* the most vicious, unrepentant criminal. *But those considerations* must no longer be allowed to obscure *the first* and *most important* reason for any law—to protect the rights of the honest, the responsible, *and* the innocent.

Without the connective words and phrases, the passage would still be intelligible. But it would not be nearly so easy to grasp. The connectives allow an easier reading of the passage, giving the readers a better understanding of its meaning. In addition, connectives subtly increase the readers' confidence in the writer by demonstrating that she has control over her ideas and is fully aware of their interrelationships.

A word of caution is in order here. Be sure to choose your connectives with care. The wrong ones can be worse than none at all, for they will not only make reading difficult, but actually set up misinterpretation. So don't just sprinkle in your connectives indiscriminately. Make them fit the relationships and convey the meaning you intend.

Exercises

1. Reread the paragraph on page 289 about violent crime and the need for reform of the legal system. Classify each of the italicized words or phrases as one of the following kinds of connectives: repeated words, echo words, pronouns, or relationship words. In the case of relationship words, indicate the kind of relationship shown.

2. Read each of the following passages closely. List each connective word or phrase in the passage. Then classify each as you did in exercise 1.

    a. Standing on our microscopic fragment of a grain of sand, we attempt to discover the nature and purpose of the universe which surrounds our home in space and time. Our first impression of the universe is something akin to terror. We find the universe terrifying because of its vast meaningless distances, terrifying because of its inconceivably long vistas of time, which dwarf human history to the twinkling of an eye, terrifying because of our extreme loneliness and because of the material insignificance of our home in space—a millionth part of a grain of sand out of all the sea-sand in the world. But above all else, we find the universe terrifying because it appears to be indifferent to life like our own; emotion, ambition and achievement, art and religion, all seem foreign to its plan. Perhaps, indeed, we ought to say it appears to be actively hostile to life like our own.[26]

b. With few exceptions, modern authorities have accepted [*Studies of a Reclining Male Nude*] as a study by Michelangelo for the figure of Adam in the "creation of Adam" section of the Sistine Ceiling. But is it really one of Michelangelo's drawings? Bernard Berenson once doubted it. He thought it more likely a very accomplished contemporary copy of a Michelangelo drawing now lost to us. Then, as sometimes happens with even the greatest connoisseurs, Berenson reversed himself. He elevated it from "School of Michelangelo" to a work by the master himself. Yet he continued to harbor doubts about it.[27]

c. Next morning my wife slipped out of the hotel successfully. The train was about an hour late in starting. I filled in the time by writing a long letter to the Ministry of War, telling them about Kopp's case—that without a doubt he had been arrested by mistake, that he was urgently needed at the front, that countless people would testify that he was innocent of any offense, etc., etc., etc. I wonder if anyone read that letter, written on pages torn out of a notebook in wobbly handwriting (my fingers were still partly paralyzed) and still more wobbly Spanish. At any rate, neither this letter nor anything else took effect. As I write, six months after the event, Kopp (if he has not been shot) is still in jail, untried and uncharged. At the beginning we had two or three letters from him, smuggled out by released prisoners and posted in France. They all told the same story—imprisonment in filthy dark dens, bad and insufficient food, serious illness due to the conditions of imprisonment, and refusal of medical attention. I have had all this confirmed from several other sources, English and French. More recently he disappeared into one of the "secret prisons" with which it seems impossible to make any kind of communication. His case is the case of scores or hundreds of foreigners and no one knows how many thousands of Spaniards.[28]

Composition Assignment

Select one of the topics, quotations, or issues listed below and write a 500-word composition on it. Don't skimp on the planning and writing stages, but pay particular attention to revising, especially to revising for paragraph effectiveness. (*Note:* If you choose one of the topics, be sure to narrow it sufficiently before generating ideas; if you choose one of the quotations, you may include it in the composition as a reinforcement for your own controlling idea, but not as a substitute for that idea.)

Topics

Tradition	National defense
Failure	Growing up
Bravery	Sisters (brothers)
Perfection	Junk mail
Science	The ghetto

Quotations

1. "A liar needs a good memory." (Quintilian)
2. "Anything which can be made funny must have at its heart some tragic implications." (Karl Menninger)
3. "Sometimes parties are more depressing than joyous." (Anonymous)
4. "There is a great man who makes every man feel small. But the real great man is the man who makes every man feel great." (G. K. Chesterton)
5. "Most often people seek in life occasions for persisting in their opinions rather than for educating themselves." (André Gide)

Issues

1. Some people believe in UFOs. That is, they believe that beings from outer space have visited us to study us and our planet. They point to a large body of evidence ranging from strange ancient ruins to unexplained events (loss of ships and planes in the Bermuda Triangle, for example) and even to contemporary eyewitness testimony. Do you accept or reject their belief? Why?

2. Do you think that those who believe that all war is wrong should be excused from serving in the armed forces? What about those who do not believe all war is wrong, but who oppose a particular war?
3. The 1970s produced a number of films, like *The Exorcist*, that dealt with the subject of possession by the devil or other evil spirits. Do you believe such spirits exist? If so, do you believe they can exercise control over a person?
4. The issue of abortion continues to rage in this country. Some claim it is morally wrong in all cases; others, that it is morally right in all cases; and still others, that it is right in some cases and not in others. Where do you stand?
5. Should the voting age be eighteen? Sixteen? Twenty-one? What is the reasoning that underlies your choice?

Part V

The Research Paper

Progress in every field of human endeavor depends upon continuing research. For that reason, training in conducting research and organizing and presenting one's findings is an important component of higher education. This section will assist you in understanding and applying the fundamental principles and approaches of research.

Strictly speaking, the research paper is not another composition form but a special application of informative or persuasive writing. Accordingly, it shares the characteristics of whichever of those forms it is applying. In other words, an informative research paper presents factual information without taking sides, whereas a persuasive research paper presents and defends the writer's judgments. (Both kinds of papers will be examined closely in the pages that follow.)

There are three significant ways in which the research paper differs from the three writing forms we have studied. First, it is more thorough. Though every good composition is based upon something more substantial than the writer's casual opinions, an effective research paper is based upon a more careful and extensive investigation of its subject. Secondly, because of its greater amount of information, the research paper tends to be longer than the average composition—instead of 500 words, well over 1,000 words. Finally, the research paper is more formal, including brief source references within the text and a list of works cited following the text. The demand for formality in the research paper is not arbitrary—it is designed to help the writer efficiently sort and arrange a greater amount of material than he or she is accustomed to handling and to present that material in a format that is useful to the readers.

Using Your Library's Resources

A good deal of the time you spend working on your research paper will be spent handling library materials. The more aware you are of your library's resources, the more efficiently you will be able to use them.

There is no reason to be intimidated by the library. It is a meticulously organized place designed to be useful and easy to use. Every book, record, tape, and other source of information stored in the library has a special identification code. No two titles have the same code. Most libraries are divided by the types of materials stored together. The divisions are as follows:

General/Circulating Collection

Usually the largest part of the library, this section contains most of the materials that may be checked out from the library. Sometimes the section is open to everyone (the "open stacks" system) and sometimes it is closed (the "closed stacks" system). In the latter system the borrower requests the books she wishes to see and a library employee obtains them.

Reference

This section, a helpful one for every researcher, contains encyclopedias, dictionaries, almanacs, and sources that tell you where to find books, articles, and other materials about your subject. The works in this section may not be taken out of the library.

Periodicals

This section usually contains all of the newspapers, journals, and magazines the library owns. Issues from the current year are often kept in open stacks. Depending on your library, older issues may be found in hardcover or in microform (microfilm or microfiche). In the latter case, machines will be available so that you can read the material and make paper copies.

Nonprint Materials

Many libraries also contain such nonprint materials as records, films, and videotapes. These are usually separately shelved rather than stored with print materials.

Government Publications

Some libraries have extensive collections of local, state, and federal government publications. These may or may not be stored in a separate collection. Since they contain a wealth of valuable information, you should always ask your librarian about them.

The Library Classification System

Libraries in the United States use either the Dewey Decimal system or the Library of Congress system to catalog their holdings. Both systems are designed to facilitate the storing and retrieving of those holdings. The Dewey Decimal system uses a number code representing the following groupings:

000 General Works
100 Philosophy
200 Religion
300 Social Sciences
400 Language
500 Pure Sciences
600 Technology
700 The Arts
800 Literature
900 History

The Library of Congress system uses a letter code and has these groupings:

A   General Works
B   Philosophy—Religion
C   Auxiliary Sciences of History
D   History and Topography (Except America)
E–F American History
G   Geography—Anthropology
H   Social Sciences
J   Political Science
K   Law
L   Education
M   Music
N   Fine Arts
P   Languages and Literature
Q   Science
R   Medicine
S   Agriculture—Plant and Animal Industry
T   Technology
U   Military Science
V   Naval Science
Z   Bibliography and Library Science

Subgroupings within each grouping, identified by a combination of numbers and letters, permit the classification of all materials. These subgroupings can be found in your campus library.

The Library Catalog

The library catalog usually provides you with three different ways to access the library's holdings: by author, by title, or by subject. You can use the catalog to determine what materials are available on a specific subject without knowing any particular author or title. Or, if you know the title or author's name, you can use the catalog to determine exactly where a work is shelved.

The traditional catalog, the "card catalog," consists of drawers of 3-×-5-inch cards containing the information shown on the samples below. However, you may find that your library's catalog is on microfilm, on microfiche, or even in a computer. Your librarian will explain which system is in use.

The preceding description is a general introduction to library resources. It may not fit your college library in every detail. In any case, becoming familiar with your library means more than understanding its general arrangement. It means learning its specific holdings in the subject area in which you will be doing your

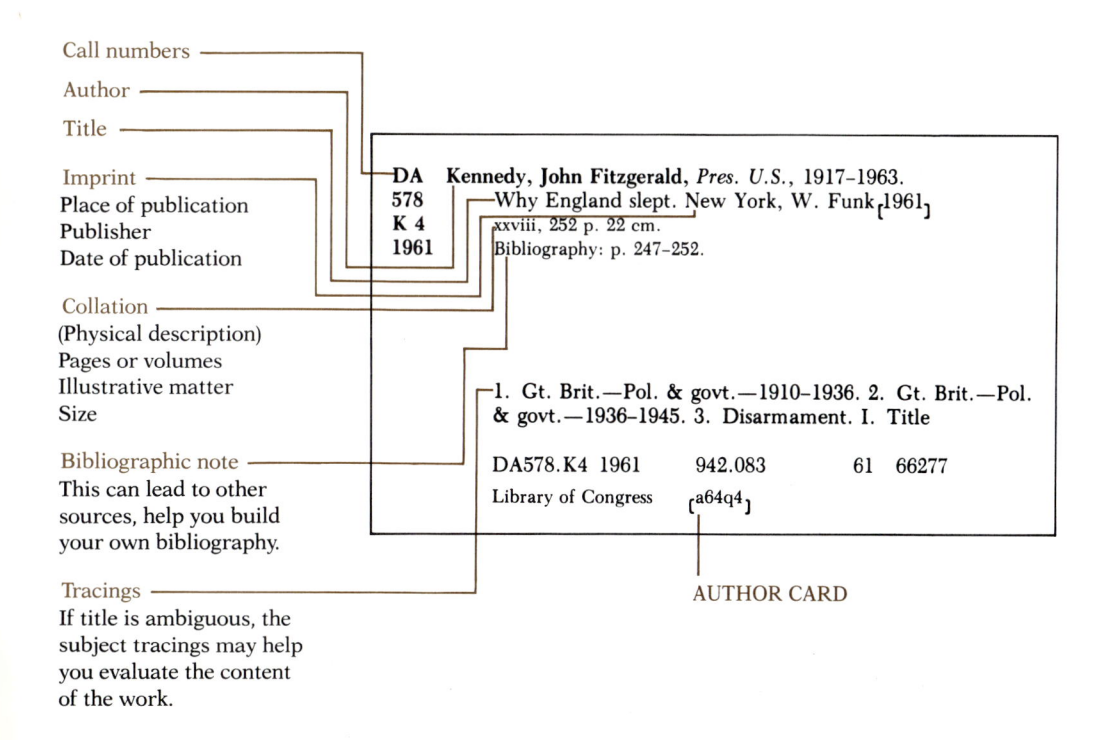

Call numbers
Author
Title

Imprint
Place of publication
Publisher
Date of publication

```
DA      Kennedy, John Fitzgerald, Pres. U.S., 1917–1963.
578       Why England slept. New York, W. Funk [1961]
K 4         xxviii, 252 p. 22 cm.
1961        Bibliography: p. 247–252.


            1. Gt. Brit.—Pol. & govt.—1910–1936. 2. Gt. Brit.—Pol.
            & govt.—1936–1945. 3. Disarmament. I. Title

            DA578.K4 1961        942.083        61    66277
            Library of Congress      [a64q4]
```

Collation
(Physical description)
Pages or volumes
Illustrative matter
Size

Bibliographic note
This can lead to other sources, help you build your own bibliography.

AUTHOR CARD

Tracings
If title is ambiguous, the subject tracings may help you evaluate the content of the work.

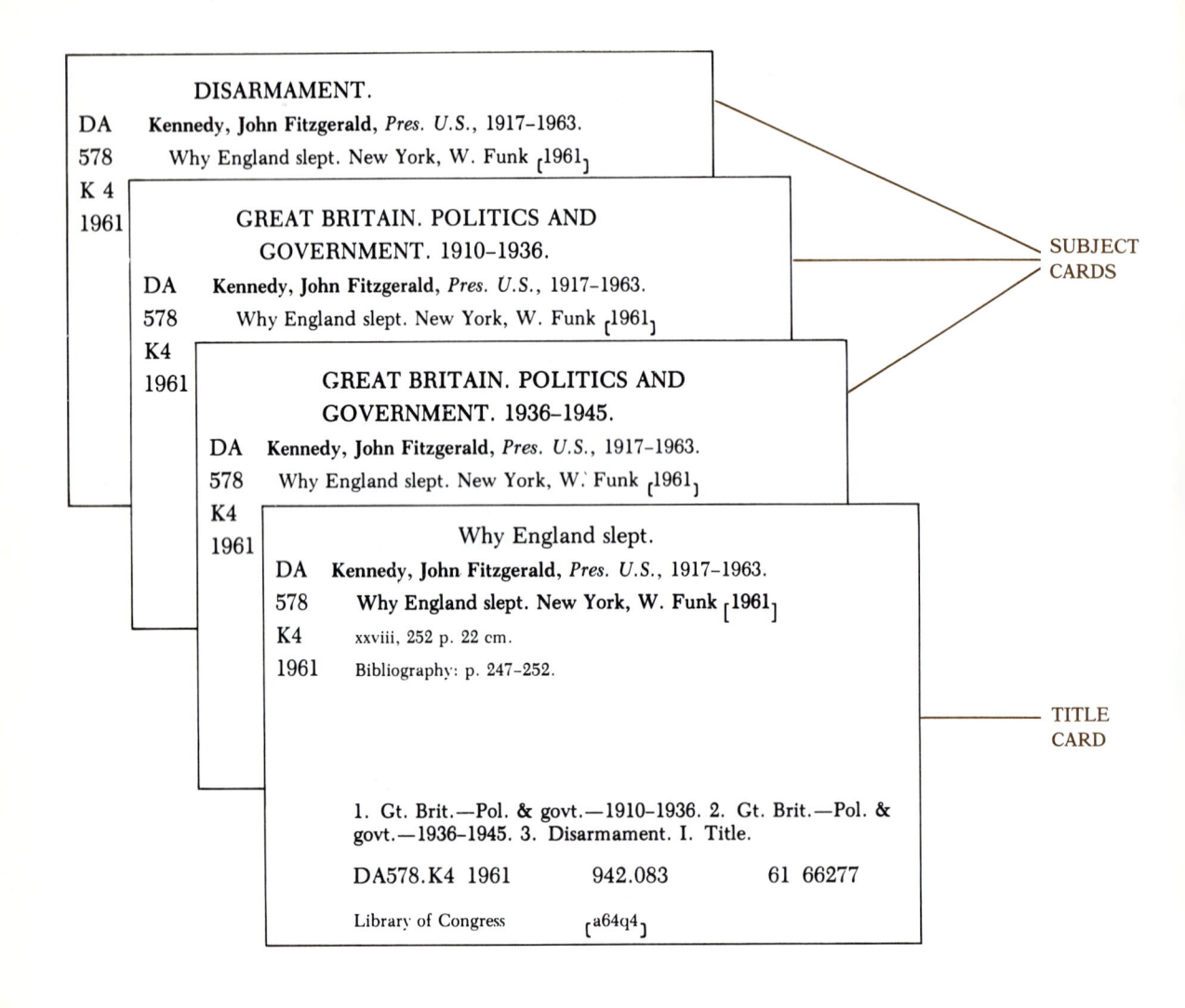

```
                                  ┌─────────────────────────────────────────┐
                                  │           DISARMAMENT.                   │
                               DA │  Kennedy, John Fitzgerald, Pres. U.S., 1917-1963.
                               578│     Why England slept. New York, W. Funk [1961]
                               K 4│ ┌─────────────────────────────────────────┐
                               1961│ │    GREAT BRITAIN. POLITICS AND         │
                                  │ │    GOVERNMENT. 1910-1936.              │         ─── SUBJECT
                                  │DA│  Kennedy, John Fitzgerald, Pres. U.S., 1917-1963.   CARDS
                                  │578│    Why England slept. New York, W. Funk [1961]
                                  │K4│ ┌─────────────────────────────────────────┐
                                  │1961│ │    GREAT BRITAIN. POLITICS AND        │
                                  │   │ │    GOVERNMENT. 1936-1945.             │
                                  │   │DA│  Kennedy, John Fitzgerald, Pres. U.S., 1917-1963.
                                  │   │578│    Why England slept. New York, W. Funk [1961]
                                  │   │K4 │ ┌─────────────────────────────────────┐
                                  │   │1961│ │       Why England slept.           │
                                  │   │   │DA│  Kennedy, John Fitzgerald, Pres. U.S., 1917-1963.
                                  │   │   │578│    Why England slept. New York, W. Funk [1961]
                                  │   │   │K4 │    xxviii, 252 p. 22 cm.
                                  │   │   │1961│   Bibliography: p. 247-252.
                                  │   │   │   │                                          ─── TITLE
                                  │   │   │   │                                              CARD
                                  │   │   │   │  1. Gt. Brit.—Pol. & govt.—1910-1936. 2. Gt. Brit.—Pol. &
                                  │   │   │   │  govt.—1936-1945. 3. Disarmament. I. Title.
                                  │   │   │   │  DA578.K4 1961        942.083          61 66277
                                  │   │   │   │  Library of Congress         [a64q4]
```

research. Does the library have extensive book holdings in that subject, or will you likely have to send for the books you need through interlibrary loan? What periodicals does it subscribe to, and what years are covered? Knowing the answers to these questions before you begin your research will enable you to allow sufficient lead time for receiving materials and to save time in using the periodical indexes.

A Strategy for Research

Many students approach the job of researching their papers haphazardly. That approach usually leaves them frustrated and yields unsatisfactory papers. You can avoid both effects by conducting your research systematically. Here is a simple yet effective strategy for doing so. Let's assume you begin your research with only the broad topic—"The Occult"—in mind. You might follow this approach.

1. *Go to the reference section of the library and find a good general encyclopedia.* Encyclopaedia Britannica *and* Encyclopedia Americana *are among the best. Consult the appropriate micropaedia volume of* Britannica* *or the index volume of* Americana. You'll find these entries:

Britannica, Micropaedia Volume VII, p. 469

one celestial body or an observer's view of another body. *See* eclipse, occultation, and transit.

occultism, a general designation for various theories, practices, and rituals based on esoteric knowledge, especially alleged knowledge about the world of spirits and unknown forces of the universe. Devotees of occultism strive to understand and explore these worlds, often by developing the higher powers of the mind. To this end they frequently study very early writings in the belief that such secrets were known to ancient civilizations and can be repossessed. A favourite text is the Chinese *I Ching* ("Classic of Changes").

   Occultism covers such diverse subjects as Satanism, astrology, Kabbala, Gnosticism, theosophy, divination, witchcraft, and certain forms of magic.

Americana, index (Volume 30), p. 588

OCCULTATION (astron.) 20–608
  Eclipse 9–582
OCCULTISM (mysticism) 20–609
  See also Devil The; Divination;
    Extrasensory Perception;
    Magic; Witchcraft
  Astrology 2–557
  Cabala 5–108
  Demonology 8–699; 9–36
  Evil Spirit 10–733
  Extrasensory Perception (ESP)
    10–804
  Fortune-Telling 11–628; 9–196
  Ghost 12–724
  Magic 18–117
  Numerology 20–543
  Parapsychology 21–287
  Psychokinesis 22–721
  Rosicrucians 23–701
  Spiritualism 25–514
  Superstition 26–35

(Both entries continued on page 302.)

**Encyclopaedia Britannica* is divided into two sets of books: the m*acropaedia* set, containing fully detailed articles on a limited number of subjects; and the m*icropaedia* set, containing brief articles and cross-references on a large number of subjects. The m*icropaedia* set functions very much like the single-volume index of *Americana*.

Britannica, Micropaedia
Volume VII, p. 469 *(cont.)*

- mystical function and ambiguous utility 12:786f
- Odin as Norse patron 8:36g
- Taoist and Confucian views 17:1034e
- theosophic affirmation of supernatural 18:276f

occupancy, in law, acquisition of unowned property by taking possession with intent of

Americana, index
(Volume 30), p. 588 *(cont.)*

Occupancy (law): *See* Possession
Occupation, Military: *See* Military Government

Note that both entries list other related subjects and give volume and page references.

2. *Next, determine whether your interest is in the broad topic of occultism or in some specific aspect of that topic.* Let's say that after reading the list of related subjects you decide that astrology is your real interest. Now consult the appropriate volume of *Britannica* (macropaedia, Vol. 2, p. 219) or *Americana* (Vol. 2, p. 557, as noted in the entry). You will find an excellent brief overview of the subject (more scholarly and detailed in *Britannica*, but more concise and readable in *Americana*).

3. *If possible, look up your topic in a subject encyclopedia.* You may find one specifically related to your subject or you may have to look in an encyclopedia that covers a broader subject area. There are, for example, various encyclopedias available in each of the following areas: art, astronomy, biology, chemistry, computer science, dance, earth sciences, economics, education, film, history, law, literature, mathematics, medicine, music, philosophy, physics, psychology, religion, science and technology, and the social sciences. For the subject of the occult, you might want to check N. Devore's *Encyclopedia of Astrology* or one of the psychology or religion encyclopedias. (*Note:* You will usually find recommended readings on your topic at the end of an encyclopedia article. These will often offer valuable information.)

4. *Look for other reference books on your topic.* By consulting a guide to reference materials, such as Eugene O. Sheehy's *Guide to Reference Books*, you will be able to identify bibliographies and other reference books that pertain to your topic and find answers to such questions as the following:

Where can I find miscellaneous facts and statistics? Sheehy lists *The World Almanac, Information Please Almanac, The New York Times Encyclopedic Almanac,* and *The People's Almanac,* among other sources.

Where can I find information about specific people? Sheehy lists *Who's Who* (British), *Who's Who in America,* and *Who's Who in the World,* among other sources.

Where can I find information about the English language? Sheehy lists the *Oxford English Dictionary,* Eric Partridge's *Dictionary of Slang and Unconventional English,* and *Webster's New Dictionary of Synonyms,* among other sources.

Where can I find significant quotations? Sheehy suggests E. M. Beck's *Familiar Quotations* and George Seldes's *The Great Quotations,* among other sources.

Where can I find publishing information about books that were or are still in print? Sheehy lists *Cumulative Book Index, Books in Print,* and *Paperback Books in Print,* among other sources.

5. *Consult the library catalog.* Look in the author and title catalogs for the books recommended in the bibliographies. (Keep in mind that on occasion you will find a book listed in one catalog section but not in another, so consult both.) If the books listed in the bibliographies are not in your library, the librarian may be able to obtain them for you through interlibrary loan. Also, consult the subject catalog for other books on your subject, looking under both the general heading of "Occultism" and the specific heading of "Astrology."

6. *Consult the appropriate periodical index in the reference section of the library.* The basic reference to nontechnical articles is the *Readers' Guide to Periodical Literature.* (This index, however, should not be used as the sole or primary tool for a college research paper.) A number of indexes are also available for specialized and technical subjects. The following are among the most commonly used:

Applied Science and Technology Index
Art Index
Biography Index
Biological and Agricultural Index
Book Review Index

Business Periodicals Index
Education Index
Engineering Index
General Science Index
Humanities Index
Index to Legal Periodicals
MLA International Bibliography
Magazine Index
Music Index
Philosopher's Index
Religion Index One: Periodicals
Social Sciences Index

Here is a sample periodical listing:

The Humanities Index, April 1975–March 1976, p. 41

    Wettlin. Sov Lit nos: 116–41 '75
  First night back; tr. by A. Shkarovsky-Raffe. Sov Lit no 1:3–29 '75
ASTBURY, R.
  Juvenal 10, 148–50. Mnemosyne 28 fasc 1: 40–6 '75
ASTRODYNAMICS
  See also
  Astronautics
ASTROLOGY
  Astrology as popular culture. M. Truzzi, J Pop Cult 8:906–11 Spr '75
  Astrology: magic or science? L. E. Jerome. il Humanist 35:10–16 S '75
  Critical look at astrology. B.J. Bok. il Humanist 35:6–9 S '75
  My flirtation with astrology. C. Lamont. Humanist 35:16 S '75
  Objections to astrology: a statement by 186 leading scientists. Humanist 35:4–6 S '75
  Science and religion in the writings of Dr William Fulke, R. Bauckham. Brit J Hist Sci 8:17–31 Mr '75
  See also
  Occult sciences
ASTROLOGY in literature

> Astrology and the Wife of Bath: a reinterpretation. B. F. Hamlin. Chaucer R 9: 153–65 Fall '74
> Chapman's Byron and Bartholomaeus Anglicus. G. F. Freije, Eng Lang Notes 12:168–71 Mr '75
> Satan in orbit and medieval demonology (Paradise lost, IX: 64–66) J. M. Steadman, Eng Lang Notes 12:161–3 Mr '75
> ASTRONAUTICS
> *See also*
> Space flight

The article entries are presented in abbreviated form. But that form is easy to decipher. The first article is read as follows: Title: "Astrology as Popular Culture." Author: M. Truzzi. Journal: *Journal of Popular Culture*. Volume: 8. Pages: 906–11. Issue: Spring 1975. (If you occasionally find an abbreviation that puzzles you, look for the explanation of the entry code at the beginning of the index volume.) Note that at the end of the listing of articles is a cross-reference to a related heading, "Occult Sciences," and that the next heading covers a more specialized aspect of the subject, "Astrology in Literature." Copy down the entries of articles you wish to read.

7. *Consult the New York Times Index. The New York Times Index* is the standard newspaper index for the United States. It covers all stories that appeared in that newspaper from 1851 to the present. Most libraries will have in their microfilm collection any *Times* story you wish to read.

8. *Check to see if your library has access to computer data bases and abstracting services.* Data bases are especially helpful when you are having difficulty finding information on your subject. Abstracting services such as *Psychological Abstracts, Sociological Abstracts,* and *America: History and Life* offer helpful summaries of journal articles. *Dissertation Abstracts International* provides summaries of doctoral dissertations.

9. *Obtain the books and articles you wish to consult in preparing your paper.* In the case of a book, turn to the index (or to the table of contents if the book does not have an index) and find which pages of the book are most relevant to your topic. Then turn to those pages and scan them. A few minutes spent in this way will often save you considerable time and frustration later. If one large part

or many smaller parts of the book prove useful, borrow the book. If only a few pages do, photocopy them and be sure to note the author, title, publisher, and date of publication on the photocopies. In the case of an article, scan it quickly to determine its value to you. If it proves valuable, photocopy all or part of it, noting author, article title, publication title, volume, number, and date. *Remember that a quotation without a source is worthless, and a return trip to the library is at best time-consuming and, if the material is not available, may be unproductive.*

10. *In all your reading, keep your purpose larger than merely acquiring information.* Make it include, as well, two other aims. The first of these is to acquire additional source references. You can do this effortlessly by noting authors' references to other books and articles on the subject. (These may be found in the body of the book or in the footnotes and bibliography that accompany it.) The second aim is to deepen your understanding, to see the connections among ideas and grasp the significance of the information. The aim here, in short, is to stimulate your thinking. That does not occur automatically when you read. It depends on the *way* you read. If, like many people, you read passively, merely absorbing the ideas of others and not forming and refining your own ideas, your thinking will not profit you very much. You must read *actively,* pausing to pursue an idea triggered in your mind by the author's words, even scribbling a note of agreement or disagreement for future reference. Most important, whenever an author offers an interpretation or judgment, you must ask appropriate questions, such as "What other interpretations or judgments are possible here?" "How substantial is the evidence the author offers for her position?" and "How reasonable is her position?"

Taking Notes

One of the most time-consuming parts of research is the taking of notes. For this reason, it is always tempting to hurry the task and take every shortcut you can think of. But there are good shortcuts and bad, and the bad ones can cost you time in the long run and create unnecessary frustration. An incomplete or illegible note, for example, can make you return to the library (often at an inconvenient time) to examine the book or article again. And many times the book or article is not available then—someone else may have

Taking Notes 307

borrowed it! The following tips are based on the experience (often painful) of countless researchers. They are designed to make note taking as fast and efficient as possible. Any other shortcuts are likely to be risky.

1. *Make a bibliography card for every work you decide is useful to you and make it the first time you handle the work.* Use a 3-×-5 index card and be sure to include all relevant information. (See the documentation guidelines beginning on page 316.) Here is a sample card:

```
QA
22
N36
1962

   Neugebauer, O. The Exact Sciences
   in Antiquity. 2nd ed. New York:
   Harper + Brothers, 1962.
```

2. *Make a separate note card for every idea.* (Some researchers prefer the 4-×-6 index card for notes because it affords a little more writing space than the 3-×-5 card.) This may seem wasteful of index cards. However, when arranging your ideas, it is much easier to shuffle cards than to recopy notes. See the top of page 308 for a sample note card.

3. *Condense the material as much as possible.* Never quote a long passage unless it is so important and so concise that a paraphrase would be unacceptable. And take the time to be sure the paraphrase does not lean too heavily on the author's phrasing. By condensing, limiting your quotations, and paraphrasing carefully, you will reduce the chances of committing unintentional plagiarism when you are writing the paper.

Page reference	Neugebauer, p. 171
Context of idea	(Discussing origins of Hellenistic science)
(Note that it's mostly paraphrased and somewhat abbreviated, yet the quotation is word for word.)	Astrology was part of Hellenistic science. Idea of bodies in universe influencing one another similar to modern mechanistic theories, yet very different from religious theory of divine intervention or magic. "Compared with the background of religion, magic and mysticism, the fundamental *doctrines* of astrology are pure science."
Researcher's own question and comment	What, then, does claim that astrology is *unscientific* mean? Examine this.

4. *Recheck for accuracy.* When you have finished taking notes on a source, check to be sure that you have not misinterpreted the source's statement or quoted out of context. Check, too, that what you have written is clear enough that you will not be confused about it when you are writing the paper. (A note that is meaningful today can be very puzzling two weeks from now.) A brief remark about the context in which the statement was made or your reaction to the statement can help provide that clarity.

Manuscript Mechanics

Unless your instructor gives you other instructions, use the following guidelines, based on the *MLA Handbook* guidelines, in presenting your research paper.

Materials

For handwritten manuscripts, use standard 8½-×-11-inch filler paper with wide spaces between lines. (Do not use paper torn out of a spiral notebook.) Use a good pen with black or blue ink, and write neatly and legibly, taking care not to run your words together.

For typewritten manuscripts, use standard 8½- × -11-inch typing paper. (Do not use onionskin paper or erasable bond.) Be sure your typewriter keys are clean and your ribbon (black or blue) is not too faint. Write or type on only one side of the paper.

Margins and Indentation

Leave a margin of one inch at the top, bottom, and at each side of the page. Indent the first word of each new paragraph five spaces. When quoting prose passages of more than four lines, indent each line of the quoted material ten spaces. When quoting poetry of more than three lines, indent each line ten spaces. However, if the poem was originally presented with unusual margins or indentation, follow the original.

Spacing

For typed manuscripts, double-space throughout, including quotations and notes. For handwritten manuscripts, indicate double-spacing by skipping one ruled line.

Syllabication

Whenever possible, avoid breaking a word at the end of a line. However, if you cannot do so without creating an unsightly space, be sure to break the word only between syllables. (If you are uncertain of the syllabication, consult a good dictionary.) For example, the word *legalization* is divided as follows: *le-gal-i-za-tion*. So you might end one line *le-* (note the hyphen) and begin the next with *galization;* or *legaliza-* followed by *tion*. However, any syllable composed of a single letter should be retained at the end of the first line, rather than carried over. So *legal-* followed by *ization* would *not* be correct (since *i* is a one-letter syllable); the word should be written *legali-* followed by *zation*.

In addition, divide hyphenated words such as *mother-in-law, ill-suited,* and *president-elect* only where they are already hyphenated. Finally, try to avoid dividing words in ways that might confuse or distract the reader. For instance, the word *barring* (meaning "in the absence of") is properly divided into *bar-* and *ring*. Yet if that division would confuse the reader momentarily (perhaps by suggesting the sense of "tavern," as in *barroom*), it should be avoided.

Page Numbers

Number *all* pages consecutively throughout the manuscript. Place each number in the upper-right-hand corner, one-half inch from the top. From page 2 on, write your last name before the page number to safeguard against misplaced pages. Use no punctuation marks with page numbers.

Tables and Illustrations

Place all tables and illustrations as close as possible to the section of the text they are related to. Label all tables "Table" plus an arabic numeral, and add a title. Both labels and titles should be placed flush left on separate lines.

Titles and Other Headings

You need not use a separate title page for your composition or research paper. Just type your name in the upper-right-hand corner of the first page, and below that type your professor's name, the course title, and the date, each on a separate line. Next, double-space twice and type your title in the center of the page, then double-space again and begin the first paragraph. (See page 325 for a sample first page.)

Capitalize only the initial letter of each important word in your title. (Do not capitalize the initial letters of articles, or those of brief conjunctions and prepositions, except when such words appear at the beginning of the title.) Do not underline your title or put quotation marks around it. Those devices are used only in your references to other people's titles. However, if your title includes a reference to another person's title, use the appropriate device for that person's title, as illustrated in the following examples:

Correct   What's Wrong with My Home Town

Correct   An Analysis of T. S. Eliot's "Ash Wednesday"

Correct   Hawthorne's Sources for *The Scarlet Letter*

If your paper contains subheadings, type them as you do your title, with double-spacing before and after to separate them from the text.

Abbreviations

In formal writing, abbreviations are usually avoided. There are, however, several exceptions to this rule. The abbreviations of personal titles or designations occurring before or after a name, such as Ms., Dr., or Ph.D., are acceptable, as are references to specific times (10:45 P.M., A.D. 1066) and Latin abbreviations (*i.e.* for "that is"; *e.g.* for "for example"; *etc.* for "and so forth").

Corrections

Corrections are acceptable in a manuscript as long as they are neatly made and are not so numerous as to be distracting. Ugly smudges, erasures, and strikeovers should always be avoided, as should the confusing rearrangement of sentences using arrows and brackets. Minor changes, however, may be made by crossing out the word or words to be deleted and printing or typing the corrections directly above it, using a caret (∧) to indicate where the correction goes. (Never make corrections in the margins.) There is no rule as to how many words may be corrected on a page. If handled carefully, one or more lines can be altered without posing a serious distraction to the reader. But it is better to write or type a page over than to risk confusing or offending a reader.

Deciding on Form

As noted earlier in this chapter, a research paper may be written in either informative or persuasive form. Let's look more closely at each and see how you should go about selecting the best one for your research paper.

The Informative Research Paper

The purpose of the informative research paper is to present the facts about an issue or scholarly topic as objectively as possible. The writer of an informative paper merely reports what he found in his research. He does not attempt to analyze or evaluate the data, nor does he offer his opinion about the issue. Where controversy exists and the sources he has consulted disagree in their interpretations, he describes the disagreement and presents relevant details about it, but he refrains from taking sides. Though it is impossible to be totally objective, he strives to be as dispassionate and impartial as he can. His aim is not to persuade but to inform.

Make your paper informative if either of these circumstances applies: After completing your research, you find that you have no strong view about any of the controversial aspects of the subject, or that your view is not substantial enough to be the focal point of the paper. (*Note:* Do not confuse this with a situation in which you do have a strong view but are timid about expressing it.)

The second circumstance in which you should write an informative paper occurs when your subject is a rather technical one about which you lack the competency to make an informed judgment, even after completing your research (for example, if you are an English major writing a research paper for an economics course or a science major writing a research paper for a poetry course).

The criteria on which the informative research paper is measured are *the quality and extensiveness of the research* and *the clarity of presentation*. To be considered excellent, the paper must include all major items of information, accurately presented. Moreover, it must contain adequate definitions, examples, explanations, and descriptive details to make it understandable to the reader, and it must be so arranged and expressed that it is easy to follow.

The Persuasive Research Paper

Like the informative research paper, the persuasive research paper presents the research findings. Nevertheless, its larger purpose is not to inform but to persuade the readers. Therefore the writer of a persuasive research paper does not only report what she found in her research; she also offers her own interpretation of those findings. Where controversy exists and the sources she has consulted disagree in their judgments, she weighs each side and explains which she finds more reasonable and why. The skill she is exercising is not merely reporting but also critical thinking.

Make your research paper persuasive if you have a significant judgment to make and you have the competency to make it. The latter condition may frighten you, but there is no reason for it to do so. If you have done your research well and are willing to exercise care in evaluating your own arguments and those of others, you should be able to make significant judgments about all but the most technical matters.

The first two criteria on which the persuasive research paper is measured are the same as those for the informative paper—that is, *the quality and extensiveness of the research* and *the clarity of presentation*. But the persuasive paper has a third, more important criterion—*the quality and force of its judgments*. Excellence in persuasion depends on the reasonableness of the views presented.

Deciding on Format

There are two formats commonly used in research papers. Either format may be used with either informative or persuasive research papers. However, each format has certain advantages and disadvantages, so your choice for a particular paper must be made in light of your topic and audience. Whenever possible, choose the format that you are more comfortable with.

The Separated Format

The divisions of the paper in the separated format are as follows:

    I. Presentation of the issue or topic
   II. Presentation of your research data
  III. Presentation of your sources' interpretations and judgments of the data
*[IV. Your interpretations and judgments]

One advantage of the separated format is that it helps you avoid much of the confusion involved with handling detailed or complicated material. You don't have to decide where to put a

---

*This division is included only if the paper is persuasive.

particular bit of information—what it is determines where it goes. In a manner of speaking, the paper organizes itself. Still another advantage of this format is that it helps you distinguish between your source's judgments and your own judgments and thereby avoid plagiarism (presenting as your own the ideas or words of someone else).

The only significant disadvantage of the separated format is that it offers less freedom of form than the integrated format. In fact, it can lead to an overly dry, mechanical presentation. That need not occur, however, if you make a special effort to keep your expression lively and interesting.

The Integrated Format

The integrated format employs the standard essay form of introduction/body/conclusion. Instead of demanding a strict separation of your research data from your sources' interpretations, and of your sources' interpretations from your own interpretations, it allows you to blend the material as you wish. You may, for example, take one item from the data, offer your sources' interpretations of it, discuss where you agree and disagree, and then move on to another item.

The principal advantage of the integrated format is that it offers you greater freedom to arrange your material to advantage, to be persuasive, to put more of your personality and style into your paper. The principal disadvantage is that it significantly increases two risks that are present in any writing situation—the risk of *superficiality* (you may be tempted to cover a lack of research by multiplying words); and the risk of *plagiarism* (lacking a clear separation between your judgments and those of your sources, you may unintentionally present their words and ideas as your own). Whenever you use the integrated format for a research paper, take special care to avoid both superficiality and plagiarism.

Documentation Defined

Documentation is acknowledgment. It is not a sign of slavishness, but of simple honesty and courtesy. It tells your readers not that you lacked the mental ability to think for yourself, but that you had the wisdom to know your limitations and consult the accumulated knowledge and interpretation of the experts in forming your views. Moreover, it provides your readers with the necessary information should they wish to pursue the subject further themselves. In short, it enhances your paper.

Not every thought that comes to you in the course of your research needs to be documented. Only those that you borrow from others and are not common knowledge need to be. How can you tell which ideas are borrowed and therefore should be documented? The question is not nearly so difficult as it may seem.

To begin with, you may develop many ideas of your own as you are reading the ideas of another person. "That reminds me of the experience I had last summer," you may think. Or, "This author's conclusion about the issue is exactly opposite that of the previous author I consulted." Or, "This interpretation is not correct—it omits an important consideration." These ideas are *yours*. True, they came to you while reading another person's ideas and may even have been prompted by her ideas. But it would be incorrect to credit them to her in a footnote, because she did not express them. *It is only by expressing ideas that a person establishes a claim to them.*

Another kind of idea that need not be credited is "common knowledge." Common knowledge is that which is accepted by those who are familiar with the subject, the kind of idea you would find expressed in most books and articles on the subject despite the differences in the authors' views. For example, the fact that Thomas Jefferson wrote the Declaration of Independence is, like the purpose and historical significance of the document, common knowledge. No reference to such a fact needs to be credited. But any idea that is not widely known or that is the subject of dispute should be credited.

The careful writer tries to avoid both underdocumentation and overdocumentation by keeping in mind that the purpose of documentation is to signal her readers when she is presenting an idea that belongs to someone else. Whenever a situation arises in which you are not really sure how to classify the idea, ask yourself whether the idea came from one specific source that you consulted. If so, document it. (If it came from a number of sources, then it is probably common knowledge. If it came from no source that you know of, then it is probably your own idea. In neither of these cases does the idea need to be documented.)

Kinds of Documentation

The Modern Language Association recommends that two kinds of documentation be used in a research paper. Those kinds, as explained in the *MLA Handbook*, 2nd edition (1984), are as follows:

1. *Brief parenthetical documentation within the research paper.* This documentation indicates to the readers exactly which ideas are borrowed, whom they are borrowed from, and the exact page references to the original works.
2. *A list of works cited in the paper.* This list, which is placed at the end of the research paper, provides all relevant publication information about the sources of the borrowed ideas.

When writers take care to provide both kinds of documentation, they enable their readers both to identify all borrowed ideas and, if they are interested in doing so, to obtain more information with a minimum of effort.

Guidelines for Brief Documentation

The *MLA Handbook* specifies that brief parenthetical documentation should meet two guidelines. The first is that it clearly point to specific sources in the list of works cited. That means that if the list of works cited contains only one work by a particular author, parenthetical documentation within the research paper need only cite the author's last name (assuming, of course, that there is no other author listed with the same last name). However, if the list of works cited contains two or more works by the same author, parenthetical documentation should contain the author's last name and the title of the particular work. (*Note:* if the title is longer than a few words, a shortened version is acceptable in parenthetical documentation.)

The second MLA guideline for brief parenthetical documentation is that it identify the location of the borrowed idea as specifically as possible. The exact page number should be given, except in the case of one-page articles or articles in alphabetically arranged encyclopedias. In addition, if the work is in two or more volumes, the particular volume number should also be given. In the case of literary works, such information as chapter number, stanza, act, scene, and line may be given with or in place of the page number.

In addition to these two guidelines, the *MLA Handbook*

stresses that parenthetical references should be kept as brief as clarity and accuracy permit and should be placed as close as possible to the borrowed material in a manner that minimizes interruptions in the flow of the writing. Documentation, remember, should aid readers, not distract them.

Following are examples of brief parenthetical documentation illustrating the basic MLA form and the most common variations of that form. Note the punctuation and spacing used, as well as the positioning of the citation.

Documentation with author's name given in text

> Carol Tavris explains how Freudianism has confused us about the nature of anger (36–39).

Documentation with author's name not given in text

> Though the system of the form of psychotherapy known as logotherapy is often associated with existentialism, its founder has not been uncritical of existentialism (Frankl 13).

Documentation of work by two authors

> Among the purposes of rumor is the justification of feelings we might otherwise feel guilty of harboring (Allport and Postman 37).

Documentation of work by author with two or more works cited in works cited list*

> Rollo May calls creativity "the struggle against disintegration" (*Courage to Create* 140).

Documentation of quoted material

> According to Carol Tavris, "the decision about whether or not to express anger rests on what you want to communicate and what you hope to accomplish, and these are not necessarily harmonious goals" (123).

---

*To avoid confusion, the title of the work or a shortened version of it should be added just before the page reference in the brief parenthetical citation, as shown.

If the work being cited is anonymous, the title should be referred to either in the text or in the brief parenthetical documentation. If the reference is not to a specific page or pages but to the work as a whole, the title should be mentioned in the text and the brief parenthetical documentation *omitted*.

Guidelines for the Works Cited List

The Works Cited list need not include works that were consulted but that contributed nothing to the research paper; however, it must include all works that contributed ideas or information to the paper. The list of works cited should begin on a new page immediately following the last page of the text. The numbering of the pages should continue that of the text, with each page number appearing in the upper-right-hand corner, one-half inch from the top. The words "Works Cited" should be centered one inch from the top of the first page of the list. Double-spacing should be used after the heading and thereafter throughout the list. Each new entry should begin flush with the left margin. If an entry runs more than one line, subsequent lines should be indented five spaces from the left margin. All entries should be alphabetized by the author's last name or, in the case of anonymous works, by the first word in the title other than *A*, *An*, or *The*.

A Works Cited list may include many kinds of materials, both print and nonprint, but the most common ones are books and periodical articles. Accordingly, the guidelines that follow are presented in three groups: books, articles, and other works. The source of these guidelines is the *MLA Handbook*, 2nd edition (1984). Because space limitations make it impossible to extend coverage in this book beyond the fundamentals, in preparing citations of unusual materials you may wish to consult the *MLA Handbook* directly.

Citing Books

Often book citations are relatively simple, involving the identification of author, title, and publication information, each followed by a period and two spaces. In some cases, however, more information is called for. Following is a list of all the information that could be required. Seldom, if ever, will you encounter a situation where all this information is required. Nevertheless, this list is a helpful reminder of the order in which the information should be presented and of the form to use in presenting it.

Author's Name	Present the last name first, followed by a comma. Give the name exactly as it appears on the title page, neither substituting full names for initials, nor changing full names to initials.
Title of the Part of the Book	This applies when you are citing a work that appears in a larger work: for example, an essay or a poem in an anthology. Enclose this title in quotation marks.
Title of the Book	Give the full title. If there is a subtitle, separate it from the title by a colon and two spaces. Underline the title and subtitle.
Name of the Editor, Translator, or Compiler	Abbreviate the word *editor* and place a period after it, in this manner: Ed. John Harrison.
Edition Used	
Number of Volumes	
Name of the Series	
Place of Publication, Name of the Publisher, and Date of Publication	Use an appropriately shortened version of the publisher's name. For example, use Knopf for Alfred A. Knopf, Inc., and Harper for Harper & Row, Publishers, Inc.
Page Numbers	Include page numbers only when citing part of a work: for example, a short story in an anthology. In such cases, cite the pages for the entire part—in the case of the short story, the beginning and ending pages.

   Here is a fictitious sample entry illustrating how all the above information would appear. Note carefully the punctuation and spacing.

Werblow, Stanley F. "Self-Knowledge and Self-Deception." *Reflective Thinking: A Symposium.* Ed. Freeman Sage. 3rd ed. Vol. 3 of *Philosophy in Everyday Life.* New York: Harper, 1982. 12–41.

Note that if a work has two authors, the name of the second author is presented in normal, rather than reverse, order. In the above case the citation would begin as follows: Werblow, Stanley F., and Ralph M. Patterson. Note too that if two or more works by Werblow were being cited, the second and subsequent references would not begin with his name but with a short rule followed by a period or comma, as in these samples:

―――, *Thinking of Thinking.* New York: Holt, 1968.

―――, ed. *Essays on Productive Thinking.* New York: Harper, 1977.

Citing Periodical Articles

Periodical article citations, like book citations, identify author, title, and publication information. Sometimes, however, as in the case of journal articles, additional information is required. Following is a list of all the information that could be required. Observe the order and the form indicated when preparing your citations of periodical articles.

Author's Name	Use the same approach as for books.
Title of the Article	Enclose the title in quotation marks.
Name of the Periodical	Underline the name.
Series Number	State this number if the periodical has appeared in more than one series.
Volume Number	Not all periodicals have volume numbers. When you are citing one that does, just use the number—do not use the word "volume" or an abbreviation.
Date of Publication	Leave a space after the volume number and give the year of publication in parentheses, followed by a colon, a space, and the page numbers.

Page Numbers — Give the page numbers for the entire article, not just a part of it. If the article does not appear on consecutive pages, give only the first page number followed by a plus sign: for example, 192+.

Here is a sample entry illustrating how all the above information would appear. Note carefully the punctuation and spacing.

> Johnson, Michael P. "Runaway Slaves and the Slave Communities in South Carolina, 1799–1830." *William and Mary Quarterly* 3rd ser. 38 (1981): 418–41.

Because there are a number of different kinds of periodical publications (quarterly journals, weekly magazines, daily newspapers, etc.), there are a number of common variations in citation form for periodical articles. The following are among the most important:

A journal article that pages each issue separately or uses only issue numbers.

In the former case, add a period and the issue number directly after the volume number. In the latter case, treat the issue as a volume number. (Only the former is illustrated below.)

> Lyon, George Ella. "Contemporary Appalachian Poetry: Sources and Directions." *Kentucky Review* 2.2 (1981): 3–22.

An article from a weekly or fortnightly periodical.

In citing an article from a weekly or fortnightly periodical, give the complete date (the day, the month in abbreviated form, and the year) instead of the volume and issue numbers.

> Friedrich, Otto. "Saying What You Mean." *Time* 9 Apr. 1984: 78.

A newspaper article.

In citing a daily newspaper use the name as it appears on the masthead, but omit the article *The*. (Thus you would cite *Washington Post* and not *The Washington Post*.) If the name of the city is not included in the newspaper's name, include it in square brackets, without underlining, immediately after the name. Then give the complete date—day, abbreviated month, and year. If the edition is indicated on the newspaper's masthead, specify the edition, preceded by a comma. If the newspaper is separated into sections, each with its own pagination, include the section designation, either with the page number if it appears that way on every page (e.g., A3), or as a separate item after the date or edition preceded by a comma and followed by a colon (e.g., late ed., sec. 3: 4+).

> Brody, Jane E. "Kinsey Study Shows Deep Predisposition." *New York Times*, 23 Aug. 1981, late ed.: 1+.

An editorial.

If the editorial is signed, begin the citation with the author's name; if it is unsigned, begin with the title. In either case, add the designation Editorial after the title, using neither underlining nor quotation marks. (Note that the city and state of the newspaper is added in brackets in the sample citation below because the name of the newspaper does not include that data.)

> "Business Need City's People, Too." Editorial. *Sunday Press* [Binghamton, NY] 23 Oct. 1983: E2.

A letter to the editor.

To identify a letter to the editor, simply write Letter after the author's last name, without underlining or quotation marks. (Note that in the sample citation given below, "N. pag." is used to signify that the letters section of the magazine was unpaginated.)

> Stewart, Douglas J. Letter. *National Geographic* 165 (May 1984): N. pag.

Citing Nonprint Materials

The *MLA Handbook* gives examples of a number of different nonprint-material citations. The following four are among the most frequently used:

A radio or television program.

This citation should include the following information in the order shown: the title of the program, underlined; the names of the director, narrator, and producer (if relevant); the network; the local station and its city; and the date of the broadcast.

> *The First Americans.* Narr. Hugh Downs. Writ. and prod. Craig Fisher. NBC News Special. KNBC, Los Angeles. 21 Mar. 1968.

An interview on radio or television.

This citation should begin with the name of the person interviewed. If the interview is the entire work, underline the title. If the interview is untitled, use the word Interview, without underlining or quotation marks. Next give the name of the interviewer if this information is pertinent (e.g., With Mike Wallace). Conclude with the network, the local station and its city, and the date of the interview.

> Gordon, Suzanne. Interview. *All Things Considered.* Natl. Public Radio. WNYC, New York. 1 June 1983.

An interview you conduct personally.

This citation should give the name of the person interviewed, the kind of interview (e.g., Personal interview or Telephone interview), and the date.

> Warren, Nathan E. Personal interview. 18 Sept. 1984.

A lecture, speech, or address.

This citation should give the speaker's name, the name of the meeting and the sponsoring organization (if applicable), the location, and the date. If the presentation was untitled, use an appropriate descriptive term (Lecture, Address, etc.).

> Ciardi, John. Address. Opening General Sess. NCTE Convention. Washington. 19 Nov. 1982.

Sample Research Papers

To help you understand the principles and approaches explained above, two sample research papers follow. Both deal with the same topic, astrology, and the same essential question—is it science or superstition? In addition, both use the same research data. But the type of paper and the format differ. (Remember, however, that either format may be used for either type of paper.) By reading each paper closely and noting the similarities and differences, you will become more familiar with the effects possible with each format and therefore better able to choose wisely for your own research papers.

An Informative Research Paper

The following paper is *informative* and is written in a *separated format.*

William J. Murphy
Professor Pelletier
English 101
November 30, 1984

Astrology: Science or Superstition?

The widespread modern interest in astrology raises once again a very old question: Is there any scientific basis for astrology or is it essentially superstition? The question is important because if astrology is scientific, then the scoffers and skeptics are denying themselves a means of making their lives happier, more successful, and more productive. On the other hand, if astrology is unscientific, then those who are influenced by it are being deceived, perhaps even harmed. This paper will examine what knowledgeable people are saying about the question.

HISTORY OF ASTROLOGY

Astrology began in Babylonia and Egypt, at approximately the same time, as a system of omen reading to predict the fates of kings (Jerome, "Magic" 10). Some scholars believe it was an aspect of star worship, since the word "astrology" (of Greek origin) means "discourse or doctrine about the stars" (Thompson 18–19). Others believe it was less formalized and more a kind of wonder; one writer calls it "an amazed and quasi-religious meditation, a vast dream in which principles and laws were slowly sketched out" (<u>Encycl. Occult</u> 45). In any case, it was part of the "magical world view" prevalent at the time, when people did not comprehend the great distances involved between us and the stars and regarded them as the homes or possessions of the gods ("Statement" 9).

As you read this paper, note how the author has kept the focus on informing the reader about what his research disclosed. Nowhere does he include his interpretation and judgment.

Though the subheadings refer to specific points made in the paper rather than its general divisions ("Presentation of Research Data," for example), close examination of the grouping of ideas will reveal that the format here is the separated format and its general divisions are followed.

By placing your name at the top of each page you ensure that if a page or two gets separated from your paper your professor will be able to tell whose it is.

Here the author abstracted the names of these people from a lengthy discussion of almost twenty pages in the original (see footnote).

The Greeks borrowed their earliest notions about astrology from the Babylonians and Egyptians. Later they combined the elements of both and developed them into a more complex and mathematical system that expressed their theory of the universe. The astrological systems used by today's astrologers are variations on Greek astrology (Jerome, "Magic" 10).

The list of famous people in Western history who reportedly accepted astrology in some form is long indeed. It includes not only literary figures, philosophers, and religious thinkers, but scientists as well. That list includes Plato and Aristotle, St. Augustine, Chaucer, Boccaccio, Jewish scholar Ibn Ezra, Albert the Great, St. Thomas Aquinas, Nostradamus, Roger Bacon, Duns Scotus, Johannes Kepler, and at least a dozen popes (Crow 179–98).

From the earliest times until the end of the sixteenth century, astrology was used in medicine to aid physicians in diagnosing illness and prescribing treatment (Thompson 103). Yet this aspect of astrology, like others, continued to be intertwined with magic at least through the Middle Ages. Talismans—objects used to attract the influence of a particular planet or of the moon or sun—were still common in the sixteenth century. Julianus Ristorus, for example, a professor at Pisa University at that time, carried two rings engraved with astrological inscriptions, one to ward off mosquitoes and the other to cure ailments of the shins and feet (<u>Encycl. Occult</u> 220). Nor is astrology completely free of magic even in contemporary times. As Derek Parker, a defender of astrology, admits, "Some astrologers still seek to preserve its past links with magic," and astrology remains "dear to those who are interested in the occult" (70).

CLAIMS AND COUNTERCLAIMS

The most basic tenets of astrology, which all the sources listed at the end of this paper acknowledge, are the following: (a) the sun, moon, and planets exert great forces on human beings; (b) the exact force of each heavenly body differs from that of all other bodies; and (c) the exact moment of decisive influence is the moment of birth. Let us consider what scientists say of each of these tenets.

The Exerting of Great Force

Scientists are divided on this question. Most seem to believe that any force exerted by the planets is at best insignificant (Thompson 284). One writer expresses his denunciation of the idea dramatically: because of the vast distances involved, Bart J. Bok says, the "gravitational force at birth produced by the doctor and nurse and by the furniture in the delivery room far outweigh [sic] the celestial forces" (30). Yet other scientists disagree. Charles J. Cazeau and Stuart D. Scott, Jr., believe it is not entirely impossible that cosmic energy may have effects on us we are not aware of. They suggest that there is already hard scientific evidence of such energy, citing the fact that radio astronomers have demonstrated that distant nebulae and galaxies do emit tremendous radio-frequency energy, one known galaxy (M 87) emitting 1,000 times more than our own galaxy. The astrological notion that the planets affect us, they say, "is indeed fantastic but is it more so than splitting and joining atoms, television, or trips to the moon?" (234).

Note how information from different sources is combined in one paragraph. The key to doing this effectively is to plan carefully, arranging your research data so that related points are grouped together.

Different Planets, Different Forces

The scientists consulted agree it is unlikely that different planets represent different forces. Bok points out that it is now known that all heavenly bodies are made of the same basic ingredients. Accordingly, he finds it unreasonable to believe that the same ingredients could exert vastly different forces and achieve vastly different effects, as astrologers claim (30–31). Further evidence that this claim of astrologers is questionable is offered by Cazeau and Scott. They point out that three of the known planets were only discovered in recent times (Ura-

Murphy 4

nus in 1781, Neptune in 1846, and Pluto in 1930). If each planet really did have a special influence, they reason, wouldn't astrological predictions made before their discovery have been in error? The authors believe so, despite the fact that they have never heard this conclusion expressed by astrologers (232).

The Influence at Birth

The science of genetics has established that at the moment of conception the genetic package is complete. Thus a person's eye color, body type, and hundreds of other characteristics are determined then (subject, in some cases, to later environmental influences). If there were one special moment in which cosmic forces were exerted, why, Bok asks, wouldn't it be the moment of conception? Why the moment of birth, which science has shown to be of relatively little significance? (31). Other scientists consulted agree with this line of reasoning without exception.

THE EVIDENCE

To support their contention that astrology is a science, its defenders argue that even in ancient times astrology was based on careful observation and reasoning. This fact, they believe, becomes blurred by the fact that the ancients lacked adequate technology to make accurate judgments and the knowledge necessary to keep their data free of superstition and pagan religion. The result, according to one source, was "a science at bottom confused, vitiated by errors and childishness, but yet rich in astounding intuitions, in millions of confirmations, and in all kinds of other knowledge...." An imperfect science, in other words, but a science nonetheless. Then, in the Middle Ages, the scientific nature of astrology became even more blurred by a split in science itself into an official side—exact, emphasizing careful experimentation and calculation—and an outlaw side composed of those disciplines that refused to give up past links with the occult (Encycl. Occult 46).

Some scientists tend to agree with this argument. Science historian O. Neugebauer, for example, says the idea of ancient astrologers that heavenly bodies exert influence on humans was very different from the idea of the gods determining fate or of people influencing events by magic. Thus, though he notes that the line between "rational science and loose speculation" was not clear, causing astrology to promote magic and superstition, he suggests that it is not incorrect to call ancient astrology scientific (171). Cazeau and Scott go even further in their agreement, stating flatly that "however astrology may be viewed today, it was the earliest exact science in history" (227).

Most opponents of astrology reject this view. Lawrence Jerome, for instance, argues that Greek astrology was not a science at all. It came to the Greeks as a "full-blown magical system, its assumptions and operating principles unquestioned. Nor, he adds, did the idea of the stars influencing human lives arrive through scientific observation. Rather, it was based on the magical "principal of correspondences," wherein what is seen as being *like* something else or reminiscent of it is considered to have the same properties ("Magic" 11-12).

This principle, according to Jerome, worked as follows. The ancients noted that a particular planet had a reddish cast, so in their primitive minds it became associated with blood, war, aggressiveness. Accordingly, they named it Mars after the god of war. Later, they linked other things associated with war—iron, for example—with the planet. Similarly, the planet Venus was named after the goddess of love, and all the mythology connected with her—beauty, sensitivity, and so on—became associated with the planet and to those born under its influence (Disproved 70-71).

Jerome admits that a detailed horoscope not only looks scientific, but actually is scientific in the sense of its intricate plottings and calculations of the stars, moon, and sun. But he stresses that the key point many people fail to notice is that all these plottings and calculations take place "against an arbitrary frame of signs rather than real stars." Hence in the most meaningful sense, in Jerome's view, astrology is decidedly not a science (<u>Disproved</u> 79).

In light of the duration and passion of the debate over whether astrology is science or superstition, there has been surprisingly little experimental research to test the matter. And what little there has been has resulted in mixed findings. One researcher, Michael Gauqelin, studied the backgrounds of 576 members of the French Academy of Medicine and another group of 508 famous physicians and found a strong statistical correlation between astrological prediction of success in medicine and actual success (Cazeau and Scott 235). Yet two other studies—J. R. Barth and J. T. Bennett's study of the influence of Mars on military careers, and Bart J. Bok's study of scientists' times of birth—reported no correlation between astrological prediction and reality (Jerome, "Magic" 15).

Still another experiment tested the accuracy of astrological indicators of personality. This study took 130 college students whose exact birth times were available. Each of the students and one of his friends was asked to rate the student's aggressiveness, ambition, creativity, intuitiveness, and extroversion. In addition, each of the 130 was given a standardized personality inventory test. The results of the ratings and inventories were compared with the students' horoscopes. The study showed "that the astrological indicators of personality were not related to either self or friends' descriptions of the subjects' personalities." Though the experimenters did not include all astrological indicators of personality, and therefore state that their findings do not prove that astrology cannot predict personality, they conclude that their failure to find a correlation in the most important astrological indicators "reduces the likelihood of this possibility being true" (Silverman and Whitmer 89, 94).

An Informative Research Paper

CONCLUSIONS OF THE AUTHORITIES

Predictably, the judgments of the authorities on whether astrology is a science are mixed. O. Neugebauer, in his discussion of ancient science, states that "compared with the background of religion, magic, and mysticism, the fundamental doctrines of astrology are pure science" (171). Building on the same perspective, Zolar offers a forceful argument for the affirmative position:

> The astrological outlook came to light as a set of attractive scientific hypotheses displacing whatever beliefs preceded them and filling a vacancy in the mind of man. These hypotheses have endured for three or two [sic] millenia, though repeatedly challenged. They have outlasted many irrelevant, purely emotional and prejudiced beliefs that conflicted with more materialistic and fatalistic tenets and they have found their supporters among the learned and the great as among the common people. Within the womb of astrology, astronomy was bred and nourished, and there never was any competition or conflict between them. Astrology is neither stupidity nor superstition. No hero of astronomy fought it as a scientific St. George; no movement of pioneers of progress speeded it toward death. No, most of the great astrologers are better known to the average person as astronomers or mathematicians. The history of astronomy is really only the history of astrology from a slightly different viewpoint (Zolar viii).

Note how this quotation of more than five lines is handled (spacing, margins, and so on). It is significant that there is only one such long quote in this paper—the emphasis is rightly on the expression of the writer of the research paper and not on the expression of his sources. Wherever possible, paraphrase or quote briefly, reserving such lengthy quotations as this for those rare occasions where their significance and compactness warrant using them.

Yet Richard Cavendish, in his comprehensive study of the occult, classifies astrology as "essentially a magical art" (219). Further, a statement signed by 192 leading scientists calls astrologers "charlatans" and warns that "those who wish to believe in astrology should realize that there is no scientific foundation for its tenets" ("Statement" 9). And a statement endorsed by the Society for the Psychological Study of Social Issues brands astrology "a magical practice that has no shred of justification in scientific fact" (Bok 32).

For C.J.S. Thompson the matter comes down to a lack of demonstration on the part of astrologers. "No proof has ever yet been furnished," he declares, "that the movements or positions in the heavens of the planets and stars can influence the life and destiny of any human being, or that they are able to impart special properties to vegetable life." For this reason, he concludes, astrology "must likewise be banished with other ancient cults to the realms of romance" (284, 288).

Is astrology science or superstition? Despite the passions of those on either side of the question, the issue is yet unsettled. Nor is it likely to be until the claims and methods of astrology are subjected to close scrutiny under the best experimental conditions.

WORKS CITED

Bok, Bart J. "A Critical Look at Astrology." Objections to Astrology. Buffalo: Prometheus, 1975. 30-36.

Cavendish, Richard. The Black Arts. New York: Capricorn, 1967.

Cazeau, Charles J., and Stuart D. Scott, Jr. Exploring the Unknown: Great Mysteries Re-examined. New York: Plenum, 1979.

Crow, W. B. A History of Magic, Witchcraft and Occultism. London: Aquarian, 1968.

Encyclopedia of Occult Sciences. New York: Tudor, 1968.

Jerome, Lawrence E. Astrology Disproved. Buffalo: Prometheus, 1977.

-----. "Astrology: Magic or Science?" Humanist Sept.–Oct. 1975: 10–16.

Murphy 9

Jones, Marc Edmund. Astrology: How and Why It Works. New York: Penguin, 1969.

Mark, Alexandra. Astrology for the Aquarian Age. New York: Essandra, 1970.

Neugebauer, O. The Exact Sciences in Antiquity. 2d ed. New York: Harper, 1952.

Parker, Derek. Astrology in the Modern World. New York: Taplinger, 1970.

Roll, W. G. "Science Looks at the Occult." Psychic 4 (June 1973): 50–55.

Silverman, T. I., and M. Whitmer. "Astrological Indicators of Personality." Journal of Psychology 87 (May 1974): 89–95.

Snyder, C. R. "Why Horoscopes Are True: The Effects of Specificity on Acceptance of Astrological Interpretations." Journal of Clinical Psychology 30 (1974): 577–80.

Standen, Anthony. "Is There an Astrological Effect on Personality?" Journal of Psychology 89 (1975): 259–60.

"Statement by Leading Indian Scientists and Intellectuals." Philosophical Forum 8 (July–Aug. 1978): 59.

"Statement by 192 Leading Scientists." Objections to Astrology. Buffalo: Prometheus, 1975.

Thompson, C.J.S. The Mystery and Romance of Astrology. New York: Brentano's, 1969.

Zolar. The History of Astrology. New York: Arco, 1972.

A Persuasive Research Paper

The following paper is persuasive rather than informative and is written in integrated rather than separated format. However, it is based on the same research as the preceding paper and uses many of the same passages of information. These similarities between the two papers will make the essential difference—the inclusion of the writer's own interpretations and judgments—all the more prominent.

William J. Murphy
Professor Pelletier
English 101
November 30, 1984

Astrology: Science or Superstition?

Astrology is very fashionable today. Newspapers and magazines carry regular horoscope columns, and respected publishing houses publish books explaining the wisdom of consulting the stars as a guide to daily living. Celebrities on television talk-shows speak enthusiastically of astrology and tell of its helpfulness in their lives. The range of areas in which astrologers offer guidance is virtually limitless. When to marry, have children, take a vacation, buy stocks and bonds, and socialize are all covered. Some astrologers even predict the most favorable days for making an appointment with a doctor or dentist.

This belief that the sun, moon, and planets influence the lives of people is not new at all. It dates from the time of ancient Babylonia and Egypt where it was associated with a system of omen reading to predict the fates of kings. The Greeks borrowed the idea and fashioned it into a more complex and mathematical system that expressed their theory of the universe. Today's astrological systems are variations of the Greek system (Jerome, "Magic" 10).

Despite astrology's long history, it still arouses controversy. Is it science or superstition? There continues to be too much disagreement among authorities to say the matter is fully settled. Yet the evidence accumulated to date suggests strongly that it is not a science. That is the position this paper will present.

Compare the introduction, conclusion, and format of this paper with those of the preceding paper. Note how this paper fits the description of the integrated format on page 314.

As in any essay, the writer makes the paper's controlling idea clear early in his presentation. In addition, the way the idea is presented communicates that the presentation is persuasive.

HOW SCIENTIFIC WAS ANCIENT ASTROLOGY?

In ancient times astrology does seem to have been an advanced idea. Science historian O. Neugebauer says that the idea of the sun, moon, and planets influencing human lives was very different from—and much more scientific than—the then-prevalent ideas of the gods determining fate and of people influencing events by magic (171). And at least two scientists state without qualification that "however astrology may be viewed today, it was the earliest exact science in history" (Cazeau and Scott 227).

Part of the problem many people have in accepting such judgments is that they conceive of science solely in modern terms and forget that it was once quite primitive and inexact. In ancient times all the sciences were lacking in technology and their approaches and data were mingled with notions of superstition and pagan religion (Encycl. Occult 46). For the critics of astrology to point to the imperfections of astrology at that time and close their eyes to the identical imperfections in other areas of science would be unfair.

Another reason for classifying ancient astrology—and, for that matter, astrology through the period of the Middle Ages—as a science is that many of the greatest thinkers in history, including great scientists, accepted it as a science and often practiced it in one form or another. Among those supporters of astrology were Plato, Aristotle, St. Augustine, Chaucer, Boccaccio, Jewish scholar Ibn Ezra, Albert the Great, St. Thomas Aquinas, Nostradamus, Roger Bacon, Duns Scotus, Johannes Kepler, and at least a dozen popes (Crow 179–98).

These arguments for classifying ancient astrology as a science do not persuade everyone. One critic of astrology, for example, maintains that astrology cannot be so classified because it came to the Greeks as a "full-blown magical system, its assumptions and operating principles unquestioned" (Jerome, "Magic" 11). Yet even if that is true and the arguments cited above are less than compelling, they are

---

This passage represents the author's own judgment. Note the pattern used here—the presentation of one or more items of data followed by the author's interpretation or judgment. This pattern, a standard one in persuasive writing, is repeated in subsequent pages.

The writer concedes a point here to those who disagree with him. This willingness to admit the complexity of the issue is characteristic of the balanced, mature thinker. (Note the pattern of pre-

Murphy 3

nevertheless strong arguments. And since the case against astrology can be made on more substantive grounds, this writer is inclined to concede that <u>ancient</u> astrology <u>was</u> a science.

sentation of data followed by interpretation and judgment.)

ASTROLOGY'S LINKS WITH MAGIC

From the beginning, astrology has had strong ties with magic and the occult. As late as the sixteenth century, astrology was used in medicine to aid physicians in diagnosing illness and prescribing treatment (Thompson 103). And talismans—objects used to attract the influence of a particular planet or of the moon or sun—were used as preventatives. Julianus Ristorus, for example, a sixteenth-century professor at Pisa University, carried two rings engraved with astrological inscriptions, one to ward off mosquitoes and the other to cure ailments of the shins and feet (<u>Encycl. Occult</u> 220). Nor is astrology completely free of magic even in contemporary times. As Derek Parker, a defender of astrology, admits, "Some astrologers still seek to preserve its past links with magic," adding that astrology remains "dear to those who are interested in the occult" (70). While the ancient link with magic may be forgiven as one of the imperfections of a primitive discipline, the modern link cannot be dismissed so easily. Science, after all, concerns itself with the natural world, and magic deals with the supernatural.

This conclusion (it is the author's own, and not that of his sources) is impressive because it makes a useful distinction between past and present "links" with magic.

THE NATURE AND TIMING OF PLANETARY INFLUENCE

We noted earlier that the idea of heavenly bodies influencing human beings is considered by some scientists to have been a valuable and scientific idea in ancient times. Somewhat more surprising, perhaps, is the fact that some scientists regard the idea as <u>still</u> within the realm of possibility, even given modern scientific knowledge and perspectives. (Others, of course, and they may be a majority, scoff at the idea.) Cazeau and Scott, for example, believe it is not entirely impossible that cosmic energy may have effects on us we are not aware of. They suggest that there is already hard scientific evidence of such energy, citing the fact that radio astronomers have demonstrated that distant nebulae and galaxies do emit tremendous radio-frequency energy, one known galaxy (M87) emitting 1,000 times more than our own galaxy. The astrological notion that the planets affect us, they say, "is indeed fantastic but is it more so than splitting and joining atoms, television, or trips to the moon?" (234).

Yet if the idea of celestial influence has met some scientific acceptance, two closely related astrological ideas have not fared so well. One is the idea that the exact force of each heavenly body differs from that of all other bodies. The scientists consulted for this paper are in agreement that it is highly unlikely that different planets would have different forces. Bart J. Bok points out that it is now known that all heavenly bodies are made of the same basic ingredients. Accordingly, he finds it unreasonable to believe that the same ingredients could exert vastly different forces and achieve vastly different effects (30–31).

The author's comment here reinforces the source's judgment and at the same time goes beyond it.

Even Cazeau and Scott, who are eminently fair-minded in their dealing with astrology, question how astrologers can have avoided making errors in their calculations before 1781, since three planets—Uranus, Neptune, and Pluto—were discovered after that time. They also question why astrologers do not now admit that such errors must have existed before 1781 (232). Their criticisms seem reasonable. The failure of astrologers to note such errors and address themselves to them does not build confidence in their claim to being scientific.

The second astrological idea that does not bear scrutiny well is that the stars work their influence at the moment of birth. The science of genetics has established that at the moment of conception the genetic package is complete. Thus a person's eye color, body type, and hundreds of other characteristics are determined then (subject, in some cases, to later environmental influences). If there were one special moment in which cosmic forces were exerted, why, Bok asks, wouldn't it be the moment of conception? Why, instead, the moment of birth, which science has shown to be of relatively little significance (31)? Other scientists consulted for this paper agree with this line of reasoning without exception. It seems clear that the ancients committed an understandable, but crucial, error in assigning so much importance to the moment of birth. But however great that error, the error of modern astrologers in refusing to admit it is far greater. For being scientific seems to demand, at very least, addressing the matter and either correcting it or showing why it does not need correction.

Note that in this judgment, as in his other judgments, the author does not parrot his source's ideas—rather, he contributes ideas, valuable ideas, of his own. This is the mark of a good persuasive paper.

WEAKNESS OF ASTROLOGY'S CENTRAL PREMISE

Lawrence E. Jerome has argued persuasively that the idea that the stars influence human lives, the central premise of astrology, did not come to the ancients through scientific observation at all. Rather, he explains, it was based on the magical "principle of correspondences," wherein what is seen as being like something else or reminiscent of it is considered to have the same properties ("Magic" 11–12). This principle, according to Jerome, worked as follows. The ancients noted that a particular planet had a reddish cast, so in their primitive minds it became associated with blood, war, aggressiveness. Accordingly, they named it Mars after the god of war. Later, they linked other things associated with war—iron, for example—with the planet. Similarly, the planet Venus was named after the goddess of love, and all the mythology connected with her—beauty, sensitivity, and so on—became associated with the planet and to those born under its influence (Disproved 70–1).

This magical basis of astrology's central premise, Jerome believes, is itself enough to disqualify any claim astrology might have to being a science. The argument seems compelling. And Jerome has stated it in at least two publications. Surely it has come to the attention of astrologers. The only effective response to Jerome's argument is a demonstration that the observed effects of the planets on human beings predated the assigning of pagan mythology, or a demonstration that despite the prior assigning of mythological notions, the effects of the planets claimed by astrology actually do occur—in other words, that Mars really does have an effect on human aggressiveness, Venus on love, and so on. Lacking such a demonstration—and it has not been forthcoming—Jerome's argument seems unassailable.

Here the author's helpful comment shows his grasp of the issue by explaining what a response by astrologers would have to consist of to answer Jerome satisfactorily.

THE CONCLUSIONS OF SCIENTISTS

One of the most important considerations in deciding whether astrology is a science is the testimony of scientists. As we noted earlier, scientists are not all in agreement on the question. Some continue to take a favorable attitude toward astrology. O. Neugebauer, for example, states that "compared with the background of religion, magic, and mysticism, the fundamental doctrines of astrology are pure science" (171). Yet that position is clearly a minority view. Richard Cavendish, in his comprehensive study of the occult, classifies astrology as "essentially a magical art" (219). A statement signed by 192 leading scientists calls astrologers "charlatans" and warns that "those who wish to believe in astrology should realize that there is no scientific foundation for its tenets" ("Statement" 9). And a statement endorsed by the Society for the Psychological Study of Social Issues brands astrology "a magical practice that has no shred of justification in scientific fact" (Bok 32). The scientific community, it is safe to say, is generally opposed to considering astrology a science.

A QUESTION OF DEFINITION

The several reasons cited so far in this paper are sufficient to support the tentative conclusion that astrology is not a science. But there is an even better reason. It does not fit the contemporary definition of science. Though the terms knowledge and science are sometimes used interchangeably, the latter is a more restrictive category:

> [The term science] ordinarily ... applies only to a body of systematized knowledge dealing with facts gathered over a long period of time and by numerous persons as a result of observation and experiment and with the general truths or laws derived by inference from such facts. The term usually connotes more exactness and more rigorous testing of conclusions than knowledge does and therefore is often used to denote knowledge whose certainty cannot be questioned (Webster's New Dictionary of Synonyms).

Considerable confusion seems to center around the history of astrology. Defenders say that astrology once fit the definition of science completely and was accepted by the most eminent thinkers as a science. And that is true. The problem comes when they reason that because it was once a science, it must still be a science. That is incorrect. To be judged a science today, astrology must meet today's definition. That definition is more restrictive than the definition in earlier times, and if the supporters of astrology wish it to be applied, then they must address the serious questions critics have raised and demonstrate their case. The burden of proof is on them.

In conclusion, reasonable people remain ready to consider impartially any new evidence advanced for astrology. But until such evidence is presented, they are justified in regarding astrology with skepticism, preferring, instead, Shakespeare's perspective on human for-

---

Here is the most impressive contribution of the author. He takes the initiative, follows what he believes to be a sound approach not found in the sources he consulted, and considers the issue from a different perspective—that of definition. (It is possible, of course, to write an effective analytical research paper without taking such bold initiative, but excellence in analysis does depend on the author's making at least some significant contribution of his or her own to the discussion.)

Note that the author does not evade the issue. Rather, he offers his considered judgment, carefully expressed to reflect the evidence presented in the paper.

tunes: "The fault, dear Brutus, is not in our stars, but in ourselves...." (Julius Caesar 1.2).

(*Note:* the Works Cited section that would normally accompany this paper is omitted because it is almost identical to the section shown on pages 332–33.)

Suggested Topics for a Research Paper

Each of the topic ideas presented here should be regarded as an idea starter rather than as a refined topic:

Nutrition: When did this science begin? What are the most important events in its development? What do nutritionists say about the current dieting craze? About specific diets? About "junk food"?

Intuition: Is there such a phenomenon as intuition, or is it a figment of people's imagination? What do the various schools of psychology say about it? (Be sure to consult humanistic as well as behavioristic schools of psychology.)

The Insanity Plea: What is the legal definition of insanity? Under what conditions may a plea of insanity be entered? What is the philosophical basis of the plea? What do judges, lawyers, psychologists, and ethicists think about the wisdom of discontinuing the insanity plea?

The Good Old Days: When were the good old days? What were the conditions then? Were they better or worse than conditions now? Why do people remember times past with such fondness? How accurate is human memory in such matters?

Prisons: What are the most pressing problems besetting our prison system? Do other countries have such problems? If not, why not? What do penologists believe are the causes of and solutions to these problems?

Mental Institutions: How did society treat the insane in centuries past? What was its understanding of mental health and illness? How has the increase in knowledge about insanity affected the conditions in mental institutions and the treatment of the inmates? What reforms do the experts believe are still needed?

Confucianism or Buddhism or Mohammedanism: How does this religion differ from Christianity and Judaism? What does it have in common with them? Where did it originate and what have been the important events in its history? In what ways, if any, does it differ today from when it was founded?

Solar Energy: What are the physical principles on which the idea of solar energy is founded? How does solar energy work? What do the experts say about the advantages and disadvantages of solar energy compared to other forms of energy?

America: Was Columbus the first non-native to visit the western hemisphere? What evidence is there that others preceded him? How reliable is that evidence? If others are thought to have preceded Columbus, how, when, and from where are they believed to have traveled?

Prohibition: Whose idea was Prohibition? Who supported it, who opposed it, and how did the idea become law? What were the effects of Prohibition on American life?

Isaac Asimov (the most prolific American writer): What is Asimov's background? How many books has he written? In how many fields? Where does he get the ideas for his books? What are his work habits? What do those who know him think of his work? Have there ever been any writers more prolific than Asimov?

Marriage: How does marriage in other cultures differ from marriage in our culture? (Consider such customs as courtship, engagement, the giving of a dowry, and arranged marriages.) How does marriage in our culture today differ from marriage in our culture 100 or 200 years ago?

Hobbies: What are some of the most unusual or dangerous or expensive hobbies people pursue? How do hobbies today compare with hobbies in colonial times or hobbies in ancient Rome?

Other sources of topic ideas: If your instructor approves, do a research paper on any one of the topics suggested in Chapters 7 and 8, provided that you did not write on it before and that you treat it in appropriate depth.

Checklist for Your Research Paper

After completing the rough draft of your research paper, examine it carefully asking the questions from either the Chapter 7 or Chapter 8 checklist, whichever is more appropriate. In addition, ask the following questions. If the answer to any question is "No," reread the appropriate section of the earlier chapter or this part to determine whether there is a weakness and, if so, how to overcome it.

1. Does the paper follow a single format (either the separated or the integrated format)?
2. Is every borrowed idea, whether expressed in your words or your source's words, documented? Do quotation marks enclose all borrowed phrasing?

Part VI

The Handbook

Editing the Composition

Amateur writers sometimes regard editing as opposed to creativity. "If I concern myself with mechanical matters like grammar, spelling, and usage," they reason, "then my creativity will suffer." Like most erroneous views, this idea contains an element of truth. Thinking about editing *during the planning or writing stage* of the composition process can detract from creativity. The larger truth, however, is that *in its proper place*, editing enhances creativity. Mechanical errors not only call attention to themselves and thus distract readers from the writer's message, they also suggest that the writer is a careless person—the kind of person whose ideas readers often dismiss summarily.

Experienced writers invest the time to edit their work not because they value creativity any less than other writers, but because they value it more. They refuse to take the chance of having their message rejected because they did not bother to correct run-on sentences or punctuate correctly.

To become an effective editor, you must learn the important conventions of grammar, punctuation, spelling, manuscript mechanics, and usage that are detailed in the pages that follow. Even more important, you must develop skill in finding errors in your writing. There is no simple formula for doing so, but these two tips will help you:

1. Become familiar with the kinds of errors you characteristically make. When your instructor discusses a particular error in class and you recognize it as one you have committed in the past, write it down in your notebook. When your instructor makes reference to something in this handbook when he or she returns your composition, read the appropriate section and add the error to the list in your notebook.
2. Whenever you write a composition, allow yourself adequate time to edit it. And don't make the mistake of looking for a number of errors at once. If you have problems with subject–verb agreement, comma splices, and pronoun reference, for

example, read through your paper three times, *once for each kind of error*. In addition, be sure to notice what you *actually* said, as opposed to what you *intended* to say. The time it takes for the extra reading will be negligible, and you will be increasing your chances of finding all your errors.

There will, of course, be occasions when the time you have to devote to editing will be severely restricted. The most common of those occasions will be when you are taking an essay exam. But even though you will be forced to streamline your editing efforts on such occasions, you should still use the basic approach outlined above.

Solving Verb Problems (VB)

Verbs are words that indicate the action or state of being of a subject. A verb that shows action and has an object is *transitive*—"I *bought* the Corvette." A verb that does not have an object is *intransitive*—"The Corvette's engine *broke down*." A verb that connects the subject with a noun or adjective that describes or renames it is a *linking* verb—"I *was* angry."

Because the form of a verb often changes when the subject of the action changes, errors in verb form can occur easily. The strategies we will discuss will help you solve your verb problems.

1. Know the Principal Parts of the Verbs You Use

The principal parts of a verb are the three forms from which the various tenses are constructed, *the present infinitive, the past tense,* and *the past participle*. Most English verbs are regular—that is, their tenses and past participles are formed by adding *-d* or *-ed* to the present infinitive. For example, the principal parts of the verb *to agree* are *agree, agreed, agreed;* the principal parts of the verb *to play* are *play, played, played*.

However, a number of English verbs do not follow this pattern. These irregular verbs form their past tenses and past participles differently, often by changing an internal vowel. Here are the principal parts of the most commonly used irregular verbs. Check this list for the verbs you are not familiar with and write their forms down several times so that you will remember them.

Infinitive	Past Tense	Past Participle
arise	arose	arisen
be	was	been
beat	beat	beaten
become	became	become
begin	began	begun
bet	bet	bet
bid	bid	bid
bite	bit	bitten, bit
blow	blew	blown
break	broke	broken
bring	brought	brought
burst	burst	burst
buy	bought	bought
catch	caught	caught
choose	chose	chosen
come	came	come
cut	cut	cut
dive	dived, dove	dived
do	did	done
draw	drew	drawn
dream	dreamed, dreamt	dreamed, dreamt
drink	drank	drunk
drive	drove	driven
eat	ate	eaten
fall	fell	fallen
find	found	found
flee	fled	fled
fly	flew	flown
forget	forgot	forgotten, forgot
forgive	forgave	forgiven
freeze	froze	frozen
get	got	got, gotten
give	gave	given
go	went	gone
grow	grew	grown
hang*	hung	hung
hear	heard	heard
hid	hid	hidden
hurt	hurt	hurt
keep	kept	kept

*Note: These are the forms of the verb *to hang* when it means *to suspend* (as with a ceiling fixture). When it means *to execute*, the forms are *hang, hanged, hanged*.

Infinitive	Past Tense	Past Participle
know	knew	known
lay (to place)	laid	laid
lead	led	led
leave	left	left
let	let	let
lie (to recline)	lay	lain
lie (to tell an untruth)	lied	lied
lose	lost	lost
make	made	made
mean	meant	meant
pay	paid	paid
prove	proved	proved, proven
read	read	read
ride	rode	ridden
ring	rang, rung	rung
rise	rose	risen
run	ran	run
say	said	said
see	saw	seen
set	set	set
shake	shook	shaken
shine	shone	shone
sing	sang, sung	sung
sink	sank, sunk	sunk
sit	sat	sat
slide	slid	slid
speak	spoke	spoken
spin	spun	spun
spring	sprang, sprung	sprung
stand	stood	stood
steal	stole	stolen
strike	struck	struck
swear	swore	sworn
swim	swam	swum
swing	swung	swung
take	took	taken
teach	taught	taught
tear	tore	torn
tell	told	told
think	thought	thought
throw	threw	thrown

Infinitive	Past Tense	Past Participle
wear	wore	worn
weave	wove, weaved	woven, weaved
weep	wept	wept
win	won	won
wind	wound	wound
write	wrote	written

2. Use the Principal Parts to Form Tenses

Tense refers to the time at which an action takes place. There are three simple tenses and three perfect tenses in English:

The Simple Tenses

Present tense indicates that the action is occurring now.

I *see* the dress I want for the party.

Past tense indicates that the action occurred in the past.

I *saw* your sister in the library last night.

Future tense indicates that the action will occur in the future.

I *will see* the World Trade Center when I visit New York City next month.

The Perfect Tenses

Present prefect tense indicates that the action was begun in the past but is completed in the present. (Or that the action was begun in the past and continues in the present.)

I *have seen* Emily every day this week.

Past perfect tense indicates that the action was completed in the past before some other past action.

I *had seen* parades before, but none as big as the one I saw that day.

Future perfect tense indicates that the action will be completed before some future time.

I *will have been* out of school for ten years by the time I repay my loans.

Each of the examples above is expressed in the first person singular, *I*. There are, of course, five other forms in addition to first person singular. The following conjugation of the verb *to see* shows all six forms. Note where the form of the verb changes and where the helping verbs *will* and *have* are used.

Present Tense

Singular	*Plural*
I see	We see
You see	You see
He (she, it) sees	They see

Past Tense

Singular	*Plural*
I saw	We saw
You saw	You saw
He (she, it) saw	They saw

Future Tense

Singular	*Plural*
I will see	We will see
You will see	You will see
He (she, it) will see	They will see

Present Perfect Tense

Singular	*Plural*
I have seen	We have seen
You have seen	You have seen
He (she, it) has seen	They have seen

Past Perfect Tense

Singular	*Plural*
I had seen	We had seen
You had seen	You had seen
He (she, it) had seen	They had seen

Solving Verb Problems

Future Perfect Tense

Singular
I will have seen
You will have seen
He (she, it) will have seen

Plural
We will have seen
You will have seen
They will have seen

Exercise

In the blanks below, write the correct form of the verb or verbs indicated in parentheses. Be sure to use the correct principal part of the verb and the appropriate helping verb if it is needed.

Sample Yesterday we _____ to Ira's house early in the morning and _____ late at night. (*drive, return*—both past tense)

Response Yesterday we *drove* to Ira's house early in the morning and *returned* late at night.

1. The snake _____ across the driveway, _____ around the sapling tree, and _____ in the tall grass. (*slither, curl, disappear*—all past tense)
2. If only I _____ how exhausting ten miles of jogging would be, I would have found an excuse not to go. (*know*—past perfect tense)
3. Henry is taking bets that we _____ State College by at least ten points next week. (*beat*—future tense)
4. I'd buy her a pair of pajamas for her birthday if I _____ her size. (*know*—past tense)
5. After Edna _____ this semester, she plans to transfer to Yale. (*complete*—present tense)
6. They barely _____ arguing about gun control when they _____ arguing about capital punishment. (*finish*, past perfect tense; *begin*, past tense)
7. My friend Bertha, the graduate student, _____ twenty years of her life in school. (*spend*—present perfect tense)
8. Harvey said that he _____ the balloons with water if you and Martin _____ them out the window. (*fill, drop*—both future tense)
9. Agnes did nothing to her roommate, and yet her roommate _____ to criticize her to others. (*continue*—present tense)

10. She swore that she _____ her last drink before her next birthday. (*have*—future perfect tense)
11. He already _____ across the lake five times that day. (*swim*—past perfect tense)
12. Sally _____ like a pro. (*dance*—present tense)
13. He _____ the books on the table when the phone rang. (*lay*—past tense)
14. It was her custom to _____ down every day at noon for a two-hour nap. (*lie*—present tense)
15. When I told you I would be free on Wednesday night, I _____ to say Tuesday night. (*mean*—past tense)
16. Because he was suspected of nonpayment of taxes, the IRS _____ his bank account. (*freeze*—past tense)
17. Angered by the taunts of his classmates, John _____ his arms about wildly, hoping to hit someone. (*swing*—past tense)
18. If Judy scores a total of eighty more points in the remaining games this season, she _____ seventeen points a game for her college career. (*average*—future perfect tense)
19. Before his death in 1983, the sexton _____ the church bell every day for fifty years. (*ring*—past perfect tense)
20. Naturally, the overweight man _____ in the flimsy antique chair. (*sit*—past tense)

3. Use *-s* and *-ed* Endings Correctly

When we conjugated the irregular verb *to see*, you might have noticed that the third person singular form of the present tense is different from the other present tense forms. We say *I see, you see, he (she, it)* **sees**, *we see, you see,* and *they see*. The difference is not peculiar to this verb—standard English requires the *-s* ending for the third person singular form of the present tense of all verbs. Here are some examples of the correct form with other verbs:

I go   We go
You go   You go
He (she, it) **goes**   They go

I do   We do
You do   You do
He (she, it) **does**   They do

Solving Verb Problems

I aggravate	We aggravate
You aggravate	You aggravate
He (she, it) **aggravates**	They aggravate

Even the verb *to be*, which changes in the second person singular as well as the third person singular, follows this rule. Note also that in the conjugation of the verb *to be*, which follows, the *-s* ending is *not* used for the second person singular.

I am	We are
You **are**	You are
He (she, it) **is**	They are

Standard English also requires the *-ed* ending for all past tense forms of regular verbs. Thus it would be incorrect to say "I *use* to eat a lot of candy." The correct form is "I *used* to eat a lot of candy." Here are two additional examples of the correct form with different verbs:

I asked	We asked
You asked	You asked
He (she, it) asked	They asked

I poisoned	We poisoned
You poisoned	You poisoned
He (she, it) poisoned	They poisoned

Exercise

In the blanks below, write the correct form of the verb or verbs indicated in parentheses. Be sure to observe the *-s* and *-ed* rules where they apply.

1. More than anything else, she _____ a dependable car. (*want*—present tense)
2. The kids were fighting, the phone was ringing, and the dog was barking, but Jethro _____ through it all. (*slumber*—past tense)
3. They _____ me to apply for the job, and then they rejected me. (*ask*—past tense)
4. It's the holiday season, and most people are happy, but Alice _____ depressed. (*feel*—present tense)
5. We _____ a new restaurant, and you wouldn't believe their salad bar. (*discover*—past tense)

6. _____ anyone want to split a pizza? (*do*—present tense)
7. When I was walking home last night, my brother jumped out from behind a bush and _____ me. (*scare*—past tense)
8. I hate to eat with her—she _____ smoke in my face before, during, and after the meal. (*blow*—present tense)
9. It _____ foolish to drive two hundred miles just to see a basketball game. (*seem*—present tense)
10. He _____ me by the arm, gave me a Charles Bronson look, and said, "Hi, honey, do you come here often?" (*pull*—past tense)

4. Make Your Subjects and Verbs Agree

A singular subject takes a singular form of the verb; a plural subject takes a plural form. This rule presents relatively little difficulty when the subject is a single word and is immediately followed by the verb. Few writers make the mistake of saying "The *dancers kicks* high in the air" or "Final *examinations is* nerve wracking." However, not all sentence constructions are quite so simple. Following are the occasions in which subject–verb agreement errors most commonly occur.

When the subject and verb are separated by other words. In many sentences the verb does not follow the subject immediately. In such cases it is easy to mistake the word closest to the verb for the subject. Consider this case:

Incorrect Verb Form	Regular exercise, she told her students, *relax* tension.
Correct Verb Form	Regular exercise, she told her students, *relaxes* tension.
Analysis	Although the plural noun *students* appears to be the subject of the sentence, the real subject is the singular noun *exercise*. The correct form of the verb is therefore the singular *relaxes*.

In editing your compositions be sure your verb choices fit the real subjects and not merely the closest nouns.

Solving Verb Problems

When a compound subject is preceded by the words each *or* every. The words *each* and *every* refer to each part of the compound subject as an *individual* person or unit. Therefore the singular form of the verb should be used. Here are some examples:

Incorrect   Every man and woman in the office *are* expected to contribute for the manager's Christmas gift.

Correct   Every man and woman in the office *is* expected to contribute for the manager's Christmas gift.

Incorrect   Each of the choir members *have* a degree in music.

Correct   Each of the choir members *has* a degree in music.

When the parts of a compound subject are joined by or *or* nor. Sometimes the subject of a sentence has two or more parts. When the word that joins those parts is *and*, there is little confusion because the sense is usually plural, as in "*John and Andy were* the first students to submit their compositions." However, when the word that joins the parts of the subject is *or* or *nor*, the sense is different. The rule that applies in such cases is this: if all parts of the subject are singular, make the verb form singular; if all parts are plural, make the verb form plural; if one part is singular and another is plural, let the part of the subject closest to the verb govern the form of the verb.

Correct   Either Agnes or her sister *is* the one responsible for the damage. (Both parts of the subject are singular.)

Correct   Neither his friends nor his relatives *recognize* his talent. (Both parts of the subject are plural.)

Correct   Neither her shoes nor her blouse *matches* her suit. (*Shoes* is plural and *blouse* singular, so the nearer one governs the form of the verb.)

In editing your compositions, be alert for the words *or* and *nor*. When you find one of them, check to be sure you have chosen the correct verb form.

When the subject is a noun with plural form but singular meaning, an indefinite pronoun, a collective noun, or a relative pronoun. A number of nouns that are plural in form usually have singular meanings and therefore take a singular form of the verb. *Athletics*, *mathematics, economics, physics, measles,* and *statistics* are examples of such nouns. Indefinite pronouns—that is, pronouns that do not refer to a specific person or thing—are also usually singular in meaning and therefore take a singular form of the verb. Examples of indefinite pronouns include *anyone, anybody, everyone, everybody, everything, each, either, neither, nobody, one, no one, someone, somebody,* and *something*. (The pronouns *all, some, any,* and *none* are exceptions to this rule and may take either a singular or a plural verb form depending on the sense of the word they refer to.)

Incorrect   *Measles are* a more serious disease than most people realize.

Correct   *Measles is* a more serious disease than most people realize.

Incorrect   I checked the house again and *everything were* in order.

Correct   I checked the house again and *everything was* in order.

A collective noun is singular in form, but it refers to a group of individual people or things. These nouns may take either a singular or a plural verb form, depending on whether they refer to the group as a whole or to each individual member of the group. *Committee, jury, council, family, group, team, panel,* and *audience* are examples of collective nouns. Similarly, the relative pronouns *who, which,* and *that,* when used as subjects, take either singular or plural verb forms, depending on the sense of the sentence, and the sense of the particular nouns they refer to.

Correct   Judging by their applause, the *audience endorses* the idea. (The audience here is referred to as a single group.)

Correct   The *committee are* in disagreement about the issue. (The group here is referred to as a collection of individuals.)

Correct   The piranha is the only *fish that displays* a total disregard of mealtime restraint. (The singular form *displays* matches the singular form *fish*.)

Correct   There are few *people* I know *who are* as two-faced as Martha. (The plural form *are* matches the plural form *people*.)

When the subject is a gerund.   A gerund is a verbal noun—that is, a noun made by adding *-ing* to a verb. *Dancing, sweating,* and *col-*

Solving Verb Problems

lapsing are examples of gerunds.* Because gerunds look like verbs, you may fail to recognize them as the subjects of sentences. When you edit your compositions, be alert for gerunds that serve as subjects and check to be sure the form of their verbs is singular.

Incorrect   Jogging with others *help* me forget the pain involved. (*Jogging*, not *others*, is the subject of the sentence, so the verb form should be singular.)

Correct   Jogging with others *helps* me forget the pain involved.

Incorrect   Copying the ideas of other writers without crediting those writers *are* both morally and legally wrong. (*Copying*, not *writers*, is the subject of the sentence, so the verb should be singular.)

Correct   Copying the ideas of other writers without crediting those writers *is* both morally and legally wrong.

Edit each of the following sentences for subject–verb agreement. If the sentence is correct as written, so indicate. If it is incorrect, revise the verb to make it correct.

Exercise

1. Bowling, golf, and wind surfing is my favorite sports.
2. The only one of my friends who always remember my birthday is Tiffany.
3. No one ever leaves her house without a piece of homemade pie.
4. Neither Tom nor Josephine is the right person for the job.
5. Watching horror movies alone late at night when imagination plays its little deceptions are inadvisable, at least for nervous individuals.
6. Tom, surrounded by the group of attractive girls, was in his glory.
7. Some of the people at the office objects to having to work on Good Friday.
8. I know I have to take another course in the math group, but statistics are just too difficult for me.

Note: When they are used as adjectives, verbs with *-ing* endings are called present participles.

9. Sandra is the only one of the sorority girls who maintain outside friendships.
10. The twenty-fifth anniversary gift that Louise plans to give her parents cost over $500.
11. Neither prayer nor all-night cramming sessions the last week of the course is going to compensate for fifteen weeks of neglecting homework.
12. Each of their eight children hold a responsible position in business or the professions.
13. If the zoning board decides to approve her request, property values in the neighborhood will plummet.
14. Athletics are his only reason for remaining in college.
15. All the churches in the community have agreed to participate in the peace vigil.
16. Has the college marching band been invited to play in the Rose Bowl parade next year?
17. In today's business world, reasoning skills are a definite requirement for success.
18. Elisa's group have fewer cavities.
19. Mike, Joan, and Eva (the division dean's daughter) is running for class president.

5. Use the Correct Sequence of Tenses

In *complex* sentences, which have one main clause and at least one subordinate clause, it is important to make the tenses of the verbs in the clauses reflect the sense of the sentence. In editing your compositions, look closely at your complex sentences to be sure the tense sequence conveys the meaning you intend. Here are some examples of tense sequences with comments on them:

Correct   Lucille *realizes* that a career in mathematics *offers* more job security than one in drama. (The sequence of present tense followed by present tense conveys the meaning that Lucille *now realizes* that a math career *now offers* greater security.)

Correct   I *know* the service station attendant *cheated* me. (The sequence of present and then past tense conveys the meaning that the writer *at present* knows that the attendant cheated him *at some past time*.)

Solving Verb Problems

Correct If I *get* a 70 or better on today's exam, I *will get* a B in the course. (The sequence of present and then future tense conveys the meaning that if the writer gets a 70 on *the present* exam, she will get a B *at some future time,* when grades are submitted.)

Correct Last week on my soap opera my favorite character *learned* that her husband *cheats* on her. (The sequence of past followed by present tense conveys the meaning that the character *at some past time* learned that her husband *regularly* cheats on her.)

Correct He *swore* that he *loved* her more than life itself. (The sequence of past tense followed by past tense conveys the meaning that *at some past time* he swore that, *at that very time,* he loved her more than life itself.)

Correct She *lamented* that she *had been* foolish to marry for money. (The sequence of past and then past perfect tense conveys the meaning that *at some past time* she regretted that she had *at some previous time* decided to marry for money.)

Exercise

For each of the following sentences, choose the form of the verb that expresses the meaning specified in parentheses.

1. Dawn knows she _____ a career in military service. (Use the verb *to want* and convey the idea that she has this knowledge now.)
2. As you'd expect, he had no sooner left when the call _____ for him. (Use the verb *to come* and convey the idea the context clearly implies.)
3. When he completes his twenty years with the firm, he _____ fifty-three years old. (Use the verb *to be* and convey the idea the context clearly implies.)
4. I gave him advice because he _____ for it. (Use the verb *to ask* and convey the idea that the request came before the advice was given.)
5. Sarah finally concluded that her roommate _____ two-faced. (Use the verb *to be* and convey the idea that being two-faced is a habit with the roommate.)
6. Laura refuses to acknowledge that she _____ a psychiatrist. (Use the verb *to visit* and convey the idea that she continues to visit the psychiatrist.)

7. Clark and Marie were very proud when their son _____ with honors. (Use the verb *to graduate* and convey the idea the context clearly implies.)
8. The hunter raised the gun and shot once, and the deer _____ dead on the spot. (Use the verb *to fall* and convey the idea the context clearly implies.)
9. Someone stole those expensive hubcaps Reggie _____ for his van. (Use the verb *to buy* and convey the idea that Reggie had gotten the hubcaps earlier.)
10. Every Christmas Maude gets perfume from her husband, and every Christmas she _____ surprised. (Use the verb *to act* and convey the idea the context clearly implies.)

6. Use the Correct Mood of the Verb

The mood of the verb indicates the writer's attitude toward the statement. There are three moods in English: the indicative, the imperative, and the subjunctive. The first two are used more frequently than the third and seldom cause writers confusion.

The *indicative mood* states a fact or judgment or asks a question:

She *volunteers* her evenings to the Red Cross. (fact)

They *deserve* to be punished for drinking and driving. (judgment)

How *does* he *manage* to live on such a low salary? (question)

The *imperative mood* gives a direction or command (note: the word *you* is understood but not expressed in the imperative mood):

Turn left at the second traffic light. (direction)

Please *hand in* your exam papers. (command)

The third mood, the *subjunctive*, is undoubtedly less familiar to you. In the present tense it differs from the indicative mood in that it uses only the plain form of the verb regardless of the subject. For example, whereas the present tense indicative mood of the verb *to go* is *I go, you go, he (she, it)* **goes**, *we go, you go, they go*, the present tense subjunctive mood is *I go, you go, he (she, it)* **go**, *we go, you go, they go*. The present subjunctive form of the verb *to be* is *be* for all persons (rather than *am, is,* or *are*). Similarly, the past subjunctive form of the verb *to be* is *were* for all persons. There are three common uses of the subjunctive mood:

Use the subjunctive mood in *that* clauses after verbs expressing commands, requests, or recommendations:

> The dean suggested that Roger *withdraw* from college.
>
> Hortense demanded that Jean *return* her clothes immediately.
>
> My psychology professor requires that a student *submit* a 1,000-word composition on the concept of responsibility if he or she is late more than three times.

Use the subjunctive form *were* in clauses beginning with *if* or expressing a wish if the idea being expressed is contrary to fact:

> I wish she *were* able to be here with us tonight.
>
> If I *were* you, I'd report those obscene phone calls to campus security.

Note that not every *if* clause expresses an idea that is contrary to fact. For example, in the sentence "If John accepts the job in Detroit, he won't be able to attend the reunion," the idea being expressed may possibly become a reality, so the indicative mood form *accepts* is correct.

Use the subjunctive in sayings where its use is customary:

> *Come* hell or high water.
>
> The politicians *be* damned.
>
> *Come* rain or *come* shine.

Exercise

Check each of the following sentences to determine whether the mood of each verb is correct. Correct those that are in error.

1. Paul type much faster now than he used to.
2. My parents asked that my brother fills the gas tank whenever it registers below half full.
3. I only wish I was there when they played the trick on Marie and her boyfriend.
4. If Harvey sell his car before Thanksgiving vacation, I'm going to have to take the bus home.
5. If I was a better student, I'd seriously consider going to law school.
6. Sally resented her landlady's suggestion that she gets home earlier at night.

7. The commission proposed that every student be required to take a course in critical thinking.
8. I couldn't love my dog any more than I do if he was purebred.
9. The jury found him guilty as charged and recommended that he receives the death penalty.
10. I wish my roommate was here now—I'd tell him what I think of his loud music.

Solving Pronoun Problems (PRON)

Pronouns have no meaning in themselves. They derive their meaning from the nouns they refer to, which are called *antecedents*. There are two broad kinds of pronoun error—incorrect case and faulty reference.

Incorrect Pronoun Case

The *case* of a pronoun reflects its function in the sentence. There are three pronoun cases—subjective, objective, and possessive. The following chart shows the correct form of pronouns in each.

Subjective	Objective	Possessive
I	me	my, mine
you*	you	your, yours
he	him	his
she	her	her, hers
it*	it	its
we	us	our, ours
they	them	their, theirs
who	whom	whose

To avoid using the incorrect pronoun case, observe the following rules:

> Use the *subjective* case if the pronoun is the subject of a clause, a complement after any form of the verb *to be* (*is, was, shall be,* etc.), or an appositive of the subject. If the subject, comple-

---

*Notice that the objective case forms for these words are the same as the subjective case forms.

Solving Pronoun Problems

ment, or appositive has two or more parts, use the subjective case for each part. If the pronoun follows the conjunction *than* or *as* and is the subject of an implied verb, use the subjective case.

Subject of a Clause	My brother is much stronger than *I* [am].
	If *he* really believes everyone is against him, *I* feel sorry for him.
Complement After a Form of the Verb *To Be*	To tell the truth, it was *she* who did it.
	If anyone stands a chance of winning the gold medal, it is *he*.
Appositive of the Subject	Only two people—*she* and Agnes—were ever suspected.
	Three members of the class will be attending the convention—Tom, Nathan, and *I*.

Exercise

Examine each of the following sentences for errors in pronoun case. Correct the errors you find and be prepared to explain your reasoning.

1. The girl in the pink taffeta dress is her.
2. Jake, Arthur, and me plan to go to Florida during semester break.
3. Him and his roommate think they should be able to play their stereos as loud as they like.
4. In my family the one whom finished dinner last had to clear the table.
5. Her mother and she look very much alike.
6. I wish I were as tall as him.
7. He is the kind of musician whom achieves more by practicing than by native talent.
8. It was me who forgot to close the garage door.
9. I hope whomever borrowed my pen will return it.
10. The boys called to say that them and their sister will be picking you up at nine o'clock.

Use the objective case if the pronoun is the direct object, the indirect object, or the object of a preposition. Also, use the objective case if the pronoun is the object of an unstated but understood verb.

Direct Object	Many people in our class liked Ted better than [they liked] *him*.
	The professor scolded *them* for being late so often.
Indirect Object	Please give *me* the change from that ten-dollar bill.
	He really should offer *her* some reason for his behavior.
Object of a Preposition	I hate conceding an argument to *them*.
	The present I received from *them* is my favorite.

Exercise

Examine each of the following sentences for errors in pronoun case. Correct the errors you find and be prepared to explain your reasoning.

1. Who are you going to the dance with?
2. Sometimes I think that course is beyond me.
3. Be sure to write Joan and I during vacation.
4. Let's keep what we learned about Edna between we club members.
5. For most enthusiastic student my vote goes to Roger rather than to he.
6. Please, Professor Blake, give we students a break and postpone the test.
7. John's late arrival prevented Sam and I from seeing him.
8. I wanted to ask their clients and they if they'd be attending the dinner.
9. Save a seat for my friend and I.
10. We couldn't have made our quota without the extra effort put forth by Edith, Betty, and, most of all, she.

Use the possessive case if the pronoun shows possession or if it precedes a gerund. (A gerund is a verb with the ending *-ing* that is used as a noun.)

Possession	*Her* coat is very expensive.
	His charm is acknowledged by everyone.
	The dog chewed *its* bone furiously.

Preceding a Gerund

Their leaving the neighborhood saddened all of us.
His stereotyping of women is very offensive.
The key to her great success is *her* refusing to yield to difficulty.

Exercise

Examine each of the following sentences for errors in pronoun case. Correct the errors you find and be prepared to explain your reasoning.

1. There's no excuse for him being rude to the dining hall staff.
2. You having to go to the hospital frightened me when I first learned of it.
3. Him sprinting the 100-yard dash in record time made the difference for our team.
4. They couldn't get they car started, so they took the bus.
5. Jim called me and asked me to come to he house for dinner next week.

Faulty Pronoun Reference

Because pronouns have no meaning in themselves but derive their meaning from their antecedents, their reference to those antecedents must be clear.

Make a pronoun refer clearly to one antecedent.

Confusing When Marie introduced Agatha to Tom, she had no idea that *she* would marry him. (Does the second *she* refer to Marie or to Agatha? There is no way to be sure.)

Clearer When Marie introduced Agatha to Tom, she had no idea that Agatha would marry him.

Be sure a pronoun refers to a word that is actually expressed in the sentence, and not merely implied.

Confusing In my psychology professor's lecture, he mentioned the work of Viktor Frankl. (*He* logically refers to *professor*, but that word is not expressed in the sentence.)

Clearer   In his lecture today, my professor mentioned the work of Viktor Frankl.

Avoid using the pronouns *this*, *that*, *which*, and *it* to refer loosely to whole statements.

Loose Reference   My sister and her husband are planning to take an extended vacation in Europe this summer, which angers my father because they've owed him money for several years. (Here *which* refers loosely to the entire first clause.)

Clearer   My sister and her husband are planning to take an extended vacation in Europe this summer, a fact that angers my father because they've owed him money for several years.

Avoid using the pronoun *they* vaguely without a specific antecedent.

Vague   I'm really disappointed with the health care in this community. *They* really should do something to improve it. (Who should do something? The pronoun *they* here has no specific antecedent.)

Improved   I'm really disappointed with the health care in this community. Interested citizens and groups should do something to improve it.

When the antecedent is a collective noun (one that can be either singular or plural) use either a singular or a plural pronoun depending on the meaning. *Army*, *team*, *committee*, and *panel* are examples of collective nouns.

Correct   The team left their uniforms for the equipment manager to wash.

Correct   The jury returned its verdict yesterday morning.

Make the pronoun agree in number with its antecedent. That is, use a singular pronoun for a singular antecedent or for a plural antecedent prefaced by the word *each* or *every*, and use a plural pronoun for a plural antecedent.

Faulty Reference   *Every student* in this class is expected to do a ten-page research paper on a topic of *their* choosing.

Improved	*Every student* in this class is expected to do a ten-page research paper on a topic of *his or her* choosing.
Faulty Reference	*Children* should never be made to do something *he* finds frightening.
Improved	*Children* should never be made to do something *they* find frightening.

When the antecedent is an indefinite pronoun—that is, a word that does not refer to a specific person or thing—use a singular pronoun. (*Anyone, everybody, no one,* and *something* are examples of indefinite pronouns.)

Faulty Reference	*Everyone* must deposit *their* books and briefcases here before entering the campus store.
Improved	*Everyone* must deposit *his or her* books and briefcase here before entering the campus store.
Alternative	*All* those entering the campus store must first deposit *their* books and briefcases here. (The plural construction is preferred whenever the passage would otherwise require repeated use of *he or she* or *his or her*.)

Exercise

Examine each of the following sentences for errors in pronoun reference. Correct the errors you find and be prepared to explain your reasoning.

1. When the committee debated the issue, its exchange of views was heated.
2. The policemen's arrival was delayed, so when they got to the scene of the crime, no witnesses were there.
3. Mary told Bertha that Hilda's husband walked out on her, adding that it had come as a complete surprise to her.
4. No one in the company I used to work for gave more than two weeks' notice when they quit.
5. If a student leaves a research paper assignment until the last minute, they shouldn't expect to get a very good grade on it.
6. She said she'd have to date more people before she could be sure we were right for each other, stressing that marriage for

her would be a lifetime commitment. I strongly objected to that.
7. When Agnes shouted at Betty, she began crying.
8. He got a second job at night so that he could save enough money to return to college, but that was difficult to do.
9. In my high school they didn't allow smoking in the halls.
10. Everyone on the team did their best.
11. The school board will announce their decision on the bond issue tomorrow.

Solving Adjective and Adverb Problems (ADJ/ADV)

Both adjectives and adverbs modify (describe) other parts of speech, but they do not modify the same parts of speech. In addition, most adverbs end in *-ly*, but not all do; moreover, some adjectives end in *-ly*. For these reasons, adjectives and adverbs are sometimes confused.

Learn to Distinguish Adjectives from Adverbs

The key to distinguishing adjectives from adverbs is to examine the function of the word that is being modified. Adjectives modify nouns or pronouns—that is, they provide descriptive detail about a person, place, or thing. Here are some examples of adjectives.

> My brother enjoys *frozen* pizza, but I can't stand it. (The word *frozen* describes the word *pizza*, a noun, so it is an adjective.)
>
> The *tall brunette* girl by the door is in my *poetry* class. (*Tall* and *brunette* modify *girl*, a noun, so they are adjectives. In addition, *poetry* modifies *class*, a noun, so it too is an adjective.)
>
> He was *hard-working* and *deserving*, but his employer gave the promotion to someone else. (*Hard-working* and *deserving* describe *he*, a pronoun, so they are adjectives.)

Adverbs, on the other hand, modify verbs, adjectives, and other adverbs, usually answering where, when, how, or to what extent. Here are some examples of adverbs.

> He ate the pizza *greedily*. (*Greedily* modifies *ate*, a verb, by telling the manner in which he ate, so it is an adverb.)

Solving Adjective and Adverb Problems

We waited a half-hour for her and *then* decided she wasn't coming. (*Then* modifies *decided*, a verb, by telling when.)

He is *very* anxious about his future with the company. (*Very* modifies *anxious*, an adjective. *Very* is therefore an adverb.)

The band I heard tonight play *really* well. (*Really* modifies *well*, an adverb, so it is an adverb.)

Exercise

Each of the italicized words in the following sentences is either an adjective or an adverb. Decide which each is by examining the word it modifies, as shown in the above examples. Be prepared to explain your choice.

1. A *smiling* face can lift people's spirits.
2. He raised the *heavy* package above his head and heaved it *mightily* on to the *waiting* truck.
3. She *often* wondered whether his *sarcastic* comments were intended to hurt other people or just to hide his *deep* sense of inferiority.
4. *Hard* drinking and *fast* driving can be a *deadly* combination.
5. "Come up and see me sometime," she whispered *breathlessly*, fluttering her *false* eyelashes, and affecting her *sexiest* Mae West pose.

Use Adjectives and Adverbs Correctly

Choosing the correct form of a word for your own writing is somewhat more difficult than being able to identify the form when you see it written. Yet if you exercise care and are willing to look up an occasional word in the dictionary, you will not find it a burdensome task. Many of the errors that occur with these two parts of speech involve relatively few words that people stubbornly resist learning. The following are among the most common:

Incorrect   He plays the guitar *good*. (The word *good* is used here to modify *plays*, a verb. But *good* is an adjective. An adverb is needed.)

Correct   He plays the guitar *well*.

Also Correct   He is a good guitarist. (The word *guitarist* is a noun, so it is proper to use the word *good* to modify it.)

Incorrect   We got home from the dance *real* late. (*Late* is an adverb signifying when, so it is incorrect to use the adjective *real* to modify it. An adverb is needed.)

Correct   We got home from the dance *really* late. (*Really* is an adverb, so it is the correct form here. *Very* is another adverb and might have been substituted for it.)

Use Comparative and Superlative Forms Correctly

Often we use adjectives comparatively. For example, we don't just say that Tim is *strong*, but that he is *stronger* than Pat, or the *strongest* in his grade. Many adjectives follow this progression, forming the comparative degree by adding *-er* and the superlative by adding *-est*. Others add the word *more* instead of the suffix *-er*, and *most* instead of *-est*. For example, we say *difficult, more difficult*, and *most difficult*. Words in both these categories are called regular adjectives.

Many other adjectives, however, follow a different progression. They form their comparative and superlative degrees not by adding a suffix or a word, but by changing to a different form altogether. *Good* is an example of such an *irregular* adjective. We don't say *good, gooder, goodest*, but *good, better, best*. Here are some further examples of both regular and irregular adjectives.

Regular Adjectives

Positive	Comparative	Superlative
dark	darker	darkest
tall	taller	tallest
swift	swifter	swiftest
angry	angrier	angriest
healthy	healthier	healthiest

Irregular Adjectives

Positive	Comparative	Superlative
many	more	most
little	less	least
bad	worse	worst

Most adverbs are regular, progressing to comparative and superlative forms by adding *more* and *most* to the positive forms. However, some progress irregularly by means of internal changes.

Solving Adjective and Adverb Problems

Regular Adverbs

Positive	Comparative	Superlative
pleasantly	more pleasantly	most pleasantly
sorrowfully	more sorrowfully	most sorrowfully
quickly	more quickly	most quickly
carefully	more carefully	most carefully

Irregular Adverbs

Positive	Comparative	Superlative
well	better	best
badly	worse	worst

In choosing comparative and superlative adjective and adverb forms, keep these three rules in mind:

1. The comparative degree is appropriate whenever the comparison involves *two* people, places, things, or actions; the superlative, when the comparison involves *more than two*.

2. It is never correct to use both the word *more* and the *-er* ending (as in *more friendlier*) or to use both the word *most* and the *-est* ending (as in *most friendliest*).

3. It is incorrect to use comparative or superlative forms with words that do not logically permit comparison. Examples of such words are *real, unique, perfect, round, square, empty,* and *dead.* (Something cannot be more real than something else, nor can anything be most dead. It is either real or unreal, dead or alive.)

Exercises

1. Decide whether each of the following words is an adjective or an adverb by determining whether it would make sense modifying a noun or pronoun, on the one hand, or a verb, adjective, or adverb, on the other. Then use each word correctly in a sentence. (If you have difficulty classifying a word, consult your dictionary.)

happy	never	acceptably
old	yesterday	sweet
heavenly	stately	strange
lovely	awkward	sensibly

2. Read the following sentences carefully to determine whether the adjectives and adverbs are used correctly. If you find an error, rewrite the sentence to eliminate it.

a. The week I spent at the beach last summer with my family was the happiest of my life.
   b. The design of the vase that brought such a high price at the auction was the most unique I have ever seen.
   c. My roommate plays the piano real well.
   d. I like Marvin, but I have least confidence in him than in my other friends.
   e. The winters in my hometown are bitter cold.
   f. If you really want to please your parents, do good in your schoolwork.

Solving Sentence Problems

Up to this point in the handbook, we have considered word-level problems. Now we will consider problems that occur at the sentence level. The most serious of these are sentence fragments, run-on sentences and comma splices, faulty predication, faulty modification, mixed or incomplete construction, and unnecessary shifts in person or tense.

Sentence Fragments (FRAG)

A sentence fragment is a group of words that is punctuated as if it were a sentence but that lacks grammatical completeness—that is, it is incapable of standing alone as a complete thought. If you have a sentence fragment problem, it is probably because you have difficulty distinguishing a phrase or a subordinate clause from a complete sentence. Here's how to do so. First check to be sure that the group of words in question has both a subject and a verb. If it does, then check to be sure that no introductory word makes it grammatically dependent on some other group of words. Any group of words that has a subject and verb and is not introduced by such a subordinating word is a complete sentence. Let's see how this simple test can be applied to actual cases:

Words in Question	Analysis
Sam and I look forward to swimming in the campus pool. At least once a week.	The first group of words set off as a sentence has both a subject and verb (*Sam and I*

Words in Question	Analysis
	and *look forward*) and has no introductory subordinating word. Therefore it is a complete sentence. But the second group of words has no verb; thus it is a fragment and should not be set off as a sentence. The passage should be revised to read: "Sam and I look forward to swimming in the campus pool at least once a week."
The dean spoke sharply to the students. Revealing her anger over the incident in the cafeteria.	The first group of words has a subject and a verb (*dean* and *spoke*) and is not introduced by a subordinating word. It is therefore a complete sentence. The second group of words, however, has neither subject nor predicate. (Though *revealing* is formed from the verb *to reveal*, it is a participle, not a verb.) The passage should be revised to read, "The dean spoke sharply to the students, revealing her anger over the incident in the cafeteria."
I love winter. Although I hate driving on slippery winter roads.	Despite its brevity, the first group of words is a complete sentence because it has a subject (*I*) and a verb (*love*) and is not introduced by a subordinating word. The second group of words, however, is not a complete sentence. Even though it has a subject (*I*) and a verb (*hate*), the introductory word *although* makes it dependent on the previous sentence. The passage may be re-

Words in Question   Analysis

vised to read, "I love winter, although I hate driving on slippery winter roads," or "I love winter. However, I hate driving on slippery winter roads." (The word *however*, unlike *although*, does not subordinate what follows it.)

Following are additional examples of sentence fragments. Each of them can be identified by using the approach demonstrated. Use that approach with each to understand why each is a fragment. (In each group of words the fragment is italicized.)

Fragment   Sentence fragments are easy to find. *If you know what to look for.*

Correction   Sentence fragments are easy to find if you know what to look for. (Or, "Sentence fragments are easy to find. You just have to know what to look for.")

Fragment   Sandy has to take her car to the garage tomorrow. *To get the front end aligned.*

Correction   Sandy has to take her car to the garage tomorrow to get the front end aligned.

Fragment   Please wait here for me. *While I run into the bank and get my check cashed.*

Correction   Please wait here for me while I run into the bank and get my check cashed.

Fragment   There is one ingredient of success more important by far than talent. *A willingness to persevere until the job is done.*

Correction   There is one ingredient of success more important by far than talent—a willingness to persevere until the job is done. (Or, "There is one ingredient of success more important by far than talent. That ingredient is a willingness to persevere until the job is done.")

Fragment   I wouldn't let anyone borrow my clothes. *Especially someone like Lisa, who doesn't even take care of her own things.*

Solving Sentence Problems

Correction   I wouldn't let anyone borrow my clothes, especially someone like Lisa, who doesn't even take care of her own things.

Many professional writers use sentence fragments on occasion for special rhetorical effects. Such use is justified because those writers have enough writing experience to distinguish between effective and ineffective (awkward) fragments. As an amateur writer, you should avoid the use of sentence fragments in all situations except those in which you are answering your own question, as in these examples:

Acceptable Fragment   Should a professor be expected to tolerate rudeness in class? *No, never.*

Acceptable Fragment   Will I accept her apology if she decides to offer one? *Of course.*

Exercise

Check each of the following groups of words to determine if it contains a sentence fragment. If it does, rewrite the passage to eliminate the fragment.

1. I've decided to cancel my membership in the book club. Because they keep sending me books after I have mailed back the cards with "send no selection" checked.
2. Every month Senator William Proxmire of Wisconsin bestows his Golden Fleece award. To the government agency that achieved the "biggest, most wasteful, or ironic" misuse of taxpayers' money.
3. She said we'd be having tofu for dinner. An announcement that made me regret I'd accepted her invitation.
4. Traveling with someone else is enjoyable. However, traveling alone is boring.
5. Woody Allen's humor may be a howl to you. To me it's just dumb.
6. She's very quick to forgive. But never to forget.
7. Some people will resort to all kinds of deceptions rather than apologize. The most pathetic of which is pretending that *they* have been offended.
8. There are no uninteresting subjects. Only uninterested people.
9. Erno Rubik became an international success in the early 1980s by inventing the cube that bears his name. A challenging

puzzle that can be solved by a child in a matter of seconds and yet can baffle an adult for months.
10. Many people favor the banning of pornographic magazines and films. Claiming that even if such material does not lead directly to sex crimes, it nevertheless fosters immature and potentially dangerous attitudes toward women.

Run-On Sentences and Comma Splices (RUN-ON, CS)

These errors consist of running two grammatically complete thoughts together, either without any punctuation (a run-on sentence) or with only a comma (a comma splice). Such errors usually occur because the writer fails to recognize that each thought is grammatically independent of the other. Both errors may be corrected in any one of the following ways:

1. Separate the independent thoughts with a comma plus a coordinating conjunction (*and, but, or, nor, for, so,* or *yet*).

Run-On Sentence	I know it's foolish to remain faithful to her when she is unfaithful to me I just can't make myself go out with anyone else.
Correction	I know it's foolish to remain faithful to her when she is unfaithful to me, but I just can't make myself go out with anyone else.
Comma Splice	That man is not fit to hold elective office, he certainly won't get my vote.
Correction	That man is not fit to hold elective office, so he certainly won't get my vote.

2. Separate the independent thoughts with a semicolon.

Run-On Sentence	The study of history is not for me I don't do well with names and dates.
Correction	The study of history is not for me; I don't do well with names and dates.
Comma Splice	I went water skiing for the first time yesterday, unfortunately, in three hours I never made it to my feet once.

Correction	I went water skiing for the first time yesterday; unfortunately, in three hours I never made it to my feet once.

3. Express each independent thought in a separate sentence.

Run-On Sentence	After two days of hoping that the throbbing in my tooth would go away by itself, I made the decision I had resisted I would visit the dentist.
Correction	After two days of hoping that the throbbing in my tooth would go away by itself, I made the decision I had resisted. I would visit the dentist.
Comma Splice	"Diamonds are forever" sounds nice, I doubt, though, that it applies if you don't keep up the payments.
Correction	"Diamonds are forever" sounds nice. I doubt, though, that it applies if you don't keep up the payments.

4. Subordinate one of the thoughts by adding an introductory word, such as *although, if, when, since,* or *because.* Or change the construction of the sentence—for example, by revising "She dropped the tray, then she started crying" to "She dropped the tray, then started crying."

Run-On Sentence	I know what it means to operate on a schedule I worked in a fast-food restaurant for two years.
Correction	I know what it means to operate on a schedule because I worked in a fast-food restaurant for two years.
Comma Splice	He wanted to remember his uncle as he had known him, he never visited the funeral home.
Correction	Because he wanted to remember his uncle as he had known him, he never visited the funeral home.

Exercise

Check each of the following passages to determine if it contains a run-on sentence or a comma splice. If it does, rewrite the sentence to eliminate the error.

1. My daughter wants more than anything to own a horse, however, she has no idea how much it costs to feed one.
2. Research shows that child abusers usually were themselves abused as children I can't understand that at all I'd think that the experience of being abused would make a person *less* likely to abuse others.
3. Less than a mile from my house is a nuclear power plant, unlike many people, though, I'm not in the least concerned about an accident.
4. Gamblers are quick to tell you about the occasions when they won, they are strangely quiet though, about the more frequent occasions when they lost.
5. According to the stereotype, men are supposed to be klutzes in the kitchen, the stereotype doesn't fit my husband, you should taste his chicken cacciatore or his fettucine Alfredo, they're scrumptious.
6. It was humiliating enough to have failed, then to make matters worse she began to receive form letters beginning "Dear Recent Graduate."
7. I've learned not to expect recognition for my successes, if I did I'd have spent most of my life in disappointment.
8. I still observe important occasions of the year, such as birthdays, Thanksgiving, and Christmas, in the way my family observed them, I believe one of the most precious gifts I can give my children is training in the art of celebrating with loved ones.
9. Baldness runs in my family, but none of my relatives has ever brought shame on us by wearing a wig.
10. She had driven away all who cared for her by her devotion to her ego, now in old age, when she desperately wanted someone to be close to, no one was there.

Faulty Predication (PRED)

Faulty predication exists whenever a subject and verb (or complement) do not fit together. In such cases the resulting sentence does

Solving Sentence Problems

not make sense. Consider this sentence: "The *meaning* of the flower in the story *symbolizes* youth and vitality." The predication here is faulty because, though a *flower* can symbolize something, a *meaning* cannot. The sentence should be revised to read, "The flower in the story symbolizes youth and vitality."

Faulty predication often occurs with forms of the verb *to be* (*is, were, are,* etc.). Because this verb links the subject of the sentence with its complement, creating a kind of equation, the subject and complement must fit together logically. Thus in the sentence "My broken *typewriter* is the *reason* I didn't complete the assignment" the predication is faulty. A typewriter can't be a reason—though, of course, the breakdown of a typewriter can be.

To correct faulty predication, rephrase the sentence to make the subject and verb, or the subject and its complement, fit together logically. Here are some examples of such revision:

Faulty Predication	Flattery is when you praise someone with an ulterior motive. (Flattery is not a time, as the word *when* indicates.)
Revision	Flattery is praise with an ulterior motive.
Faulty Predication	Her only objection was the price of the tickets. (The price itself cannot constitute the objection, though the *unreasonableness* of the price can.)
Revision	Her only objection was that the price of the tickets was excessive.
Faulty Predication	The actor's strong voice was an outstanding performance. (A *voice* is not a *performance*.)
Revision	The actor's strong voice contributed to his outstanding performance.

Exercise

Check the predication in each of the following sentences. If it is faulty, revise it.

1. Capital punishment is a national debate today.
2. In a democratic society voting is both a right and a privilege.
3. A preconception is when you have your mind made up in advance.

4. Any person who drinks and drives spells danger to innocent people.
5. The choice of Edgar as class president was chosen without regard for experience and ability.
6. Abstract painting is a personal impression of reality.
7. North Carolina is where many people are choosing to live in retirement.
8. That dark walkway between the library and the dormitory was where the assault occurred.
9. Prayer in the schools is an argument people get very excited about.
10. Rock music creates negative attitudes in children.

Faulty Modification (MOD)

Faulty modification exists whenever a modifier does not clearly modify the word it was intended to modify. There are three types of faulty modification: squinting, dangling, and misplaced.

Squinting Modification Modification is squinting if the reader cannot tell whether the modifier refers to the preceding or the following word. For example, in the sentence "I explained last week I would be absent from class," it is not clear whether the explanation was given last week or whether the absence was to have occurred then. To correct squinting modification, rephrase the sentence to make the intended modification clear. In the above case, the corrected sentence might read, "Last week I explained that I would be absent from class," or "I explained I would be absent from class last week." Here are some additional examples.

Squinting   The inn I work at often has a band playing on weekends. (Does the writer work there often, or does a band play often?)

Correction   The inn I often work at has a band playing on weekends.

Squinting   The material he had memorized completely failed to come to mind during the exam. (Did he memorize it completely or did his effort to remember it fail completely?)

Correction   He had memorized the material, but he completely failed to recall it during the exam.

Dangling Modification   A modifier is dangling if it does not logically modify some word in the sentence. This error usually occurs in sentences with introductory participial, prepositional, or infinitive phrases. It can be corrected by placing the words you intend the phrase to modify directly after the phrase. Here are some examples of dangling modification:

Dangling   Sprinting toward the finish line, Ace's feet got tangled and he fell on his face. (Who was sprinting? Ace, not just Ace's feet.)

Correction   Sprinting toward the finish line, Ace got his feet tangled and fell on his face.

Dangling   While driving on Interstate 95, a terrible accident happened. (Who was driving? Surely not the accident.)

Correction   While driving on Interstate 95, I saw a terrible accident happen.

Dangling   To be fully awake for my eight o'clock class, six-thirty is the latest I can get up. (Who is awake? You or six-thirty?)

Correction   To be fully awake for my eight o'clock class, I can't get up any later than six-thirty.

Misplaced Modification   Modification is misplaced if the word modified is not the one the writer intended to modify. This error frequently occurs with such words as *almost, even, exactly, hardly, just, simply, nearly,* and *only,* which modify the word or words immediately following them. Notice how the meaning of the following sentences is affected by the position of the word *only*:

She *only* smiled to him as she passed him in the hall. (She didn't speak to him; she only smiled.)

She smiled *only* at him as she passed him in the hall. (She didn't smile at anyone else, only at him.)

She smiled at him *only* as she passed him in the hall. (She never smiled at him anyplace else, only in the hall.)

The error of misplaced modification can also occur with prepositional phrases or adjective clauses. Such phrases and clauses are usually understood to modify the word (or words) that immediately precede them. If that word is not the one the writer intended to modify, confusion will result. To correct misplaced modification, move the misplaced word, phrase, or clause so that it conveys the meaning you intend.

Misplaced Phrase We had just finished dinner when the doorbell rang on the patio.

Revised We had just finished dinner on the patio when the doorbell rang.

Misplaced Clause The blue car belongs to my brother that was parked in front of my house.

Revised The blue car that was parked in front of my house belongs to my brother.

Exercise

Check each of the following sentences to determine if it contains squinting, dangling, or misplaced modification. If it does, rewrite the sentence to eliminate the error.

1. Inching her way up the sheer face of the cliff, the climber's thoughts were focused on finding the best place to drive the piton.
2. A song played on the radio frequently reminds me of a particular person or incident.
3. While dancing with another guy, my boyfriend walked into the room.
4. Being frightened to begin with, every noise made me jump.
5. To be licensed to drive a car, a demonstration of skill under crowded highway conditions, as well as under quiet city street conditions, should be required.
6. Hoping to get the endorsement of the pressure group, the senator's vote on the issue supported their position.
7. The expensive watch drew admiring glances from everyone in the office that Jim's wife had gotten for his birthday.
8. She looked lovely descending the stairs to meet her date in a pale blue evening gown.

9. I lost one of my contact lenses somewhere on the football field that I paid $200 for.
10. Misplaced modifiers can make a poor impression on the reader in a composition.
11. On the chance that Agatha might have forgotten how he had embarrassed her, Chuck called her for a date.
12. Walking through the woods, a rattlesnake threatened me.
13. She watched the porpoises frolic in the surf with her boyfriend.
14. While playing the video game, someone called me on the telephone.
15. As a rule, people who only think now and then think poorly.

Mixed or Incomplete Construction (CON)

Mixed construction occurs when two incompatible grammatical constructions are used together in a sentence. In such a sentence the writer begins to express a thought one way and then shifts to another way in mid-sentence, thereby violating grammar and making the meaning unclear.

Given the fact that ideas often come to us in rapid succession, it is understandable that from time to time two slightly different ideas will compete for expression in a single sentence. Here's how that can happen. A writer is thinking of these two thoughts simultaneously: "Although Sam is not an honor student, he is very conscientious" and "The fact that someone is not an honor student does not necessarily mean that he or she is irresponsible." But when the writer expresses the thoughts, she does not state one and then the other. Instead, she writes this mixed construction: "Although Sam is not an honor student does not mean he is irresponsible."

Not all mixed constructions, however, occur because the writer combined two separate thoughts. Sometimes they occur because the writer failed to choose between two ways of expressing a single thought. Here are two examples of this error:

Mixed   Because of his recent surgery is the reason he couldn't complete the physical education requirement.

Correction   Because of his recent surgery, he couldn't complete the physical education requirement.

Alternative Correction	His recent surgery is the reason he couldn't complete the physical education requirement.
Mixed	By doing it this way is the fastest way to achieve our goal.
Correction	Doing it this way is the fastest way to achieve our goal.
Alternative Correction	By doing it this way we can achieve our goal most quickly.

Incomplete construction occurs when the writer omits one or more words necessary to convey the meaning intended or required by the sense of the sentence. Not all omissions are errors, of course. Here are some examples of acceptable omissions:

Acceptable Omission	My life has been easy; my sister's, hard. (The omission of the words *life has been* in the second half of the sentence is acceptable because they are stated in the first half and the omission causes no confusion.)
Acceptable Omission	Some people prefer Italian food, others Chinese, and still others French. (The omission of the verb *prefer* from the middle and end of the sentence is acceptable because it is the correct form for each of the three parts of the sentence and is clearly implied by the sentence structure.)

The omission of *necessary* words, on the other hand, is an error. Here are some examples of such incomplete construction:

Incomplete	Marie needs twelve more hours of social science; Susan and I, nine each. (The omission of the verb in the second half of the sentence implies that the verb *needs* is intended. However, unlike the subject *Marie*, the subject *Susan and I* is plural, and so requires the plural form of the verb, *need*.)
Correction	Marie needs twelve more hours of social science; Susan and I need nine each.
Incomplete	I like Brunhilda better than Yvonne. (Expressed this way the sentence is confusing. Does the writer like

Solving Sentence Problems

	Brunhilda better than she likes Yvonne, or better than Yvonne likes Brunhilda?)
Correction	I like Brunhilda better than Yvonne likes her. (Or "... better than I like Yvonne.")
Incomplete	My group had fewer cavities. (Fewer cavities than during the last testing period? Fewer cavities than other groups? Fewer cavities than a dog has fleas? The comparison must be completed to be meaningful.)
Correction	My group had fewer cavities this year than last year.

When editing your composition for mixed or incomplete constructions, be sure to look closely at what you actually said, instead of merely letting your eyes scan the paper as you think of what you *meant* to say.

Exercise

Check each of the following sentences to determine if it is a mixed or incomplete construction. If it is, rewrite it to eliminate the error.

1. Her husband was more interested in sports than his friends.
2. After jogging for six miles every day is the time I enjoy a tall glass of lemonade.
3. Bill has taken music lessons for eight years; Kathleen, for three.
4. By studying the works of the masters is the best way to learn painting technique.
5. Drinking moderately makes more sense than drinking excessively.
6. He was a very excitable person and not because he was really lying was the reason he failed the lie detector test.
7. Tim plans to enter medical school when he graduates; Pat and Charles, law school.
8. Even though you like a subject does not mean it represents a good career choice for you.
9. He comes from a poor family is the reason he appreciates things the rest of us take for granted.
10. Some dogs are easy to train, others difficult, but mine is so stupid he failed the entrance exam to obedience school.

Unnecessary Shifts in Person or Tense (SHIFT)

Shifts in person or tense often cause difficulties for beginning writers. Some shifts cannot be avoided—the thought being expressed demands them. For example, if you were writing about automobile accidents and turned from one involving several friends to one in which you alone were involved, you would have to shift from "my friends" to "I." Similarly, if you were contrasting the attitude you had toward studying in high school with your present attitude, you would correctly begin with past tense and then, at the appropriate time, switch to present tense.

Not all shifts in person or tense are necessary, however, as these examples illustrate:

Unnecessary Shift in Person	*The student* who comes to college deficient in basic skills is often required to take remedial courses. Whether or not *they* succeed in these courses depends on *their* attitude. If *the student* does not realize that the requirement reflects the fact that basic skills will be demanded in later courses, *he or she* may exert only token effort. When that happens, *the students* not only fail to learn the basic skills but also reinforce their poor study habits and increase *their* chances of failing in later courses.
Correction	*Students* who come to college deficient in basic skills are often required to take remedial courses. Whether or not *they* succeed in these courses depends on *their* attitude. If *students* do not realize that the requirement reflects the fact that basic skills will be demanded in later courses, *they* may exert only token effort. When that happens, *they* not only fail to learn the basic skills but also reinforce *their* poor study habits and increase *their* chances of failing in later courses.
Alternative Correction	*The student* who comes to college deficient in basic skills is often required to take remedial courses. Whether or not *the student* succeeds in these courses depends on *her* attitude. If *she* does not realize that the requirement reflects the fact that basic skills will be demanded in

later courses, *she* may exert only token effort. When that happens, *she* not only fails to learn the basic skills but also reinforces *her* poor study habits and increases *her* chances of failing in later courses.

Note that in both corrected versions, wherever a change in person is made, the verb is also changed to agree with the subject. Note also that in the alternative corrected version, only the pronoun *she* is used, and not *he or she*, which becomes distracting when it must be repeated several times. (The pronoun *he* could have been used in place of *she*.)

Unnecessary Shift in Tense	One consideration in judging the quality of instruction *is* so obvious that it *is* often overlooked. That is, *is* the teacher well-educated, knowledgeable, and interested in the subject. Surely if a teacher barely *knew* what he or she *was* talking about, or *was* bored with the subject, the students *will* have difficulty grasping the lesson.
Correction	One consideration in judging the quality of instruction *is* so obvious that it *is* often overlooked. That is, *is* the teacher well-educated, knowledgeable, and interested in the subject. Surely if a teacher barely *knows* what he or she *is* talking about, or *is* bored with the subject, the students *will* have difficulty grasping the lesson.

If your instructor indicates that you tend to have a problem with shifts in person or tense, check each noun and pronoun or tense in your composition while editing. If you find any shift that cannot be justified, change the wording to achieve consistency.

Exercise

Check each of the following passages for unnecessary shifts in person or tense. If you find any, revise them to eliminate the error.

1. Many students on this campus lack table manners. A student will shovel food into his mouth without pausing to breathe, reach across someone else's tray for the salt, talk with his

mouth full of food, and burp at his neighbor. On more than one occasion I've actually seen students bend over and lick their plates. These and similar experiences have prompted my friend to term any trip to the dining hall "a visit to the kennel."

2. The dark clouds threatened rain all morning and by noon they delivered. It poured with no let-up for about three hours, and then, just when I was about to give up any hope of playing tennis, the sun suddenly begins to shine. Within an hour the courts are dry and Agnes and I are enjoying our weekly match.

3. Professor Schwartz promised that he'd make economics interesting and relevant for nonmajors, and he kept his word. I enjoyed every minute of that course. If you have room in your schedule this term, I recommend that you take it.

4. A thirteen year old is a curious creature. One moment they're giggling uncontrollably or otherwise acting like small children, and the next they're so sophisticated that they're shocked if their parents use slang in public.

5. The media share responsibility for the casual attitude many Americans have about violence. Every evening during the Vietnam war, for example, TV news treated viewers to film footage of maimed and bloodied human beings and of cities and towns reduced to rubble. Even today, when our nation is not at war, they miss no opportunity to display the gory details of whatever violent episode occurs in some remote corner of the world.

Solving Spelling Problems (SP)

Many poor spellers regard their problem as a challenge to become excellent spellers. They try to memorize spelling rules and keep a dictionary handy to look up every word they are unsure of. Some succeed with this approach, but others soon grow weary of forgetting the rules, becoming confused in applying them, or spending so much valuable time flipping through the dictionary. Not infrequently, these people eventually admit defeat and resign themselves to producing writing filled with spelling errors and receiving low grades.

If you are growing weary of the effort to become a good speller, or if you have already abandoned hope, then this spelling section is designed for you. It does not aim to teach you how to write without committing spelling errors. Instead, it aims to teach you how to

Solving Spelling Problems

correct your errors, quickly and effectively, after you have made them. In other words, it treats spelling not as a writing problem but as an *editing* problem.

In the pages that follow you will find no spelling rules to memorize (though if you already have learned such rules, you should certainly go on using them). Nor is the approach presented here a complicated one to use. It may be summed up in two simple guidelines:

1. *Forget about spelling while you are writing—turn your attention to it only after you have finished revising your rough drafts.* Looking up words while you are writing can interfere with the flow of thought and cause writer's block. In addition, since it is impossible to be sure during the writing stage which words will survive the revision stage, it is inefficient to look up words then.
2. *Use your own personal spelling list and a spelling dictionary.* A speller's dictionary is more compact and easier to use than a regular dictionary because it contains no definitions. (There are a number of good spelling dictionaries on the market—ask your instructor or campus bookstore manager for help in choosing one.) Your personal spelling list should include any words your instructor indicates you have misspelled in your compositions. But you needn't wait to begin your list until you have received one or more corrected compositions. The rest of this section will help you begin creating your list immediately.

There are numerous causes of spelling errors. The five presented below are the most common. Read them carefully and circle all those words that have posed problems for you in the past. Then include them in your spelling list and use that list to edit your compositions.

Words That Are Often Mispronounced

Each of the following correctly spelled words is frequently misspelled because it is mispronounced.

apt	children	government
arctic	congratulate	grievous
athlete	drowned	history
athletic	February	hundred
boundary	generally	hungry

interest
kindergarten
laboratory
library
literature
memory
mischievous
nuclear
pertain
probably
recognize
relevant
represent
sophomore
strictly
surprise
temperament
temperature
veteran
Wednesday

Words That Are Similar in Sound

Each of the words in the following list is often confused with a word that sounds like it. The result is not only a spelling error but also an error in meaning. (Each pair listed here is also listed in the glossary of usage, p. 430. Consult the glossary about any of these words you are unsure of.)

accept, except
affect, effect
allot, a lot
allude, elude
already, all ready
altogether, all together
always, all ways
anyway, any way
are, our
ascent, assent
beside, besides
board, bored
capital, capitol
censor, censer, censure
choose, chose
conscience, conscious
diner, dinner
forth, fourth
gorilla, guerrilla
hear, here
hole, whole
illusion, allusion
its, it's
lay, lie
lead, led
lightning, lightening
loose, lose
maybe, may be
moral, morale
passed, past
patience, patients
personal, personnel
petition, partition
phase, faze
presence, presents
principal, principle
propose, purpose
quite, quiet
rain, reign, rein
raise, raze
right, rite, write
rise, raise
road, rode
sent, cent, scent
sight, site, cite
since, sense
sit, set
so, sow, sew
stationary, stationery
straight, strait

Solving Spelling Problems

then, than
there, their, they're
through, threw
to, too, two
tortuous, torturous

waist, waste
weak, week
were, where
whose, who's
your, you're

Related Words That Are Spelled Differently

Some words are spelled differently in their different forms. Spelling errors result from using the spelling of one form where it does not apply. Here are some examples of such words.

advice, advise
argue, argument
breath, breathe
comedy, comic
courtesy, courteous
descend, descent
describe, description
destroy, destruction
disaster, disastrous
enter, entrance
envy, enviable, envious
explain, explanation

generous, generosity
grief, grieve, grievance
high, height
hunger, hungry, hungrily
influence, influential
judge, judgment
marry, marriage
omit, omission
paralyze, paralysis
varied, various
vengeance, vengeful

Words with Prefixes, Suffixes, or Troublesome Internal Letter Combinations

The most common prefixes include *im-*, *a-*, *in-*, *un-*, *dis-*, *mis-*, *per-*, *pre-*, and *pro-*. Some spelling errors occur in words with prefixes because the writer is uncertain whether the root word stays the same or changes with the addition of the prefix. *Immoral* and *disappear*, for example, are commonly misspelled for this reason. Other errors occur because of confusion about the meaning of the prefix and thus about what prefix is appropriate to use in a particular situation. That is the case when a writer uses *per*scription to mean *prescription*. To gain more confidence in using prefixes correctly, use this approach—the next time you look up a word beginning with a particular prefix, look up several other common words beginning with that prefix and add to your list any that you are unsure of. Your investment in time will be minimal, and you will very soon have gained control over all your problem prefixes.

Suffixes cause even more spelling problems than prefixes. You will have to choose between *-able* and *-ible; -ant* and *-ent; -cede, -ceed,* and *-sede; -ery* and *-ary; -or, -er,* and *-ar;* and so on. Unfortunately, you can't put the alphabetical format of the dictionary to work for you with suffixes as you can with prefixes, so you must be prepared to look up each word with a problem suffix once. Nevertheless, by writing it down on your list when you look it up, you will at least ensure that you will not have to look it up more than once. Moreover, if you are alert to the correct spelling of words when you read, you can often save yourself even that first lookup.

Troublesome internal letter combinations are yet another cause of spelling errors. *Thief*, for example, may be incorrectly spelled *theif*, or *receive* incorrectly spelled *recieve* because the writer is not sure which vowel comes first. Or, to take a somewhat different problem, *existence* may be incorrectly spelled *existance* or *separate* incorrectly spelled *seperate* because the sound of the correct vowel is indistinguishable from the sound of the incorrect vowel. You need have no great difficulty overcoming these nagging problems if you write the troublesome word on your list correctly and consult the list when you write. (If any of the words used as examples in this paragraph are problem words for you, be sure you write down the correct spellings given here.)

Words with Unusual Plural Forms

Sometimes a writer spells a word correctly in the singular, but incorrectly in the plural. Not all English nouns form their plurals by adding a final *s*. Here are some of the other plural forms:

body, bodies
potato, potatoes
leaf, leaves
mother-in-law, mothers-in-law

child, children
phenomenon, phenomena
analysis, analyses

Whenever you look up a noun in the dictionary, note not only the singular form but the plural form as well, and write both on your spelling list. That will help you avoid errors caused by unusual plural forms.

A Basic Spelling List

The list that follows contains more than a thousand of the most frequently misspelled words in the English language. Surely many of the words will pose no problem for you. But just as surely there are some that you have misspelled many times in the past. To expand your personal list of problem words, take the time now to read each word in the list, making a check mark by the ones you have had trouble with. Then write them down in a notebook, ideally one you use just for this purpose, being sure to list them alphabetically and to leave sufficient room for the addition of at least two or three dozen words under each letter of the alphabet. Finally, add words whenever you have an opportunity to do so, and use your list when you edit all your compositions.

A

absence
abundance
abundant
academic
academically
academy
accept
acceptable
acceptance
accepting
access
accessibility
accessible
accessories
accidental
accidentally
acclaim
accommodate
accompanied
accompanies
accompaniment
accompanying
accomplish
accomplishment
according
accumulate
accuracy
accurate
accurately
accuse
accuser
accuses
accusing
accustom
ache
achievement
acquaint
acquaintance
acquire
across
activities
actual
actuality
actually
adequately
adjacent
admission
admittance
adolescence
adolescent
advantageous
advertisement
advertiser
advertising
advice
advise
affect
affidavit
afraid
against
aggravate
aggressive
aisle
alleviate
allot
allotment
allotted
allowed
allows
all right
all together
almost
alphabet
already
altar
alter
although
altogether
amateur
among
amount
analysis
analyze
anecdote
annually
another
answer
anticipated
antidote
antiseptic
anxiety
apologetically
apologized
apology
apparatus
apparent
apparently
appear
appearance
applied
applies
applying
appreciate
appreciation
approach
approaches
appropriate
approximate
aqueduct
arctic
area
argue
arguing
argument

arise
arising
arouse
aroused
arousing
arrangement
article
ascend
asinine
atheist
athlete
athletic
attack
attempt
attempts
attendance
attendant
attended
attitude
audience
author
authoritative
authority
autumn
auxiliary
available
awkward

B

bachelor
ballistic
bargain
basically
basis
beauteous
beautified
beauty
become
becoming
before
began
beginner
beginning
behavior
belief
believe
beneficial

benefited, or
   benefitted
beyond
bigger
biggest
bookkeeping
boundary
breath
breathe
brilliance
brilliant
Britain
Britannica
brought
burial
buried
bury
business
busy

C

cafeteria
calendar
campaign
capital
capitalism
career
careful
careless
carried
carrier
carries
carrying
categorically
category
caught
celebrate
cemetery
certain
certainly
challenge
changeable
changing
character
characteristic
characterized
chauffeur

cheerfulness
chief
children
choice
choose
chose
chosen
Christian
Christianity
cigarette
cite
clothes
coincidence
college
colossal
column
comfortably
coming
commercial
commission
committee
communist
companies
comparative
compel
competent
competition
competitive
competitor
complete
completely
compliment
comprehension
concede
conceivable
conceive
concentrate
concern
condemn
confuse
confusion
congratulations
connoisseur
connotation
connote
conscience
conscientious
conscious

consensus
consequently
consider
considerable
considerably
consistency
consistent
contemporary
contempt
continue
continuous
continuously
controlled
controlling
controversial
controversy
convalescent
convenience
convenient
convertible
copyright
correlate
correspondence
council
councillor,
   or councilor
counselor
countries
courageous
court
create
criticism
criticize
cruelly
curiosity
curious
curriculum
cylinder

D

dangerous
daughter
dealt
deceive
decided
decidedly
decision

Solving Spelling Problems

deficient
define
definite
definitely
definition
delinquent
democracy
dependent
descendant
descent
describe
description
desert
desirability
desire
despair
dessert
destruction
detriment
devastating
develop
device
devices
dictionary
dietitian
difference
different
difficult
dilemma
diligence
diminish
dining
dining room
diphtheria
disappoint
disastrous
discernible
disciple
discipline
discoveries
discrimination
discuss
discussion
disease
disgusted
disillusioned
dissatisfied
distinguished

divide
divine
doctor
doesn't
dominant
dormitories
doubt
dropped
drunkenness
due
during

E

eager
easily
ecstasy
edition
effect
efficiency
efficient
eighth
either
eligible
eliminate
eloquently
embarrass
embarrassed
emigrate
emperor
emphasize
emptiness
encourage
endeavor
enemies
enjoy
enormous
enough
entangle
enterprise
entertain
entertainment
enthusiasm
enthusiastically
entirely
entrance
enviable
envious

environment
envy
epidemic
episode
epitaph
equality
equipment
equipped
escapade
escape
especially
etc.
eventually
every
everybody
everything
evidently
exaggerate
exaggerating
exceed
excellence
excellent
except
excess
excitable
exercise
exhausted
exhibit
exhilarate
existence
existent
expense
experience
experiment
explanation
extravagant
extremely
eyeing, or eying

F

facilities
faithfulness
fallacy
familiar
families
fantasies
fantasy

fascinate
fascinating
fascist
fashions
favorite
feasible
February
fictitious
field
finally
financially
financier
foreign
foreigners
formally
formerly
forty
forward
fourteen
fourth
friendliness
fulfill
fundamentally
funeral
further

G

gaiety
gauge
gazing
generally
genius
genuine
goggles
government
governor
grammar
grammatically
grandeur
grievance
grievous
group
guarantee
guaranteed
guard
guess
guidance
guiding

H

handicapped
handkerchief
handled
happened
happening
happiness
harassed
harassment
haughtiness
healthy
hear
heard
heavier
height
helpful
hemisphere
hemorrhage
here
hereditary
heredity
heretic
heroes
heroic
heroine
heroism
hesitate
hindrance
hopeless
hoping
hospital
hospitalization
hostile
huge
human
humanist
humiliate
humorist
humorous
hundred
hunger
hungrily
hungry
hurriedly
hygiene
hypocrisy
hypocrite

I

ideally
ignorance
ignorant
imaginary
imagination
imagine
immediate
immediately
immense
importance
important
inadequate
inauguration
incalculable
incidentally
increase
incredible
indefinite
independence
independent
indictment
indispensable
individual
individually
industries
inevitable
influence
influential
ingenious
ingredient
initiative
innocence
inoculate
inseparable
insistence
instead
instructor
intellect
intellectual
intelligence
intelligent
interest
interference
interpretation
interrupt
intolerance
introductory
invariable
involve
irrelevant
irreligious
irresistible
irritable
island
issue
its
it's

J

January
jealousy
jewelry
Judaic
Judaism
judgments

K

kindergarten
knowledge
known

L

labeled
laboratory
laborer
laboriously
laid
language
later
laugh
least
led
leisurely
length
lengthening
license
lieutenant
lightening
lightning
likable
likelihood
likely
likeness
listener
literary
literature
liveliest
livelihood
liveliness
lives
loneliness
lonely
loose
lose
losing
loss
loyalty
luxuries
luxury

M

magazine
magnificence
magnificent
maintenance
management
maneuver
manner
manufacturers
manufacturing
marriage
material
mathematics
matter
maybe
meant
mechanics
medical
medicine
medieval
melancholy
mere
methods
metropolitan
might
miniature
minimum

minutes
miscellaneous
mischief
misspelled
modern
monotonous
moral
morale
morally
mosquitoes
movement
multiplication
muscle
mysterious

N

naphtha
narrative
naturally
necessary
Negro
Negroes
neighbor
neither
newsstand
niece
ninety
ninth
noble
notice
noticeable
noticing
numerous

O

obstacle
occasion
occur
occurred
occurrence
occurring
off
offense
often
omit

omitted
operate
opinion
opponent
opportunities
opportunity
oppose
opposite
optimism
optimistic
organization
origin
original
overwhelming

P

paid
palpitate
pamphlets
pandemonium
pantomime
parallel
paralysis
paralyzed
paraphernalia
parliament
particular
particularly
passed
past
peace
peculiar
peculiarities
people
perceive
performance
permanent
permissible
permit
persistent
personal
personnel
perspiration
persuade
pertain
phase
phenomenon

philosophy
physical
picnicking
piece
planned
plausible
playwright
pleasant
political
politician
portrayed
possession
possible
practical
practically
practice
prairie
precede
precedent
predominant
prefer
preferred
prejudice
prepare
prescription
presence
present
prestige
prevalent
preventive
previous
primitive
principal
principle
prisoners
privilege
probably
procedure
proceed
produce
profession
professor
prominent
pronounce
propaganda
propagate
prophecy
proprietor

psychoanalysis
psychology
psychopathic
psychosomatic
punctuation
pursue

Q

qualities
quantity
quarter
question
questionnaire
queue
quiet

R

realize
really
rebel
receipt
receive
receiving
recognize
recommend
reference
referred
referring
regard
regrettable
relative
relativism
relieve
religion
remember
reminisce
renowned
repetition
repetitious
represent
representative
research
resistance
resources
response
restaurant

result
revealed
reverend
rhythm
ridicule
ridiculous
righteous
rivalry
roommate

S

sacrifice
sacrilegious
safety
sandwich
satire
satisfaction
satisfied
satisfy
saucer
scarcity
scene
schedule
scheme
scholarship
school
scientific
secretary
seize
sense
sentence
separate
separation
sergeant
several
shepherd
shining
should
shoulder
shriek
siege
significance
similar
simile
simple
simply

since
sincerely
situation
sizable
skiing
sociology
soldier
soluble
sometimes
sophomore
sorrowful
source
sovereignty
speaking
special
specifically
specimen
speech
sponsor
stabilization
stationary
stationery
stenographer
stepped
stopping
stories
story
straight
straighten
strength
strenuous
stretch
strict
stubborn
studying
substantial
substantiate
subtle
succeed
success
successful
succession
suddenly
suddenness
sufficient
summary
summed

supersede
supervisor
supply
suppose
suppress
surprise
surrounding
surveillance
susceptible
suspense
suspicious
swimming
syllable
symbol
symmetrical
symmetry
synonymous
system

T

technical
technique
temperament
temperature
temporarily
tenant
tendency
tenement
than
their
themselves
then
theories
theory
there
therefore
they're
third
thirtieth
thorough
thoroughly
those
though
thought
through
to

together
tomorrow
too
tragedy
transferred
tremendous
trespass
tried
tries
twelfth
twentieth
twenty
two
tying, or tieing
typical
tyranny

U

unbelievable
unconscious
uncontrollable
undesirable
undoubtedly
uneasiness
unencumbered
unforgettable
unmanageable
unnecessary
until
unusually
useful
useless
using
usual
usually

V

vacuum
valleys
valuable
varies
varieties
various
vaudeville

Solving Spelling Problems

vegetable	voice	weird	wonderful
vengeance	volume	whenever	write
ventilate		where	writing
veteran	**W**	wherever	written
vicinity		whether	
victim	waive	which	**Y**
view	warrant	while	
village	wave	whole	yacht
villain	wealthiest	wholly	yield
vinegar	weather	whose	your
visible	Wednesday	witnessed	you're
vitamin	weight	woman	

Exercise

Check each of the following sentences for spelling errors. For every misspelling you find, write the correct spelling of the word.

1. He is the best sophmore athlete this college has ever enrolled.
2. The U.S. goverment has more nucular weapons than the Soviet goverment.
3. I had a long arguement with my stubburn roommate Paul over the existance of God.
4. The questionaire I recieved in the mail yesterday is similiar to the one you filled out last week.
5. Her professer gets really upset when a composition contains mispelled words.
6. The author of the book my mother sent me for my brithday is a born-again Christain.
7. In my part of the country it's unusual to have thunder and lightening in Febuary.
8. Our misteak in Vietnam was to respond conventionally to gorilla warfair.
9. Believe me, it's hard to allude women and remain a batchler when you have good looks and verbil stile.
10. It wouldn't phase me to walk through a sematary on a dark night—I don't scair easily.
11. When the leafs and the temperture begin to fall, New Englanders brace themselves for the onslought of winter.
12. Another page off the calender—it won't be long before final exams are here again.

13. She was a mischievious child, always ready to play a prank on someone.
14. According to stereotype, mother-in-laws always make life difficult for their daughter-in-laws.
15. That war was fought during the rein of Napoleon.
16. This is strickly confidential—those aichs and pains Agnes is always complaning about are more imaginary then real.
17. Who is he to pass judgement on matters of hypocrasy? He's the biggest phoney of them all.
18. The way that doctor harrasses his patients, it's a wonder anyone goes to him.
19. Alcohol has been known to indeuce a certain paralasis of the tongue.
20. More and more people today seem to be demonstrating a complete lack of morale principal.
21. So far the attempts to inforce quiet hours in the dormatories have been disasterous.
22. Maude has an ingenius way of injecting her narrow little opinions into every discussion.
23. Seperate checks please, waiter—I don't want my freind here to develope a dependancy on my generosity.
24. The personal policy of this company is to hire people on their merits, and not on the bases of age, color, or sex. There has never been a charge of descrimination against the company in its twenny-year history.
25. I find it hard to conceive of any hire form of estasy then listening to my English instructor lecher on literature.
26. Talk about clumsiness—that's the forth time in recent weeks I've seen him brake a dish.
27. Allow me to purpose a toast—to loyalty, the hallmark of freindship.
28. The present administration is similiar to the previus one in at least one respect—its contempt for the common worker.
29. Any act that excedes the boundries of good taste is in my view a grievious offense.
30. The dean is accessable, all right, but there's little benefit in that because you can't recieve a strait anser from her.

Solving Punctuation Problems (PUNCT)

Punctuation serves a very practical purpose—to enable readers to follow the writer's thinking and grasp his or her message not vaguely, but precisely. The contribution of punctuation to the overall effectiveness of a composition is much greater than is commonly realized. To appreciate this fact more fully, try to unravel the meaning of the following passage from the writing of T. S. Eliot, a master of English prose and poetry, with all his punctuation removed.

> For literary judgment we need to be acutely aware of two things at once of what we like and what we ought to like few people are honest enough to know either the first means knowing what we really feel very few know that the second involves understanding our shortcomings for we do not really know what we ought to like unless we also know why we ought to like it which involves knowing why we don't yet like it it is not enough to understand what we ought to be unless we know what we are and we do not understand what we are unless we know what we ought to be the two forms of self-consciousness knowing what we are and what we ought to be must go together.

If you were able to understand the passage, it wasn't without difficulty. Reading it undoubtedly took you much longer than was necessary. You may even have had the feeling you were working your way through a maze or piecing together a puzzle. To read that way is hardly an efficient or pleasurable activity. Now take another look at the same passage, this time as it was originally written by the author.

> For literary judgment, we need to be acutely aware of two things at once: of "what we like," and "what we *ought* to like." Few people are honest enough to know either. The first means knowing what we really feel: very few know that. The second involves understanding our shortcomings; for we do not really know what we ought to like unless we also know why we ought to like it, which involves knowing why we don't yet like it. It is not enough to understand what we ought to be, unless we know what we are; and we do not understand what we are, unless we know what we ought to be. The two forms of self-consciousness, knowing what we are and what we ought to be, must go together.[1]

Your second reading was surely faster and easier, for the punctuation significantly aids your understanding of the rather complex idea that T. S. Eliot is communicating. This example should make abundantly clear that the words and sentence structure writers use are not enough to convey meaning. *The way they mark the spaces between words is as important as the words themselves.* Those marks are the reader's signposts along the path of meaning.

We will examine four broad areas of punctuation and the various punctuation marks classified under each. These four areas are end punctuation, internal punctuation, the punctuation of quoted material, and the punctuation of words.

End Punctuation

End punctuation is used at the ends of sentences. End punctuation marks are the period, the question mark, and the exclamation point.

The Period

Use a period to signal the end of a statement or command.

> We all did well on the examination.
> Try to keep your room neater.

Use a period after abbreviations.

> Dr.   Mr.   Mrs.   Ms.   B.A.   D.D.S.

The Question Mark

Use a question mark after a direct question.

> Did that movie really receive rave reviews?

The Exclamation Point

Use the exclamation point after an interjection or exclamatory statement.   Do not overuse it, or you will reduce its effectiveness.

Help! Police!
The building is on fire!

Internal Punctuation

Internal punctuation is used within sentences to separate words, phrases, and clauses. Internal punctuation marks are the comma, the semicolon, the colon, the dash, and parentheses.

The Comma

Use a comma to separate main clauses joined by a coordinating conjunction (and, but, or, nor, for, so, yet).

> Many farmers were financially harmed by the government's embargo on the sale of grain to the Soviet Union, and they instructed their representatives to oppose any similar action in the future.
>
> They may decide to stay in the dormitory and study despite the noise, or they may work in the library instead.
>
> My brother didn't get his application in on time to take the civil service examination, so he'll have to wait until they offer the examination again.

Use a comma to separate introductory phrases and clauses from a main clause.

> Happy at receiving the promotion, Ethel took her husband and children out to dinner at an expensive restaurant.
>
> According to the director of admissions, this college's enrollment has dropped four percent a year for the past three years.
>
> If you plan to go to that game, you'd better get your ticket early.

Use commas to set off sentence elements that do not restrict the meaning of the sentence.

> Stan, the leader of the protest, rose to speak.
>
> Her clothes, which she bought exclusively at the finest stores, were always in good taste.

Use commas to set off all absolute phrases. (An absolute phrase consists of a noun or pronoun followed by a present or past participle. In some cases, the pronoun or the participle or both are clearly implied but unexpressed.)

> The dog stood quietly, its head lowered, its tail curved between its legs, expecting to be scolded.
>
> The cadet stood at attention, back straight, shoulders braced, eyes directly to the front. (Note that the pronoun "his" or "her" is unexpressed, as are the participles "being held" in the first two phrases and "being focused" in the last phrase.)

Use commas to separate items in a series.

> Their team was faster, taller, and more aggressive than ours.
>
> Be sure to bring a tent, a sleeping bag, food for four days, and an extra pair of boots.
>
> My duties at home kept me busy—helping my mother with the cooking and cleaning, taking care of my younger sister, and washing and ironing clothes for the whole family.

Use commas to set off elements that interrupt the flow of a sentence.

> My view, in short, is that the insanity plea should be abolished.
>
> Professors, unlike students, are allowed to park near classroom buildings.
>
> You can do it, Edna, if only you try.

Use commas to separate adjectives that modify a noun separately.

> She is a determined, popular, able candidate.

(*Note:* when the adjectives modify the noun collectively, as in the sentence "I'm heading for my quiet mountain hideaway," use no commas between adjectives.)

Use commas for dates if the month, date, and year are given (one comma following the date and another following the year if it occurs in the middle of a sentence); for addresses (but not for the ZIP code); for the names of geographical places, such as cities and states; and for separating people's names from their professional titles.

Solving Punctuation Problems

His last letter was postmarked January 23, 1956.

Her address is 233 Montgomery Street, Los Angeles, California 94101.

My parents have a summer home in Bovina Center, New York.

She introduced him as Chauncey M. Borstin, Jr., M.D.

Exercise

In each of the following sentences add one or more commas, following the rules for the comma explained in the preceding pages.

1. Although Arthur tried his best to get me a ticket to the concert he failed.
2. His face and hands filthy his clothing rumpled and worn the stranger definitely looked down on his luck.
3. Brunhilda who was rather plain in high school is a glamorous movie star today.
4. My professor expects students to do their work neatly thoroughly and on time.
5. The eggs were dried out and flaky the toast cold and soggy the coffee bitter.
6. Moreover the regulation about freshman parking is discriminatory.
7. Go to bed right after supper buy three alarm clocks hire two strong men to shake you awake and do whatever else is necessary to get to class on time.
8. Because I registered late most of the courses I wanted to take were closed.
9. If this country doesn't do something about inflation the dollar will soon be as valueless as the penny.
10. We spent thirteen hours driving to Cape Cod so when we got there we were more ready for bed than for a party.
11. Ella Louise Mabel and Clarissa are the only ones who didn't acknowledge the invitation.
12. Unlike the student living in a dormitory the student living off campus faces few distractions.
13. Having walked through the freezing woods for most of the night without food or drink or adequate clothing Nathan was becoming desperate.
14. If Pete doesn't pass every subject this term he'll lose his scholarship.

15. Next summer I plan either to get a job in my field or failing that to bum around the beach.
16. When confronted with a problem I study it react to it examine my reaction and try to draw a conclusion.
17. You can do your studying each day of the term or you can neglect it all term and spend the night before the final exam cramming.
18. The speaker at the next meeting will be Eduardo Gomez Ph.D. a visiting professor from Lima Peru.
19. She was ready willing and able to take on the assignment but her supervisor gave it to someone else.
20. She wrote January 4 1984 on her check forgetting that the new year had begun.

The Semicolon

Use a semicolon to separate closely related main clauses when no coordinating conjunction (and, but, or, nor, for, so, yet) *connects them.*

> The road to excellence is long and hard; only those who are dedicated can survive its rigors.
>
> Henry has half a dozen girls wild about him; Bart can't even get a date.

Use a semicolon to separate main clauses joined by a conjunctive adverb. (Examples of conjunctive adverbs are *however, consequently, moreover,* and *therefore.*)

> He attacked the problem with real style; unfortunately, more than style was needed to solve it.
>
> I've used every dollar I had to get my car fixed; therefore, I can't even think about going to Florida for spring vacation.

Use a semicolon to separate items in a series if one or more of the items contain internal commas.

> There are three kinds of people that I find insufferable: those who value money and position above friendship; those who derive enjoyment from mockery and ridicule; and those who,

lacking a particular virtue themselves, find ways to harm those who possess it.

The Colon

Use a colon to separate from the main clause any material that explains, illustrates, or amplifies it.

> There is one thing that no teacher need tolerate in class: loud snoring.
>
> Daydreamers seldom accomplish much: they exhaust themselves in imagining.

Use a colon to set off a list or series.

> Only three people are graduating with distinction: Bertha, Henry, and Clyde.
>
> My reasons for remaining here are the following: the trip is too costly, I can't take the time from my studies, and my part-time employer needs me to work this weekend.

Use a colon to introduce a formal quotation.

> G. K. Chesterton once offered this wry definition of journalism: "Journalism largely consists in saying 'Lord Jones Dead' to people who never knew Lord Jones was alive."

Use a colon to separate titles and subtitles.

> Someday I'm going to write a book. It will be titled *The Art of Procrastination: A Guide to Goofing Off.*

Exercise

In each of the following sentences add one or more semicolons or colons, following the rules explained on the preceding pages.

1. My landlord must be getting rich he has two large houses, each with twelve students, and charges an outrageously high rent.
2. There are at least three problems that threaten to plague the United States throughout the 1980s meeting energy needs without continuing to depend on Middle Eastern oil breaking the spiral of inflation and countering the efforts of countries

that, while deploring capitalist intervention, foment revolution wherever they can.
3. If Anna thinks she can get away with browbeating me, she'd better think again I've had more than enough of her nonsense.
4. Few people in her class ever got to know her well she kept to herself during school hours and never attended after-school functions.
5. In some states the legal drinking age is 21 in others, 19 in still others, 18.
6. Hypocrisy is a kind of willful schizophrenia the hypocrite has two personalities, one of which he or she keeps hidden from public view.
7. He is the least valuable player on our baseball team he leads the league in errors is a weak hitter and runs slowly, shuffling when sprinting is in order.
8. I'm not going to give up on the problem however, I am going to put it aside until my frustration subsides.
9. I'm going to title my paper "Marriage A Risky Enterprise."
10. Of all the proverbs I've read, this one is my favorite "The person who can't dance says the band can't play."

The Dash

In recent years the distinction between the dash* and the colon has all but disappeared. Today many respected writers use them almost interchangeably—many even prefer the dash. (Two uses have resisted this change—the introduction of formal quotations and the separation of titles and subtitles. The colon alone is acceptable there.) Unless you are writing for an audience you have reason to believe will prefer the more traditional colon (for example, the readers of a scholarly journal), you may use the dash instead. Thus you may:

Use a dash instead of a colon to separate from the main clause any material that explains, illustrates, or amplifies it.

> There is one thing that no teacher need tolerate in class—loud snoring.

Note: Most typewriters do not have a dash key. To make a dash in typing, use two hyphens with no spacing before, after, or between them.

Daydreamers seldom accomplish much—they exhaust themselves in imagining.

Use a dash instead of a colon to set off a list or series.

Only three people are graduating with distinction—Bertha, Henry, and Clyde.

My reasons for remaining here are the following—the trip is too costly, I can't take the time from my studies, and my part-time employer needs me to work this weekend.

In addition, you may use the dash to set off a parenthetical element that occurs within a sentence and that you want to emphasize. Use one dash before the element and another after it, unless it occurs at the end of the sentence, in which case omit the second dash. Here are some examples of this use:

His table manners—specifically, the way he chomps his food, wields his knife and fork like primitive weapons, and drools all over himself—leave something to be desired.

Many a time she sat at home until the early hours of the morning—worried and angry and at a loss to understand—while her husband drank himself blotto at some bar.

He dug the well by hand—an exhausting procedure that left him lame for a week.

Parentheses

Parentheses may be used to de-emphasize certain elements in a sentence; specifically, elements that do not restrict the meaning of the sentence. For example, in the sentence "Only one boy, Tom, was late for class," "Tom" is a nonrestrictive element. It adds a specific detail, but the meaning of the sentence would not be changed if that detail were omitted. So we could place it in parentheses instead of commas if we wanted to de-emphasize it. (However, if the sentence were changed to "Only Tom was late for class," then we could not place "Tom" in parentheses, because the sentence depends on that word for its meaning.) In addition, parentheses are used for "asides," elements that interrupt the thought of the sentence. Careful writers avoid using parentheses too frequently, for frequent interruption of the flow of thought can be distracting to the reader.

Bill Johnson (whose father graduated from this college in 1950) earned the highest grade point average in this year's graduating class.

The men on this campus (excluding, of course, my boyfriend and yours) are incredibly ugly.

Mr. Norton holds (Can you believe it?) a *distinguished* teaching professorship at this college.

My roommate was arrested last night for littering (a charge that anyone who has seen his side of our room would find eminently believable).

Note that in the third example the question mark is placed inside the parentheses. This is the case whenever the words within the parentheses express a question. When the words outside the parentheses express a question, then the question mark is placed outside. Note too that in the last example the period is placed outside the parentheses. That is usually where it is placed. (The only exception to that rule is in cases where the parenthetical element comprises the entire sentence, as it does in this sentence.)

Exercise

Each of the following sentences contains a parenthetical element set off by commas (or one comma if it occurs at the end of the sentence). Decide whether the sense of the sentence suggests it should be left as it is, emphasized, or de-emphasized. If a change is desirable, rewrite the sentence providing the appropriate punctuation.

1. The widely supported tax measure was today vetoed by the governor, an action that dramatically demonstrates her "taxpayers-be-damned" attitude.
2. The two best players on the team, Ace and Brian, have had offers from several professional organizations.
3. My dormitory, affectionately known as "The Pit," is an experience in less-than-elegant living.
4. She worked hard to attain her lifelong dream, the presidency of a large corporation.
5. The know-it-all tone, which implies that the writer thinks he has all the answers and is unwilling to consider the views of others, makes readers resentful and uncooperative.

Punctuation of Quoted Material

Three punctuation marks are used to present quoted material. They are quotation marks (both double and single), brackets, and ellipsis marks. (We will consider here both end and internal punctuation used with quotation marks.)

Quotation Marks

Use double quotation marks for direct quotations. For indirect quotations, use no quotation marks at all.

Correct   "Keep your eye on the ball," my tennis coach yelled.

Correct   My tennis coach yelled at me to keep my eye on the ball.

Use single quotation marks for a quotation within a quotation.

> He paused for a moment and then said, "What is the basic rule of philosophy? D. E. Trueblood's answer is best: 'It is not intellectually honest to hold a position after it is known that the position leads inevitably to other positions which are recognized as false.'"

Omit quotation marks for prose quotations of more than four lines and poetry quotations of more than three lines. Instead, separate the quotations from the text of your paper by triple-spacing after your last line, then typing the quotation double-spaced, with every line indented ten spaces. (Present the lines of poetry exactly as they appear in the original.)

A sample prose quotation:

Before he died, my uncle wrote me a long letter and shared with me some of the thoughts that guided his life. One in particular has always struck me as an excellent principle for anyone who aspires higher than the herd:

> Never shape a thought or a deed by what others want to hear or see. It's impossible to please others for more than a moment—their desires are fleeting because they never really know what they want.

Think and do what you believe is right and good and let the reaction of others fall where it may.

A sample poetry quotation:

What human characteristic can most effectively corrupt judgment? Alexander Pope believed it to be pride:

> Of all the Causes which conspire to blind
> Man's erring judgment, and misguide the mind,
> What the weak head with strongest bias rules,
> Is *Pride*, the never-failing vice of fools.

Use a slash mark between two or three lines of poetry which are run into the text rather than separated.

My girlfriend is truly, in Wordsworth's words, "Fair as a star, when only one / Is shining in the sky."

Use a comma to separate an opening quotation from the rest of the sentence. (However, if the quotation ends with a question mark or an exclamation point, omit the comma.)

Correct   "You mind your business and I'll mind mine," he said brusquely.

Correct   "Isn't it my business when you disturb me with your stereo?" she responded.

Use commas around words that interrupt a quotation to provide information.

"If I never see him again," she sobbed, "it'll be too soon."

Use quotation marks for the titles of songs, short stories, and newspaper and magazine articles. However, do not use them for the names of newspapers, the titles of magazines, or the titles of books. Those names and titles should be *italicized* (underlined).

"The Love Song of J. Alfred Prufrock" is a famous poem by T. S. Eliot.

My favorite Beatles song is "Let It Be."

The assignment in Introduction to Fiction is to read Hemingway's "The Killers."

The editorial in this morning's newspaper, "Teaching the Russians a Lesson," is an exercise in superficial thinking.

Always place commas and periods inside quotation marks, even when the marks set off only a word or phrase and not the entire sentence. However, always place semicolons and colons outside.

Correct   His reaction to failing was philosophical. "I gave it my best shot," he said, "but that just wasn't good enough—I have no regrets."

Correct   To be creative, we must be "alive to the moment"; in other words, we must be ready to seize the hints of meaning and challenges to problem solving that present themselves.

Put dashes, question marks, and exclamation points inside quotation marks if they apply to the quotation only and outside if they apply to the whole statement.

Correct   The professor asked plaintively, "Doesn't anyone know the answer to the question?"

Correct   Did Charles say "I hate Lola"?

Brackets

Brackets are not the same as parentheses. They are used to set off editorial comments from the quotations in which they are inserted for clarification or comment.

> Elbert Hubbard's tongue-in-cheek definition of an editor is often quoted: "[An editor is] a person employed on a newspaper, whose business it is to separate the wheat from the chaff, and to see that the chaff is printed."

The brackets in the above sentence make clear that the words "An editor is" were not in the original material but were added by the author to fit the quotation into her sentence structure.

Ellipsis Marks

Use an ellipsis mark (three spaced periods) to indicate an omission from quoted material. When the omission occurs at the end of the sentence, use an additional period.

Contemporary feminism inaugurated its existence as a movement with an attack on the teachings and principles of Sigmund Freud. Those women who have come to represent the movement to the news media have insisted that if any one man promoted the oppression of women it was he. Freud—that slave driver of the unconscious—chased women from the consulting room to the nursery and kitchen, they say, and generations of analysts and psychiatrists who came after him kept them bound to pots and pans, diapers and baby carriages. The liberation of women, feminists claimed, depended on exposing the errors of these theories which have chained women to traditional stereotypes and prevented them from taking charge of their lives and their worlds.[2]	"Contemporary feminism inaugurated its existence as a movement with an attack on the teachings and principles of Sigmund Freud. Those women who have come to represent the movement to the news media have insisted that if any one man promoted the oppression of women it was he. Freud . . . chased women from the consulting room to the nursery and kitchen, they say, and generations of analysts and psychiatrists who came after him kept them bound to pots and pans, diapers and baby carriages. The liberation of women, feminists claimed, depended on exposing the errors of these theories. . . ."

As this example demonstrates, ellipses can save space, an important consideration in articles and essays with a word limit. But it is important to preserve the grammatical structure of the original sentences. Careless omission of words can turn a meaningful sentence into gibberish.

Exercise

Each of the following sentences contains one or more violations of the rules for using quotation marks, brackets, and ellipsis marks.

Rewrite each sentence, making the necessary corrections. Be prepared to explain your changes.

1. "Please come as soon as you can", he said. "I need your help."
2. Who was the person who said "I'll take a second helping of steak?"
3. Agnes told me "to stop making eyes at her boyfriend or I'd be sorry."
4. Sometimes we come upon an idea that's so obvious we wonder why we hadn't thought of it ourselves. That's the way I felt recently when I read this quote from Max Lerner", There has been a succession of women's revolutions in America. But watch out for the revolt of the father, if he should be fed up with feeding others, and get bored with being used, and lay down his tools, and walk off to consult his soul".
5. She turned to him and whispered, "Why don't you get lost, jerk"?
6. "My husband will drive five miles to save five cents on a can of vegetables," she lamented, "and then buy some expensive new gadget we don't even need. To borrow a phrase from Benjamin Franklin, he's "penny wise and pound foolish.""
7. Professor Monahan announced, "Tomorrow's exam will be no more rigorous than usual:" in other words, the highest mark in the class will be a D.
8. "Moby Dick" is a long novel, but it's well worth reading.
9. My grandmother told me there was a popular song in her younger days titled *Tea for Two*. Can you believe that hokey title?
10. "Most of the things we do," Oliver Wendell Holmes, Jr., wrote, "we do for no better reason than that our fathers have done them or that our neighbors do them . . ."

Punctuation of Words

The four punctuation conventions we will now consider are associated with the smallest unit of written expression—the individual word. These conventions are italics, capitalization, the apostrophe, and the hyphen.

Italics

Use italics for the title of any separately published work. (In typing, the equivalent of italics is underlining.)

>   *The New York Times   Newsweek   Roots   The Scarsdale Diet*

Use italics for the names of ships, aircraft, works of art, movies, phonograph albums, and television shows.

>   H.M.S. *Queen Mary   The Spirit of St. Louis   The Mona Lisa
>   Gone with the Wind*   Michael Jackson's album *Thriller
>   Sixty Minutes*

Use italics for letters, words, and numbers used as words.

>   If you want to speak Italian like a native, learn to roll your *r*'s.
>   The word *can't* is not in his vocabulary.
>   When you write a *7*, make it look like a *7* and not a *1*.

Use italics for foreign expressions.

>   In logic a conclusion that does not follow from its premises is called a *non sequitur*.
>   She graduated *cum laude*.

Use italics to emphasize a word, phrase, or clause. (Effective writers exercise restraint in this use of italics, confining it to those occasions where special emphasis is needed.)

>   Did you say you earned *forty thousand dollars* last year?

Capitalization

Modern usage demands that capitalization be used in the following situations.

Capitalize the personal pronoun, I:

>   I said that I would be glad to volunteer.

Capitalize people's names:

> Robert A. Jones
> Sam

Capitalize specific titles when they precede a name, but not when they follow it (unless the title denotes very high office):

> Professor Schwartz
> Judge Paul Wilmarth
> Andrew Owens, president of Topper Transmission Company
> Theodore Roosevelt, President of the United States

Capitalize names of the Deity:

> God
> Creator

Capitalize specific races, religions, nationalities:

> Negro
> Jew
> Italian
> Protestant

Capitalize specific places:

> Houston
> Los Angeles
> Japan

Capitalize common nouns when they are part of a place name:

> Second Street
> the Delaware River

Capitalize days of the week and months of the year. (Note that the names of seasons are not capitalized.)

Monday
March
spring

Capitalize the names of specific events, documents, and courses or programs:

the War of 1812
the Gettysburg Address
Psychology 102

Capitalize the names of institutions and organizations:

The Urban League
Siena College
Ford Motor Company

Capitalize titles of published works, whether separately published or part of larger publications. (Note that articles [*a, the*], conjunctions [*and, but, or*], and prepositions of fewer than five letters [*for, to, from, near*] are not capitalized in titles, unless they are the first word of the title.)

"Ode to a Nightingale"
Reader's Digest

Capitalize nouns indicating family relationships when they are used in conjunction with proper names or are used as names themselves:

my aunt, Aunt Ruth
my father, Father

Capitalize specific regions of the country. (Note that the words *east, south, north,* and *west* are not capitalized when they refer to simple direction.)

the South
the Midwest
Drive north for two miles, then east for one mile.

Solving Punctuation Problems

Exercise

Each of the following sentences contains one or more omissions or misuses of italics or capitalization. Rewrite each sentence, making the necessary corrections. Be prepared to explain your changes.

1. The word tantalize has an interesting etymology.
2. My Mother's family came to this country from lithuania.
3. I plan to visit the united nations building when I visit New York City next month.
4. The one magazine I read carefully each week is "U.S. News and World Report."
5. My uncle lives twenty miles West of Cooperstown, New York, the Home of the Baseball Hall of Fame.
6. I used to have trouble pronouncing the letter "s."
7. We lost all the money we took to the race track, but as the French say, "c'est la vie."
8. My scholarship was awarded by Reginald O'Shaughnessy, President of O'Shaughnessy Plumbing Corporation.
9. In comparative religion 103 we're now studying buddhism.
10. For Christmas I'm going to buy my Father a copy of Rodin's famous statue, "The Thinker."
11. This year Spring is supposed to be warmer than usual.
12. My sister Sally had her poem *Whispers of Love* selected for inclusion in "Best Poems of 1984."
13. In my hometown five streets are named after trees, including my street, Elm street.
14. The name hiroshima will always be a reminder of the horror of nuclear war.
15. My instructor holds the title of distinguished professor of humanities.

The Apostrophe

Use the apostrophe to show possession or ownership. (If the noun in question ends in *s*, add only an apostrophe. If it does not end in *s*, add an apostrophe and an *s*.)

> John's anger
>
> the dog's bone

the child's game
the children's game

Agnes' car
Lois' dress
the princess' carriage

the boy's shoes [one boy]
the boys' shoes [more than one boy]
the dinosaur's habitat
the dinosaurs' habitat

Bob and Bill's room [one room, joint possession]
Bob's and Bill's books [more than one book, individual possession]

the mother-in law's kindness
the mothers-in-law's kindness

Use the apostrophe to form contractions.

can't
won't
there's
shouldn't

Use the apostrophe to form the plurals of numbers, letters, and words used as words. (It is also acceptable to form such plurals without an apostrophe.)

Mind your *p*'s and *q*'s. [or *p*s and *q*s]

His *u*'s and *n*'s are indistinguishable.

He makes his *4*'s strangely, too. [or *4*s]

We are halfway through the 1980's. [or 1980s]

There'll be no *if*'s, *and*'s, or *but*'s [or *if*s, *and*s, or *but*s] about it.

The Hyphen

Use a hyphen to divide a word when it will not fit at the end of a written or typed line. Convention requires that the break occur between syllables rather than within a syllable. For example, the word *experimentation* could be broken as follows: *ex-peri-men-ta-tion*. (Notice that where a syllable consists of a single letter, *i* in this case, that syllable is usually not carried over to the next line.) A good dictionary is your best guide in questions of syllabication.

Use a hyphen to form compound numbers up to ninety-nine; to express fractions (two-thirds, one-fifth); *to join two or more words used as a single adjective* (a fur-lined jacket); *and to separate some prefixes, notably* self-, all-, *and* ex-, *from the words they modify* (a self-made man, all-embracing policies, *and* ex-champion).

Use a hyphen to form compound words.   Since such words in time become a single unhyphenated word (*wallboard, baseball, handyman*), no list of compounds will remain accurate for very long. A current dictionary is your best guide here.

Exercise

Each of the following sentences contains one or more omissions or misuses of apostrophes or hyphens. Rewrite each sentence, making the necessary corrections. Be prepared to explain your changes.

1. He said he wouldnt be able to afford the tuition next year.
2. Freds sister is a lawyer in Philadelphia.
3. When it came to drooling, Pavlovs dog had no peer.
4. There are eighty six students in my biology lecture section.
5. She spends three quarters of her allowance on junk food.
6. No one would guess that Gerry is an ex convict.
7. I know she's a successful author, but buying a gold plated typewriter is a bit extravagant.
8. If you lack self esteem you cant really be happy.
9. My cars exhaust system has to be replaced.
10. Proficiency in writing doesnt depend so much on talent as on willingness to refine your first efforts.

Punctuating Paragraphs

Many professional writers view punctuation more as a paragraph-level task than as a sentence-level task. Of course, they punctuate their sentences as they write them. But they do not regard that punctuation as fixed and final. It is to them highly tentative. And when they are editing their work, they look at each paragraph to decide whether the punctuation suits their audience and the occasion and whether it contributes to the overall effect they intend. If it does not, they change it.

Let's consider how this approach works in an actual situation. Here is a paragraph as originally written and then as revised for different audiences and effects.

The unusually long second sentence in this passage is made readable by the careful use of the colon and semicolons. Such punctuation is quite common in scholarly articles and books written for well-educated readers.

Observers are generally agreed that divorce is rapidly approaching epidemic proportions in this country. The causes of this phenomenon are varied: the increasing mobility of the modern family and resulting lack of a sense of belonging; the decline in the birthrate and the corresponding reduction in the demands of homemaking and child-rearing; a growing sense of dissatisfaction in many middle-aged women with the roles of wife and mother, prompting them to resume their education or find employment, in many cases developing interests and associations that compete with family life; the difficulty many husbands have, largely because of insecurity or unreasoning fear of change, to accept the changing roles of wives and mothers; and perhaps most important, a widespread tendency to view marriage as a temporary, qualified commitment rather than a lifelong, absolute one, and a widespread acceptance of casual sex.

This version contains seven sentences instead of two. The use of periods instead of colons and semicolons increases the pace and, by breaking the idea into more easily digested pieces, makes it more readable. The liberal use of connecting words—"first," "second," "in addition," "moreover," "finally"—also aids clarity. This style is appropriate in most writing situations.

Observers are generally agreed that divorce is rapidly approaching epidemic proportions in this country. The causes of this phenomenon are varied. First, the modern family is increasingly mobile and as a result lacks a sense of belonging. Second, the birthrate has declined and the demands of homemaking and child-rearing have been reduced. In addition, many middle-aged women have experienced a growing sense of dissatisfaction with the roles of wife and mother and have been prompted to resume their education or find employment, in many cases developing interests and associations that compete with family life. Moreover, many husbands have difficulty, largely because of insecurity or unreasoning fear of change, in accepting the changing roles of wives and mothers. Finally, and perhaps most important, there is a widespread tendency to view marriage as a temporary, qualified commitment rather than a lifelong, absolute one, and there is a widespread acceptance of casual sex.

This version has thirteen sentences—almost double the number in the second

Most observers agree that divorce has become almost epidemic in this country. Why? For a number of reasons. The modern family, to begin with, is more and more mobile. People lack roots and so lack a sense of belonging. Then, too, the birthrate has declined. That means taking care of the home and raising children is less demanding. Another reason is that many middle-aged women have become dissatisfied being just wives and mothers and have returned to college or taken jobs. In many cases, that has meant developing interests and associations that compete with family life. Moreover, many husbands are too insecure or afraid of change to accept the changing roles of wives and mothers. The most important reason, though, is probably the new view of marriage and sex. In that view marriage is not a lifelong and absolute commitment, but a temporary, qualified one. And casual sex is accepted.

Adopting the professional attitude toward punctuation described above offers you an important benefit—it helps you view your rough drafts as rough drafts and be willing to change them when change is desirable. For example, regarding your semicolon between two main clauses as a tentative choice will remind you that the structure of the sentence is itself open to change. After looking closely at the rest of the paragraph, you might decide that a different structure, with different punctuation, might serve your purpose and audience better.

version. It is very fast-paced. And it too has many helpful connectives, though they are more subtle than those of the second version ("to begin with," "then, too," "Another reason"). The style of this passage is used in most newspapers and popular magazines. It is well-suited to the reader who has little time to devote to reading, as well as to the less sophisticated reader. However, the fastidious, well-educated reader would undoubtedly find its style a bit too clipped.

Exercises

1. Each of the following passages is effectively written. However, all punctuation—including capital letters and apostrophes—has been removed from *within the sentences*. Only end punctuation remains. Read each carefully and decide what internal punctuation is necessary to make the meaning clear. Consult the appropriate principles whenever you are uncertain what mark would be appropriate.
    a. Emphasis is force stress prominence. We say that a word or sentence or paragraph has emphasis if it stands out from other words sentences or paragraphs around it if it in some way attracts the readers attention more than the others do. Why should you want any one part to stand out from the rest? Because not every part of what you say will be of equal weight. Some parts will always be more important than others more deserving of special attention. Your ability to convey the exact meaning you intend will therefore depend on your ability to give emphasis to those parts and not others. To do that you will have to make a conscious effort to control the emphasis.
    It is virtually impossible to write a single paragraph with-

out creating some emphasis consciously or unconsciously for certain words or phrases. If you tried to write without emphasis the result would be a primer style in which every detail was set off in a separate sentence to compete with all others for the readers attention. But such a style would be inferior to the mature balanced style that effective adult communication demands.

b. The search for identity is not new however in american thought though in every generation each man who writes about it discovers it anew. In america from the beginning it has somehow been understood that men must thrust into the future the pace has always been too rapid for mans identity to stand still. In every generation many men have suffered misery unhappiness and uncertainty because they could not take the image of the man they wanted to be from their fathers. The search for identity of the young man who cant go home again has always been a major theme of american writers. And it has always been considered right in america good for men to suffer these agonies of growth to search for and find their own identities. The farm boy went to the city the garment makers son became a doctor abraham lincoln taught himself to read these were more than rags to riches stories. They were an integral part of the american dream. The problem for many was money race color class which barred them from choice not what they would be if they were free to choose.[3]

c. The term subordinate and its companion term coordinate refer to grammatical rank or importance. Subordinate refers to unequal rank coordinate to equal rank. The concepts are easier to understand if we use examples. Suppose you wanted to state that you attended an exciting party last night and that you left early. There are two ideas involved great party and left early. If you wanted to express these two ideas more or less equally you'd say i went to a marvelous party last night but i had to leave early. In this case you'd be using two independent clauses each capable of standing as a complete sentence. If however you wanted one idea to dominate you would place only that idea in an independent clause the other you would make grammatically subordinate. In other words you'd say last night i had to leave a marvelous party early. Since the fact that the party was marvelous is expressed only in the subordinate adjective phrase the emphasis here is on leaving.

Solving Punctuation Problems

    d. Seventy-five years ago white slavery was rampant in england. Each year thousands of young girls were forced into brothels and kept there against their will. While some of the victims had been sold by their families a large proportion were seized and held by force or fraud. The victims were not from the lower classes only. No level of english society was immune to having its daughters seized. Because this practice continued in england for years after it had been largely wiped out on the continent thousands of english girls were shipped across the channel to supply the brothels of europe. One reason why this lasted so long as it did was that it could not be talked about openly in victorian england. Moral standards as to subjects of discussion made it difficult to arouse the community to necessary action. Moreover the extreme innocence considered appropriate for english girls made them easy victims helpless to cope with the situations in which they were trapped. Victorian standards besides perpetuating the white slave trade intensified the damage to those involved.[4]

2. This exercise is a little more challenging than the previous exercise because in each of the following passages *all* punctuation has been removed. Read each carefully and decide what punctuation is necessary to make the meaning clear. (Since the wording is exactly the same as in the originals, no rephrasing will be necessary.) Consult the principles discussed in the previous pages whenever you are uncertain about what mark would be appropriate.
    a. Perhaps somewhere there is an extraordinary individual who consistently arranges her ideas automatically as she produces them and who never has an irrelevant idea or a relevant idea out of its proper order but it is highly unlikely such an individual exists the human thought process simply does not work that way so for amateurs and professionals alike the way to effective expression lies in composing thoughts creating the order that will be most effective.
    b. Professional writers combine techniques of development not because they wish to complicate their writing but because in many cases it is the most natural and interesting way to express their ideas a freelance writer for example may be writing an account of a trip to an exotic country for a travel magazine she may have many facts to tell about the country its people and its places of interest and she may have many

vivid descriptions to share dozens of little sights and sounds that shaped her reaction to the country and its inhabitants yet her larger purpose in writing may be to persuade her audience that such a trip offers many exciting and inexpensive things to do because of this purpose the writer will probably emphasize what she and her family did on their trip.

c. In all but the briefest writing as you probe your topic more and more deeply and move from one point to another you can easily forget your controlling idea this forgetting often results in a blurring or shifting of focus that is it makes you deal with a supporting idea as if it were the main idea devoting more attention to it than it deserves or allowing it to lead you off on a tangent thereby undermining the controlling idea and confusing your readers the best defense against a blurring or shifting of focus is to spend a little time establishing the focus while arranging your ideas this can be done quite simply all you have to do is check each idea in your list to be sure it helps to clarify or support the controlling idea then make a brief marginal note of the relationship between each idea and the preceding idea these notes will help you maintain the focus of the paper as you are writing it and make your presentation more coherent.

d. One rather simple way of getting interest into your paper is to take the side of the argument that most [other people] will want to avoid if the assignment is an essay on dogs you can if you choose explain that dogs are faithful and lovable companions intelligent useful as guardians of the house and protectors of children indispensable in police work in short when all is said and done man's best friends or you can suggest that those big brown eyes conceal more often than not a vacuity of mind and an inconstancy of purpose that the dogs you have known most intimately have been mangy ill-tempered brutes incapable of instruction and that only your nobility of mind and fear of arrest prevent you from kicking the flea-ridden animals when you pass them on the street.[5]

e. It is heartening to gaze back over the history of learning and see how often mighty minds have appeared in lonely lands and savage tribes and eras full of repression and violence how wonderful it is in the midst of some bloody epoch resounding with dull groans and choked hymns to meet a serene and gracious mind studying nature and making poetry or to discover among lazy bourgeois or glum earthbound peasants a powerful intellect grappling with abstractions of number producing unique inventions or building a systematic interpretation of the universe.[6]

A Glossary of Usage

Accept, Except

Accept is a verb meaning "to take willingly." **Except** is a preposition meaning "but."
>*Correct*   John can't **accept** the invitation.
>*Correct*   Everyone was on time **except** Tim.

Affect, Effect

Affect is a verb meaning "to influence." **Effect** can be either a verb or a noun. As a verb it means "to cause"; as a noun, its more common use, it means "a result."
>*Correct*   Don't let her nagging **affect** your disposition.
>*Correct*   Researchers have been unable to **effect** a cure.
>*Correct*   The **effect** of his drinking has been tragic.

Allot, A Lot

Allot is a verb meaning "to distribute or apportion." **A lot,** which is always written as two words, means "much."

All Right, Alright

All right is the preferred form. **Alright** is generally avoided by educated people.

Allude, Elude

Allude is a verb meaning "to refer to indirectly." **Elude** is a verb meaning "to avoid."
>*Correct*   Did he **allude** to her recent accident?
>*Correct*   They were trying to **elude** their creditors.

Allusion, Illusion

See Illusion, Allusion

Already, All Ready

Already means "before that time." But ***all ready*** means "completely prepared" (in colloquial usage, "all set").
    Correct   He was ***already*** at the party when she arrived.
    Correct   She was ***all ready*** to leave for the play when the phone rang.

Altogether, All Together

Altogether means "entirely" or "completely." ***All together*** means "everyone at the same time" or "with one another" and is usually separated by other words.
    Correct   It was an ***altogether*** useless experience.
    Correct   They ***all*** banded ***together*** against the common foe.

Always, All Ways

Always means "all the time, forever." ***All ways*** means "every method" and is often separated by another word or words.
    Correct   Must you ***always*** criticize my mother?
    Correct   They tried ***all*** honest ***ways*** to obtain the tickets.

Am Not, Ain't

Ain't is never an acceptable substitute for ***am not*** or related forms (***are not, is not***).
    Correct   I ***am not*** going to the party.
    Correct   You ***are not*** going to the party.
    Correct   Pam ***is not*** going to the party.

Among, Between

See Between, Among

Amount, Number

See Number, Amount

Anyway, Any Way, Anyways

Anyway means "nevertheless" or "in any case." ***Any way*** means "any manner" or "any method" or "any direction." ***Anyways*** is a nonstandard form.
    Correct   I didn't want to be Prom Queen ***anyway.***
    Correct   ***Any way*** we travel to Syracuse will take us at least two hours.

Are, Our

Are is part of the verb "to be." ***Our*** is a possessive pronoun.
    Correct   My brothers' names ***are*** Bill and Ted.
    Correct   It's ***our*** turn to do the dishes.

As, Like

See Like, As

Ascent, Assent

Ascent is a noun meaning "a rise." **Assent** is a verb meaning "to agree."
- *Correct*   The **ascent** of the mountain was risky.
- *Correct*   I'll never **assent** to her plan to cheat.

Awful, Awfully, Very

See Very, Awfully, Awful

Beside, Besides

Beside means "next to." **Besides** means "anyway" or "moreover."
- *Correct*   Why does she always have to sit **beside** me?
- *Correct*   I haven't any money to lend you; **besides,** you didn't pay me back the ten dollars you borrowed.

Between, Among

Between is used when two persons, places, or things are involved; **among,** when more than two are involved.
- *Correct*   There has never been any hostility **between** Tim and me.
- *Correct*   There has never been any hostility **among** Tim, Ed, and me.

Board, Bored

Board is a noun meaning "a wooden plank." **Bored** means "uninterested."
- *Correct*   I'll use that **board** for my bookcase.
- *Correct*   Going to class leaves him **bored.**

Can, May

Can means "able to do something." **May** means "having permission to do something." (There is one exception to this difference—a question in which the negative form of the expression is used. Thus "Why can't I go to the movies tonight?" is preferable to "Why may I not go to the movies tonight?" because it is less awkward.)
- *Correct*   I know I **can** do better than D work in that course.
- *Correct*   **May** I have an extension of the deadline for the assignment?

Can Hardly, Can't Hardly

Hardly in such expressions is synonymous with *barely.* The sense intended is therefore "I **am** able to, but just barely so." **Can hardly** conveys that intention. But **can't hardly** does not—it suggests inability rather than ability. For this reason, **can't hardly** is never acceptable.

    Correct   I **can hardly** wait for the tournament to begin.

Capital, Capitol

Capital has a number of meanings. Two of the most common are the town or city that is the seat of government in a country, state, or nation; and money. **Capitol** refers to the building in which government business is conducted. (When capitalized, it refers to the building where the U.S. Congress conducts its business.)

Censor, Censer, Censure

Censor is both a verb and a noun. As a verb it means "to examine that which may be objectionable and, if it is, to suppress it." As a noun it means "the official who examines and decides whether to suppress." **Censer** is a noun meaning "a vessel containing incense, usually used in worship." **Censure** is both a verb and a noun: as a verb it means "to disapprove, blame, or condemn"; as a noun, "the expression of disapproval, blame, or condemnation."

    Correct   They've decided to **censor** the book.
    Correct   The **censors** seem to have missed that scene in the film.
    Correct   The altar boy carried the **censer** in the procession.
    Correct   He's more to be pitied than **censured.**
    Correct   If ever there was a congressman deserving of **censure,** it's ours.

Cent, Sent, Scent

See Sent, Cent, Scent

Choose, Chose

Both words are parts of the same verb—**to choose.** But **choose** is a present tense form and **chose,** the past tense form. (**Choose** rhymes with **news, chose** with **those.**)

    Correct   Help me **choose** between these two dresses.
    Correct   He's not sorry he **chose** to study instead of party.

Cite, Sight, Site

See Sight, Site, Cite

Conscience, Conscious

Conscience is a noun meaning "inner moral guide, sense of right and wrong in ethical matters." **Conscious** is an adjective meaning "mentally awake, aware."

    Correct   Let your **conscience** be your guide.
    Correct   He was the only one **conscious** after the accident.
    Correct   Public servants must be **conscious** of their obligation to constituents.

Consensus, Consensus of Opinion

Consensus means "the opinion of a group of people." Therefore, the expression **consensus of opinion** is redundant.

Could Have, Could've, Could Of

Could have is standard English. **Could've** is an acceptable contraction of **could have** that is commonly used in speaking, but seldom in writing. **Could of** is never correct and probably results from hearing the contraction spoken but not recognizing it as such. (Note: The same rule applies to **would have** and **should have**.)

Couldn't Care Less, Could Care Less

Couldn't care less is an expression of total lack of concern. It means one cares so little that it would be impossible to care less. **Could care less** is not a logical substitute because it violates the sense of the expression. (If one could care less than he does, then he does care somewhat).

    Correct   I **couldn't care less** whether he has a date for the prom.

Different From, Different Than

Different from refers to a difference between two or more people, places, or things. **Different than** refers to a difference in the **same** person, place, or thing over a period of time.

    Correct   Your idea of an interesting course is **different from** mine.
    Correct   My idea of an interesting course is **different** now **than** it was in high school.

Diner, Dinner

Diner means "an informal restaurant" or "a person who dines." **Dinner** means "the main meal of the day." (**Diner** rhymes with **miner;** **dinner,** with **thinner.**)

Disinterested, Uninterested

Despite their similarity, these words have very different meanings. **Disinterested** means "free of bias, impartial." **Uninterested** means "not interested, indifferent."

 Correct What we need here is a **disinterested** opinion.
 Correct She was **uninterested** in him as a suitor.

Each Other, One Another

Each other is used in references to two people: **one another**, in references to more than two people.

 Correct John and Agnes can't stand the sight of **each other.**
 Correct The students in my division seem to like **one another.**

Effect, Affect

See Affect, Effect

Elude, Allude

See Allude, Elude

Enthusiastic, Enthused

Enthusiastic means "eager" or "intensely interested." **Enthused** is a substitute form that is considered acceptable in informal writing but not in formal writing.

Etc., &

Etc. is an abbreviation of the Latin **et cetera**, which means "and others" or "and so forth." The symbol **&** is used in place of **and**. Although both are widely used in informal writing, many authorities still consider them (especially **&**) unacceptable in formal writing.

Except, Accept

See Accept, Except

Farther, Further

Farther refers to distance; **further,** to degree.

 Correct I live **farther** from college than you do.
 Correct Each week I get **further** into debt.

Faze, Phase

See Phase, Faze

Fewer, Less

Fewer is used when speaking of things usually considered as individual units; **less,** when speaking of things not usually considered as individual units.

>*Correct*   fewer people, fewer potatoes, fewer towns, fewer paper clips
>*Correct*   less mashed potatoes, less hostility, less sugar

Flaunt, Flout

Flaunt means "to show off." **Flout** means "to show disrespect for, to scorn."

>*Correct*   At every opportunity she **flaunted** her knowledge of French.
>*Correct*   Must you **flout** every rule of etiquette?

Forth, Fourth

Forth means "forward." **Fourth** is the numerical reference between third and fifth.

>*Correct*   They went **forth** like the victors they were.
>*Correct*   This aspirin is the **fourth** I've taken today.

Gorilla, Guerrilla

A **gorilla** is a primate. A **guerrilla** is a soldier in an unconventional war.

>*Correct*   If it weren't for the hair all over his body, that **gorilla** could be mistaken for my roommate.
>*Correct*   A **guerrilla** is often more dedicated to his cause than a conventional soldier is.

Healthy, Healthful

Healthy means "in good health" or "conducive to health in an indirect or figurative sense." **Healthful** means "nutritious," or "health-producing in a direct, literal sense."

>*Correct*   He is an unusually **healthy** old man.
>*Correct*   This climate is not too **healthy.**
>*Correct*   The food served in my dining hall may be **healthful,** but it is rather unappealing.

Hear, Here

Though these words sound alike, their meanings are quite different. **Hear** is a verb, and **here** is an adjective indicating place.

>*Correct*   Please play your stereo quietly, so I don't have to **hear** it.
>*Correct*   **Here** I am—let the party begin.

Himself, Hisself

Himself is the correct form. **Hisself** is unacceptable.
    Correct   He decided to do his taxes **himself.**

Hole, Whole

A **hole** is an opening. **Whole** means "complete."
    Correct   The draft is coming through that **hole.**
    Correct   I can't believe you ate the **whole** pizza.

Hopefully

Many educated people object to the use of this word in constructions that express some particular person's hoping. For example, they would object to the sentence "**Hopefully,** this lecture will be more interesting than the one last week." They would prefer "I hope this lecture . . ." or "Let us hope this lecture. . . ." Nevertheless, its use is widespread and there is at least one accepted precedent for such an adverbial construction—the use of **admittedly,** as in "Admittedly, the error was mine." Therefore, it may be considered an acceptable form in many situations, but one that should be avoided when writing for a fastidious audience.

I, Me

See Me, I

Ignorant, Stupid

Ignorant means "lacking knowledge or education." **Stupid** means "unintelligent."

Illusion, Allusion

Illusion means "a false idea or impression or that which creates such an impression." **Allusion** means "a casual reference to a person, place, or thing."
    Correct   She is obsessed with the **illusion** that I love her.
    Correct   His writing is filled with biblical **allusions.**

Immoral, Amoral

Immoral means "not conforming to a moral code one endorses in theory." **Amoral** means "not having a moral code."

Imply, Infer

Imply means "to suggest indirectly, to hint at." **Infer** means "to judge or conclude."
    Correct   You seem to be **implying** that I got this job by dishonest means. I resent that **implication.**

Correct   The essay **infers** that nuclear war is unavoidable. I reject that **inference**.

In, In To, Into

These words have different uses. **In**, as a preposition, is used mainly to indicate position, location, or condition. **In to** (two words) is used when **in** is an adverb. And **into** indicates direction or movement or, in a figurative sense, a change of condition.

Correct   The key is not lost. It's **in** your hand.
Correct   My uncle is in the county jail, but no one is allowed **in to** see him.
Correct   The hero and heroine rode off **into** the sunset.

In Regard To, In Regards To

In regard to is the accepted form of this expression; **in regards to** is a nonstandard form.

Irregardless, Regardless

See Regardless, Irregardless

Its, It's

Its is a possessive pronoun. **It's** is the contraction of **it is**.

Correct   A dog will give **its** affection more quickly than a cat will.
Correct   Hurry, please—**it's** closing time.

Kind Of, Sort Of

In informal writing, as in conversation, both **kind of** and **sort of** are commonly used instead of **somewhat** or **rather**. But in formal writing the latter expressions are preferred.

Lay, Lie

These words are both verbs. They are confused because one of the principal parts of each is the same. Remembering those principal parts is the key to overcoming confusion.

Lay means "to place or put." Its principal parts are lay/laid/laid.

Present tense—lay	I **lay** [am **laying**] my pencil on the desk.
Past tense—laid	Yesterday I **laid** my pencil on the desk.
Present perfect—have laid	I **have laid** my pencil on the desk.

Lie means "to rest or recline." Its principal parts are lie/lay/lain.

Present tense—lie	I **lie** down for a nap each day at noon.

Past tense—lay   I *lay* down yesterday at noon.
Present perfect—have lain   I *have lain* down regularly because the doctor ordered me to.

Lead, Led

Lead has two uses—as a present tense form of the verb *to lead* (rhymes with **seed**); as a noun meaning a type of metal (rhymes with **dead**). However, *led* (which also rhymes with **dead**) is the past tense of the verb *to lead.*

Correct   Agnes is the best one to **lead** the group.
Correct   The **lead** in your pencil is really graphite.
Correct   Bill **led** his team to the championship.

Leave, Let

Leave means "to depart or to cause to remain." **Let** means "to permit."

Correct   Please don't **leave** me—we've been through too much together.
Correct   You can't **leave** all that junk in my closet.
Correct   He'll join us if his mother will **let** him.

Less, Fewer

See Fewer, Less

Lightning, Lightening

Lightning accompanies thunder. **Lightening** means "making lighter."

Correct   A flash of **lightning** lit up the sky.
Correct   He removed the bundle, **lightening** the camel's load.

Like, As

Contemporary usage, particularly in the field of advertising, has blurred the traditional distinction between these words in some constructions. Nevertheless, most educated people avoid substituting **like** for **as** when the meaning intended is "in the same manner or way that." For example, "Wowies taste good **like** dogyummies should" would be unacceptable in formal writing.

Loose, Lose

Loose means "unattached" or "free from restraint." **Lose** means "to misplace or be deprived of." (**Loose** rhymes with **moose**, **lose** with **blues**.)

Correct   His tie was **loose,** his jacket unbuttoned.
Correct   Whatever you do, don't **lose** the tickets to the game.

Many, Much
Many means "a large number of individual units." **Much** means "a large quantity of something not usually considered in individual units."
- *Correct*   many horses, many nations, many postage stamps, many grapes
- *Correct*   much sand, much affection, much stupidity, much corn, much coffee

May, Can
See Can, May

Maybe, May Be
These expressions have essentially the same meaning. However, **maybe** is an adverb and **may be** is a verb form (the verb **to be** plus its auxiliary **may**). Which you use depends on the part of speech your sentence calls for.
- *Correct*   **Maybe** I'll order a pizza.
- *Correct*   I **may be** fat but she's fatter.

Me, I
Me and **I** are both personal pronouns. But **me** is in the objective case; and **I**, in the nominative. The most common error with these words is using **I** instead of **me** as the object of a preposition.
- *Correct*   Bill went to the movies with Tom and **me.** (The word used here is the object of the preposition **with,** so **me** is correct.)
- *Correct*   Bill, Tom, and **I** went to the movies. (The word used here is a subject of the sentence, not an object, so **I** is correct.)

Moral, Morale
Moral, as an adjective, refers to right conduct, knowing the difference between right and wrong. As a noun, it refers to a lesson. **Morale** refers to a person's mental state, his degree of confidence, cheerfulness, enthusiasm.
- *Correct*   Agnes is a very **moral** person.
- *Correct*   The **moral** of the story is don't hitchhike.
- *Correct*   The players' **morale** was high.

Most, Almost
Most means "the highest degree." **Almost** means "nearly."
- *Correct*   This is the **most** unusual course I've ever taken.
- *Correct*   It is **almost** time to leave.

Much, Many
See Many, Much

Nauseated, Nauseous
Although the use of **nauseous** has become widespread, particularly in speaking and informal writing, the word continues to be considered nonstandard. Careful writers use **nauseated** instead.

Number, Amount
Use **number** when referring to persons, places, or things usually considered as individual units. Use **amount** when referring to things not usually considered as individual units.
- *Correct* a number of dogs, a number of seashells, a large number of cars, a small number of oilwells
- *Correct* an amount of oil, a large amount of corn, a small amount of paint

Numbers
In formal writing, all numbers that can be expressed in one or two words are written out. All others are expressed in figures. However, when several numbers are being mentioned in close proximity, at least one of which is expressed in figures, for the sake of consistency they all may be expressed in figures.
- *Correct* one hundred women, three billion dollars, thirty-eight elephants
- *Correct* 73,300 paid attendance, $250,000, $14.75

OK, O.K., Okay
All three forms are acceptable in informal writing, but not in formal writing. (In formal writing choose a more exact word.)

One Another, Each Other
See Each Other, One Another

Passed, Past
Passed is a past tense form of the verb **to pass**. **Past** as an adjective means "gone by, ended"; as a noun, "that time which no longer is present."
- *Correct* I **passed** all my midterm examinations.
- *Correct* The **past** month has been my busiest this year.
- *Correct* It's foolish to try to live in the **past**.

Patience, Patients

Patience means "forbearance." **Patients** are a doctor's clients.
>Correct **Patience,** she reminded him, is a virtue.
>Correct With all his **patients,** no wonder he drives a Mercedes.

Percent, Percentage, Part

Percent is used in references to "rate per hundred" when numbers are also used. **Percentage** is used in such references when numbers are **not** used. **Part** is used in references to divisions of things that do not concern rate per hundred.
>Correct I spend more than thirty **percent** of my salary on food.
>Correct A large **percentage** of the national budget is allocated to defense spending.
>Correct He gave **part** of his wardrobe to his roommate.

Personal, Personnel

Personal (pronounced *per'-son-al*) is an adjective meaning "private." **Personnel** (pronounced *per-son-nel'*) is a noun meaning "employees."
>Correct This is a **personal** matter that doesn't concern anyone but Jan and me.
>Correct All college **personnel** are expected to attend the meeting.

Petition, Partition

A **petition** is a formal request or the document that expresses such a request. A **partition** is something that divides two or more things; for example, a wall.
>Correct They are circulating a **petition** to fire Dean Borden.
>Correct I wish I could build a **partition** in my room so I wouldn't have to see my roommate.

Phase, Faze

Phase is usually used as a noun meaning "one of a series of forms or stages." **Faze** is a verb meaning "to disturb."
>Correct I'm afraid I'm in the most boring **phase** of adolescence.
>Correct His threats didn't **faze** me a bit.

Principal, Principle

Principal as a noun means "the chief administrative officer of a school"; as an adjective, "main or primary." **Principle** is a noun meaning a "rule."

Correct   The **principal** called Arthur into her office.
Correct   The **principal** reason he left college was the poor quality of his work.
Correct   The law of supply and demand is one of the most important **principles** of economics.

Propose, Purpose

Propose is a verb meaning "to offer or suggest." **Purpose** is a noun meaning "reason or intention."
Correct   I **propose** we use the money for a concert.
Correct   A student's chief **purpose** in college should be to develop his mind.

Provided, Providing

Provided means "cared for" or "with the provision that." Providing means "furnishing."
Correct   She **provided** well for her family.
Correct   You may have the night off **provided** you get someone to work in your place.
Correct   He was responsible for **providing** refreshments.

Quite, Quiet

Quite is a one-syllable word that rhymes with **bite**. **Quiet** is a two-syllable word that rhymes with **diet**. **Quite** means "rather"; **quiet** means "silent."
Correct   His parents are **quite** concerned about his partying.
Correct   Sam has difficulty being **quiet** when someone else is talking.

Rain, Reign, Rein

Rain, like snow, is a form of precipitation. **Reign** is a verb meaning "to rule." A **rein** is a strap for controlling a horse, and is usually used in the plural.
Correct   We haven't had as much **rain** as usual this year.
Correct   Long may the queen **reign.**
Correct   He held the **reins** loosely in his hand.

Raise, Raze

Raise is a verb meaning "to build up" (or "to lift up"). **Raze** is a verb with the exactly opposite meaning—"to tear down."
Correct   Let's **raise** our glasses in honor of Sharon.
Correct   The building where I was born was **razed.**

Reasoning, Rationalizing

Reasoning means "the process of thought that leads to judgment." **Rationalizing** can have the same meaning, but since it also has the meaning of "defective reasoning, reasoning that aims at self-satisfaction rather than truth," it can confuse the reader as to your intended meaning. Careful writers, therefore, never use these words interchangeably.

Reason Is That, Reason Is Because

The accepted expression is **reason is that.** Since both the word "reason" and the word "because" refer to cause, the expression **reason is because** is redundant.

    Correct   The **reason** I am in college **is that** I want to learn.

Regardless, Irregardless

The prefix **ir-** and the suffix **less** both mean "without." Therefore, **regardless** means "without regard" and **irregardless,** "without without regard." Because of its redundancy, **irregardless** is not accepted in modern usage.

Respectfully, Respectively

Respectfully means "with respect." **Respectively** means "pertaining to what has preceded, and in the same order."

    Correct   Bill treats everyone **respectfully.**
    Correct   Bill, Bob, and Alice go to Georgia Tech, Indiana University, and Colgate, **respectively.**

Right, Rite, Write

Right means "correct." A **rite** is a religious ceremony. **Write** is a verb meaning "to form letters."

    Correct   He gave the teacher the **right** answer.
    Correct   That ceremony is part of the pagan fertility **rite.**
    Correct   **Write** more legibly next time.

Rise, Raise

Rise means "to get up or go up." **Raise** means "to cause to rise, to lift."

    Correct   I **rise** early in the summer.
    Correct   My spirits **rise** when summer approaches.
    Correct   He tried his best to **raise** the sunken treasure ship.

Road, Rode

A **road** is a surface on the ground. **Rode** is the past tense of the verb "to ride."

Glossary

Correct   The **road** is long and lonely.
Correct   He **rode** a wild horse on his uncle's ranch.

Sent, Cent, Scent
Sent is a form of the verb **to send**. **Cent** means "penny." And **scent** means "odor."

Should Have, Should've, Should of
See Could Have, Could've, Could of

Sight, Site, Cite
Sight refers to vision, viewing, or that which is viewed. **Site** means "a location, often a building location." And **cite** means "to make reference to" or "to credit."
Correct   The mountains near my home are a majestic **sight**.
Correct   He has a serious **sight** problem.
Correct   We've finally picked out a **site** for our new home.
Correct   The professor said to **cite** all our sources for the term paper.

Since, Sense, Sence
Since means "from a former time until now." **Sense** as a verb means "to perceive or feel intuitively"; as a noun, "the relative quality of one's judgment" or "one of the means of sensory perception." **Sence** is an incorrect form sometimes substituted for **since** or **sense**.
Correct   I haven't had a good night's sleep **since** I left home.
Correct   He seemed to **sense** what was about to happen.
Correct   I hope you'll have the good **sense** to drive safely.
Correct   His **sense** of smell was blocked by a powerful perfume.

Sit, Set
Both words are verbs. But **sit** means "to rest or recline" and **set** means "to place or put."

Present tense—sit	Please **sit** down.
Past tense—sat	Everyone but Tom **sat** quietly.
Present perfect—have sat	I **have sat** in this seat every day this term.
Present tense—set	**Set** the books on the table.
Past tense—set	Yesterday you **set** them on the bookcase.
Present perfect—have set	After you **have set** them down, you may go to lunch.

So, Sow, Sew

So has a variety of meanings. The most common ones are "in the way indicated," "in order," "in that degree," "very." **Sow** means "to scatter seed on the ground." And **sew** means "to stitch material."

    Correct   I arrived early **so** I could avoid the crowd.
    Correct   A man will reap only what he **sows**.
    Correct   I hope you'll be able to **sew** this shirt before tonight.

So Do I, So Don't I

In some parts of the country, the expression **so don't I** is used in place of **so do I**. But **so don't I** makes no sense—it says the exact opposite of what is meant. Avoid this and related errors (for example, *so can't I, so won't I, so wouldn't I, so couldn't I*).

Stationary, Stationery

Stationary is an adjective meaning "fixed, not moving." **Stationery** is a noun meaning "writing materials" (paper and envelopes).

Straight, Strait

Straight is the opposite of crooked. A **strait** is a water passageway.

    Correct   He's headed **straight** for success.
    Correct   Steer the boat gently through that **strait**.

Stupid, Ignorant

See Ignorant, Stupid

Than, Then

See Then, Than

Them, Those

Never use **them** as an adjective—that is, to modify a noun. Only **those** can be used that way.

    Correct   He served **them** an eviction notice.
    Correct   **Those** shirts are the ones on sale.

Themselves, Themself, Theirselves

Only the first form—**themselves**—is standard English. The others are never acceptable.

Then, Than

Then indicates time. **Than** introduces the second part of a comparison.

    Correct   First we visited my aunt; **then** we went shopping.
    Correct   There is no more dedicated athlete **than** my brother.

There, Their, They're

These words are pronounced the same. But **there** is an adverb indicating place, **their** is a pronoun showing possession, and **they're** is a contraction of **they are.**

    Correct   **There** she is—Miss Commercialism.
    Correct   The students placed **their** library books in the book depository.
    Correct   Al and Chris called to say **they're** going to be late.

Through, Thru, Threw

Through means "between" or "in one side and out the other." **Thru** is an abbreviated form of **through** that is unacceptable in formal (and most informal) writing. **Threw** is a past tense form of a verb meaning "projected or propelled."

    Correct   The stake was driven **through** the werewolf's heart.
    Correct   Our pitcher **threw** just nine pitches that inning.

Thus, Thusly

Thus means "accordingly." **Thusly** is an unacceptable substitute for **thus.**

To, Too, Two

To has many meanings, most of which you are familiar with. But it cannot be used as a substitute for **too,** which means "more than enough" or "also." Nor should either word be confused with **two,** which is the number between one and three.

    Correct   Give the pencil **to** me.
    Correct   When are you going **to** wash your clothes?
    Correct   Henry says he is **too** tired to go to class.
    Correct   Are you going **too**?

Tortuous, Torturous

Tortuous means "twisting, turning, winding, crooked." **Torturous** means "very painful."

    Correct   The river winds its **tortuous** way to the sea.
    Correct   English class is for some people a **torturous** experience.

Try to, Try and

Try to means "make an attempt." Never use **try and** as a substitute for **try to** because it wrongly suggests that **two** actions are taking place. (In "try and learn grammar," the suggestion is that there is trying **and** there is learning, when that is not the sense of the sentence.)

    Correct   If you **try to** learn grammar, you will learn it.

Uninterested, Disinterested
See Disinterested, Uninterested

Unique
Unique means "without parallel, one of a kind." Therefore, the words ***more, most,*** and ***very*** shouldn't be used with it. (To say something is "more unique" than something else is a contradiction—if it is unique, then no comparison can properly be made. To say something is "very unique" is redundant.)

Use, Usage
Use may be either a verb or a noun. As a verb it rhymes with ***news*** and means "to employ or put into service." As a noun it rhymes with ***loose*** and means "the employment or application of something." ***Usage*** is a more specialized noun whose most common use concerns language.

    Correct   Be sure to ***use*** the correct tool for the job.
    Correct   Contemporary English ***usage*** frowns on slang in formal writing.

Used To, Use To
The correct expression is ***used to,*** never ***use to.*** The error of using ***use to*** undoubtedly arises from the fact that the ***d*** and ***t*** sounds blend together when the expression is spoken.

    Correct   I ***used to*** be a careless driver, but I've reformed.

Very, Awfully, Awful
Very means "in high degree, extremely." ***Awfully*** means "extremely badly, terribly." Thus, ***awfully*** is really not a synonym for ***very.*** Still, it is an acceptable substitute in ***informal*** writing (and speaking). ***Awful*** is an adjective and should never be substituted for either ***very*** or ***awfully.***

Always correct	Tim is a ***very good*** tennis player.
Always correct	Joe is an ***awful*** tennis player.
Correct informally	Tim is an ***awfully good*** tennis player.
Never correct	Tim is an ***awful good*** tennis player.

Waist, Waste
The ***waist*** is the middle of the body. ***Waste*** is misused or discarded material.

    Correct   My ***waist*** is a bit larger than it used to be.
    Correct   I've decided that dieting is a ***waste*** of time.

Weak, Week

Weak means not strong. A **week** is seven days long.

    Correct   I'd rather be mentally strong and physically **weak** than the reverse.

    Correct   Only one more **week** until semester break!

Were, Where

Were is a form of the verb **to be;** **where,** an adverb denoting place.

    Correct   We **were** the last ones to leave the library.

    Correct   I want to go **where** you go, do what you do.

Which, That

Which refers to places and things, never to people. **That,** however, though it usually refers to places and things, can also refer to people.

    Correct   The farm **which** my family used to own is just around the bend.

    Correct   The dog **that** I'll always remember was a Saint Bernard named Agatha.

    Correct   The man **that** steals my purse won't get much for his efforts.

Who, Whom

Who and **whom** are pronouns referring to people. When the word used will be the subject of a verb, use **who.** When the verb already has a subject, use **whom.**

    Correct   The man **who** runs the restaurant is sitting in the next booth. (**Who** is the subject of **runs. Man** is the subject of **is sitting.**)

    Correct   The man **whom** I introduced Sally to last night just came in the door. (The verbs in this sentence—**introduced** and **came in**—already have subjects, so **whom** is the correct form to use.)

Whoever, Whomever

The distinction between these two words is the same as that between **who** and **whom.**

    Correct   I'll sell my car to **whoever** gives me a reasonable offer. (**Whoever** is the subject of **gives.**)

    Correct   It is my right to sell it to **whomever** I wish. (**Is** and **wish** already have subjects.)

Whole, Hole

See Hole, Whole

Whose, Who's

In modern usage, **whose** is the possessive form of both **who** and **which**. **Who's,** though it is pronounced the same, is an entirely different word. It is the contraction of **who is.**

Correct The man **whose** wife just left is a well-known actor.
Correct The car **whose** engine caught on fire belonged to Ed.
Correct Can you tell me **who's** in charge here?

Word Endings

Learning to **hear** your writing as you proofread it will help you to avoid omitting word endings.

Ending omitted I have **listen** to him long enough.
Corrected I have **listened** to him long enough.
Ending omitted He was very jealous of what **belong** to him.
Corrected He was very jealous of what **belonged** to him.
Ending omitted I can't believe this is **happen** to me.
Corrected I can't believe this is **happening** to me.

Would Have, Would've, Would Of

See Could Have, Could've, Could Of

Write, Right, Rite

See Right, Rite, Write

You, One, A Person, We

Traditionally, **you** has been frowned upon in most formal writing. **One** has been preferred. For example, unless the sentence "You should never waste your breath arguing with a bigot" were addressed to a specific person, it would have been considered appropriate only in speech or informal writing. It would have been written, "One should never waste his breath arguing with a bigot." Today many writers consider **one** too stilted for most writing situations. They prefer **a person** (or a more specific term, such as **a man** or **a woman**). **You** is also considered acceptable as long as it is not obtrusive or too personal in the particular context. In many writing situations, **we** offers a desirable balance between formality and casualness. There is no clear-cut rule, however, in this matter. To decide what is appropriate in a given situation, you should consider the occasion, the audience, and your purpose in writing.

Your, You're

Your is a possessive pronoun. **You're** is a contraction of **you are.**

Correct **Your** coat is in the hall closet.
Correct **You're** the only one I really care for.

Notes

Chapter 1

1. Malcolm Cowley, ed., *Writers at Work* (New York: Viking, 1957) 88.
2. *Writers at Work* 46.
3. George Orwell, "Shooting an Elephant," *Shooting an Elephant and Other Essays*. Copyright 1950 by Sonia Brownell Orwell; renewed 1978 by Sonia Pitt-Rivers. Reprinted by permission of Harcourt Brace Jovanovich, Inc., and the estate of the late Sonia Brownell Orwell and Martin Secker & Warburg Ltd.
4. Joan Didion, *The White Album* (New York: Simon & Schuster, 1979).
5. Eric Hoffer, *In Our Time* (New York: Harper, 1976).
6. Carin C. Quinn, "The Jeaning of America—And the World," *American Heritage* Apr.–May 1978.
7. Sidney J. Parnes, *Creative Behavior Guidebook* (New York: Scribner's, 1967) 49.

Chapter 2

1. See, for example, the sources discussed in Sidney J. Parnes, *Creative Behavior Guidebook* (New York: Scribner's, 1967) 54f.

Chapter 3

1. Hyman Kublin, *Encyclopedia Americana* (Danbury: Americana, 1978) vol. 5, 618.
2. George Leonard, "Physical Education for Life," *Today's Education* Sept.–Oct. 1975: 75–76.
3. Edward Hughes, "Nature's Elegant Oddity: the Giraffe," *Reader's Digest* Oct. 1979: 206–10.
4. William Brashler, "Donahue! Darling of the Daytime Dial," *Reader's Digest* Oct. 1979: 125–28.
5. Andrew Jones, "The American in Cell No. 5," *Reader's Digest* Sept. 1979: 81–87.
6. John Underwood, "Football's Unfolding Tragedy," *Reader's Digest* Sept. 1979: 93–97.

Chapter 4

1. *Reliable Knowledge*, rev. ed. (New York: Houghton, 1964) 143–44.
2. Siegfried Giedion, *Mechanization Takes Command: A Contribution to Anonymous History* (New York: Oxford, 1948) 652–55.
3. "Male and Female Created He Them," *New York Times Book Review* 10 June 1979: 11+.
4. William J. Reilly, *The Twelve Rules for Straight Thinking* (New York: Harper, 1947) 15.
5. James Harvey Robinson, *The Mind in the Making* (New York: Harper, 1921) 41.

Chapter 6

1. Francis L. Wellman, *The Art of Cross-Examination*, 4th ed. Copyright 1923, 1936 by Macmillan Publishing Co., Inc., renewed 1951, 1964 by Ethel Wellman. Reprinted with permission of Macmillan Publishing Company.
2. Colin M. Turnbull, *The Forest People*. Copyright © 1961 by Colin M. Turnbull. Reprinted by permission of Simon & Schuster, Inc.
3. G. Reichel-Dolmatoff, "Jungle Gods of San Agustin," *Natural History* Dec. 1966: 41.
4. George Orwell, "A Hanging," *Shooting an Elephant and Other Essays*. Copyright 1950 by Sonia Brownell Orwell; renewed 1978 by Sonia Pitt-Rivers. Reprinted by permission of Harcourt Brace Jovanovich, Inc., and the estate of the late Sonia Brownell Orwell and Martin Secker & Warburg Ltd.
5. Malachi Martin, *Hostage to the Devil: The Possession and Exorcism of Five Living Americans* (New York: Reader's Digest, 1976) 5.

Chapter 7

1. Ron Alexander, "At the Plaza You Ring for the Bellperson." Copyright © 1978 by The New York Times Company. Reprinted by permission.
2. "The Brain's Opiate." Copyright 1978 Time, Inc. All rights reserved. Reprinted by permission from *TIME*.
3. Cecil Roth, *A Bird's-Eye View of Jewish History* (New York: Schocken, 1954) 278–80. Reprinted by permission.
4. Herndon G. Dowling, "Snake," *Encyclopedia Americana* (New York: Americana, 1974), vol. 25, 86.
5. Warren R. Young, "Peerless Pelé: Rebirth of a Superstar," *Reader's Digest* Sept. 1976: 114–15.
6. Mortimer Adler, *Great Ideas from the Great Books*. Copyright © 1961, 1963 by Mortimer J. Adler. Reprinted by permission of Pocket Books, a division of Simon & Schuster, Inc.
7. Theodore H. Gaster, "Immortality," *Encyclopedia Americana* (New York: Americana, 1974), vol. 14, 808.
8. John L. Wilhelm, "Black Holes: The Darkest Riddle of the Universe," *Reader's Digest* Sept. 1977: 69–70. Reprinted by permission.
9. S. I. Hayakawa, *Language in Thought and Action*, 4th ed. (New York: Harcourt, 1978).
10. Bob Beecroft, "The Winning of the West," *New York Sunday News Magazine* 28 Aug. 1977: 4.
11. Edmund S. Morgan, *The Puritan Family* (New York: Harper, 1966) 100–1.

Notes 453

12 George H. Gallup, "What Mankind Thinks of Itself," *Reader's Digest* October 1976: 134.
13 Adler, *Great Ideas* 149. Reprinted by permission.
14 Morgan, *The Puritan Family* 42–43.
15 James Webb, "What We Can Learn from Japan's Prisons," *Parade* 15 Jan. 1984: 6+.
16 S. Alexander Rippa, *Education in a Free Society: An American History*, Fifth Edition. Copyright © 1967, 1971, 1976, 1980, and 1984 by Longman, Inc. Reprinted by permission of Longman, Inc., New York.
17 "Hitler Without Cheers or Tears." Copyright 1977 Time, Inc. All rights reserved. Reprinted by permission from *TIME*.
18 Julie Baumgold, "Agoraphobia: Life Ruled by Panic." Copyright © 1977 by The New York Times Company. Reprinted by permission.
19 "The ABCs of School Violence," *Time* 23 Jan. 1978: 73–74.
20 James Horwitz, "The Bounty Hunter." Copyright 1978 New York News, Inc. Reprinted by permission.
21 Alan Levy, "Spending a Weekend in Liechtenstein." Copyright © 1978 by The New York Times Company. Reprinted by permission.
22 Anne Hollander, "When Fat Was in Fashion." Copyright © 1977 by The New York Times Company. Reprinted by permission.
23 Robert V. Barron, "From Con to Pro," *Writer's Digest* Feb. 1978: 26–28.
24 James Stewart-Gordon, "The Mystery of the Missing Bones," *Reader's Digest* Sept. 1976: 177–86. Reprinted by permission.
25 Frank Trippet, "There's No Madness Like Nomadness." Copyright 1977 Time, Inc. All rights reserved. Reprinted by permission from *TIME*.
26 Michael Halberstam, "Hey, You Ought to Sue the Doctor," *American Educator* Summer 1977: 7–8.

Chapter 8

1 John Wilson, *Philosophy* (London: Heinemann, 1968) ix.
2 Wellman, *Art of Cross-Examination* 27. Reprinted by permission.
3 Mortimer J. Adler, "How to Mark a Book," *Saturday Review* 6 July 1940: 11.
4 Rudolf Flesch, *How to Write, Speak and Think More Effectively* (New York: NAL, 1951) 42.
5 Gilbert Keith Chesterton, *Orthodoxy* (Garden City: Doubleday, 1959) 124. Reprinted by permission of Dodd, Mead & Co., Inc.
6 C. S. Lewis, *The Abolition of Man*. © C.S. Lewis Pte. Ltd., 1947. Reprinted by permission of Collins Publishers, London.
7 J. B. Rhine, "Occultism," *Encyclopedia Americana* (New York: Americana, 1974) vol. 20, 610.
8 Jimmy Breslin, "Dig We Must—Into Oil's Books." Copyright 1979 New York News, Inc. Reprinted by permission.
9 George F. Kneller, *The Art and Science of Creativity*. Copyright © 1965 by Holt, Rinehart and Winston. Reprinted by permission of Holt, Rinehart and Winston, CBS College Publishing.
10 "Telling It Like It Isn't." Copyright 1969 Time, Inc. All rights reserved. Reprinted by permission from *TIME*.
11 Harry A. Overstreet, *The Mature Mind*. Copyright 1949, © 1959 by W. W. Norton & Company, Inc. Copyright renewed 1976 by Bonaro Ovestreet. Reprinted by permission of W. W. Norton & Company, Inc.
12 Ethel Marbach, "Appalachia: A Witnessing for Christ?" *Ave Maria* 25 July 1964.

13 Walter Lippmann, *Public Opinion* (New York: Harcourt, 1927) 95.
14 Stokely Carmichael, "What We Want," *New York Review of Books* 22 Sept. 1966: 1+.

Chapter 10

1 Gilbert Highet, "Man's Unconquerable Mind," *Reader's Digest* Aug. 1954: 277–78. © 1954, Columbia University Press. Reprinted by permission.
2 Douglas MacArthur, Address at West Point, 12 May 1962, in *Reminiscences* (New York: McGraw-Hill, 1964) 424.
3 John F. Kennedy, Inaugural Address, rpd. in Theodore C. Sorensen, *Kennedy* (New York: Harper, 1965) 245.
4 Norman Cousins, "What Matters About Schweitzer," *Saturday Review* 25 Sept. 1965: 30–31.
5 Quoted in Leon A. Harris, *The Fine Art of Political Wit* (New York: Dutton, 1964) 167.
6 H. L. Mencken, *The American Scene: A Reader*, sel. and ed. Huntington Cairns (New York: Knopf, 1965) 206. Reprinted by permission.
7 Lewis, *The Abolition of Man* 91. © C. S. Lewis Pte. Ltd., 1947. Reprinted by permission of Collins Publishers, London.
8 R. Z. Sheppard, "Return to the Planet of the Apes," *Time* 26 June 1978: 75.
9 Gilbert Keith Chesterton, in *The Man Who Was Chesterton* (Garden City: Doubleday, 1960) 138. Reprinted by permission of Miss D. E. Collins.
10 MacArthur, *Reminiscences* 426.
11 Mike Royko, "Hayseeds Just Like Other Hustlers," *Binghamton* [N.Y.] *Evening Press* 14 July 1976: 6a.
12 Rex Reed, "Five Dums and a Doobie-Doobie," *New York Daily News* 19 Mar. 1978: 11c.
13 James Stewart-Gordon, "Houdini, the Man No Lock Could Hold," *Reader's Digest* Feb. 1976: 153. Reprinted by permission.
14 Eldridge Cleaver, *Soul on Ice* (New York: McGraw-Hill, 1968) 20. Reprinted by permission.
15 "Can't Anyone Here Read English?" Copyright 1975 Time, Inc. All rights reserved. Reprinted by permission from *TIME*.
16 Jack London, "The Story of an Eyewitness: An Account of the San Francisco Earthquake," *Collier's Weekly* 1906.

Chapter 11

1 Anthony Lewis, *Gideon's Trumpet* (New York: Vintage Books, 1964) 214–15.
2 Carl T. Rowan and David M. Mazie, "Our Immigration Nightmare," *Reader's Digest* Jan. 1983: 89–90.
3 Hoffer, *In Our Time*.
4 Lance Morrow, "A World of Exaggeration," *Time* 14 Dec. 1981.
5 George F. Kennan, *Democracy and the Student Left* (Boston: Little, Brown, 1968).
6 Francois Boucher, *20,000 Years of Fashion* (New York: Abrams, 1967) 411. Reprinted by permission.
7 John Knox Jessup, introd. to Russell W. Davenport, *Dignity of Man* (New York: Harper, 1955) 1–2.
8 Mortimer J. Adler, *The Paideia Proposal: An Educational Manifesto* (New York: Macmillan, 1982) 21.

9 Grant H. Hendrick, "When Television Is a School for Criminals." Copyright © 1977 by Triangle Publications, Inc., Radnor, Pa. Reprinted with permission from *TV Guide*® Magazine.
10 William Golding, "Thinking as a Hobby," *Holiday* Aug. 1961: 10.
11 Steven R. Weisman, "28% Are Held in Mental Hospitals Needlessly, New York Study Says," *New York Times* 15 Jan. 1978: 1.
12 L. David Mech, "Where Can the Wolf Survive?" *National Geographic* Oct. 1977: 518. Reprinted by permission.
13 Roger A. Garrison, *The Adventure of Learning in College* (New York: Harper, 1959) 11–13.
14 Adapted from a paragraphed passage in Vincent Ryan Ruggiero, *Beyond Feelings* (Port Washington: Alfred, 1975) 9–10.
15 Adapted from a paragraphed passage in Elisabeth Kübler-Ross, *Death: The Final Stage of Growth* (Englewood Cliffs: Prentice-Hall, 1959). Reprinted by permission.
16 Theodore C. Sorensen, *Kennedy* (New York: Harper, 1965) 13.
17 Thomas Ellis Katen, *Doing Philosophy*, © 1973, p 347. Reprinted by permission of Prentice-Hall, Inc., Englewood Cliffs, N.J.
18 T. S. Eliot, *On Poetry and Poets* (New York: Farrar, 1957) 24.
19 Jacques Barzun, *The Teacher in America* (New York: Little, Brown, 1945) 49.
20 George Orwell, "Politics and the English Language," *The Orwell Reader* (New York: Harcourt, 1956) 362.
21 George Bernard Shaw, in *Shaw on Religion*, ed. Warren Sylvester Smith (New York: Dodd, 1967) 162.
22 Joseph Wood Krutch, *The Twelve Seasons* (New York: Sloane, 1949) 109.
23 Alfred North Whitehead, *Science and the Modern World* (New York: NAL, 1948) 92.
24 Robert Penn Warren, *Who Speaks for the Negro?* (New York: Random, 1965) 432.
25 Lewis Mumford, *The Myth of the Machine: The Pentagon of Power* (New York: Harcourt, 1970) 215.
26 Sir James Jeans, *The Mysterious Universe* (London: Cambridge UP, 1948) 2–3. Reprinted by permission.
27 Hilton Kramer, "Michelangelo and Connoisseurship," *New York Times* 6 May 1979: sec. 2, 1+.
28 George Orwell, "Homage to Catalonia," in *The Orwell Reader*. Copyright 1952, 1980 by Sonia Brownell Orwell. Reprinted by permission of Harcourt Brace Jovanovich, Inc., and the estate of the late Sonia Brownell Orwell, and Martin Secker & Warburg Ltd.

Handbook

1 T. S. Eliot, "Religion and Literature," *Essays Ancient and Modern* (New York: Harcourt, 1936) 83.
2 Suzanne Gordon, "Helene Deutsch and the Legacy of Freud," *New York Times Magazine* 30 July 1978: 23.
3 Betty Friedan, *The Feminine Mystique*. Copyright © 1963, 1973 by Betty Friedan. Reprinted by permission of W. W. Norton & Company, Inc.
4 Herman Kahn, *Thinking About the Unthinkable* (New York: Horizon, 1962) 17. Reprinted by permission.
5 Paul Roberts, *Understanding English* (New York: Harper, 1958) 409.
6 Highet, "Man's Unconquerable Mind" 150. © 1954, Columbia University Press. Reprinted by permission.

Index

Abbreviations, 311, 404
Absolute phrase, 406
Abstracting services, 305
Abstract words, 242
Acknowledgment. *See* Documentation
Active voice, 256–57
Addresses, comma with, 406
Adjective(s), 370–72
   adverb vs., 370–71
   comma with, 406
   comparative form of, 372
   correct use of, 371–72
   hyphenation of, 423
   parallel, 228
   as sentence opening, 231–32
   superlative form of, 372
Adjective clauses
   misplaced modification with, 384
   parallel, 228
Adverb(s), 372–74
   adjective vs., 370–71
   comparative form of, 372, 373
   conjunctive, 408
   correct use of, 371–72
   irregular, 373
   regular, 373
   as sentence opening, 232
   superlative form of, 372, 373
Agreement
   points of, 93
   subject–verb, 356–60
Almanacs, 303
Ambiguity, 241
Analogy
   faulty, 203–4, 211
   in informative compositions, 137–38, 151
   in persuasive compositions, 181, 183
And, 286
Antecedents, 364, 368–69
Apostrophe, 421–22
Appeals, irrational, 206–7, 212
Appositive, 364–65
Arguments, limiting, 92
Article, documentation of, 320–22
As, 365
Associations, 31–32
Assumptions, 76
Attacks on people, 201–2, 211
Audience, 83–87
   familiar, 85–86

   of persuasive compositions, 186
   unfamiliar, 86–87
   writing *to* vs. *for*, 83–87
   See also Readers
Authority
   appeal to, 206
   as influence on judgment, 74
   quoting of, 179
   as source of evidence, 95

Base clause
   defined, 224
   expansion of, 226–27
   forms of, 220
Be, 355, 365
Beck, E. M., 303
Bernard, Saint, 26
Bibliography, 154, 160, 187, 189
   See also Documentation
Blake, William, 25
Book citations, 318–20
Books in Print, 303
Brackets, 143, 415
But, 287–88

Capitalization, 310, 418–21
Card catalog, 299–300, 303
Case (pronoun), 364–67
   objective, 364, 365–66
   possessive, 364, 366–67
   subjective, 364–65
Causation, faulty, 204–6, 211–12
Cause-to-effect order, 167
Central idea. *See* Controlling idea
Certainty, qualifications of, 59
Chesterton, G. K., 26, 245
Chronological order, 112, 133
Churchill, Sir Winston, 245–46
Citation. *See* Documentation
Clarity
   degrees of, 241
   in sentences, 228–30, 241
Classification
   Dewey Decimal system of, 297–98
   Library of Congress system of, 297, 298
   as persuasive technique, 170, 181
Clauses
   adjective, 228, 384
   base, 224–27
   colon with, 409
   commas with, 405
   dash with, 410–11

   order of, 233
   semicolon with, 408
   subject of, 365
Climactic moment, 113, 127
Collective noun, 358, 368
Colloquialisms, 240
Colon, 409–10, 415, 424
Comma, 405–7, 414, 415
Command, 362
Comma splice, 378–80
Comparative form
   of adjective, 372
   of adverb, 372, 373
Comparisons, 171–73, 289
   See also Figurative language
Complement, 364, 365
Complexity, order of, 133
Complex sentence, 360–61
Composite description, 123
Composition
   choices in, 5
   creativity in, 5–11
   defined, 5
   stages in, 11–14
   See also Informative composition; Narrative composition; Persuasive composition
Composition forms, 41–53
   combinations of, 48–49
   informative, 18, 44–45, 48, 49, 50
   narrative, 18, 42–44, 50, 111–29
   persuasive, 18, 46–47, 48–49, 50
   selection of, 49–51
Compound subject, 357
Compound words, 423
Concessions, 92–93
Conclusions
   flaws in, 68–69
   hasty, 207–8, 212
   of informative compositions, 155, 157, 160
   of narrative compositions, 113, 125–26, 128
   of persuasive compositions, 182, 183, 189
Conclusion-to-evidence order, 167
Concreteness, degree of, 242–43
Condition, qualification of, 59
Conjunction, coordinating, 378, 405
Conjunctive adverb, 408
Connectives, 285–91, 424, 425
Connotative meaning, 237–38

456

Contractions, 422
Contradictions, 202–3, 211
Contrast, 171, 172, 287–88
Controlling idea, 53–61
   comparisons and, 171
   defined, 53
   expressing, 56–60
   in introduction, 158
   selecting, 54–56
   in title, 158
Conversational diction, 240
Coordinating conjunction, 378, 405
Coordination, in sentences, 221–23
Corrections, in manuscript, 311
Creative thinking, 63
Creativity, 5–11
   development of, 11
   editing and, 347
   examples of, 6–10
Credits. *See* Documentation
Critical thinking, 64–81
   assumptions and, 76
   attitude in, 65–66
   characteristics of, 64–70
   connecting ideas and, 68–70
   defined, 64
   distinctions in, 76–77
   fact vs. opinion in, 66–67
   flawed conclusions and, 68–69
   judgments in, 72–79
   logic and, 68–70
   questioning and, 72–79
   self-serving reasoning in, 75
   taste vs. judgment in, 67–68
Cumulative Book Index, 303
Cumulative sentence, 225

Dangling modification, 383
Dash, 170, 410–11, 415
Data bases, 305
Dates
   capitalization in, 419–20
   comma with, 406–7
Definition
   figurative, 118–19, 149, 182, 183
   literal, 138–39, 149, 150, 151, 183
Demosthenes, 26
Denotative meaning, 237–38
Describing
   in informative composition, 149, 150
   as narrative technique, 116–17, 123–24, 127
   See also Narrative composition
Devore, N., 302
Dewey Decimal system, 297–98
Dialogue
   imaginary, 32–37
   in narrative composition, 119–20, 127
   paragraphing with, 277–78
Diary, 14n
Diction, level of, 240–41
Dictionary, speller's, 391
Dictionary of Slang and Unconventional English, 303
Didion, Joan, 8
Direct address, 154
Direct object, 366
Distinctions, making, 76–77
Documentation, 143, 154–55, 187, 314–23
   bibliography, 154, 160, 187, 189
   book citations, 318–20
   defined, 314–15
   kinds of, 316–23
   nonprint-material citations, 322–23
   parenthetical, 316–18
   periodical citations, 320–22
   of quotations, 142n, 306, 317
   Works Cited list, 318
Drafts
   guidelines for, 18–19
   by professional writers, 4
   revision of, 18–19

Echo words, 285
Economy, in sentences, 245–54, 261
Editing, 347–429
   for adjective and adverb problems, 370–74
   importance of, 13, 347–48
   for pronoun problems, 364–70
   for punctuation problems, 402–29
   for sentence problems, 374–90
   for spelling problems, 374–90
   for verb problems, 348–64
   See also Planning; Writing
Effect-to-cause order, 167
Either/or, 357
Either–or thinking, 200, 211
Eliot, T. S., 403
Ellipsis marks, 143, 144, 416
Emotions, appeal to, 206
Emphasis, italics for, 418
"Emphasis added," 143
Encyclopaedia Britannica, 301–2
Encyclopedia Americana, 301–2
Encyclopedia of Astrology, 302
English language
   finding information about, 303
   sensitivity to, 231
   See also Language

Errors in logic. *See* Fallacies
Evaluation, 173–74, 178, 180, 182, 189
Evidence, 93–97
   evaluating, 96
   interpreting, 96–97
   kinds of, 94–96
   proof vs., 93
Evidence-to-conclusion order, 167
Exactness, of sentences, 236–43, 261
Examples
   citing of, 135–37, 150, 151, 158, 159
   in persuasive compositions, 177–78, 179, 180, 181, 187, 188
Exclamation point, 404–5, 415
Exclamatory statement, 404–5
Experience, as evidence, 94–96
Explanation, 168–70, 179, 180, 181
Explanatory notes, 59
Expressions, overworked, 238–39

Fact
   defined, 66
   examples of, 73
   opinion vs., 66–67
Factual data
   in persuasive compositions, 187, 188
   presentation of, 134–35, 149, 150, 151, 156, 157, 158, 159
Faith, appeal to, 206
Fallacies, 199–211
   attacking the person, 201–2, 211
   and contradiction, 202–3, 211
   either–or thinking of, 200, 211
   faulty analogy of, 203–4, 211
   faulty causation of, 204–6, 211–12
   hasty conclusion of, 207–8, 212
   irrational appeal of, 206–7, 212
   and overgeneralization, 208–9, 212
   and oversimplification, 78–79, 210–11, 212
   and stereotyping, 200–1, 211
Familiar audiences, 85–86
Familiar Quotations, 303
Figurative definition, 118–19, 149, 182, 183
Figurative language, 258–59
5W formula (*who, what, when, where, why*), 154
Flashbacks, 112, 122
Footnotes, 143
   See also Documentation
For, 288

Foreign expressions, 418
Formats, 313–14
  integrated, 314, 334–42
  separated, 313–14, 324–33
Fractions, 423
Fragments, 374–78
France, Anatole, 26
Free modifiers, 224–25
Freewriting, 29–31
Fromm, Erich, 26
Fuller, Thomas, 26
Future perfect tense, 351, 353
Future tense, 351, 352

Generalizations, 78, 208
Gerund
  pronoun case with, 366–67
  as subject, 358–59
Gerund phrases, parallel, 228
Gibran, Kahlil, 27
Government publications, 297
Grammatical problems, 348–429
  with adjectives and adverbs, 370–74
  with pronouns, 364–70
  with punctuation, 403–29
  with sentences, 374–90
  with verbs, 348–64
Great Quotations, The, 303
Guide to Reference Books, 302–3

Halifax, Lord, 26
Hasty conclusions, 207–8, 212
Headings, 310–11
Hoffer, Eric, 10
Hubbard, E., 26, 27, 415
Huxley, T. H., 27
Hyphenation, 309–10, 422–23

I, 418
Idea(s)
  connecting, 68–70
  controlling, 53–61
  evaluating, 63–81
  profound, 250
  quantity and quality of, 17
  separating from person, 90
  See also Judgment
Idea generation, 17, 28–37
  forcing associations, 31–32
  freewriting, 29–31
  imaginary dialogue, 32–37
Illustrations, 310
Imaginary dialogue, 32–37
Imperative mood, 362
Importance, order of, 167
Incomplete construction, 386–87
Indefinite pronoun, 358, 369

Indicative mood, 362
Indirect object, 366
Infinitive, 348–51
Infinitive phrase, 233, 383
Inflated writing, 247–50
Information Please Almanac, 303
Informative composition, 18, 44–45, 48, 49, 50, 131–62
  characteristics of, 131–33
  checklist for, 161–62
  patterns of organization for, 133
  persuasive composition vs., 132
  sample, 158–60
  strategies for, 153–58
  title of, 155, 156, 157, 158
  topics for, 160–61
Informative research paper, 312, 324–33
Informative techniques, 133–53
  citing examples, 135–37, 150, 151, 158, 159, 179, 180, 187, 188
  combining, 148–53
  defining literally, 138–39, 149, 150, 151, 183
  making analogies, 137–38, 151, 181, 183
  paraphrasing, 142, 144–45, 159
  in persuasive compositions, 177–78, 179, 180, 181, 183, 187, 188
  presenting factual data, 134–35, 149–51, 156–59, 187, 188
  presenting a process, 139–40, 158, 159
  quoting, 142–44, 151, 159, 179, 188
  summarizing, 141–42
  tracing, 140–41, 149
Integrated format, 314, 334–42
Interest, order of, 133
Interjection, 404–5
Interpretation, 173
  See also Evaluation
Interview citations, 323
Intransitive verb, 348
Introductions
  in informative compositions, 155–58
  in narrative compositions, 125–126
  in persuasive compositions, 169, 174, 177, 187
Irrational appeal, 206–7, 212
Irregular adverbs, 373
Irregular verbs, 348–51
It, 368
Italics, 143, 414, 418

Jargon, 249–50
Journal articles, documentation of, 320–22
Judgment
  of authorities, 74, 95
  critical reasoning and, 72–79
  defined, 66
  examples of, 73
  hasty, 75–76
  identifying, 72–73
  in persuasive compositions, 166, 173–74, 177–82, 186–89
  preconceived notions and, 73–75
  reasonableness of, 77–79
  supporting, 93–97
  taste vs., 67–68

Language, literal vs. figurative, 258–59
  See also English language
Larrabee, Harold A., 63
Library
  catalog, 299–300, 303
  classification systems, 297–98
  divisions, 296–97
Library of Congress classification system, 297, 298
Linking verb, 348
List, punctuation of, 409, 411
Literal definition, 138–39, 149–51, 183
Liveliness, in sentences, 254–61
Logic, 199–216
  in connections between ideas, 68–70
  fallacies in, 199–211
  revision guide for, 211–12

Magazine articles, documentation for, 320–22
Majority opinion, 74
Manuscript preparation, 308–11
Marcellinus Ammianus, 245
Meaning
  connotative, 237–38
  denotative, 237–38
Mencken, H. L., 246
Metaphor, 259
Metonymy, 259
Misplaced modification, 383–84
Mixed construction, 385–86
MLA Handbook, 316–23
Moderation, appeal to, 206
Modern Language Association, 316
  See also MLA Handbook
Modification, 382–85
  dangling, 383
  misplaced, 383–84

Modification (*continued*)
  squinting, 382–83
Modifiers
  free, 224–25
  in predicate, 57–58
Moods, 362–64
  imperative, 362
  indicative, 362
  subjunctive, 362–63

Names, capitalization of, 419, 420
Narrating, 113–16, 123–24, 149–50, 156
Narrative composition, 18, 42–44, 50, 111–29
  characteristics of, 111–13
  checklist for, 129
  dialogue in, 119–20, 127
  flashbacks in, 112, 122
  sample, 126–28
  strategies for, 125–26
  title of, 126
  topics for, 128–29
Narrative techniques, 113–24
  combining, 121–24
  defining figuratively, 118–19, 149, 182, 183
  describing, 116–17, 123–24, 127, 149, 150
  dialogue, 119–20
  in informative compositions, 149–50, 156
  narrating, 113–16, 123–24, 149–50
  in persuasive compositions, 182–83
Neither/nor, 357
Newspaper articles, documentation for, 320–22
New York Times Encyclopedic Almanac, 303
New York Times Index, 305
Nonrestrictive elements, 405, 411
Note taking, 306–8
Nouns
  capitalization of, 419–20
  collective, 358, 368
  parallel, 228
  plural form with singular meaning, 357–58
Numbers, hyphens in, 423

Object, 366
Objective case of pronouns, 364, 365–66
Observation, as evidence, 94–96
O'Connor, Frank, 4, 53n
Opinion
  defined, 66
  fact vs., 66–67
  See also Judgment
Order
  cause-to-effect, 167
  chronological, 112, 133
  of complexity, 133
  conclusion-to-evidence, 167
  effect-to-cause, 167
  evidence-to-conclusion, 167
  flashback, 112, 122
  of importance, 167
  of interest, 133
  reverse, 167
  of space, 133
  of time, 112, 133
Organizational patterns
  in informative compositions, 133
  in narrative compositions, 112
  in persuasive compositions, 166–67
Orwell, George, 7, 247
Overgeneralization, 208–9, 212
Oversimplification, 78–79, 210–11, 212
Oxford English Dictionary, 303

Page numbering, 310
Paper. *See* Composition; Research paper
Paperback Books in Print, 303
Paragraph(s), 269–93
  coherence of, 283–89
  connections between, 12, 289–91
  length of, 273–83
  patterns of, 270–73
  punctuation of, 423–29
  topic sentence of, 270–73
Paragraph breaks, 274–78
Parallel structure, 228–30
Paraphrasing, 142, 144–45, 159
Parentheses, 411–12
Parenthetical comments, 170
Parenthetical documentation, 316–18
Participial phrase, 383
Participle, 232
  past, 348–51
Partridge, Eric, 303
Passive voice, 256–57
Past participle, 348–51
Past perfect tense, 351, 352
Past tense
  defined, 351
  of irregular verbs, 348–51, 352
  parallel, 228
  verb endings for, 355
People's Almanac, The, 303
Period, 404, 415

Periodical(s), 297, 303–5
Periodical citations, 320–22
Person, unnecessary shifts in, 388–89
Personification, 259
Persuasion, 88–102
  anticipating readers' reactions, 98, 102
  building a balanced case, 91–93
  examples of, 99–102
  respecting readers, 89–91
  supporting judgments, 93–97
  understanding opposing side, 88–89
Persuasive composition, 18, 46–47, 48–49, 50, 165–92
  characteristics of, 165–67
  checklist for, 191–92
  informative composition vs., 132
  informative techniques in, 177–81, 183, 187, 188
  judgment in, 166, 173–74, 177–82, 186–89
  patterns of organization in, 166–67
  sample, 187–89
  strategies for, 185–87
  title of, 187
  topics for, 189–91
Persuasive research paper, 312–13, 334–42
Persuasive techniques, 168–85
  classifying, 170, 181
  combining, 177–85
  comparing, 171–73
  evaluating, 173–74, 178, 180, 182, 189
  explaining, 168–70, 179, 180, 181
  interpreting, 173
  presenting reasons by, 168, 178, 181
  and speculating, 174–75, 180
Phrases
  absolute, 406
  comma with, 405, 406
  gerund, 228
  infinitive, 233, 383
  participial, 383
  prepositional, 231, 383, 384
Place(s)
  capitalization of, 419, 420
  comma with, 406–7
  qualifications of, 58
Plagiarism, 314
Planning, 21
  guidelines for, 17–18
  as stage in composition, 11–12, 13, 21

Plurals
    apostrophe with, 422
    unusual, 394
Poetry, punctuation of, 413, 414
Pope, Alexander, 414
Possession, apostrophe with, 421–22
Possessive case of pronouns, 364, 366–67
Preconceived notions, 73–75
Predicate, 57–58
Predication, faulty, 380–82
Predictability, 254–55
Prefixes, 393–94, 423
Premise, 68
Preposition, object of, 366
Prepositional phrase, 231
    dangling modification in, 383
    misplaced modification in, 384
Present infinitive, 348–51
Present perfect tense, 351, 352
Present tense
    defined, 351
    examples of, 352
    verb endings for, 354–55
Pretentiousness, 248
Process, presenting, 139–40, 158, 159
Professional titles
    capitalization of, 419
    comma with, 406–7
Profound ideas, 250
Pronoun(s), 364–70
    capitalization of *I*, 418
    effective use of, 284
    faulty reference of, 367–70
    indefinite, 358, 369
    relative, 358
Pronoun case, 364–67
    objective, 364, 365–66
    possessive, 364, 366–67
    subjective, 364–65
Pronunciation, and spelling, 391–92
Proof, 93
Publication, 14n
Publilius Syrus, 27
Punctuation, 403–29
    apostrophe, 421–22
    brackets, 143, 415
    capitalization, 310, 418–21
    colon, 409–10, 415, 424
    comma, 378–80, 405–7, 414, 415
    dash, 170, 410–11, 415
    ellipsis marks, 143, 144, 416
    end, 404–5
    exclamation point, 404–5, 415

hyphen, 309–10, 422–23
internal, 405–12
italics, 143, 414, 418
of paragraphs, 423–29
parentheses, 411–12
period, 404, 415
question mark, 404, 412, 415
of quotation, 413–17
quotation marks, 413–15
semicolon, 378–79, 408–9, 415, 424
slash, 414
of words, 417–23

Qualifications, 58–59
Questioning, 72–79
Questioning attitude, 65–66
Question mark, 404, 412, 415
Quotation(s)
    from authority, 179
    colon with, 409
    documentation of, 142n, 306, 317
    as informative technique, 142–44, 151, 159
    in persuasive compositions, 179, 188
    punctuation of, 413–17
    sources of, 303
Quotation marks, 143, 144, 413–15

Readers, 83–105
    anticipating reactions of, 86, 98
    contract with, 14–15
    expectations and, 102
    familiar, 85–86
    persuasion of, 88–102
    respecting, 89–91
    understanding opposing views of, 88–89
    unfamiliar, 86–87
    writing *to* and *for*, 83–87
Reader's Digest, 59
Readers' Guide to Periodical Literature, 303–5
Reading, speed of, 270
Reasonable judgment, 77–79
Reasoning. *See* Critical thinking
Reasons, presenting, 168, 178, 181
Reference materials, 297, 301–6
Reilly, William J., 75
Relationship words, 285–89
Relative pronoun, 358
Research
    library resources for, 296–300
    note taking in, 306–8
    strategy for, 301–6
Research paper, 295–345

checklist for, 344–45
documentation of, 314–23
format of, 313–14
informative, 312, 324–33
manuscript guidelines for, 308–11
persuasive, 312–13, 334–42
selecting form of, 311–13
topics for, 343–44
Reston, James, 26
Reverse order, 167
Revising, 195–97
    approaches to, 196–97
    for logic, 199–216
    for paragraph effectiveness, 269–93
    for sentence style, 219–66
    as stage in composition, 11, 13–14
Rewriting
    guidelines for, 19
    by professional writers, 4
Robinson, James Harvey, 75
Rogers, Will, 26
Rough draft. *See* Drafts
Run-on sentences, 378–80

Sabatier, Paul, 26
Santayana, George, 27
Schweitzer, Albert, 27
See, 352–53, 354
Seldes, George, 303
Semicolon
    comma splice vs., 378–79
    in long sentences, 424
    problems with, 408–9
    with quotation marks, 415
    in run-on sentences, 378
Sentence(s), 219–66, 374–90
    clarity in, 228–30
    comma splice in, 378–80
    complex, 360–61
    coordination in, 221–23
    cumulative, 225
    economy in, 245–54, 261
    exactness of, 236–43, 261
    faulty modification in, 382–85
    faulty predication in, 380–82
    liveliness of, 254–61
    parallel structure in, 228–30
    run-on, 378–80
    shifts in person or tense in, 388–90
    simple, 219–23
    subordination in, 221–23
    texture of, 224
    topic, 270–73

Sentence(s) (*continued*)
  varying style of, 260–61
  word order in, 230–33
Sentence construction, 385–87
  incomplete, 386–87
  mixed, 385–86
Sentence elements, nonrestrictive, 405, 411
Sentence fragment, 374–78
Sentence patterns
  basic, 219–21
  combining, 221–23
  expanding, 224–27
Separated format, 313–14, 324–33
Series
  colon with, 409
  comma in, 406
  dash with, 411
Sheehy, Eugene O., 302–3
Sic, 143
Simile, 258
Simple sentence, 219–23
Simplification, 210
Slang, 240, 303
Slash, 414
Smith, L. P., 27
Socrates, 26
Sources. *See* Documentation
Space order, 133
Specificity, degree of, 242–43
Speculation, 151, 155, 160, 174–75, 180
Speedreading, 270
Speller's dictionary, 391
Spelling, 390–402
Spelling list, 391, 395–401
Squinting modification, 382–83
Standard conversational diction, 240
Standard written diction, 240
Statistics, as evidence, 94
Stereotyping, 200–1, 211
Stevenson, R. L., 25, 26
Subject
  appositive of, 365
  of clause, 365
  collective noun as, 358
  compound, 357
  faulty predication and, 380–82
  gerund as, 258–59
  indefinite pronoun as, 358
  plural form with singular meaning, 357–58
  relative pronoun as, 358
Subjective case of pronouns, 364–65
Subject–verb agreement, 356–60

Subjunctive mood, 362–63
Subordination, in sentences, 221–23
Subtitles, 409
Suffixes, 394
Summarizing, 141–42
Superlative form
  of adjective, 372
  of adverb, 372, 373
Supporting examples. *See* Examples
Syllabication, 309–10, 422–23
Synecdoche, 259

Tables, 310
Taste
  defined, 66
  examples of, 73
  judgment vs., 67–68
Taylor, Sir Henry, 26
Tense. *See* Verb tense
Texture, 224
Than, 365
That, 363, 368
Thesis. *See* Controlling idea
They, 368
This, 368
Thoreau, Henry David, 26
Thurber, James, 4
Time, qualifications of, 58
Time order
  in informative composition, 133
  in narrative composition, 112
Titles (of works)
  capitalization of, 310, 420
  colon with subtitles, 409
  of informative compositions, 155–58
  italics with, 414, 418
  manuscript, 310–11, 325, 335
  of narrative compositions, 126
  of persuasive compositions, 187
  quotation marks with, 414–15
To be, 355, 365
Topics
  for informative compositions, 160–61
  for narrative compositions, 128–29
  narrowing, 37–39
  for persuasive compositions, 189–91
  possibilities for, 24–28
  for research papers, 343–44
  selecting, 17, 23–24
  See also Subject
Topic sentence, 270–73

To see, 352–53, 354
Tracing, 140–41, 149
Tradition, appeal to, 206
Transitive verb, 348
Trueblood, D. E., 413

Underlining, in quotations, 143, 144
  See also Italics
Understatement, 79, 92, 259
Unfamiliar audiences, 86–87

Verbs, 57–58, 348–64
  agreement with subject, 356–60
  endings of, 354–56
  faulty predication and, 380–82
  intransitive, 348
  irregular verbs, 348–51
  linking, 348
  mood of, 362–64
  parallel past-tense, 228
  principal parts of, 348–51
  transitive, 348
Verb tense
  defined, 351
  formation of, 351–54
  future, 351, 352
  future perfect, 351, 353
  meaning and, 57
  past, 228, 348–51, 352, 355
  past perfect, 351, 352
  perfect, 351, 352–53
  present, 351, 352, 354–55
  present perfect, 351, 352
  sequence of, 360–62
  shifts in, 389
  simple, 351
Vivid words, 257–58
Voice, active vs. passive, 256–57
Vowels, 394

Webster's New Dictionary of Synonyms, 303
Which, 368
Who's Who, 303
Who's Who in America, 303
Who's Who in the World, 303
Word(s)
  abstract, 242
  compound, 423
  concrete, 242
  confusion between, 238
  connecting, 285–91, 424, 425
  echo, 285
  frequently misspelled, 391–401
  mispronounced, 391–92
  punctuation of, 417–23

Word(s) *(continued)*
    relationship, 285–89
    repetition of, 284–85
    vivid, 257–58
Wordiness, 249
Word order, variations of, 230–36
Working conditions, 17
Works Cited list, 318
World Almanac, The, 303
Writer's block, 23

Writing, 107–8
    clarity in, 228–30, 241
    diction and, 240–41
    difficulty of, 3–4
    drafts in, 4, 18–19
    economy in, 245–54, 261
    format of, 270
    guidelines for, 16–19
    learning by doing, 15
    liveliness in, 254–61
    specificity in, 11
    topics for, 23–28
    working conditions for, 17
    writing *to* vs. *for* readers, 83–87
    See also Editing; Planning
Written diction, 240
Wylie, I.A.R., 26

DATE DUE

WITHDRAWN

MONTGOMERY COLLEGE LIBRARIES
germ, circ   PE 1408.R8351985
Composition :

0 0000 00223693 3

48720878
PE1408.R8351985
RUGGIERO   VINCENT RY
COMPOSITION   THE
CREATIVE RESPONSE